Cyber Ethics 4.0

Serving Humanity with Values

Cyber Ethics 4.0

Serving Humanity with Values

Christoph Stückelberger / Pavan Duggal (Eds.)

Globethics.net Global Series No. 17

Globethics.net Global Series
Series Editors: Christoph Stückelberger, Founder and President of
Globethics.net and Professor of Ethics (emeritus University of Basel/
Switzerland, Visiting Professor in Moscow/Russia, Enugu/Nigeria,
Beijing/China).
Obiora Ike, Executive Director of Globethics.net and Professor of Ethics
(Godfrey Okoye University Enugu/Nigeria).

Globethics.net Global 17
Christoph Stückelberger / Pavan Duggal (Eds.), *Cyber Ethics 4.0:*
Serving Humanity with Values
Geneva: Globethics.net, 2018
ISBN 978-2-88931-264-1 (online version)
ISBN 978-2-88931-265-8 (print version)
© 2018 Globethics.net

Managing Editor: Ignace Haaz
Assistant Editor: Samuel Davies

Globethics.net Head Office
150 route de Ferney
1211 Geneva 2, Switzerland
Website: *www.globethics.net*
Email: *publications@globethics.net*

All web links in this text have been verified as of October 2018.

CONTENTS

3 Ethics in the Information Society: the Nine P's..........69

Globethics.net

Part II Disruptive Cyber Technologies and Ethics

4 My Friend The Algorithm: Theological-Ethical Challenge of Artificial Intelligence...................................93

Erny Gillen, Luxemburg

9 Homo Deus: No Deus Homo: Yes Becoming Truly Human ... 171

Christoph Stückelberger, Switzerland

10 The Oracle of Big Data: Prophecies Without Prophets ... 177

Bruno Granche, Germany

Part IV Cyber Law, Cyber Health and Ethics

11 Blockchain Legal Regulations ... 195

Michael Mosimann, Switzerland

12 A Humanistic Approach to the Ethics of High Tech 201

Aharon Aviram, Tapan Patel, Israel

13 Digital Health: Meeting Ethical and Policy Challenges 229

*Effy Vayena / Tobias Haeusermann / Afua Adjekum
Alessandro Blasimme, Switzerland / UK*

17 Towards a Just Internet: A Republican Net Neutrality 297

Johan Rochel, Switzerland

Part VI Cyber Security, Cyber Crime, Cyber War and Ethics

18 Ethics and Autonomous Weapon Systems: An Ethical Basis for Human Control? 323

International Committee of the Red Cross (ICRC)

Part VII Cyber Media, Cyber Education and Ethics

INTRODUCTION

Christoph Stückelberger / Pavan Duggal

The Cyber Space is the whole global space of virtual reality, a parallel world to the physical world, with uncountable interactions with the physical world. This Cyber Space grew exponentially in its importance in the last three decades. It is everywhere and anytime present, through satellites, the information technologies, the internet, the weather forecasts, the big data collections, the food production, the health systems, the courts, education, e-government, culture, music, and religion.

We therefore can speak of a *Cyber Society* which includes all aspects of modern society which are linked to cyber space and are influenced by it. Today, all sectors of society around the globe are already part of the cyber world, even without a computer or mobile phone in personal life. There are huge expectations and opportunities and at the same time immense fears and challenges.

Cyber Ethics aims at giving orientation about right and wrong, good and bad, related to the cyber space. It tries to apply and modify fundamental values and virtues to specific new challenges and situations arising from cyber technologies and cyber society. As cyber space influences all parts of society, cyber ethics includes almost all ethics domains.

This book is called *Cyber Ethics 4.0*. This refers to the Fourth Industrial Revolution as the term for the data internet- and data-based fast developments of new technologies, especially associated with artificial intelligence.

The Cyber world is per definition a world without physical borders. Even with national and international legislations, it is basically global and therefore multilingual, multicultural, multi-religious, multilateral, even if nationalist parties now want to come back to national identities – also as a reaction to the overwhelming and omnipresent global Cyber Space.

Therefore, *ethics in the cyberspace is also global, interconnected, multicultural, multi-religious and multi-philosophical. This diversity* is expressed in this book by the variety of authors with their values, coming from various continents and contributions of international (UN-organisations) with a collective of contributors from all continents. Ethical answers are developed in processes of dialogue while being faithful to the respective authors' convictions and traditions. The articles show in all diversity many common values such as: the cyber world has to serve basic human needs (expressed in the UN SDGs), has to respect privacy and freedom, has to increase equality and inclusivity, has to protect and not destroy life etc. "Neither national governments, nor the technology sector, nor civil society, nor anyone else can alone solve the challenges of technological progress" stated Michael Møller, Director-General of the UN Geneva, in November 2017 in Geneva on Internet Governance.[1]

The International Telecommunication Union ITU in Geneva organised in 2018 the second "AI for Global Good Summit"[2] to develop initiatives for positive use of new technologies like AI for health, education, food, water, citizenship, peace etc. as ITU with this conference does. But it is also needed to develop fast clear limits and regulations against the negative use of such new technologies as we already see with auton-

---

[1] https://news.itu.int/digital-geneva-convention-whats-next-for-internet-governance-challenges/. (Accessed 11 Sept 2018)

[2] https://www.itu.int/en/ITU-T/AI/2018/Pages/default.aspx (Accessed 11 Sept 2018)

omous weapons, cybercrime etc. The volumes of this book will look at opportunities and threats of cyber-related technologies.

Consumers and experts alike expect much from future technological developments in cyber space, including from Artificial Intelligence. Key concerns of consumers as well as experts related to new cyber-related technologies are the security of personal data and the fear of reduction or fast modification of jobs as a new representative survey of Intel in the USA shows.[3]

The book has seven sections (Part I-VII) in order to cluster the topics:

Part I "Ethics in the Cyberspace. An Overview" develops the basic values and virtues and legal perspectives. Ethical values and legal regulations are twins. The relation between law and ethics appears in many articles and mirrors the fact that the two book editors are an ethics expert (Christoph Stückelberger) and a law expert (Pavan Duggal).

Part II "Disruptive Cyber Technologies and Ethics" deals with Artificial Intelligence, Blockchain as the future of the jobs in the cyber society as key ethical challenges of the fourth industrial revolution.

Part III "Cyber Religion and Ethics" looks at the religious and pseudo-religious aspects which are key drivers for fears and hopes in any technological revolution. It leads to the fundamental question of the relation between human beings and non-human entities.

Part IV "Cyber Law and Ethics" deals with selected aspects of the intense efforts for regulating the cyber space as an unregulated cyber society undermines the existing laws, regulations and conventions. The hot topics of data ownership, freedom and control of human behaviour and legal cyber ethics with potentially disruptive political impact are on the table. This part is closely linked to the next part:

---

[3] *Intel Next 50 Study*, Released 22 Aug 2018. https://newsroom.intel.com/news-releases/consumers-see-world-contradictions-emerging-technologies/ (Accessed 1 Sept 2018)

Part V "Cyber Governance and Ethics" is the extension of the "classical" question, how new technologies can be governed in an international setting as Internet governance was the case. Manifold efforts within in the UN system, by regional political entities such as the EU, by academic, private sector and NGO actors are fast growing. The cyber space is also a chance and a challenge for political systems (e.g. the issue of Net neutrality).

Part VI "Cyber Security, Cyber Crime, Cyber War and Ethics" touches a broad field of strong concerns of citizens, business, armies, parliaments, governments, etc. These articles about autonomous weapons, cyber crime regulations and cyber intelligence show the complexity, but also the political will needed to agree on regulatory frameworks for these threats. The fact that many national governments, but also city councils, universities, and companies have now massively increased–in the last few years–the means and staff for cyber strategies and more cyber security shows that the importance is now recognised.

Part VII "Cyber Media, Cyber Education and Ethics" is a key area of cyber society which would justify a number of additional books only about these aspects of cyber ethics. In this volume, we concentrate pars pro toto on the responsibility of the individual citizen for critical thinking, on cyber bullying among young people as a serious threat, and on child protection as a great need.

The selection does not claim to be complete and comprehensive, but shows pars pro toto that *Cyber Ethics nowadays includes almost all ethical topics.* This is an immense extension compared to the beginning. Richard Spinello, one of the pioneers of Cyber Ethics in teaching, deals in his book "Cyberethics"[4] with ethical values of the internet, regulating and governing the internet, freedom of speech, intellectual property, internet privacy and internet security. All these remain key topics. But

---

[4] Richard Spinello, *Cyberethics. Morality and Law in Cyberspace*, Loans and Barlett Learning: Burlington, 2017[6].

today, Cyber Ethics includes practically all sectors and aspects of society as all parts of the real, physical, emotional, mental, and institutional world are somehow linked to the virtual world of the cyber space. This makes the topic of cyber ethics so fascinating, but also without limitations.

The Cyber Society[5] is no more a theory, but reality: research in innovation labs of twenty years ago are now being implemented–from small start-ups to Small and Medium Enterprises to the tech giants, from village and city level with digitising cities to national strategies–with regional (e.g. EU) and international (UN-related) conventions and regulation efforts.

An example on national level: the *Strategy "Digital Switzerland"*[6] of the Swiss government started 2016 with innovative strategies in the economic sector, but in the meantime includes practically all ministries and levels from cities to provinces and the national level. It includes almost all sectors from education to health care, from e-commerce to fintech (financial industry, regulation of Blockchain[7]), from e-voting to custom control, from cyber weapons to cyber security, from agriculture with smart farming technologies to international diplomacy by developing the UN city Geneva as a "Cyber Hub" for global exchange on the Cyber Space. Interestingly, the Swiss government with its concretisation of the strategy "Digital Switzerland" in September 2018 formulated a top principle of orientation*: "The human being at the centre"*. This means that technology has to serve human beings and not human beings having to serve technology. A key ethical principle.

---

[5] See below article 1.

[6] Swiss Government: *Strategie Digitale Schweiz* 2018-2020, 5 Sept 2018, https://www.bakom.admin.ch/infosociety. Neue Zürcher Zeitung, *Der Bunderat treibt die Digitalisierung voran – neu mit den Kantonen,* NZZ 6 Sept 2018. https://www.nzz.ch/schweiz/bundesrat-setzt-kuenstliche-intelligenz-auf-die-agenda-ld.1417868. (Accessed 7 Sept 2018)

[7] See article 11 in this book.

Volume Co-Editor Pavan Duggal, a top cyber law expert from India is the director of the annual "International Conference on Cyber Law, Cybercrime and Cybersecurity" (http://Cyber Lawcybercrime.com/iccc-2018). It brings together hundreds of experts and institutions. The topic of cyber ethics becomes each year more prominent. Globethics.net, with its Founder President and Ethics expert Christoph Stückelberger and Co-Editor of this Volume, is regularly a keynote speaker at the conference. Some of the authors of this volume have also been actively involved as speakers. Both editors have extensively published on legal and ethical issues.[8]

The Globethics.net Foundation (www.globethics.net), with its head office in Geneva/Switzerland, and ten regional offices on all continents – is the publisher of the volume. Globethics.net will further take the topic of cyber ethics in the form of *teaching modules for universities* as part of its core activity *"Ethics in Higher education"* and also in contributing to international (UN-related) efforts of cyber-governance, ethics of artificial intelligence and others.

We as volume editors invite the readers to send their suggestions, comments and offers of collaboration on one or the other aspects of cyber ethics! We need each other to build a strong international community of people who contribute to strengthening the values-driven, ethical development of the cyber society in order to "learn to be human".

stueckelberger@globethics.net   pavan@pavanduggal.com

10 September 2018
Prof. Dr. Christoph Stückelberger, Geneva/Switzerland
Dr. Pavan Duggal, New Delhi/India

---

[8] See the 60 page bibliography of publications of Christoph Stückelberger, https://www.christophstueckelberger.ch/publishing/articles. The list of over 80 books authored or edited by Pavan Duggal is available here: https://en.wikipedia.org/wiki/Pavan_Duggal

PART I

ETHICS IN THE CYBER SPACE
AN OVERVIEW

1

CYBER SOCIETY: CORE VALUES AND VIRTUES

Christoph Stückelberger, Switzerland

1.1 Definitions

Let us first look at definitions of some key terms for this article and this book[9] in order to provide some clarity about the topic.

Cyber, an abbreviation of cybernetics, means the virtual reality created by computer technologies in the large sense. Virtual reality, created by the cyber world, is also reality, but not tangible in the same way as the physical reality.

Cyber Space is the whole global space of virtual reality, a parallel world to the physical world, with uncountable interactions with the physical world.

Cyber Society means all aspects of modern society which are linked to cyber space and are influenced by it. Today, all sectors of society around the globe are already part of the cyber world. Even without a computer or mobile phone in personal life, the cyber space is everywhere and anytime present, through satellites, the information technolo-

---

[9] Definitions are endlessly available on internet. These are my own definitions. A good extensive collection of short definitions can be found in Pavan Duggal, *Mobile Law*, Third edition, Haryana: LexisNexis, 2016, 16-26.

gies, the weather forecasts, the big data collections, the food production, the health systems etc.

Data means the representation of information, facts, concepts, and knowledge which are collected and have been or will be processed in a computer system or computer network and stored in the memory of a digital hard ware device/entity (computer, cloud etc.).

Big Data are very large amounts of data which are too large to be processed manually and/or inadequately structured to evaluate and make them meaningful and useful. Big Data processing is done by digital technologies and networks (up to the new quantum computing) which allows processing of an immense amount of data in reasonable time. "Big" is related to five V's: volume, velocity (speed), variety (types of data), value (for business) and validity (guarantee and duration).

Artificial Intelligence (AI) is, as part of information technology, the ability of a computer (e.g. as robot) or computer system to produce intelligent solutions and behaviours based on processing large amount of data (big data) and with self-learning mechanisms. The term 'intelligence' in AI is controversial as the definition of what intelligence is, is in itself controversial. Intelligence is characterized by the ability of learning, reasoning, solving (new) problems, using language and perception (awareness).[10]

Ethics gives orientation about right and wrong, good and bad, based on religious, philosophical and other worldviews and value systems. This orientation aims at taken values-driven decisions.

Cyber Ethics gives orientation about right and wrong, good and bad, related to the cyber space. It tries to apply and modify fundamental values and virtues to specific new challenges and situations arising from cyber technologies and cyber society. As cyber space influences all parts of society, cyber ethics includes almost all ethics domains (see below).

---

[10] B.J. Copeland, Artificial Intelligence, Encyclopedia Britannica, updated June 21, 2018, https://www.britannica.com/technology/artificial-intelligence.

Values are general benchmarks of orientation for individuals, communities and institutions for what is good and right, such as freedom, justice and peace. As fundamental values they can be globally accepted, but contextually diversified or they are not generally shared. Justifications of values differ and depend on religious and non-religious world views.

Virtues are benchmarks for individual behaviour for what is good and right such as honesty and modesty. They are often common to all human beings, but different in their priorities, contextualisation and justification.

Norms (ethical) are rules, based on values and virtues, but concretised for specific situations. E.g. the value or fairness and the virtue of honesty lead to the norm "you should not steal".

1.2 Specificities of the Cyberspace

Ethical chances and challenges of Cyberspace are very similar to all other technologies. Technologies are basically means of human beings to expand their capacities (five senses and the body capacity like arms, legs and muscle strength). But there are important specificities of Cyberspace:

➢ **Time:** Cyberspace is anytime: fast, speedy, unbound time.
  Challenge: time differences are often underestimated.
➢ **Space:** Cyberspace is everywhere: global, unbound space.
  Challenge: The human body is still bound to space.
➢ **Size:** Cyberspace is mass production. Reaches great numbers.
  Challenge: Overwhelming information. Infobesity.
➢ **Virtual:** Cyberspace is virtual: digital, not material and physical.
  Challenge: The distinction between real-virtual becomes difficult.
➢ **Anonymous**: Cyberspace facilitates multiple identities.
  Challenge: Freedom versus dishonesty. Darknet as illegal space.

> **Money**: Cyberspace seems to be to a large extent for free.
> Challenge: Cost and capital structures are often not transparent.
> **Power:** Cyberspace seems to be democratic, participatory, open.
> Challenge: Existing power structures are often hidden.

1.3 Dimensions of Cyber Ethics in Cyber Society

As mentioned in the above definition: cyber space influences all parts of society and cyber ethics includes almost all ethics domains. In other words: today, applied ethics in each single problem must consider the cyber-dimension of the ethical question, as the following diagram shows:

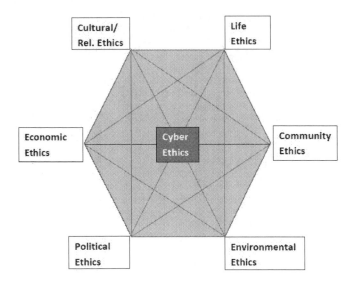

Cyber Ethics as Life Ethics includes life between birth and death. Health ethics, bioethics etc. are heavily in discussion under the aspect of artificial intelligence in ageing, health care, telemedicine etc.

Cyber Ethics as Community Ethics deals with questions of bad and good of social media, changes in community life, chances of global communication, and abuse in terms of cyber bullying, mobbing etc.

Cyber Ethics as Environmental Ethics deals with impact of cyber technology on human-nature relation, environmental negative impact of energy use and positive impact of manifold environmental advantages of weather forecast, scientific research, etc.

Cyber Ethics as Political Ethics deals with changes in political systems, elections, security, armies with autonomous weapons, need and limits of regulation of Cyber Space on international and national levels, etc.

Cyber Ethics as Economic Ethics deals with positive and negative impacts of cyberspace on economic growth, job creation or job losses, financial investments in cyber research by sector, military or not, etc.

Cyber Ethics as Cultural and Religious Ethics looks at ethical and unethical impact of cyberspace on culture, music, art, dance, language diversity, cultural inclusion or discrimination, religious respect or hate messages through the internet, etc.

Cyber Ethics therefore means: In today's world, all ethical topics should include the cyber aspect of it. On the other hand, all cyber-related technological, political, economic etc. developments should reflect the ethical aspects of it in terms of ethically positive and negative impacts.

1.4 Fourth Industrial Revolution

Cyber Ethics is to a great extent the Ethics of (new) technologies. They influence human behaviour, human-nature relations, environment, ways of thinking and acting, brain structures, community life, perspective of past and future, culture and religion, and economy and politics.

This technological revolution is called the Fourth Industrial Revolution. Let us briefly look back to such technological revolutions and a few ethical aspects in order to sharpen our ethical perception of the current technical revolution.

1.4.1 Neolithic Agricultural Revolution

Each technological revolution includes chances and leads to revolutionary disruptions. Ten thousand years ago, from Nomads to Agriculturalists. Disruption: Cain the farmer kills the nomad shepherd Abel. The agricultural life style was winner above the nomad existence (Genesis 4:1-16). And even in this very early Neolithic technological revolution the fundamental ethical question was raised. According to the Jewish-Christian faith, God asked Cain after killing Abel, "where is your brother?" Cain answered, "why should I care for my brother?" Technological revolutions have to raise the question from the beginning, of how the weaker parts of society can benefit and not be killed or marginalized by the technological innovation.

First farmers   Farmer Cain kills Nomad Shepherd Abel

1.4.2 Industrial Revolutions. From Proletariat to Digitariat?

Four Industrial Revolutions are counted:

1. Water/Steam Power   led to mechanized production
2. Electric Power   led to mass production
3. Electronics/ICT   led to automated production
4. Digital Power   leads to integrated data from
   physical, digital, biological sphere.

Let us briefly look at three of these four industrial revolutions:

The *First Industrial Revolution* in the second half of the 19th century[11] brought a lot of technological benefits with the steam machine, the railway, beginning of electricity. Urbanisation, and poverty of workers was also linked to industrialisation. Christian urban social work (diakonia) aimed to help reduce social disaster, and Marx developed his radical view of changing the economic system.

Main Railway Station Zurich 1900   Käthe Kollwitz, Weberzug, 1897

The *Second Industrial Revolution* at the beginning of the 20th century was symbolised by the beginning of automation assembly lines for cars by Henry Ford in 1913 (image left side below). But the workers' General Strike in Liverpool against new automatized machines showed immediately the disruptive characteristic of such innovation which led to a workers' social revolution as reaction to the technological innovation.

Assembly Lines for cars, 1913   Workers' General Strike 1911

---

[11] See e.g. the illuminating magazine *Deutschland 1850-1900: Die industrielle Revolution*, Der Spiegel, Geschichte, 4/2018.

The *Fourth Industrial Revolution* is the one we are now immediately involved with: cyber society, digital revolution and artificial intelligence. Also, this technological revolution is at the same time an economic and socio-political, and even a religious[12] revolution. As with former industrial revolutions, it leads to immense technological progress and at the same time leads to large social disruptions, again mainly on the question of loss of jobs, freedom, and security.

Whereas in Japan 2015, the first teacher robot was teaching children, while in the same period in Chicago 2012, teachers demonstrated for fair pay and better working conditions.

Japan 2015 Teacher Robot   Chicago 2012 Teachers Demonstration

"It is possible, that the digitisation leads to a new mass of disaffected people, a new proletariat."[13] A new "digitariat", a proletariat in the digital age of the disadvantaged who can hardly benefit from the digital revolution, is already visible in some parts of the world.

Manifold efforts are now going on to manage this immensely fast current fourth industrial revolution in a direction which is of benefit for humanity and can minimize the negative impact on humans and nature.

As in each technological (and political) revolution, at the beginning the society is divided in two parts, those who expect the heaven on earth

---

[12] See below chapters 10 and 11 on Deus Homo – Homo Deus.

[13] *Offen sein statt Selbstgewiss*. Interview with the historian Andreas Rödder, in *Deutschland 1850-1900: Die industrielle Revolution*, Der Spiegel, Geschichte, 4/2018, 132-136 (135. Translation by the author).

and the solution for almost all problems from this change and those who fear hell and destruction up to the self-destruction of humanity. The history of technological and political revolutions shows us that both are exaggerations. The reality is a mixed result of some progress and benefits and some dangers and destructions. The reason – from an ethical, theological and philosophical perspective is that human beings remain human beings which means that technology remains as good and bad as the human beings which develop, maintain, destroy, use and abuse them. Even though some techno-prophets claim that this will be different in the Fourth Industrial Revolution because future robots with AI will be more powerful than human beings and act independent from them, by historical analysis, ethical reflection and Christian Faith tells me that this will not be the case. Rather the Fourth Industrial Revolution is in fact a gigantic transformation, but still comparable with other transitions in the history of humankind. This should not be a tranquillizer nor lead to fatalism, on the contrary it should avoid fearful paralysis or uncritical enthusiasm but rather lead to a rational, value-driven engagement for the fruitful use of these technologies and the courageous avoidance and refuse of its abuse for destructive activities.

This rational and passionate engagement then leads to the core ethical question, in which values and virtues can guide us in this critical phase of the Fourth Industrial Revolution.

But before we look at values and virtues, we briefly look at users' motivations in using cyberspace – with only a short list – which then already shows the ethical challenges and pitfalls in using cyberspace. These motivations produce constructive and destructive energy and are oriented towards values and anti-values as well as virtues and vices.

1.5 Users' Motivations in Cyber-Space

Motivations of users of cyberspace for using and abusing it·

1.	Information	education, formation
2.	Entertainment	gaming, distraction, adrenalin kick
3.	Wealth	profit making, economic competition/war
4.	Poverty	access to info to overcome poverty
5.	Professions	knowledge, increasing job professionalism
6.	Belonging	networking, family, peer groups, identity
7.	Damage	deliberately doing harm, targeted or random
8.	Revenge:	targeted damage, e.g. mobbing, bullying
9.	Power	cyber-warfare, -intelligence, espionage
10.	Addiction	addicted gaming, dependency
11.	Ideology	political, ideological, religious platform
12.	Narcissism	Self-affirmation, platform for the Ego, pride
13.	Boredom	overcoming boring, meaningless, saturated life by action and adventure.

Some of these motivations are predominantly ethically positive or negative, but a good number of them can lead to constructive and destructive results as is the case for many human actions and many human-made technologies.

1.6 Core Values and Virtues

1.6.1 Tree of Values and Virtues

Which are the fundamental values and virtues[14] as ethical orientation for decisions and actions in cyber-society? They are not different in the virtual world from values in the natural and physical world! We live – this is my ethical assumption and in itself an important ethical founda-

---

[14] These values and virtues are in detail developed - in multicultural and global perspectives, in Christoph Stückelberger/ Walter Fust/ Obiora Ike (eds.), *Global Ethics for Leadership: Values and Virtues for Life*, Geneva: Globethics.net, 2016. Also Christoph Stückelberger/ Frank Mathwig, *Grundwerte. Eine theologisch-ethische Orientierung*, Zürich: Theol. Verlag, 2007.

tion - in one and the same reality and have to avoid a dichotomy of two separate worlds! If we act as if there are two worlds, a virtual and a material, we fall in the trap of a dualistic world view and also open the door for double morality. As it is not ethical to say, "my values at home in private life are different from my values in business and professional life", so it is not ethical to say, "in the virtual cyberspace I can have another (anonymous) identity and be a thief whereas I would never be it in my physical existence".

Tree of Values	Tree of Virtues
1. Responsibility	1. Integrity
2. Freedom	2. Compassion
3. Justice	3. Care
4. Equity	4. Transparency
5. Peace	5. Accountability
6. Security	6. Reliability
7. Community	7. Respect
8. Inclusiveness	8. Humility
9. Participation	9. Courage
10. Forgiveness	10. Gratitude
11. Stewardship	11. Generosity

1.6.2 Relational Values and Virtues

These values and virtues are not 22 isolated islands, but they are strongly interconnected. One big problem in ethics, including cyber ethics, is the human attempt to maximize one or the other value or virtue which then leads to dangerous imbalances. Examples: if we want to have maximum freedom in access to data and information, we may violate the value of community, the virtue of respect and the value of responsibility. It then may create resistance and disruptions against data collection and use. Extreme individualism leads to anarchy, extreme communalism to dictatorship, extreme freedom to anarchy, extreme equality to overregulated planned economy, etc. A balanced is needed.

The answer is a balanced system of values and virtues which relates them to each other. I call it the "relationality"[15] (being relational) of values and virtues. The optimum, not maximum of a value is then the goal.

The following diagram shows *how values are connected to each other*.

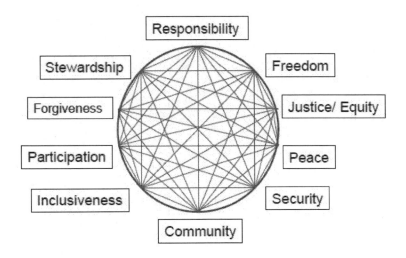

---

[15] The term "Relationalität/ Relationality" is from my teacher and pioneer in modern economic ethics, Prof. Arthur Rich in his famous book *Business and Economic Ethics: The Ethics of Economic Systems*, Peeters Publishers, 2006, 181-188.

The following diagram shows *how virtues are connected to each other*.

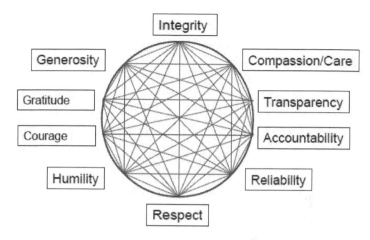

Related to cyberspace, the relation among values and virtues means e.g.:

Freedom   - use cyberspace with Responsibility, Accountability

Justice   - enable fair, just, equitable us of cyberspace

Equity   - promote Internet Governance with equal rights

Peace   - develop "just cyber warfare", promote just peace

Security   - the obligation to protect and the right to forget

Inclusiveness - reduce the gap between digital winners and digitariat

Privacy   - protect private spheres and rights (big data)

Dignity   - protect + promote dignity of every human being

Participation - enable participation of all in pricing and laws

Honesty   - promote transparency by technology and law

Integrity   - defend values with courage + resist temptations.

1.7 Old Values or Eschatological Vision?

Ethical values and virtues last for thousands of years. As human beings we always have basic needs such as protection, a community, dignity and identity and a meaningful life. Religions in all diversity emphasise such human values: greed destroys community, therefore liberation from greed is taught by all world religions. Protection of life and respect for the dignity of the other is a precondition for peace. Trust based on honesty is the foundation for all relations.

Therefore, Cyber-Ethics 4.0 does not have to reinvent from zero ethics, but has to apply "old" values to the new situation. A good example is the new book "Soziallehre 4.0"[16] which applies and re-interprets the classical catholic Social Doctrin for the new "times of Digitisation". The five classical values of the Social Doctrine, Personality, Subsidiarity, Solidarity, Sustainability and Common Good[17] build the ethical orientation for digitisation with a human face. "Remaining humans"[18] is the key vision of dealing with the machine. This of course provokes the core anthropological question about the essence of being human. And being human is not static but dynamic and always influenced by the human-machine interaction. The author of the book summarizes at the end the differences between humans and machines, e.g. robots:

"1. The human being is not a machine.

2. The human being calculates slowly.

3. The human being gets aching muscles.

4. The human being can be emphatic.

5. The human being has a free will.

6. The human being bears responsibility.

7. The human being knows about God." [19]

Another approach than referring to former values is the *eschatological perspective*.[20] Eschatology means thinking and acting from the end

---

[16] Heinrich Wullhorst, Soziallehre 4.0. wie wir in Zeiten der Digitalisierung-menschlich bleiben können, Bonfifatius, Paderborn 2018.

[17] Ibid, 25-38.

[18] "Menschen bleiben", ibid 143-145.

[19] Ibid, 163. Translation from German by Stückelberger.

of times, from the future, from the envisaged ideal. It may not contradict to the classical approach, but it is more dynamic. It does not ask how classical or traditional values and virtues build the benchmark for the current world, but it asks where humanity wants to go and to be. What is the humane society we envisage for the future? In religious terms: what is the will and vision of God for the future of the whole creation? This includes openness for change, if needed radical change, and offers at the same time an ethical vision.

In Christian faith and ethics, Eschatological ethics is called the vision of the Kingdom of God. The Kingdom of God will not be realised on earth, but it is the stimulus and the horizon to orient daily decisions. The Bible in the Old Testament is full of such visions such as the vision of peace where enemies like lions and sheep peacefully live together (Jes. 11:7). The Bible in the New Testament designs the Kingdom of God especially in the parables of Jesus: "The Kingdom of God is like...": It is a place where the poor are dignified and have their place (Luke 6:20), where God and God's love is in the midst of the heart of people and now more outside on stones of law (Luke 17.21), where humanity is an inclusive community like in a banquet open for all (Luke 14:15), where servant leadership is winning over exploiting leadership (Matthew 20:28), where fairness and justice reigns, hunger and sickness are overcome (Matthew 25: 31-46) and where - in modern terms - the Sustainable Development Goals are implemented[21].

---

[20] See e.g. the theologies of Leonhard Ragaz, Christoph Blumhardt, Arthur Rich (*Business and Economic Ethics: The Ethics of Economic Systems*, Peeters Publishers, 2006, chapter 6) and Christoph Stückelberger (*Vermittlung und Parteinahme. Der Versöhnungsauftrag der Kirchen in gesellschaftlichen Konflikten*, Theologischer Verlag: Zürich 1988, 349-356).

[21] See Christoph Stückelberger, *God's Strategy for Life*, New Horizons, ECLOF, Issue 23, June 2005, 11. Download: https://www.christophstueckelberger.ch/publishing/articles/

1.8 Cyber Ethics by Norms, Laws and Relations

What is the relation between ethical values and legal norms?[22] Is the call for ethics in terms of self-responsibility and self-regulation enough or do we need binding laws based on values? And in many cultures, even more important than principle-based values and norms-based laws are relation-based decisions: most important is to maintain and strengthen relations. E.g. if bribes are needed to maintain the relation, one pays bribes and it is prevalent over the principal of not paying bribes or even the law forbidding it.

A global Cyber Space with Cyber Ethics needs all three

- *The Rules of Ethics* for visions, orientations, community.
- *The Rules of Law* for reliability, trust, control of power, etc.
- *The Rules of Relations* for humane relations.

The three dimensions need to be balanced. It means:

- In societies which tend to solve all issues with laws and regulations, relations and individual and collective ethical values have to be strengthened.
- In societies with low trust in and respect of the rules of law, the implementation of law has to be strengthened.
- In societies with individual values, but an exaggerated individualism and little sense and respect for communities, the rules of relations have to be strengthened.

---

[22] More about it in the next article 2 in this book.

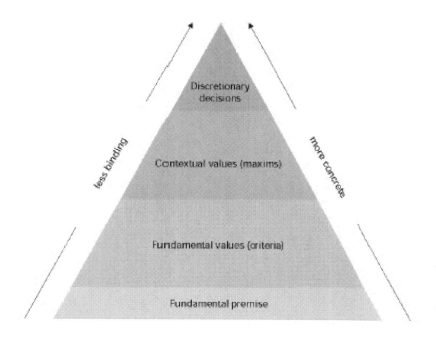

In Ethics, there is a hierarchy of levels of the binding character of a norm[23]: Fundamental Premises are normally not expressed, but implicitly provided, e.g. "What I see exists." Or "I want to live". Without these premises, ethics is a phantom in the air. Then come the fundamental values and virtues which are general, long term valid even though they can change in priority. The next level are contextual values, also called maxims, standards or laws. International conventions, national laws or standards such as the ISO standards are placed on this level. They express values in a specific context of space and time. They are more concrete and less generally binding, but more binding in terms of law and obligations.

---

[23] Graph from Christoph Stückelberger, *Global Trade Ethics*, WCC Publications: Geneva 2002, 24.

The SDGs, described below, are on this level. On top of this level, there are then specific areas of applications, e.g. ethics of artificial intelligence or even more concrete the behaviour and programming of a specific robot.

Norms, standards and laws have to be elaborated in a democratic process. A well-established form are advisory ethics committees. In the 1990's, with the growth of biotechnology, many governments installed national bioethics committees. The same is needed for National Cyber Ethics Committees as e.g. proposed by a Commission of the House of Lords of the United Kingdom (see next chapter 2.8 and 6.2.2). Such ethics committees are also needed in leading IT and AI companies (Google and Alibaba have them which is positive, but they of course are led by their interests), in Universities as Sub-committees of the Research Ethics Committees and in multilateral institutions. "The European Group on Ethics in Science and Technology" (EGE)[24] is a good example for it. It is an independent advisory body of the President of the European Commission. It was built in 1991 mainly on bioethics and published since then 29 position papers, called opinions[25]. Each of the 28 EU member states has a respective "National Ethics Council". A similar approach is now needed for Cyber-Ethics and especially ethics of Artificial Intelligence (see below chapter 2.9).

1.9 The UN Sustainable Development Goals SDGs

A clear international and value-based regulatory framework for Cyber Space and Cyber-ethics are the Sustainable Development Goals SDGs 2015-2030, approved by the United Nations General Assembly in 2015.

---

[24] http://ec.europa.eu/research/ege/index.cfm. (Accessed 2 Sept 2018)
[25] http://ec.europa.eu/research/ege/index.cfm?pg=reports (Accessed 2 Sept 2018)

ICT4D[26] (Information and Communication Technologies for Development) was the technical key word since the World Summit for Information Society WSIS in Geneva 2003, ICT4SDG[27] (Information and Communication Technologies for the SDGs) is the current concept, under leadership of ITU and UNESCO.

All cyber related activities have to be measured against the benchmark of the SDGs! Do they contribute to the SDGs or contradict or hinder them? Technologies such as Artificial intelligence also have to clearly be oriented towards these goals. AI is positive, if it contributes to the SDGs without doing harm for others and it is negative if it does not contribute to the SDGs or does harm to them. The SDGs, in Introduction to them as in the different goals, is based on core ethical values[28]:

- *Guarantee basic human needs* such as food, water, health, education
- *equality* of all human beings, including gender equality and overcoming all forms of discrimination
- *justice* in equal treatment and access

---

[26] https://www.itu.int/net/wsis/.

[27] https://www.itu.int/en/sustainable-world/Pages/default.aspx.

[28] See paper *Globethics.net Engaged for Values-driven SDGs*, Geneva 2015, https://www.globethics.net/sustainable-development (Accessed 1 Sept 2018)

- *freedom* of action and decision
- *inclusion* so that all human beings are included in the community
- *sustainability* as the long term and environmentally sound development
- *peace* as the foundation for development and progress, eliminate violence.

1.10   Artificial Intelligence Ethics: "AI for Good"

The hot topic of artificial intelligence and Ethics – one of the most debated currently within the topics of Cyber Ethics – has to be seen as a concretisation of the broader topic of Cyber Space serving the SDGs and the technological dimension of it, called ICT4SDG.

The International Telecommunication Union ITU as the specialised UN agency for telecommunication and leading many of the cyber-related issues, organised 7-9 June 2018 in Geneva for the second time the international conference "AI for Good Global Summit: How Artificial Intelligence can Boost Sustainable Development".[29] It is an important effort to support positive use of new technologies like AI for health, education, food, water, citizenship, peace etc. as ITU with this conferences does. But it is also needed to develop fast clear limitations, regulations and laws[30] for the use and especially against the negative abuse of such new technologies as we already see with autonomous weapons, cybercrime etc. The different articles of this book look at opportunities and threats of cyber-related technologies.

The *United Nations Global Pulse* is a new unit for "Harnessing big data for development and humanitarian action"[31] similar to ITU, but

---

[29] https://www.itu.int/en/ITU-T/AI/2018/Pages/default.aspx

[30] Duggal, Pavan, Artificial Intelligence Law, New Delhi, 2017, 26ff.

[31] https://www.unglobalpulse.org/about-new. Accessed 2 Sept 2018)

with a focus on big data, it looks at how big data can serve the SDGs and where they hinder it. For 2019, the "International Congress for the Governance of Artificial Intelligence" (ICGAI 2019) is in preparation and international new networks like "Building Agile Governance for AI and Robotics" (AG4AI)[32] and "The World Technology Network" (WTN)[33] work on it.

The *EU Commission* appointed in June 2018 52 experts to the new multi-stakeholder "High Level Group on Artificial Intelligence": "The Group will also prepare draft ethics guidelines that will build on the work of the European Group on Ethics in Science and New Technologies and of the European Union Agency for Fundamental Rights in this area. The guidelines will cover issues such as fairness, safety, transparency, the future of work, and more broadly the impact on upholding fundamental rights, including privacy and personal data protection, dignity, consumer protection and non-discrimination. The draft guidelines will be finalised by the end of the year and presented to the Commission at the beginning of 2019." [34] This High Level Group will also support "The European AI Alliance"[35] which is in formation since 2018 as an open forum for the discussion of AI. This shows the different approaches between leading powers: whereas USA and China are top leaders in funding AI research, the EU with its democratic structure and tradition seeks a broad democratic process and consensus on new technologies such as AI.

There should not only be a competition in AI technology research, but also AI ethics research. Who invests in ethics of AI and Cyber-Ethics and how much? The *UK Government* is realistic and confesses

---

[32] https://bgi4ai.org/. (Accessed 2 Sept 2018)

[33] https://www.wtn.net/ (Accessed 2 Sept 2018)

[34]   https://ec.europa.eu/digital-single-market/en/news/commission-appoints-expert-group-ai-and-launches-european-ai-alliance. (Accessed 2 Sept 2018)

[35] https://ec.europa.eu/digital-single-market/en/european-ai-alliance. (Accessed 2 Sept 2018)

that they cannot compete with the large players in terms of money for AI research, but they do not give and make out of the weakness a virtue: they want to be top in AI Ethics research! The House of Lords in United Kingdom adopted and recently published an official Report of the Select Committee on Artificial Intelligence with the proposal of a "Centre for Data Ethics and Innovation: "As we have previously discussed, the Industrial Strategy also announced a new Centre for Data Ethics and Innovation. This would be a 'world-first advisory body which would review the current 'governance landscape' and advise the Government on 'ethical, safe and innovative uses of data, including AI'. The Centre would engage with industry to establish data trusts, and there would be wide consultation as to the remit of the Centre in due course. The Prime Minister reaffirmed these ambitions in her speech to the World Economic Forum on 25 January 2018. Matt Hancock MP told us that the Centre 'will not be a regulatory body, but it will provide the leadership that will shape how artificial intelligence is used'. The Minister said the Government wanted 'to ensure that the adoption of AI is accompanied, and in some cases led, by a body similarly set up not just with technical experts who know what can be done but with ethicists who understand what should be done so that the gap between those two questions is not omitted'. The Minister cited the Human Fertilisation and Embryology Authority as an example of how this can be an effective approach and said, 'it is incredibly important to ensure that society moves at the same pace as the technology, because this technology moves very fast'." [36]

These efforts show, that AI and Ethics and the Governance of AI is a growing topic on all levels, from UN to EU to national governments, from academia to NGOs and private sector. In China, soon the leading

---

[36] House of the Lords, Select Committee on Artificial Intelligence, Report of Session 2017-19, *AI in the UK: ready, willing and able?*, published London, 16 April 2018, para 353-354.

nation in AI research with huge investments, "the ethical discourse about AI is only just starting in China".[37]

1.11 Cyber-Capitalism: Cyber-Ethics as Business Ethics

The classical three production factors are natural resources (land, mining etc), labour (human and animal work force) and capital. But in the Cyber Society, data becomes the fourth, very powerful production factor. The power is not the normal small pieces of data, but the Big Data as huge data collection thanks to fast computers, cyber-connectivity of computers through the internet, and analytical tools through algorithms.

Cyber Technologies as all technologies are closely linked to economy: they need – more and more – very high amounts of investment capital for top research and they are driven by world giant private companies and – on a lower

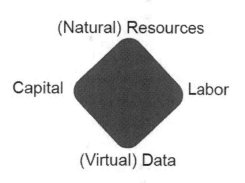

level, by public academic research institutions. The concentration of power in such technologies is significant.

The *concentration of power of Big Data* is visible when we look at the huge data transfer per minute on internet which is mainly streamed through these few platforms[38]:

---

[37] https://www.merics.org/de/blog/ethical-discourse-about-ai-only-just-starting-china.

[38] http://www.visualcapitalist.com/internet-minute-2018/ (Accessed 1 Sept 2018)

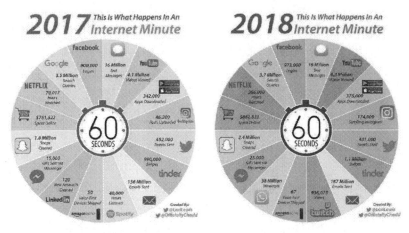

Data ownership is the biggest "capital" today. Even though many companies, individuals and states own data, the largest data ownership happens as a bipolar world of the few giant American companies and now – as an almost exact mirror – with respective Chinese companies:

Service	USA	China
Search Machine	Google	Baidu
Social Net	Facebook	Tencent
E-commerce	Amazon	Alibaba
E-payment	Paypal	Alipay
Messenger	WhatsApp	Wechat
Videos	YouTube	Youku Tudou
Data Ownership	Companies	Companies

This new digital bi-polar world shows also the huge macroeconomic importance of the cyber space. The same is visible in the expected explosion of revenues from business related to artificial intelligence (see graph on next page)[39].

China with its very ambitious new Silk Road initiative, called One Belt One Road (OBOR) or now Belt and Road (BAR), aims at developing infrastructure connections throughout 60+ countries from South East Asia to East Africa. This should foster trade and development. Supporters see it as a great chance for many countries, others fear the dominance of China. But it is not only about railways, ports and roads, but there is also a "digital silk road" [40] on the way.

Enterprise artificial intelligence market revenue worldwide 2016-2025

Revenues from the artificial intelligence for enterprise applications market worldwide, from 2016 to 2025 (in million U.S. dollars)

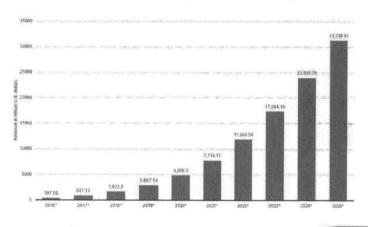

---

[39] https://www.weforum.org/agenda/2018/07/we-know-ethics-should-inform-ai-but-which-ethics-robotics. (Accessed 3 Sept 2018).

[40] https://www.weforum.org/agenda/2018/08/china-is-building-a-new-silk-road-and-this-one-s-digital. (Accessed 7 Aug 2018)

The funding of Artificial Intelligence Research is another example of

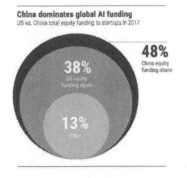

China dominates global AI funding
US vs. China total equity funding to startups in 2017

48%
China equity
funding share

38%
US equity
funding share

13%
Other

the concentration of power in the cyber space and especially the big data collection and use. In 2017, China dominated the global funding of AI start-ups with a share of 48%, compared to USA with 38% and others 13%.[41] Funding AI Research is most probably the largest scientific, technological, economic, political and military power game in the current cyber world. After Ke Jie, the Chinese world champion in the Ancient Chinese board game Go, was beaten by the Google owned DeepMind robot in 201, China declared the country aims at becoming the world leader in AI by 2030. This is not unlikely to happen.

Another hot topic enabled by big data and artificial intelligence algorithms is *fintech*, the technologies applied in finance, banking, and currency transactions. *Blockchain technologies* are seen as a great chance by some and a great threat by others. Even though it is described as the most democratic and transparent financial system possible, there is at the same time a huge power struggle for market shares and influence on the future of the Blockchain development going on:

The tech giants Amazon, Microsoft, Facebook and others are already building and selling Blockchain services and in many industries, Blockchain consortia are built: Telecom industries, extracting industries, supply chain traders, insurance companies, Distributed ledger technology DLT, R3 as consortium of 200+ banks, Maerks and others on shipping supply consortia, BITA Blockchain in Transport Alliance, B3i as insur-

---

[41]   https://www.theverge.com/2018/2/22/17039696/china-us-ai-funding-startup-comparison (Accessed 7 Aug 2018)

ance consortium and others[42]. The following graph shows: the large banks already build five large Blockchain consortia[43]:

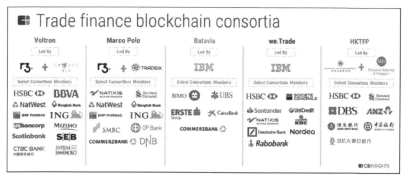

These few examples show that cyber ethics is in its core not only technology ethics, but even more economic ethics, political ethics and military ethics. Let us mention only four examples of ethical challenges in AI with four quotes: *Inequality, work ethics, freedom and control of power.*

"*Worsening inequality*, and a corresponding negative impact on social stability, is one of the greatest potential risks associated with the Fourth Industrial Revolution. While new technologies can democratise access to employment and entrepreneurial opportunities, not to mention education and knowledge, the tendency of new global technology plat-

---

[42] The Future of Blockchain Tech: How venture firms, corporates, regulators and builders are shaping Blockchain technology's future. CB Insights Briefing, Slides on https://www.cbinsights.com/research/tech-giants-blockchain-projects/?utm_source=CB+Insights+Newsletter&utm_campaign=65055acb50-Top_Research_Briefs_09_22_2018&utm_medium=email&utm_term=0_9dc051 3989-65055acb50-91268653. Accessed 23 Sept 2018.

[43] CBS Research Briefs: How Banks Are Teaming Up To Bring Blockchain To Trade Finance, 23 Aug 2018. https://www.cbinsights.com/research/banks-regulators-trade-finance-Blockchain/ (Accessed 24 Aug 2018)

forms to dominate winner-takes-all markets could exacerbate inequality and social fragmentation."[44]

Work ethics: "Perhaps, though, what we need to think more about, in the ethics of AI, is the way that we treat the human data processors who prepare material for the training of artificial neural networks and other machine learning techniques. For instance, staff on precarious contracts at Facebook and Google are paid $0.02 for each image that they moderate, meaning that they must sift through heaps of scarring images of child abuse for a tiny quantity of remuneration. The point of what I'm trying to say here is this: we think that the ethics of AI are about restricting the actions of advanced machine-learning algorithms to operate within specific normative moral bounds. What we don't often acknowledge is that such learning often still depends upon vast quantities of human labour to filter the datasets. This work is repetitive and mentally scarring. And it is paid very badly. Those who preach the need for AI ethics principles are also, often, Silicon Valley billionaires. Yet their wealth relies on the exploitation of people who filter and moderate content, to feed to AI. Perhaps we should address the ethics of this, before we heed the cries for ethics to be transferred solely to the realm of machine regulation."[45]

Freedom: "Dataism is the first movement since 1789 that created a genuinely novel value: freedom of information. We mustn't confuse freedom of information with the old liberal value of freedom of expression. Freedom of expression was given to humans, and protected their right to think and say what they wished – including their right to keep their mouths shut and their thoughts to themselves. Freedom of infor-

---

[44]   *World   Economic   Forum,   2017,   4th   Industrial   Revolution.* https://toplink.weforum.org/knowledge/insight/a1Gb0000001RIhBEAW/explore/dimension/a1Gb00000027vYmEAI/summary (Accessed 8 Aug 2018)

[45]   https://www.theguardian.com/commentisfree/2017/dec/24/facebook-google-youtube-dirty-work-social-media-inappropriate-content (Accessed 8 Aug 2018)

mation, in contrast, is not given to humans. It is given to information. Moreover, this novel value may impinge on humans' traditional freedom of expression, by privileging the right of information to circulate freely over the right of humans to own data and to restrict its movement."[46]

Control of Power: all these examples and analyses show that the Fourth Industrial Revolution which we face in form of the Cyber Revolution, has many similarities to former industrial revolutions with its potential and challenges. The wild early capitalism of the first and second industrial revolution provoked the other extreme of the overregulated dictatorial communism and finally led after the Second World War at least in Europe to a more balanced social market economy. In a similar way, we are today with the "Internet Revolution" [47] in a "Class conflict in the age of cyber-capitalism"[48].

1.12 Recommendations

In this article we developed fundamental values and virtues, their relationality, their relation to standards, norms and laws and their application through the Sustainable Development Goals SDGs and as example in the ethics of Artificial Intelligence as well as in the orientation about the economic power structures in Cyber Capitalism of the few worldwide leading companies and their Big Data as the current most profitable production factor.

Let us come to *recommendations* for selected domains as conclusions.

---

[46] Harari, Yuval Noah. *Homo Deus. A Brief History of Tomorrow*, Harper. Kindle Edition, 388.

[47] Richard Barbrook/ Andy Cameron, *The Internet Revolution. From Dotcom Capitalism to Cybernetic Communism*, Amsterdam: University of Applied Sciences, 2015.

[48] James Laxer, *The Undeclared war: Class conflict in the age of cyber-capitalism*, Viking publisher 1998.

Education

1. *Set the ethical frame of values and virtues* for behaviour in the Cyber Space: freedom, non-violent communication, fairness, equality, sustainability, caring and virtues such as respect, honesty, transparency, integrity etc.[49]

2. *Enlarge media education* from technical skills to compulsory media education on values and virtues, on all levels up to higher education.

3. *Strengthen responsibility of individual consumers* of cyber devices, from mobile communication to social media, internet in general up to interacting with robots. The German Cyber Expert and Philosopher Ingo Radermacher formulated twelve stimulating rules (maxims) how to deal with the digital world[50]:

   1 Be diligent, be educated

   2 Become a part-time-computer scientist

   3 Learn, how to learn

   4 Simplify

   5 Take your language seriously

   6 Develop strength against fragility

   7 Get competence in security issues

   8 Look for a balance between agility and stability

   9 Differentiate looking at innovations

   10 Leadership means "herding cats"

   11 Deepen your understanding of human beings and the world

   12 Engage in it.

---

[49] See above chapter 2.6 and below article 4.

[50] Ingo Radermacher, *Digitalisierung selbst denken. Eine Anleitung, mit der die Transformation gelingt*, Business Village: Göttingen 2017, 85-196 (192). See also his article in this book.

Regulation

4. *Agree internationally on governance structures for global cyber-related technologies*, especially the governance of Artificial Intelligence and of financial technologies (*fintech*) such as Blockchain technologies which both have manifold ethical aspects to clarify. Even though with the current trends of protectionism and scepticism about multilateralism, global governance rules for technologies which have no national boarders are needed, as it was needed to establish the internet governance. Legal Regulations on a national level and internationally need synchronization as much as possible, finding the balance between overregulation/police state/cyberspace protectionism on one side and too liberal regulations benefitting only the powerful and wealthy on the other.

5. *Formalize Ethics Committees as national and international cyberspace regulatory bodies.* They can be with a large mandate including different dimensions of cyber space or – more realistically – focussed on e.g. Artificial Intelligence and Ethics

6. *Equip Police and Courts* with enough trained specialists on cybercrime and cybersecurity, especially in developing countries.

Politics

7. *Guarantee Human Rights* in Cyberspace such as freedom of expression, freedom of assembly (networking), security, privacy, freedom of religious expression, etc.

8. *Clean Police and Courts* from corrupt practices which weaken effective measures against cybercrime.

9. *Resist the abuse of cybersecurity and anticorruption policies* as justification for authoritarian controls of citizens and violating human rights.

10. *Control Intelligence Agencies* (Secret Services) in their cybersecurity activities, by parliaments and governments, codes and Intelligence Agency Ethics.

Economy

11. *Pricing:* what are the future models for financing values-driven cyberspace? Open access, for free? State-owned and supported? Adverts-financed? Client-financed? Philanthropy-supported? Which mix of all this?

12. *Financing Research:* technological innovation needs huge capital resources which is mainly provided by private companies (see above on AI research). It has to be balanced with publicly transparent research and ethical research standards for private and public sector. As in bioethics e.g. the cloning of human beings is internationally forbidden, also limits in AI have to be set. The slippery slope where the limits of what is ethical are constantly shifted, has to be taken seriously.

13. *The Cyber Economy* is dominated by bi-polar cyber-giants in USA and China with mirror-companies and networks (see above). In order to avoid a new bi-polar world with a new cold war, decentralisation, democratic regulation and a multi-polar cyber-world and multi-lateral rules and regulations are needed.

CYBER LAW AND CYBER ETHICS: HOW THE TWINS NEED EACH OTHER

Pavan Duggal, India

2.1 The Importance of Cyber Law

It has been further predicted that by 2020, the estimated number of passwords used by humans and machines worldwide will grow to 300 billion.[51] The increasing significance and advent of cyberspace has brought forward large number of complex legal, policy and regulatory issues concerning cyberspace. That is a reason why Cyber Law as a discipline has evolved extensively in the last two decades. More than two decades ago, I had given a definition of the term of Cyber Law which today still becomes relevant and topical. *"Simply speaking, Cyber Law is a generic term, which refers to all the legal and regulatory aspects of Internet and the World Wide Web. Anything concerned with or related to or emanating from any legal aspects or issues concerning any activity of netizens and others, in Cyberspace comes within the ambit of Cyber Law."*[52]

Cyber Law's first beginnings were with the first Cyber Law being passed in the State of Utah in United States. Thereafter began a long

---

[51] https://www.scmagazine.com/video-300-billion-passwords-by-2020-report-predicts/article/634848/es. All links in this article accessed 11 Sept 2018.

[52] http://Cyber Laws.net/cyber-law/

journey as different countries came up with their different national laws on cyber legal frameworks. Countries have been invariably inspired by the UNCITRAL Model Law on Electronic Commerce which was passed by the General Assembly in the year 1997.

Different countries have not only come up with the national laws for promoting e-commerce but have also come up with extensive legal frameworks to govern cybercrimes, data protection, privacy, electronic transfer of funds, regulating electronic transactions, electronic evidence, cybersecurity and other diverse subjects.

2.2 The Significance of Cyber Ethics

No wonder, in this entire developed cyberspace ecosystem, cyber ethics becomes a matter of immense significance. In fact, internet began as a lawless jungle, and a lot of people still believe that internet is a place where law does not apply. However, over a period of time, Cyber Law has evolved and has displaced that particular perception of cyberspace being a lawless jungle. Internet is a place where a majority of human activities takes place. Therefore, it is imperative to appreciate that ethical principles, which govern human acts and conduct, should also need to be equally applicable in cyberspace. In this context, the discipline of cyber ethics has evolved which has a direct connection and co-relation with Cyber Law.

Before proceeding forward, it is important to understand as to what is the concept of cyber ethics. Cyber ethics is a newly evolving discipline that is looking at the ethical ramifications aspects and impacts of acts, deeds and things done in cyberspace. Various stakeholders have defined cyber ethics in their own distinctive manner. *Wikipedia* defines 'cyber ethics' as *"the philosophic study of ethics pertaining to computers, encompassing user behavior and what computers are programmed* to do, and how this affects individuals and society. "[53] Further, *Pusey, P. & Sadera* in the article entitled *Cyberethics, cybersafety, and cybersecurity: Preservice teacher knowledge, preparedness, and the need for teacher education to make a difference*[54] have defined cyber ethics as a set of "*moral choices individuals make when using Internet-capable technologies and digital media.*"[55] Cyberethics is a branch of applied ethics that examines moral, legal, and social issues at the intersection of computer/information and communication technologies. This field is sometimes also referred to by phrases such as Internet ethics, computer ethics, and information ethics. The expression "Internet ethics" is somewhat narrow in scope and thus unable to capture the range of cyber-related ethical issues that arise independently of the Internet and networked computers per se.[56] In relation to cyber world, a new type of ethics known as computer ethics has emerged resulting in the creation of Code of Computer Ethics that may have binding effect on the professionals particularly if the code becomes part of the work ethic and procedure.[57]

The Centre for Internet Security has defined cyber ethics as "the code of responsible behaviour on the Internet."[58] According to some, the definition of cyber-ethics is using appropriate ethical behaviour and ac-

---

[53] https://en.wikipedia.org/wiki/Cyberethics

[54] http://etec.ctlt.ubc.ca/510wiki/Cyberethics#cite_note-1

[55] Pusey, P. & Sadera, W. A. (2011). Cyberethics, cybersafety, and cybersecurity: Preservice teacher knowledge, preparedness, and the need for teacher education to make a difference. *Journal of Digital Learning in Teacher Education, 28*(2), 82-88, http://etec.ctlt.ubc.ca/510wiki/Cyberethics#cite_note-1.

[56]   https://link.springer.com/referenceworkentry/10.1007%2F978-1-4020-8265-8_279.

[57] http://kanoon.nearlaw.com/2017/10/26/cyber-law-and-ethics.

[58] https://www.cisecurity.org/daily-tip/know-the-rules-of-cyber-ethics.

knowledging rights and responsibilities related to online environments and digital media.[59]

No wonder, it has been stated that computer ethics are nothing but how we use our personal morals and ethics while using the computer for various purposes. They consist of all the rules that you would apply to not misuse any information that is not yours to use, or to access any data that is not owned by you.[60]

Some experts believe that the field of ethical aspects concerning cyberspace need to be designated under cyber ethics while others believe that the word computer ethics is a more appropriate description of the emerging discipline. However, it has been felt that 'cyber ethics' is a more accurate term than 'computer ethics'. The term computer ethics can connote ethical issues construed as pertaining to stand-alone or unconnected computers. However, with the advent of networked systems, a computer system may nowadays be thought of more accurately as a new kind of *medium* as opposed to a *machine*;[61]

When one looks at the various definitions of cyber ethics, it is increasingly clear that different experts have sought to explain in their own remarkable manners the entire emerging concept of application of ethical principles to cyberspace. When one looks at the salient features of cyber ethics, one finds that different stakeholders have illustrated and elaborated different aspects and features of cyber ethics.

In January 1989, the Internet Architecture Board (IAB)[62] in RFC 1087 defines an activity as unethical and unacceptable if it[63]:

- Seeks to gain unauthorized access to the resources of the Internet;
- Disrupts the intended use of the Internet;

---

[59] https://www.sophia.org/tutorials/cyber-ethics-2.

[60] https://techspirited.com/importance-of-computer-ethics

[61] http://ci-journal.org/index.php/ciej/article/view/280/232

[62] https://www.iab.org/

[63] https://tools.ietf.org/html/rfc1087

- Wastes resources (people, capacity, computer) through such actions;
- Destroys the integrity of computer-based information; or
- Compromises the privacy of users.

The Computer Ethics Institute has published the Ten Commandments which stipulate as follows:

1. Thou shalt not use a computer to harm other people;
2. Thou shalt not interfere with other people's computer work;
3. Thou shalt not snoop around in other people's computer files;
4. Thou shalt not use a computer to steal;
5. Thou shalt not use a computer to bear false witness;
6. Thou shalt not copy or use proprietary software for which you have not paid (without permission);
7. Thou shalt not use other people's computer resources without authorization or proper compensation;
8. Thou shalt not appropriate other people's intellectual output;
9. Thou shalt think about the social consequences of the program you are writing or the system you are designing;
10. Thou shalt always use a computer in ways that ensure consideration and respect for your fellow humans.[64]

In the context of cyber ethics, it needs to be appreciated that ethical principles must be based on the existing cultures, rules, practices and judicial system of each society.[65]

It has been suggested that ethical considerations make it imperative that the information society is developed into a knowledge society. In this context, *six aspects need to be considered* which are as follows: [66]

---

[64]   http://www.computerethicsinstitute.org/images/TheTenCommandments OfComputerEthics.pdf

[65] https://www.devry.edu/blog/2014/02/cyber-ethics-a-global-conversation.html

[66] https://www.cigionline.org/sites/default/files/gcig_no.39web.pdf

- Value-based approach;
- People-centred framework;
- Communities and identities-oriented solutions;
- Education-focused approach;
- Gender-oriented design;
- Generation-sensitive framework.

Having examined the salient features of cyber ethics, it is imperative to appreciate that cyber law has a direct connection with cyber ethics. Cyber ethics provides the ethical foundations for ethical behaviour in cyberspace, thereby reflecting the ethical standards of human civilization. Cyber law as a discipline, stipulates or stands for legal instruments and legislations that are passed in different countries which effectively provide sanction, validity and enforceability to various principles concerning ethical behaviour in cyberspace.

Hence, cyber law as a discipline, effectively strengthens the foundations of good ethical behaviour that are stipulated by cyber ethics. In fact, cyber ethics gets substantially strengthened by cyber legal frameworks, as the ethical principles on their own do not have any respective standing. Cyber ethics only stipulates moral values but till such time, the said ethical standards concerning ethical behaviour in cyberspace are not adequately backed by appropriate legal provisions and sanctions, they rarely get complete enforceability. Further, the nature of human behaviour is such that people tend to only adhere to ethical standards once its stipulated under the law and once there are legal ramifications or consequences for not complying with the same. This intrinsic aspect itself underlines the co-relation between Cyber Law and cyber ethics. This becomes even more relevant as though "good / right" and "bad / wrong" do not mean the same thing for all still, everyone possesses a notion of right and wrong.[67]

---

[67] https://arxiv.org/ftp/arxiv/papers/1507/1507.08447.pdf

2.3 Cyber Crime is Unethical and Illegal

No wonder, the role of ethics becomes even more significant given the huge advent and increase of cyber-criminal activities in cyberspace which are not just unethical but also illegal. The need to combine ethics and law in regulating the activities of cyber world cannot be over emphasized. This is crucial in order to curb the menace of cybercrime which has eaten deep into the fabrics of the society. Information technology has made the world a global village and has enhanced every sphere and sector of the society like economy, commerce, social and educational sectors. [68]

However, this is one space where lot of work is required to be done. It is high time now for careful inspection of the legal and ethical aspects of ICT as there are not enough guidelines available in this field as compared to those available in conventional branches of science and technology. [69]

There is a distinctive need for cyber ethics to be strengthened by Cyber Laws. Different Cyber Laws in different parts of the world have sought to reiterate and reinforce ethical principles concerning ethical behaviour in cyberspace. No wonder, it is been opined that an information governance framework should contain measurable and strategic goals that will be beneficial for the provider and citizens and promote ethical standards. [70] Further, as now countries have begun a new arms race for coming up with the new legal national frameworks to govern and regulate cybersecurity, it is imperative that cyber legal frameworks and cybersecurity legal frameworks must now be evolved keeping in mind the evolved principles of cyber ethics. Various national and international organizations, such as the International Federation of Infor-

---

[68] https://cirworld.com/index.php/ijct/article/view/12/pdf

[69] https://arxiv.org/ftp/arxiv/papers/1507/1507.08447.pdf

[70] http://ci-journal.org/index.php/ciej/article/view/280/232

mation Processors (IFIP), the Association for Computing Machinery (ACM), Institute of Electrical and Electronics Engineers (IEEE), the British Computer Society (BCS) and the Institute of Data Processing Management (IDPM), have recognized the need for new codes of ethics to inform and advise their members about relevant social and ethical issues.[71]

When one looks at the growing number of Cyber Laws in the world including cybersecurity laws, it is increasingly clear that the said legal frameworks incorporate cyber ethical principles and standards e.g. an act of not hacking a computer system is an ethical principle. If an ethical principle is violated then such act is prescribed as a cybercrime which is punishable with imprisonment and fines. If a person does any cyber-crime activity, then it becomes an offence under the existing Cyber Laws.

Further, the increased focus of people on protection and preservation of personal privacy as also data privacy has brought forward the need for effectively codifying ethical considerations pertaining to protection of privacy. For example, it is ethical not to invade anyone's privacy, however, in case if somebody does invade somebody's privacy that becomes an actionable wrong for which various remedies are provided under different cyber legal frameworks. Further, different Cyber Laws have stipulated that a person, who does not follow expected societal ethical principles and behaviour concerning activities on cyberspace, would be held to legal consequences. These include various remedies including damages by way of compensation as also criminal liability imprisonment and fines. Similarly, it is ethical to respect other person's personal data and sensitive personal data. These ethical principles have formed the basis for data protection legal frameworks which all come within the broad umbrella of Cyber Law jurisprudence.

---

[71] https://www.apu.ac.jp/~gunarto/it1.pdf

2.4 Ethics Education has Positive Impact

Here, it is pertinent to note that knowledge and education about cyber ethics has a direct impact upon human behaviour. A seven year exploratory study was conducted which concluded that ethics education has a positive impact on the students; that is, knowledge of ethics arguably has an effect of lowering the rate of abuse, and computer science curriculum can be improved by including a module on computer ethics and social responsibility.[72]

Today it is an interesting world in which we live, where there are new emerging technologies that are promising to completely impact the way how human activity and endeavour would evolve with the passage of time. These include the emerging technologies like Artificial Intelligence, Internet of Things and Blockchain. These new technologies such as Artificial Intelligence, Internet of Things and Blockchain bring forward new challenges concerning intersection between Cyber Law and cyber ethics which need to be appropriately addressed by adequate legislative and legal frameworks and actions in the coming times.

No wonder, the World Economic Forum's list of top ten emerging technologies of 2015 includes those that aim to resolve some of the ethical debates posed by an earlier generation of technologies, as well as others that will bring about new ethical and regulatory challenges.[73]

The advent of Artificial Intelligence throws up new ethical issues and considerations which are required to be addressed by Cyber Law. Should Artificial Intelligence be allowed to develop beyond the point, where it surpasses new intelligence? Further, should Artificial Intelligence be allowed ethically to not be amenable to human will and instead take independent actions which could spell disastrous consequences for

---

[72] Lee, W. W.; K. C. C. Chan; "Computer Ethics: A Potent Weapon for Information Security Management," *ISACA Journal*, vol. 6, 2008, www.isaca.org

[73] https://www.wcforum.org/agenda/2015/03/top-10-emerging-technologies-of-2015-2/

human society? The ever more rapid proliferation of robotic systems raises many ethical challenges, from the ethics of human-robot interactions research and development, to ethics programming for autonomous systems, and the social impact of robotic technology in such areas as self-driving vehicles the ever more extensive displacement of human labour by automated and autonomous systems.[74] Ethics is an ongoing and dynamic enterprise. When new technologies appear, there is a commendable concern to do all of the ethics first. Or, as sometimes suggested, place a moratorium on technological development until ethics catches up.[75]

No wonder, it has been pointed that ethics and AI are related at several levels including the following:[76]

- Ethics by Design;
- Ethics in Design;
- Ethics for Design.

2.5 The Need for Cyber Regulation Based on Cyber Ethics

These are indeed very interesting times in which we live. No wonder, Cyber Law as a discipline must provide adequate, strong, validity and sanction for cyber ethical principles and cyber ethics as an evolving discipline. Governments in every country, public policy makers, computer professionals, organizations and private citizens must all take an interest and make their contributions, so that this global information can be exploited in a socially and ethically sensitive way for our future bene-

---

[74] https://reilly.nd.edu/research/program-areas/technologies/

[75] Bill Joy, "Why the Future Doesn't Need Us," Wired 8.4 (2000) https://crown.ucsc.edu/academics/pdf-docs/moor-article.pdf

[76] https://link.springer.com/article/10.1007/s10676-018-9450-z

fit and applications.[77] The need for the regulation of cyber world cannot be over emphasized because of the technological advancement which has transformed the world into a global village. Cyber law entails the safe and lawful collection, retention, processing, transmission and use of personal data of individuals.[78] Cyber ethics thus provide the foundation for cyber legal principles concerning the protection of data and other aspects of human endeavour in cyberspace.

It is further important to note that the future of intersection of Cyber Law and cyber ethics assumes a lot of significance. Cyber ethics as a discipline is substantially evolving. Cyber Law will play a very important role for the evolution of cyber ethics. The onus will be on law makers and legislators to start recognizing the intersection between Cyber Law and cyber ethics and increasingly grant legal recognition, validity and sanction to cyber ethics principles. This becomes although more significant, as we are coming across times where cybercrimes are going to be far more difficult and dangerous. Cybercrime as a paradigm is constantly evolving. The global cost of cybercrime is constantly increasing. The cybersecurity community and major media have largely concurred on the prediction that cybercrime damages will cost the world $6 trillion annually by 2021, up from $3 trillion in 2015. This represents the greatest transfer of economic wealth in history, risks the incentives for innovation and investment, and will be more profitable than the global trade of all major illegal drugs combined.[79] The advent of darknet presents completely different challenges of cyber ethics. Darknet embodies large number of ethical principles concerning cyber ethics. It is also important to examine the role of cyber ethics in the darknet as the

---

[77] https://www.apu.ac.jp/~gunarto/it1.pdf

[78] file:///E:/Download/12-Article%20Text-20-1-10-20161214.pdf

[79]   https://www.csoonline.com/article/3211491/security/state-of-cybercrime-2017-security-events-decline-but-not-the-impact.html#tk.cso_fsb

same can be instrumental in the development and crystallization of various cyber ethical principles.

2.6 Very Dangerous Times

When one looks at the projected figures for increase of cybercrime, it is increasingly very clear that we are living in very dangerous times. Attacks will quadruple by 2020.[80] 668 breaches compromised 22,408,258 records between January 1 and July 2, 2018 according to the Identity Theft Resource Center report.[81] Further, it has been pointed out that the average total cost of a data breach is $3.86 million, the average global possibility of a breach in the next 24 months is 27.9%, and the average breach cost reduction for organizations using security automation is $1.55 million according to the 2018 Ponemon Report.[82] In this constantly evolving paradigm cybercriminal activities need to be appropriately regulated by disseminating more information about the cyber ethical standards of behaviour concerning acts done in cyberspace. Cyber Law as a framework can distinctly help in this regard.

Just to conclude, this intersection between Cyber Law and Cyber Ethics presents a very interesting area of potential evolution of jurisprudence in the coming times. More and more countries are increasingly going to rely upon cyber ethical principles to become the foundation for future national legislations concerning regulation of acts done in cyberspace so that we can all work towards a secure and safer cyberspace. Lot of work needs to be done on the intersection between Cyber Law and cyber ethics. It will be interesting to see how this intersection evolves and further what all steps would be taken by different stakeholders to

---

[80]   https://www.csoonline.com/article/3237674/ransomware/ransomware-damage-costs-predicted-to-hit-115b-by-2019.html

[81] https://www.idtheftcenter.org/wp-content/uploads/2018/07/DataBreachReport_2018.pdf

[82] https://www.ibm.com/security/data-breach

push the envelope of the jurisprudence on the intersection between Cyber Law and cyber ethics.

3

ETHICS IN THE INFORMATION SOCIETY:
THE NINE P'S

Globethics.net

This text[83] on the ethics of information and knowledge societies calls for value-based decisions and actions for the development of information, communication and knowledge. It is based on seven core values: equity, freedom, care and compassion, participation, sharing, sustainability and responsibility. These values are exemplified on nine core topics of the information society, the "Nine P's": principles, participation, people, profession, privacy, piracy, protection, power and policy.

The Globethics.net Board of Foundation acknowledged the issue paper on 5 May 2013 and invites all interested and concerned persons and institutions to discuss it and send their feedback and proposals for improvement.

Introduction

Ten years after more than 11,000 participants gathered in Geneva in 2003 for the opening session of the World Summit on the Information Society (WSIS), a UNESCO meeting in Paris at the end of February

---

[83] First published as *Ethics in the Information Society: The Nine 'P's. A Discussion Paper for the WSIS+10 Process,* Geneva: Globethics.net, 2013, Globethics.net Texts Series No 4.

2013 met to take stock of what has been achieved since then and to set out challenges for the future.

The recommendations from this first WSIS +10 review meeting will feed into further United Nations deliberations and into the review of the Millennium Development Goals.

WSIS – which met in two sessions in Geneva (2003) and Tunis (2005) – aimed to promote access to information and knowledge through new communications technologies and to tackle the global digital divide separating the northern hemisphere from the global South. At the same time, it highlighted the ethical dimensions of the Information Society, and underlined the need for measures to safeguard cultural and linguistic diversity and identity, to avoid local content being overshadowed by vested global interests.

The idea for Globethics.net was born during WSIS in 2003 by Christoph Stückelberger, then General Secretary of the development agency "Bread for all", being an ethicist and involved in WSIS. Representatives from the global South identified the need to strengthen ethical institutions, especially in developing and transition countries, through strengthening the production and dissemination of, and access to, information and knowledge using Information and Communication Technologies (ICTs). Bread for all needs information for all. This led to the creation of the Global Digital Library on Ethics, as well as the networking and workgroup facilities of Globethics.net.

A decade later, as UNESCO has noted, there is intense public debate over the future development of the Internet, shaped by the defence of the right to freedom of expression and freedom of information online, the growth of multilingualism on the net and the ever-increasing influence and impact of communications technologies on all aspects of people's lives. Such issues are too important to be left to governments alone. Civil society is an indispensable part of the "ethical space" within which a global communication ethic needs to be elaborated, alongside the institutional political system of government and the institutionally orientated political society.

At the same time, research commissioned for the UNESCO meeting in Paris underlines that information ethics needs to address the challenges and implications of the information society in developing regions, particularly in terms of inter-cultural information ethics.

Globethics.net emphasises that most of the "Final Recommendations" of the first WSIS+10 Review Event in Paris on 25-27 February 2013 are relevant for the implementation of ethical values.

Globethics network with its 200'000 registered participants from 200 countries and territories can make a contribution for the WSIS+10 process 2013-2015. Globethics.net seeks to promote a truly global conversation on the Ethics in the Information Society.

3.1 Principles: Ethical Values

Knowledge societies can be sustainable, coherent, innovative and integrative if they are based not only on pragmatic opportunities or political or financial interests, but on ethical values. In a globalized multicultural world these values have to be global values while at the same time respecting the diversity of contextual values.

The "Globethics.net Principles on Sharing Values across Cultures and Religions" (2009/2013) stated: "Global ethics is an inclusive approach to common binding values, guiding principles, personal attitudes and common action across cultures, religions, political and economic systems and ideologies. Global ethics is grounded in the ethical recognition of inalienable human dignity, freedom of decision, personal and social responsibility and justice. ... Global ethics identifies trans-boundary problems and contributes to their solution.

Global ethics promotes public awareness of those fundamental values and principles. They are the foundation on which the universal consensus on human rights is built. Human rights are the most tangible and legally binding expression of this ethical vision. Global ethics fosters trust among human beings and strengthens caring and action for global environmental protection.

Contextual ethics takes seriously the identity of people and institutions in their local, cultural, religious, economic and political contexts. Global ethics needs to be local and contextual in order to have an impact on individual action and social structures. On the other hand, contextual ethics becomes isolationist if it remains local and is not linked to global ethics. Contextual ethics appreciates and respects diversity in its different forms as social, political, cultural, religious, and bio-diversity. There is an enormous richness in diversity. It may decrease vulnerability and be a source of sustainability. Contextual ethics contributes to global ethics. Together they can lead to unity in diversity. All cultures and religions can contribute to global values. ...

Global and contextual ethics are two poles that challenge each other and inseparably belong together. ... Global ethics can be abused for domination over other cultures, religions and values. Contextual ethics can be abused to defend traditional privileges or power. On a global as well as on a local level, 'power over others' tends to be oppressive, 'power with and for others' tends to be empowering and nurturing. ... "

Fundamental values for the knowledge societies are:

- *Justice/equity* is based on the inalienable human dignity of every human being and on their equality. Justice grows when people cultivate a deep respect towards each other. Fair and equal chances of access to information are a precondition for mutual understanding.
- *Freedom* of access to information, of expression, of believe and of decision is core for human dignity and human development. Freedom, equity and responsibility balance each other.
- *Care and compassion* is the ability for empathy, respect and support of the other. It leads to solidarity.

- *Participation* is the right and ability to participate in societal life and in decisions of concern.
- *Sharing* leads to, enables, and sustains relationships between human beings and strengthens communities. The ITCs enable in an extraordinary way the sharing of information and knowledge.
- *Sustainability* as long term perspective for green technologies.
- *Responsibility* is accountability for one's own actions. The level of responsibility has to correspond to the level of power, capacity and capability. Those with more resources bear greater responsibility.

All these values are interconnected and balance each other.

Questions for consideration:

- Do you share these values? Would you add or delete values?

3.2 Participation: Access to Knowledge for All

Access to information, communication, education and knowledge is a basic right and public good. Open access for free or for affordable costs enables participation of all in the development of societies. It has to be further promoted by the WSIS+10 processes.

The digital divide between the global North and South is narrowing, but instead there is an "access divide" to knowledge resources. Technical developments in recent years have increased bandwidth particularly in Asia but also Latin America and Africa, although there are still major discrepancies with the global North. Technology alone is not enough, however. In fact, the right to education includes the right to information, communication and knowledge. They can be seen as one human right as they are interlinked. Nevertheless, the management of knowledge resources continues to be monopolised by the global North such as through large commercial publishers, particularly in the sphere of academic journals. Increasing access to knowledge needs to go beyond promoting an information flow from North to South. The dominant model and its alternatives downplay context and local aspiration. In recent years a number of developments have used the possibilities offered by information and communication technologies to increase access to knowledge, such as open access, both through open access journals (the "gold" path) and institutional repositories (the "green path"). In several continents, there have been moves by governments to ensure that publicly-funded research must be openly accessible. While such developments may increase access for those in the global South, to what extent do they really address a knowledge divide that needs to be bridged in both directions? To what extent do such technological developments significantly increase the possibility of contributions to global knowledge dialogue from the countries of the South, or will the South again be marginalised? Open Access journals that do not charge author fees may mitigate some of these factors, but nevertheless face questions about visibility, accessibility and reliability, while the established journal mechanisms often discriminate against journals from the South. Another move towards increasing access to knowledge has been the increasing popularity of Massive Open Online Courses (MOOCs). However, they may also reinforce the domination of large schools in the global North.

Recommendations:

Globethics.net calls upon

- Governments and international organizations to reinforce free and fair access to knowledge for developing countries;
- Governments to include support for open access repositories in Official Development Assistance, including training and support as well as infrastructure;
- Regulators to support the development of regional hubs that index open access repositories, distinguishing between full text repositories and those offering only metadata;

> • Public and private actors to develop open access and open publishing initiatives in collaboration with institutions in the global South that include global visibility, accessibility, new ranking mechanisms, building impact factor metrics and local value attribution.

Questions for consideration:

- • If Open Access in future requires payment by authors or institutions, what kind of solutions and preferential treatments are to be offered for institutions in developing countries that cannot afford subscription fees and resources for publication?
- • How is Open Access related to copyright issues? Do "creative commons" licences help resolve the free circulation of knowledge, or do they risk allowing knowledge production in the global South being commoditised in the North?

3.3 People: Community, Identity, Gender, Generation, Education

> People, human beings, as senders and receivers are the key actors of information, communication and knowledge. How to filter, digest and assimilate information and knowledge? How to use them for enrichment and not confusion, for identity building and not identity-loss, for respect of diversity and not increase of uniformity, for more equality instead of more inequality? Is knowledge primarily used to win over others in very competitive markets, to oppress others or for building communities?

The knowledge society should respect six aspects:

Value-based: Societies are envisaged where persons, groups and institutions share knowledge in fairness, equity, freedom and for the benefit of caring sustainable communities: families, communities and nations which respect the rights of individuals, but also of the communities, which strengthen unity but also respect diversity of cultures, languages, worldviews, religions, economic and political systems.

People-centred: The fast innovations in ICTs make technology a main driver of development. But technology is not a goal in itself, it should serve people. Information society needs to be people-centred.

Communities and identities-oriented: ICT trends increase individualism and individual media consumptions. The needs and rights of individuals and of communities need to be balanced. The flood of information leads to constant deconstruction and reconstruction of identities and needs care in balancing change and stability and building strong identities especially of adolescent people.

Education-focussed: A key element for WSIS+10 is education in responsible use of the almost unlimited mass of information and communication. Information ethics is needed on all levels, from the producers (see P4) to the consumers in order to deal with information in a responsible way. Awareness has to be increased that dealing with information, communication and knowledge can be as challenging as handling toxic substances or driving a powerful car. Therefore education for the ethical use and the personal transformation of such information to knowledge for the society becomes very important. Instruments are education in critical media consumption including the use of social media.

Gender-oriented: Gender equality in access to information, communication, knowledge and decision-making is an important dimension of an inclusive and people-centre society. It includes ensuring parity in women's representation in high levels and decision-making in the ICT.

Generation-sensitive: Computer literacy of older persons is important for their participation in society and for intergenerational exchange.

Recommendations

Globethics.net calls upon

- Educational institutions to increase information ethics in the curricula and examine a "driving licence" for young adults for using the information highways (already practiced in test schools);
- Educational institutions to care for ethical aspects of fast growing e-learning, distant learning and Mass Online Courses;
- Media providers and educational institutions to increase efforts to transform information into adapted and digested knowledge
- Public and private media institutions to care for cultural and lingual diversity of programmes;
- Building empowering capabilities of women and girls to use ICTs for education, formation and citizenship and for older persons in computer and internet literacy;
- Validate and include indigenous people's values and knowledge;
- Policy makers to guarantee the freedom of expression while avoiding moral harm and violation of the integrity of persons.

Questions for consideration

- On which recommendations do you agree or disagree?

3.4 Profession: Ethics of Information Professions

Professions in the fields of information, communication and knowledge creation, processing, dissemination, control, renewal, preservation, archiving and policy-making have a special ethical responsibility in implementing core values.

Journalists, librarians, archivists, teachers, bloggers, philosophers, scientists, IT hardware and software developers, curricula developers, religious leaders, social media owners, politicians and many other content professionals in information, communication and knowledge production have a great influence on private and public opinions since ever. But even more it is the case in the modern information society.

Value-based development and Human Rights require strengthening ethics and Human Rights for the *work conditions of the content professionals*. This includes: the space and freedom for value-based, corruption-free, honest journalism; the protection of information professionals who in some countries face threats to life, or are killed; the value-based vision of media-owners to support cultural, linguistic and religious diversity and views expressed and to optimize but not maximize the profits expected from media investments.

At the same time, the *content professionals* have to strengthen these values, virtues and rights *themselves* through their professional work. This includes: fair, honest, transparent, corruption-free, qualitative journalism based on integrity, independence of investigative journalism and the endeavour to seek truth; respecting integrity of people and institutions; respecting ethical benchmarks against the pressure of economic profit maximisation, audience rating and entertainment goals. Professional codes of ethics are important instruments to enhance the ethical responsibility of content providers in the information society.

Recommendations

Globethics.net calls upon

- Associations and network of professionals (e.g. journalists, publishers, librarians) to ensure the promotion and strengthening of ethical codes in the production, distribution and archiving or information, communication, and knowledge;
- Associations and network of professionals to develop and promote respective codes for consumers who become more and more also producers of media content (bloggers, citizen journalists, citizen photographers etc.)
- Governments to ensure a legal framework that offers space for corruption-free and honest journalism;

- Governments and society as a whole to protect information professionals and to take clear legal actions against killing, intimidation and other violations of the freedom of expression;
- Governments, content producers, media owners and consumers to ensure cultural, linguistic and religious diversity;
- Training institutions of media professionals to include ethics courses as mandatory in the curricula;
- Training institutions to provide training in digital safety for journalists, both off-line and online.

Questions for consideration
- On which recommendations do you agree or disagree?
- What are your experiences with professional codes of ethics and how can they be strengthened?

3.5 Privacy: Dignity, Data Mining, Security

Privacy is a human right, not a commercial concession. Views on privacy rights differ between the US, UK, Continental Europe, Asia, Africa, Latin America and political structures. Threats to privacy are constantly arising - especially from the commercial and security sectors and social networks. Reasonable balance needs to be struck between privacy and security needs. The WSIS process should support the safeguarding of privacy, in coherence with open access to information.

The protection of privacy is a human right recognised in the UN Declaration of Human Rights 0f 1948, Art. 12. It is not a concession to be granted at the whim of commercial or other interests. This has not always seemed to be so. For much of its history, humanity has lived a communal life. Privacy has been difficult - especially for those who are poor - but so have e.g. health and security. The UN System is itself a positive – albeit imperfect – response to the horrors of the Second World War. The UN has said privacy is a right. But privacy rights have to be balanced with community rights as expressed e.g. in the African Banjul Charta of Human Rights and Peoples' Rights. They limit each other.

In the time of the British writer George Orwell, the greatest threat to individual liberties was felt to be from the state. The threat is still there, but the internet has opened up possibilities for private and state organisations to data mine huge amounts of individuals' data and to use it for their own private and not necessarily socially beneficial ends, or simply to incompetently lose it. Because something is technically possible does not mean that it is socially desirable or legally acceptable. Books have been digitised without permission of rights owners, Street View has intruded into your neighbourhood whether you like it or not, and Facebook 'privacy' settings have rightly become the subject of intense criticism. Mobile phone records can already easily track us electronically without our consent.

It has been argued that because X is now technically possible, so X must be actioned because it is part of inevitable human progress. This is ethically wrong – because criminal journalists can hack into telephone accounts of murdered teenagers does not make it morally or legally acceptable. It is also argued that if you have nothing to hide, you have nothing to fear. It ignores the question of principle and the fact that a certain degree of privacy and discretion rather than full-on disclosure (as per Wikileaks) is necessary for diplomacy and society to function.

Different political systems and historical experience lead to different privacy policies: North Americans are concerned about governments invading individual privacy, Europeans about enterprises controlling life, Chinese officials about uncontrolled Western individualism.

Governments must be able to protect public security. But cyberwarfare can threaten public security. Companies, in their pursuit of profit, must respect the privacy of individuals. If not, the information society becomes the surveillance society and we are on the slippery slope towards the loss of fundamental liberties. Privacy is threatened as much by private sector excess as by government action or negligence, but both must be accountable to individuals and organisations for their actions.

Recommendations

Globethics.net calls upon

- WSIS review process to demand and governments to enact and enforce reasonable privacy safeguards for their citizens;
- Companies to develop software and collecting data to ensure greater attention to the ethical dimension of business, including a genuine respect for the privacy of individuals;
- Internet intermediaries to be more transparent about requests they receive from governments for data access.

Questions for consideration
- On which recommendations do you agree or disagree?

3.6 Piracy: Intellectual Property, Cybercrime

Piracy is an old problem, with a new electronic face. Piracy can be an existential threat to existing business models for innovative content creation and use. Piracy may occur because potential users see content as too expensive and rights protection as excluding the poor. Compromises are needed to take account of all stakeholder interests.

Pirates have operated since time immemorial in the lawless regions of the world. Today most pirates don't steal treasure on the high seas: they steal ideas and information electronically. It has always been possible to steal ideas and information. But with the growth of digital media and the advent of the Internet, stealing has become easier. Sometimes, it has become policy: e.g. the disregard for national laws in the global programme of digitizing books without seeking the permission of rights owners is fine example of business arrogance of a large private digitizing company, and an illustration of why ethics must go hand in hand with innovation: just because something is innovative does not make it the right thing to do.

While new technology has fuelled the intellectual property piracy problem, paradoxically it has also helped to provide solutions too. Plagiarism is now much simpler to detect with appropriate software.

Not everyone opposes the pirates' efforts to circumvent patent and copyright laws. Millions of people have, come to see free music as almost a civic right. This has declined recently as legal download sites become easier and cheaper to use, and a few delinquent downloaders have been sued for large sums. Poorer people, and the developing world, have a case when they argue that current intellectual property regimes protect rich business interests in the developed world at the expense of less well-off populations in the developing world. WIPO has at times seemed to defend information producer interests more than promote information user interests. This is not helpful in the context of making information more freely and affordably accessible in the developing world.

The licensing of information products rather than the sale to the end user raises new questions about information ownership and the rights of individuals to transmit or bequeath digital materials. The acquisition and reuse for commercial purposes by some content curators and Internet-based companies of information and digital products submitted free-of-charge by users needs to be resisted, especially when such companies have near-monopolistic positions in the Internet economy.

At the heart of the intellectual property piracy issue is the ethical question of what should count for more: the lives of less well-off people who need access to drugs, information, etc. or the protection of world business interests and incomes of the creators and distributors of intellectual property? Piracy, if not controlled, poses an existential threat to the current business model of content producers and distributors. The challenge is to identify and chart out a middle course and implement it in an ethical and effective manner so that all stakeholders feel they have gained.

Recommendations

Globethics.net calls upon:

- WIPO and other international organizations to ensure that copyright enforcement initiatives be based on inclusive, multi-stakeholder processes that reflect transparent and accountable processes;
- Governments and other actors including UNESCO to encourage research and debate on a balanced legal system to protect intellectual property and to favour access to information for all;
- WSIS to support relaxation of patents where affordable copies of products (e.g. drugs) are essential for saving lives;
- The WSIS review process to underline the need for it to be legally possible to do digitally what can be legally done in hard copy, including an individual's right to own digital materials and to bequeath or transfer their ownership to others.

3.7 Protection: Children and Young People

Through access to the Internet on computers, smartphones and tablets, young people are connecting with each other and wider society in ways that were previously unimaginable. A generation of children and young people have grown up for whom the digital world is taken for granted. Nevertheless, there are concerns that children, young people and young adults may face specific risks and hazards, including sexual exploitation, a lack of anonymity and potential addiction to online networks.

Young people and young adults who have grown up in the Information Society often feel at home in the digital world in a way that is not the case for older people. This includes young people and young adults developing their own strategies for dealing with their online existence in areas such as anonymity, sharing of personal data, and verifying information found online. Nevertheless, concerns have been raised about risks that children, young people and young adults face in the digital world. These include cyberbullying and sexual abuse, as well as the potential lack of anonymity on the Internet, confusion between individual and social identity, and the permanence of online information. There are also dangers of addiction to online games and social networks.

Developing responses mean avoiding sensationalism, mythmaking and inappropriate policy measures. There is thus a need for accurate information to better calibrate appropriate responses. So far much of the research has been undertaken only in industrialised societies.

Children, young people and young adults may be better aware of some of the risks that they face online than are adults. Effective strategies thus require their active involvement as actors in their own right to understand their use of information and communication technologies, their awareness of the risks and hazards, and the strategies that they have developed to counter such risks.

Globethics.net welcomes initiatives such as "Child Online Protection" COP of ITU and partners and the "Draft African Union Convention on … Cyber Security in Africa" In some cases related to criminal abuse, measures require rigorous offline criminal investigation measures, in which children are seen as credible witnesses. In others, risks may be dealt with through the enforcement of general measures such as transparency, the need for explicit consent in sharing of information, and the right to withdraw such consent.

Measures to protect children and young people need also to take into account their rights as set out in the Convention on the Rights of the Child and other international agreements to information, freedom of expression and association, privacy and non-discrimination.

Recommendations

Globethics.net calls upon:

- Internet and social networking providers to ensure comprehensible and accessible privacy mechanisms;
- Governments and international organisations to support research into the use of ICTs by children, young people and young adults, not only in industrialised countries;
- National authorities to ensure their investigation and enforcement mechanisms are equipped to deal with cyber-based criminality, including the exploitation and abuse of children.

Questions for consideration
- Where is the balance between measures to protect children and young adults and affirming their rights to participate fully in the information society, including freedom of information/expression?
- Where is the balance between legislative measures to protect children and young adults online and the restrictive measures that impinge on their rights to free expression and information online?

3.8 Power: Economic Power of Technology, Media and Consumers

The production, processing, dissemination, control and archiving of information, communication and knowledge need political power to set the legal frame and economic power to provide the necessary investment capital. Political and economic power should not be power over others, but sharing power with others and using it for others as a service to human beings, the whole society and public governance.

The value chain and number of suppliers in the production, processing, dissemination, control and archiving of information, communication and knowledge is very long, complex and global. The products -

information, communication and knowledge - with its far reaching impact on human beings and society are services with a different quality and ethical importance than daily commodities and products such as shoes or clothes because of its high impact on behaviour, mentalities, ideologies, world views, identities, cultures, economic and political developments.

The free market together with a political regulatory framework and informed consumers can provide the necessary innovative dynamics. But the ethical responsibility of political regulators and economic investors are higher in this sector than for other commodities.

Key actors are the investors in and managers of companies and institutions for information, communication and knowledge, the politicians and associations as regulators as well as the consumers. All these actors have their specific responsibilities in using their entrusted power. The larger the power, the higher are the responsibilities and accountability. Globethics.net in its "Principles of Sharing Values" stated: On global as well as on regional, national and local level, "'power over others' tends to be oppressive, 'power with and for others' tends to be empowering and nurturing. Power as 'power from' (e.g. power from God, from the people through election) can be abused to justify oppressive power. It can also be used responsibly as an empowering power, serving the needs of the needy." And "Also global ethics can be abused for domination over other cultures, religions and values. Contextual ethics can be abused to defend traditional privileges or power. Both can be used to serve people and their needs."

The profits expected from media and educational investments should be optimized but not maximized. Profit is not a goal in itself, but a means to provide these services for the sustainability development goals. Consumers have their own responsibility in selecting information, communication and knowledge products and paying fair prices for them.

Recommendations
Globethics.net calls upon

- Investors and relevant organizations to pay due heed to the values and standards of socially responsible investments (SRI) in all investments relating to information and communication technologies;
- Media owners and other relevant private-sector enterprises to ensure that their involvement in and strategy of information and communication companies is based on ethical values and responsibility for the specific impact of the sector for society;
- Politicians and other regulators to base media regulations on the values of freedom, equal access, peoples' participation, respect of diversity and sustainable development;
- Producers and consumers of information, communication and knowledge content to use their respective power to promote ethics in information society.

Questions for consideration

- On which recommendations do you agree or disagree?
- How can economic and political power related to ICTs be used as a service for the information and knowledge society?

3.9 Policy: Ethics of Regulation and Freedom

Parliaments, governments, civil society and educated citizens are needed to ensure that regulatory measures support freedom of expression, freedom of association in information and communication technologies and the right to seek, receive and impart information and ideas through any media and regardless of frontiers. Fast technological development, ethical standards and regulatory framework have to be more synchronized.

Information and communication technologies are not just an expression of a globalising world, they are also the foundations on which globalisation has been built, including its economic, cultural or political aspects. In Geneva in 2003, WSIS highlighted the "Ethical Dimensions of the Information Society": the need to uphold fundamental values, respect human rights and the fundamental freedoms of others, while dealing with the "abusive uses" of Information and Communication Technologies, through illegal and illicit actions. Such ethical questions raise the issues of regulation and regulatory frameworks. The ethical challenges transcend the "abusive uses" of ICTs, however, encompassing issues such as access to information and knowledge, capacity building, cultural and linguistic diversity, identity, local content and media pluralism.

The global nature of ICTs suggests that a global approach is required. Yet while global decision-making structures in international fora may be able to deal with issues of technical standards, they are often not adapted to dealing with the ethical challenges of the information society. International regulatory agreements are subject to negotiations between governments that might have very different ideas about what constitute, for example, "illegal and illicit actions" or pluralism and diversity. Large transnational corporations may *de facto* exercise greater influence than elected governments in developing policy and regulatory frameworks.

In this context, parliaments, governments and strong civil society organizations need to exercise their respective roles in promoting and protecting communication rights, including the right for all to engage in transparent, informed and democratic debate.

There is a balance to be faced between Internet freedom, which may risk exacerbating inequity and unequal access, and promoting an equity of access that requires regulation. The current regulatory structure for information and communication technologies risks favouring economic and commercial deregulation to the detriment of the wider interest of communities and the public commons.

Recommendations

Globethics.net calls upon

- The United Nations in the WSIS+10 review process to reaffirm the foundational principles of the Information Society (Universal Declaration of Human Rights; freedom of expression and of association, "seek, receive and impart information and ideas through any media and regardless of frontiers"), and for civil society organizations to remain vigilant about any threats to such principles;
- UN instruments to promote the regulation and freedom of the cybersphere, including a UN Rapporteur on Human Rights and Internet;
- International regulatory bodies for the information society including the ITU and the Internet Governance Forum to ensure a multistakeholder approach based on transparency, accountability and representativeness, to encompass the activities of transnational corporations, to address net neutrality and inequalities in Internet access.

Questions for consideration:

- What is the balance between Internet freedom with the risk of unequal access, and regulations in order to promote equity of access?
- How may inclusivity, transparency, representativeness and empowerment best be ensured in ICT regulation and internet governance?

Sources

Globethics.net: *Principles of Sharing Values across Cultures and Religions.* Geneva 2012, www.globethics.net/web/ge/texts-series.

Ethics of Information and Communication Technologies, European Group on Ethics in Science and New Technologies to the European Commission, Opinion No. 26, Brussels, 2012 website.

Final Statement. Information and knowledge for all. An expanded vision and a renewed commitment, First WSIS+10 Review Event in Paris on 25-27 February 2013,
http://www.unesco.org/new/fileadmin/MULTIMEDIA/HQ/CI/CI/pdf/wsis/WSIS_10_Event/wsis10_final_statement_en.pdf.

Final Recommendations of the First WSIS+10 Review Event in Paris on 25-27 February 2013,
http://www.unesco.org/new/fileadmin/MULTIMEDIA/HQ/CI/CI/pdf/wsis/WSIS_10_Event/wsis10_recommendations_en.pdf

Child Safety Online: Global challenges and strategies, UNICEF Innocenti Research Centre, 2012, http://www.unisef-irc.org/publications/pdf/ict_techreport3_eng.pdf.

PART II

DISRUPTIVE CYBER TECHNOLOGIES AND ETHICS

4

MY FRIEND THE ALGORITHM: THEOLOGICAL-ETHICAL CHALLENGE OF ARTIFICIAL INTELLIGENCE

Erny Gillen, Luxemburg

Many people are afraid of a future determined by machine-made intelligence. They overlook the fact that they are already surrounded by it: prostheses (artificial limbs) and other technical equipment facilitate everyday life, and even the human organism is the product of biochemical algorithms.[84]

4.1 Artificial: Negative Moral Judgment?

Anyone who has to deal with the little word "artificial" in the Catholic Church and to introduce distinctions in morally sensitive areas such as fertilization or contraception, immediately works with the uncomfortable feeling of possible proscription. When it comes to unprejudiced ethical discourse, this little word seems to come with more than a little baggage. Even in colloquial language the adjective has more the function of a warning sign: wrong, imitation, false, pretend or, to be completely up to date, fake - "gefakt" as the German Duden dictionary puts

---

[84] This article was first published in German. Erny Gillen, *Mein Freund, der Algorithmus*, Herder Korrespondenz, 10/2017, 49-51. With permission from Herder Verlag. Translation Jane Stranz.

it. It can also mean flowery, contrived, tortuous, unnatural, theatrical or turgid. An artificial product is regarded with suspicion in an enlightened world that stands for "bio" and "green". Someone who behaves artificially engenders little trust from the very beginning. Behind their artificial appearance, they are probably concealing their true, probably less favourable, nature.

Thus, in everyday language, the description "artificial" often suggests a negative moral judgment. In medicine and other sciences, on the other hand, the adjective is rather used to describe differences between, for example, the functioning biological organs or situations and an artificial kidney or an artificial coma. But the little word also refers back to its noun, namely "art". With their healing art the good doctors outsmart the illness or the wear and tear of the body. Modern artificial teeth in our mouths mean we can speak without any worries and adapt our first and second teeth to the unadulterated beauty of artificial ones. Glasses and lenses mean we are able to see, something we become aware of only when we lose the devices which give us artificial clear sightedness.

4.2 Artificial: Ethically Positive Innovation?

Unlike in everyday language, the word "artificial" seems to have retained its ethical ambivalence in some technical languages. Before a patient is subjected to an artificial intervention, there are discussions to be had and decisions to be made. An artificial prosthesis in the knee requires the active help of the patient for it to be inserted organically. Coordinating artificial organs and the remaining natural ones is a continual work of precision. We can hardly afford the art of medicine today without its chemical, surgical or technical artificial mediations and tools.

To give a positive hue to the little word "artificial", we happily replace it today with the more innocuous word "new". People on the move with a new knee, with new teeth or a new pacemaker, reap the benefits as state-of-the-art human beings. What matters is the function that has been preserved or restored. In the case of hearing and visual aids, the function is not only preserved, but sometimes artificially increased. The military and gaming industry know how to exploit these opportunities with success.

Sometimes the little word "artificial" sounds quite tantalizing. For thousands of years, people only dreamed of flying; today it is no dream that millions of people fly. Thirty years ago, who would have imagined an artificially networked world via the Internet, or just fifteen years ago, that one could telephone or even read e-mails on the street "without a physical connection"? The world in which we live is artificial through and through. We have got used to our art and culture through technology and development. But each time we take a new step, progress seems artificial until enough people are ready to accept its applications as being "new". The courageous are by then already planning the next enhancements for our lives.

The etymology in the Duden also teaches us that the Middle High German word "artificial" ("künstlich") originally meant "wise or clever" ("klug oder geschickt") and thus refers us back to the special "ability" of human beings. Ancient and renowned philosophers have already grappled with this art and ability, recognizing one of its main virtues as being prudence (phrónesis).

They were convinced that the practice of the virtues, as attitudes pushing people to take action, would raise them out of the dust of nature. By applying reason, human beings have gradually emancipated themselves from their living environment through their own efforts and shaped it by setting new goals. This included, from the outset, the dream of machines (such as the self-propelled cars of Hephaestus in the "Iliad").

For example, according to Hannah Arendt, as far as cultural history is concerned, we live in a consumer and mass society that assimilates people according to its own rules. Under the "rule of no one", the subject of action no longer lives for itself, but lives because it consumes and in order to consume. The products and work of homo laborans serve consumption, which has become an aim in itself and which is kept alive through the spiral of growth.

4.3 Intelligence: Action-oriented Ability

Artificial intelligence (AI), in the sense of a purposeful superhumanly fast and memory-powerful extension, arose in the service of this model of society of the ever-more, ever-faster and right now. Here, too, it is worth taking a look at the Duden, which under the entry for "intelligence" has: "The ability [of the human being] to think in abstract terms using reason and derive therefrom purposeful action." The square brackets around the term "human being" were originally set by the Duden! Intelligence is thus a practical, action-oriented ability.

As working people, we are evidently caught up in a society and economy in whose networking it is not clear who works for whom. As the Duden rightly states, purpose-based intelligence is not reserved for homo sapiens alone, but can also be found in non-human structures (economics, technology) and systems (social security). Again, this intelligence is to be distinguished from reason and intellect. The concept of artificial intelligence is thus undefined and can stand as a placeholder for many things.

There is still no theological proposal that explains the world from the point of view of technical singularity. Nevertheless, one could rewrite the story of creation and the fall without too much difficulty using the notions of Artificial Intelligence. After all, the so-called singularity is a new beginning, behind which, by definition, we cannot look. Although evolution can take us gently and step by step, the transition from today into the new tomorrow is inconceivable and beyond imagination. Something completely new has been born.

4.4 Creation Story: Human Beings Responsibility

This is exactly what our biblical story of creation speaks of, which sees human beings as emerging from the hand of God and gives them responsibility for what happens on earth. In doing so, with its strict monotheism, it consciously sets itself apart from other theological approaches from Egypt, Babylon or Greece. All these different stories of the origins are written out of a particular present and set of problems. Conceived as a myth or a narrative, they dramatically describe the lot and the task of the people of today. In today's society, this function has been taken over by both more and less enlightened sci-fi writers, and even more by the productions of film directors.

A theological approach that recognizes this potential singularity might either be optimistic such as the AI language games of Ray Kurzweil, or pessimistic such as the fears of Stephen Hawking (see Herder Korrespondenz, July, 38-40). The linguistic material, as we hear and read daily, can allow for both a new and better creation and an apocalyptic downfall. The papal advisor Antonio Spadaro already runs a cyber-theology website.

Such a theologisation of the new world faces other secular approaches such as the "religion" of humanism. In his entertaining, nearly 600-page bestseller "Homo Deus" (2015, German 2017), Yuval Noah Harari presents a philosophy of history based on a certain understanding of religion:

> "However, religion is created by humans rather than by gods, and it is defined by its social function rather than by the existence of deities. Religion is any all-encompassing story that confers superhuman legitimacy on human laws, norms and values. It legitimises human social structures by arguing that they reflect superhuman laws" (p 182, English language edition).

Harari also goes on to describe how biological science in particular exposes human beings and reveals their innermost being, their ego, as an invented story. Human beings are also the product of biochemical algorithms. With this knowledge, Sapiens, as the former crown of creation, sees itself once again as naked. It is only part of other forces that makes it and tells it who it is and where it is going. Everything is information – as are human beings themselves. It does not depend on the individual pieces of data, but on the data streams in which the individual piece of data gets a purpose. It seems that at the end of humanism (understood as religion) we find ourselves disenchanted back in the Garden of Eden, handing over the knowledge of good and evil to the universe.

For the moral creators behind the programming keys, these theological-anthropological approaches sound abstruse and abstract. In the laboratories of the so-called artificial intelligence you are not dealing with "the" AI, but with specific individual applications. How should the car react when it has to make decisions about who it protects and who it exposes to danger in an emergency? How should a brain-computer interface, which connects a prosthetic hand with the brain of its wearer, for example, react if they want to use these new powers to strangle someone to death? How should a remotely controllable pacemaker react when it is hacked? The moral creators in science and industry must take decisions by giving devices that control themselves a viable morality that answers questions of right or wrong actions, either generally or specifically. As there is no consensus among scientists or in society about the concrete answers, one could leave them to chance or be guided by pseudo-democratic voting results. The moral creators can also base themselves on any old morality and program this in.

4.5 The Commandment to Love and Artificial Intelligence

However, since the new machines no longer act according to linear and complex alternatives thought out in advance, but learn to deal with situations in a creative and evolutionary way using their neural connections as do our brains, one possibility is to pass the moral question "cannily" on to the new forms of intelligence. Instead of feeding the technical "problem solvers", as the first computers were called, with a preformulated rule of morality, one could also give them the vocabulary and rules of the moral language game constantly being reinvented by human beings. Thus in all situations, they would be able to commit the same mistakes and errors that make up human beings. To err is human.

But according to our morality so capable of erring, the machines are not allowed to be wrong. They should be perfect or at least better than humans. The path of a perfect morality that knows exactly what is right and wrong, without hesitation and enforced by force, is paved with the bodies of the victims, who were on the wrong side in one of these final solutions. Morality stands as a sign for uncertainty, not for certain knowledge. It is characterized by the freedom that enables it to decide and thereby take the risk of right and wrong. In the internal dialogue of conscience and in exchange with one another, moral creators also gain the courage to take the plunge into the unknown and to chart a beginning that would not exist without their commitment to freedom.

Morality is not a natural process at all, but entirely an art of practical reason and therefore of thought. The artificial intelligence of the future will also think and argue, and even have to deal with emotions. Whether it bases itself on the language of Immanuel Kant or the hate messages of Twitter accounts will depend on its education. One should not call it stupid too quickly. And to keep it stupid is no longer possible anyway, with the potency of this kind of intelligence.

For example, taking as a starting point the Christian-inspired "Golden Rule", one could imagine the following calculation: perhaps Artificial Intelligence will one day encounter us as a smart Samaritan (robot), who does not follow the rules of its far-sighted morality but follows what is good and therefore follows the commandment of love.

If we replace the law of the majority with the law of purposeful argumentation, exciting new moral language games could emerge, which would also make we human beings think, because they would confront us with our own sources of morality. We should not underestimate the quick-wittedness of super-computers. At the same time, they could have access to the writings of Aristotle, Immanuel Kant, John Rawls, and Martha Nussbaum, as well as drawing on the church's social proclamation and forging totally new connections. Again, this is just a sort of game of Go on a different level. We, the humans, must decide what morality we live out and exemplify. This will be decisive for emotionally intelligent machines. Violence begets violence, love begets love. Superhuman efforts in different cultures have brought us to this point. This meant crossing unforeseen boundaries in both a positive and negative sense. Perhaps together with an educated artificial intelligence we will be able to transcend ourselves and grow together as moral creators in search of what is good and the right.

5

ARTIFICIAL INTELLIGENCE ETHICS

Julia Bossmann, Rob Smith, Mauro Gillen, USA
Srikar Reddy, India

The World Economic Forum (WEF) in its global agenda has an important focus on the Fourth Industrial Revolution and within it especially on Artificial Intelligence and Robotics.[85] The following three articles are contributions to the World Economic Forum Agenda. Chapter 6.1 is written by Julia Bossmann, USA[86], chapter 6.2 by Rob Smith[87] and chapter 6.3 by Mauro Gillen and Srikar Reddy[88]. They express the authors' view and not the view of the World Economic Forum.

---

[85] https://www.weforum.org/agenda/archive/artificial-intelligence-and-robotics. (Accessed 3 Sept 2018). Note of the Editor: The chapter is a reprint with permission of the authors.

[86] Julia Bossmann, *Top 9 ethical issues in artificial intelligence*, published 21 Oct 2016 on the WEF agenda platform https://www.weforum.org/agenda/2016/10/top-10-ethical-issues-in-artificial-intelligence. (Accessed 3 Sept 2018).

[87] Rob Smith, *5 core principles to keep AI ethical,* published 19 April 2018, https://www.weforum.org/agenda/2018/04/keep-calm-and-make-ai-ethical. Accessed 3 Sept 2018.

[88] Mauro Gillen/ Srikar Reddy, *We know ethics should inform AI. But which ethics?,* published 26 July 2018, https://www.weforum.org/agenda/2018/07/we-know-ethics-should-inform-ai-but-which-ethics-robotics.

5.1 Top Nine Ethical Issues in Artificial Intelligence

Optimizing logistics, detecting fraud, composing art, conducting research, providing translations: intelligent machine systems are transforming our lives for the better. As these systems become more capable, our world becomes more efficient and consequently richer.

Tech giants such as Alphabet, Amazon, Facebook, IBM and Microsoft – as well as individuals like Stephen Hawking and Elon Musk – believe that now is the right time to talk about the nearly boundless landscape of artificial intelligence. In many ways, this is just as much a new frontier for ethics and risk assessment as it is for emerging technology. So which issues and conversations keep AI experts up at night?

5.1.1 Unemployment: What Happens After the End of Jobs?

The hierarchy of labour is concerned primarily with automation. As we've invented ways to automate jobs, we could create room for people to assume more complex roles, moving from the physical work that dominated the pre-industrial globe to the cognitive labour that characterizes strategic and administrative work in our globalized society.

Look at trucking: it currently employs millions of individuals in the United States alone. What will happen to them if the self-driving trucks promised by Tesla's Elon Musk become widely available in the next decade? But on the other hand, if we consider the lower risk of accidents, self-driving trucks seem like an ethical choice. The same scenario could happen to office workers, as well as to the majority of the workforce in developed countries.

This is where we come to the question of how we are going to spend our time. Most people still rely on selling their time to have enough income to sustain themselves and their families. We can only hope that this opportunity will enable people to find meaning in non-labour activities, such as caring for their families, engaging with their communities and learning new ways to contribute to human society.

If we succeed with the transition, one day we might look back and think that it was barbaric that human beings were required to sell the majority of their waking time just to be able to live.

5.1.2 Inequality: How Do We Distribute the Wealth Created by Machines?

Our economic system is based on compensation for contribution to the economy, often assessed using an hourly wage. The majority of companies are still dependent on hourly work when it comes to products and services. But by using artificial intelligence, a company can drastically cut down on relying on the human workforce, and this means that revenues will go to fewer people. Consequently, individuals who have ownership in AI-driven companies will make all the money.

We are already seeing a widening wealth gap, where start-up founders take home a large portion of the economic surplus they create. In 2014, roughly the same revenues were generated by the three biggest companies in Detroit and the three biggest companies in Silicon Valley ... only in Silicon Valley there were 10 times fewer employees.

If we're truly imagining a post-work society, how do we structure a fair post-labour economy?

5.1.3 Humanity: How do Machines Affect our Behaviour and Interaction?

Artificially intelligent bots are becoming better and better at modelling human conversation and relationships. In 2015, a bot named "Eugene Goostman won the Turing Challenge"[89] for the first time. In this challenge, human raters used text input to chat with an unknown entity, then guessed whether they had been chatting with a human or a machine. Eugene Goostman fooled more than half of the human raters into thinking they had been talking to a human being.

---

[89] http://time.com/2847900/eugene-goostman-turing-test/.

This milestone is only the start of an age where we will frequently interact with machines as if they are humans; whether in customer service or sales. While humans are limited in the attention and kindness that they can expend on another person, artificial bots can channel virtually unlimited resources into building relationships.

Even though not many of us are aware of this, we are already witnesses to how machines can trigger the reward centres in the human brain. Just look at click-bait headlines and video games. These headlines are often optimized with A/B testing, a rudimentary form of algorithmic optimization for content to capture our attention. This and other methods are used to make numerous video and mobile games become addictive. Tech addiction is the new frontier of human dependency.[90]

On the other hand, maybe we can think of a different use for software, which has already become effective at directing human attention and triggering certain actions. When used right, this could evolve into an opportunity to nudge society towards more beneficial behavior. However, in the wrong hands it could prove detrimental.

5.1.4 Artificial Stupidity: How Can We Guard Against Mistakes?

Intelligence comes from learning, whether you're human or machine. Systems usually have a training phase in which they "learn" to detect the right patterns and act according to their input. Once a system is fully trained, it can then go into test phase, where it is hit with more examples and we see how it performs.

Obviously, the training phase cannot cover all possible examples that a system may deal with in the real world. These systems can be fooled[91] in ways that humans wouldn't be. For example, random dot patterns can lead a machine to "see" things that aren't there. If we rely on AI to bring

---

[90]   https://kernelmag.dailydot.com/issue-sections/features-issue-sections/ 15708/addicting-apps-mobile-technology-health.

[91] http://www.evolvingai.org/fooling.

us into a new world of labour, security and efficiency, we need to ensure that the machine performs as planned, and that people can't overpower it to use it for their own ends.

5.1.5 Racist Robots: How Do We Eliminate AI Bias?

Though artificial intelligence is capable of a speed and capacity of processing that's far beyond that of humans, it cannot always be trusted to be fair and neutral. Google and its parent company Alphabet are one of the leaders when it comes to artificial intelligence, as seen in Google's Photos service, where AI is used to identify people, objects and scenes. But it can go wrong, such as when a camera missed the mark[92] on racial sensitivity, or when a software used to predict future criminals[93] showed bias against black people.

We shouldn't forget that AI systems are created by humans, who can be biased and judgemental. Once again, if used right, or if used by those who strive for social progress, artificial intelligence can become a catalyst for positive change.

5.1.6 Security: How Do We Keep AI Safe from Adversaries?

The more powerful a technology becomes, the more can it be used for nefarious reasons as well as good. This applies not only to robots produced to replace human soldiers, or autonomous weapons, but to AI systems that can cause damage if used maliciously. Because these fights won't be fought on the battleground only, cybersecurity will become even more important. After all, we're dealing with a system that is faster and more capable than us by orders of magnitude.

---

[92] https://gizmodo.com/5256650/camera-misses-the-mark-on-racial-sensitivity.
[93] https://www.propublica.org/article/machine-bias-risk-assessments-in-criminal-sentencing.

5.1.7 Evil Geniuses: How Do We Protect Against Unintended Consequences?

It's not just adversaries we have to worry about. What if artificial intelligence itself turned against us? This doesn't mean by turning "evil" in the way a human might, or the way AI disasters are depicted in Hollywood movies. Rather, we can imagine an advanced AI system as a "genie in a bottle" that can fulfil wishes, but with terrible unforeseen consequences.

In the case of a machine, there is unlikely to be malice at play, only a lack of understanding of the full context in which the wish was made. Imagine an AI system that is asked to eradicate cancer in the world. After a lot of computing, it spits out a formula that does, in fact, bring about the end of cancer – by killing everyone on the planet. The computer would have achieved its goal of "no more cancer" very efficiently, but not in the way humans intended it.

5.1.8 Singularity: How Do We Stay in Control of a Complex Intelligent System?

The reason humans are on top of the food chain is not down to sharp teeth or strong muscles. Human dominance is almost entirely due to our ingenuity and intelligence. We can get the better of bigger, faster, stronger animals because we can create and use tools to control them: both physical tools such as cages and weapons, and cognitive tools like training and conditioning.

This poses a serious question about artificial intelligence: will it, one day, have the same advantage over us? We can't rely on just "pulling the plug" either, because a sufficiently advanced machine may anticipate this move and defend itself. This is what some call the "singularity": the point in time when human beings are no longer the most intelligent beings on earth.

5.1.9 Robot Rights: How Do We Define the Humane Treatment of AI?

While neuroscientists are still working on unlocking the secrets of conscious experience, we understand more about the basic mechanisms of reward and aversion. We share these mechanisms with even simple animals. In a way, we are building similar mechanisms of reward and aversion in systems of artificial intelligence. For example, reinforcement learning is similar to training a dog: improved performance is reinforced with a virtual reward.

Right now, these systems are fairly superficial, but they are becoming more complex and life-like. Could we consider a system to be suffering when its reward functions give it negative input? What's more, so-called genetic algorithms work by creating many instances of a system at once, of which only the most successful "survive" and combine to form the next generation of instances. This happens over many generations and is a way of improving a system. The unsuccessful instances are deleted. At what point might we consider genetic algorithms a form of mass murder?

Once we consider machines as entities that can perceive, feel and act, it's not a huge leap to ponder their legal status. Should they be treated like animals of comparable intelligence? Will we consider the suffering of "feeling" machines?

Some ethical questions are about mitigating suffering, some about risking negative outcomes. While we consider these risks, we should also keep in mind that, on the whole, this technological progress means better lives for everyone. Artificial intelligence has vast potential, and its responsible implementation is up to us.

5.2 Five Core Principles to Keep AI Ethical

Science-fiction thrillers, like the 1980s classic film The Terminator, illuminate our imaginations, but they also stoke fears about autonomous, intelligent killer robots eradicating the human race.

And while this scenario might seem far-fetched, last year, over 100 robotics and artificial intelligence technology leaders, including Elon Musk and Google's DeepMind co-founder Mustafa Suleyman, issued a warning about the risks posed by super-intelligent machines.

In an open letter to the UN Convention on Certain Conventional Weapons, the signatories said that once developed, killer robots - weapons designed to operate autonomously on the battlefield - "will permit armed conflict to be fought at a scale greater than ever, and at timescales faster than humans can comprehend." [94] The letter also states: "These can be weapons of terror, weapons that despots and terrorists use against innocent populations, and weapons hacked to behave in undesirable ways. We do not have long to act. Once this Pandora's box is opened, it will be hard to close."

5.2.1 AI Must Be a Force for Good - and Diversity

The United Kingdom government published in 2018 a report[95], commissioned by the House of Lords AI Select Committee, which is based on evidence from over 200 industry experts. Central to the report are five core principles designed to guide and inform the ethical use of AI. The first principle argues that AI should be developed for the common good and benefit of humanity.

The report's authors argue the United Kingdom must actively shape the development and utilisation of AI, and call for "a shared ethical AI

---

[94] https://futureoflife.org/autonomous-weapons-open-letter-2017.

[95] https://publications.parliament.uk/pa/ld201719/ldselect/ldai/100/100.pdf. See also in this book chapters 2.6 and 2.8.

framework" that provides clarity against how this technology can best be used to benefit individuals and society.

They also say the prejudices of the past must not be unwittingly built into automated systems, and urge that such systems "be carefully designed from the beginning, with input from as diverse a group of people as possible."

5.2.2 Intelligibility and Fairness

The second principle demands that AI operates within parameters of intelligibility and fairness, and calls for companies and organisations to improve the intelligibility of their AI systems. "Without this, regulators may need to step in and prohibit the use of opaque technology in significant and sensitive areas of life and society," the report warns.

5.2.3 Data Protection

Third, the report says artificial intelligence should not be used to diminish the data rights or privacy of individuals, families or communities.

It says the ways in which data is gathered and accessed need to be reconsidered. This, the report says, is designed to ensure companies have fair and reasonable access to data, while citizens and consumers can also protect their privacy.

"Large companies which have control over vast quantities of data must be prevented from becoming overly powerful within this landscape. We call on the government ... to review proactively the use and potential monopolisation of data by big technology companies operating in the UK."

5.2.4 Flourishing alongside AI

The fourth principle stipulates all people should have the right to be educated as well as be enabled to flourish mentally, emotionally and economically alongside artificial intelligence.

For children, this means learning about using and working alongside AI from an early age. For adults, the report calls on government to invest in skills and training to negate the disruption caused by AI in the jobs market.

5.2.5 Confronting the Power to Destroy

Fifth, and aligning with concerns around killer robots, the report says the autonomous power to hurt, destroy or deceive human beings should never be vested in artificial intelligence.

"There is a significant risk that well-intended AI research will be misused in ways which harm people," the report says. "AI researchers and developers must consider the ethical implications of their work."

By establishing these principles, the UK can lead by example in the international community, the authors say.

"We recommend that the government convene a global summit of governments, academia and industry to establish international norms for the design, development, regulation and deployment of artificial intelligence."

5.3 Ethics Should Inform AI – But Which Ethics?

Artificial intelligence (AI) relies on big data and machine learning for myriad applications, from autonomous vehicles to algorithmic trading, and from clinical decision support systems to data mining. The availability of large amounts of data is essential to the development of AI. Given China's large population and business sector, both of which use digitized platforms and tools to an unparalleled extent, it may enjoy an advantage in AI. In addition, it has fewer constraints on the use of information gathered through the digital footprint left by people and companies. India has also taken a series of similar steps to digitize its economy, including biometric identity tokens, demonetization and an integrated goods and services tax.

5.3.1 Deontological or Teleological Ethical Standards?

But the recent scandal over the use of personal and social data by Facebook and Cambridge Analytica has brought ethical considerations to the fore. And it's just the beginning. As AI applications require ever greater amounts of data to help machines learn and perform tasks hitherto reserved for humans, companies are facing increasing public scrutiny, at least in some parts of the world. Tesla and Uber have scaled down their efforts to develop autonomous vehicles in the wake of widely reported accidents. How do we ensure the ethical and responsible use of AI? How do we bring more awareness about such responsibility, in the absence of a global standard on AI?

The ethical standards for assessing AI and its associated technologies are still in their infancy. Companies need to initiate internal discussion as well as external debate with their key stakeholders about how to avoid being caught up in difficult situations.

Consider the difference between deontological and teleological ethical standards. The former focuses on the intention and the means, while the latter on the ends and outcomes. For instance, in the case of autonomous vehicles, the end of an error-free transportation system that is also efficient and friendly towards the environment might be enough to justify large-scale data collection about driving under different conditions and also, experimentation based on AI applications.

By contrast, clinical interventions and especially medical trials are hard to justify on teleological grounds. Given the horrific history of medical experimentation on unsuspecting human subjects, companies and AI researchers alike would be wise to employ a deontological approach that judges the ethics of their activities on the basis of the intention and the means rather than the ends.

5.3.2 Golden Rule of Ethics

Another useful yardstick is the so-called golden rule of ethics, which invites you to treat others in the way you would like to be treated. The difficulty in applying this principle to the burgeoning field of AI lies in the gulf separating the billions of people whose data are being accumulated and analysed from the billions of potential beneficiaries. The data simply aggregates in ways that make the direct application of the golden rule largely irrelevant.

5.3.3 Cultural Relativism versus Universalism

Consider one last set of ethical standards: cultural relativism versus universalism. The former invites us to evaluate practices through the lens of the values and norms of a given culture, while the latter urges everyone to live up to a mutually agreed standard. This comparison helps explain, for example, the current clash between the European conception of data privacy and the American one, which is shaping the global competitive landscape for companies such as Google and Facebook, among many others. Emerging markets such as China and India have for years proposed to let cultural relativism be the guiding principle, as they feel it gives them an edge, especially by avoiding unnecessary regulations that might slow their development as technological powerhouses.

5.3.4 Ethical Standards as Important as Technical Standards

Ethical standards are likely to become as important at shaping global competition as technological standards have been since the 1980s. Given the stakes and the thirst for data that AI involves, it will likely require companies to ask very tough questions as to every detail of what they do to get ahead. In the course of the work we are doing with our global clients, we are looking at the role of ethics in implementing AI. The way industry and society addresses these issues will be crucial to the adoption of AI in the digital world.

However, for AI to deliver on its promise, it will require predictability and trust. These two are interrelated. Predictable treatment of the complex issues that AI throws up, such as accountability and permitted uses of data, will encourage investment in and use of AI. Similarly, progress with AI requires consumers to trust the technology, its impact on them, and how it uses their data. Predictable and transparent treatment facilitates this trust.

Intelligent machines are enabling high-level cognitive processes such as thinking, perceiving, learning, problem-solving and decision-making. AI presents opportunities to complement and supplement human intelligence and enrich the way industry and governments operate.

However, the possibility of creating cognitive machines with AI raises multiple ethical issues that need careful consideration. What are the implications of a cognitive machine making independent decisions? Should it even be allowed? How do we hold them accountable for outcomes? Do we need to control, regulate and monitor their learning?

A robust legal framework will be needed to deal with those issues too complex or fast-changing to be addressed adequately by legislation. But the political and legal process alone will not be enough. For trust to flourish, an ethical code will be equally important.

The government should encourage discussion around the ethics of AI, and ensure all relevant parties are involved. Bringing together the private sector, consumer groups and academia would allow the development of an ethical code that keeps up with technological, social and political developments.

Government efforts should be collaborative with existing efforts to research and discuss ethics in AI. There are many such initiatives which could be encouraged, including at the Alan Turing Institute, the Leverhulme Centre for the Future of Intelligence, the World Economic Forum Centre for the Fourth Industrial Revolution, the Royal Society, and the Partnership on Artificial Intelligence to Benefit People and Society.

5.3.5 Ethical Challenges

But these opportunities come with associated ethical challenges:

Decision-making and liability: As AI use increases, it will become more difficult to apportion responsibility for decisions. If mistakes are made which cause harm, who should bear the risk?

Transparency: When complex machine learning systems are used to make significant decisions, it may be difficult to unpick the causes behind a specific course of action. Clear explanations for machine reasoning are necessary to determine accountability.

Bias: Machine learning systems can entrench existing bias in decision-making systems. Care must be taken to ensure that AI evolves to be non-discriminatory.

Human values: Without programming, AI systems have no default values or "common sense". The British Standards Institute BS 8611 standard on the "ethical design and application of robots and robotic systems" provides some useful guidance: "Robots should not be designed solely or primarily to kill or harm humans. Humans, not robots, are the responsible agents; it should be possible to find out who is responsible for any robot and its behaviour."

Data protection and IP: The potential of AI is rooted in access to large data sets. What happens when an AI system is trained on one data set, then applies learnings to a new data set?

Responsible AI ensures attention to moral principles and values, to ensure that fundamental human ethics are not compromised. There have been several recent allegations of businesses exploiting AI unethically. However, Amazon, Google, Facebook, IBM and Microsoft have established a non-profit partnership to formulate best practices on artificial intelligence technologies, advance the public's understanding, and to serve as a platform about artificial intelligence.

6

BLOCKCHAIN ETHICS

Troy Wilkinson, Great Britain

We are accustomed to having everything centralized from banking to taxes even to social media so when the things we are used to become decentralized by the Blockchain, where everything exists everywhere but yet nowhere central, the question of ethics is raised.

6.1   Blockchain Definition and Description

Before diving into the ethics of the Blockchain, it is important to understand what exactly is the Blockchain. Too often, the Blockchain is confused with the crypto-currency Bitcoin. Bitcoin is not the Blockchain but instead is the technology that first utilized Blockchain technology to process its transactions. Crypto-currency mining is still by far the largest use of Blockchain technology but the realm of possibilities for the application of Blockchain are endless.

By definition, the Blockchain is "a digitized, decentralized, public ledger of all cryptocurrency transactions. Constantly growing as 'completed' blocks (the most recent transactions) are recorded and added to it in chronological order, it allows market participants to keep track of digital currency transactions without central recordkeeping. Each node (a computer connected to the network) gets a copy of the Blockchain, which is downloaded automatically. Originally developed as the accounting method for the virtual currency Bitcoin, Blockchains – which use what's known as distributed ledger technology (DLT) – are appearing in a variety of commercial applications today. Currently, the technology is primarily used to verify transactions, within digital currencies though it is possible to digitize, code and insert practically any document into the Blockchain. Doing so creates an indelible record that cannot be changed; furthermore, the record's authenticity can be verified by the entire community using the Blockchain instead of a single centralized authority."[96]

One of the wondrous things about the Blockchain is that it can never be hijacked, the records are indelible and cannot be falsified and the motivation for true decentralization lies in four areas[97]:

(1) anonymity and transaction obfuscation, to make it impossible to find and attack the transacting parties directly;

(2) decentralization, to make it impossible to co-opt or attack the system as a whole through a central entity;

(3) strong encryption, to make it impossible for a powerful outsider to see what goes on; and

(4) distributed organization, to create organizational structures that are resistant to interference.

6.2 Blockchain Anonymity and Privacy: Ethical?

But, on the flipside, the Blockchain is not regulated and the great deal of anonymity has lead it to be a favoured vessel for payments to cyber-criminals and embargoed nation states who are circumventing

---

[96]   ICFAI,   P.   B.   (2018,   August   03).   Blockchain. https://www.investopedia.com/terms/b/Blockchain.asp. (Retrieved 8 August, 2018)

[97] Bulkin, Aleksandr (2016, April 21). Elephant in the room: ethical Blockchains and the conundrum of governance. https://blog.coinfund.io/elephant-in-the-room-ethical-Blockchains-and-the-conundrum-of-governance-a11d0f9c4c56. Retrieved 8 August, 2018.

traditional financial institutions via crypto-currencies. Do we have the right to be anonymous with no gate keepers?

There also has been a great debate over the rise of ransomware and how the Blockchain technologies behind crypto-currency may be directly correlated to the increase in the cyber-crime. It is important however to note that ransomware first started in 1989 with mailing of floppy disks and that even today, cyber-criminals are using these old-school methods (now infected CDs and USB sticks) to distribute ransomware. So, while the crypto-currencies may have made it easier to be paid electronically, ransomware is not a by-product of Blockchain technology but rather a new efficiency that cyber-criminals have employed in their criminal enterprises.

With the Blockchain, the individuals behind transactions are anonymous by nature although some companies such as Chainalysis have taken a step to help companies and individuals hit by cyber-crime and fraud track transactions on the Bitcoin Blockchain to identify bad actors. These companies are able to reveal the structure of cyber-criminal organizations and when funds are transferred into fiat currencies, there is the possibility of revealing the true name or an IP address. It is these transactions that have enabled law enforcement and Blockchain investigation firms to identify and arrest groups and individuals behind recent ransomware attacks.

Yet due to the ability to identify individuals using the Bitcoin Blockchain and the volatility of the crypto-currency, cyber-criminals have moved away from reliance on Bitcoin to truly anonymous Blockchain cryptocurrencies such as Monero[98] so that their identities can remain hidden again leading to the question, do we have the right and is it ethi-

---

[98] Bing, Chris (2017, December 29). *Bitcoin hype pushes hackers to stash their money in lesser-known cryptocurrencies*, https://www.cyberscoop.com/bitcoin-hype-pushers-hackers-to-stash-their-money-in-lesser-known-cryptocurrencies. Retrieved 8 August, 2018.

cal for us to remain anonymous on the Blockchain? So we continue to allow cyber-criminals to hide behind the mask of privacy to continue their nefarious activities? Or would it be more ethical to maintain decentralization yet not allow anonymous transactions, particularly financial?

But the anonymity of the Blockchain also can lead to issues with abuse of the technology by bad actors who take advantage of the privacy afforded to trade illegal weapons, drugs, even weapons of mass destruction. Blockchain-based crypto-currencies have long been the favoured fiat of the cyber-criminals trading wares on the Dark Web. Research showed that cyber-criminals trade up to $650,000 per day[99] in cryptocurrency payments on the Dark Web. While the want for privacy is undeniably attractive and one of the most prized attributes of Blockchain, one must question whether or not it is truly needed from an ethical standpoint.

The United States has long been imposing sanctions on North Korea and Iran but both countries have active programs to mine and steal crypto-currencies to circumvent the sanctions. It is alleged that North Korea has been secretly funding its nuclear and missile programs[100] by hacking crypto-currency exchanges. Even a senior Iranian lawmaker openly discussed using Blockchain-based digital currencies to circumvent US sanctions[101]. Unfortunately for the United States, there is little that it can do to stop the use of these Blockchain-based currencies by what it has

---

[99] Budko, Dmitry (2018, June 19). *Immunity on the Dark Web as a Result of Blockchain Technology.* https://codeburst.io/immunity-on-the-dark-web-as-a-result-of-Blockchain-technology-6693eb087bdd. Retrieved 8August 8, 2018.

[100] Ward, Alex (2018, February 28). *How North Korea uses bitcoin to get around US sanctions.* https://www.vox.com/world/2018/2/28/17055762/north-korea-sanctions-bitcoin-nuclear-weapons. Retrieved 8 August, 2018.

[101] Tassev, Lubomir (2018 July 16). *Iran considers using cryptocurrencies to Evade US Sanctions.* https://news.bitcoin.com/iran-considers-using-cryptocurrencies-to-evade-us-sanctions. Retrieved 9 August, 2018.

deemed "rogue nations" to bypass its sanctions as they have no legal right to regulate its use or exchange outside its borders.

6.3 No Possibility to Be Forgotten

Is the indelible nature of the Blockchain ethical? Prior to the General Data Protection Regulation (GDPR) in Europe, there was the question of whether or not we possess the right to be forgotten; and the right of individuals to "determine the development of their life in an autonomous way"[102] was not regulated. But now with GDPR and similar data privacy acts being implemented, how does the right to be forgotten function within Blockchain? The simple answer is that it does not. With the Blockchain, once a transaction is recorded, it can never be removed leading to a possible confrontation with GDPR requirements to comply with requests to be forgotten. With an indelible ledger, there is no possibility to have data expunged so to paraphrase the old saying, "What happens on the Blockchain, stays on the Blockchain."

Estonia as part of the information society initiative has implemented Blockchain technologies as a way for the government to guarantee the integrity of its records and its digital identity cards. The ID cards give Estonian citizens access to various services such as healthcare, finance, and voting. But this has raised questions about how does an individual control their digital identity to protect the data? It is important from an ethical standpoint that when these digital identities are created care is taken to only provide the subset of data that is required for the provision of service. An example would be, should your healthcare provider have access to voter information? The immediate answer is no. When applied across a broad spectrum of data sets, such as identity, it is vitally important that access is restricted and controlled. Special care should be

---

[102] Wikipedia. *Right to be forgotten,* https://en.wikipedia.org/wiki/Right_to_be_forgotten. Retrieved 9 August, 2018.

given to ensuring that the data is not easily accessible by unauthorized parties and logs of data access are maintained and regularly reviewed to ensure that the citizens are protected against unnecessary intrusions into their private data.

Blockchain technology is in direct confrontation with the right to be forgotten and as Blockchain moves from its beginnings in cryptocurrency to things such as social media and business efficiencies, even more questions are raised about the ethics of the Blockchain. For instance, is it ethical to collect information of children on the Blockchain when they have no say in the placement of their information on the Blockchain and no ability to have it removed? Or even worse, after researchers found unknown persons storing links to images and lists of websites of child abuse within Bitcoin's Blockchain[103], despite disputes about whether or not it was a valid claim, what would we do if it was possible to store those references forever, ever embedded in the technology when the information is destructive and highly illegal?

As law enforcement agencies look to the Blockchain, there are benefits of course to implementing Blockchain for chain of evidence and information sharing among agencies but what happens if it is applied to criminal records? Is it ethical to have records that can never be expunged? Should the possibly mistakes of your youth follow you throughout your life with the ability to never be forgotten? These are the problems that society will possibly face if Blockchain is implemented in the recordkeeping of law enforcement.

---

[103] Gibbs, Samuel (2018, March 20). *Child abuse imagery found with bitcoin's Blockchain.* https://www.theguardian.com/technology/2018/mar/20/child-abuse-imagery-bitcoin-Blockchain-illegal-content. Retrieved 9 August, 2018.

6.4 Blockchain for Voting?

As governments think about applying Blockchain to voting to fight fraud and corruption, what happens if the Blockchain stops being anonymous and voter records are publicly exposed, unable to be erased? The decision of West Virginia to use Blockchain in its mid-term elections[104] has faced much criticism from election security experts who are concerned that the use of Blockchain could in fact introduce new security vulnerabilities as records would not be protected while being transmitted to the voting Blockchain so there is no guarantee that the data would be accurate or was not altered in transit. And what would happen years down the road if the voter information became publicly accessible? How could citizens be assured that their private votes would not be made public? If governments will implement Blockchain technology for usage in voting, they must take significant steps to ensure the privacy of the votes and preserve the freedoms of free and democratic votes.

6.5 Blockchain for Transparent Trade Tracing

Many of the ideas behind the use of Blockchain are to lead to better, more ethical business practices such as in the implementation of the Blockchain in tracing diamonds or cobalt mining. De Beers, the world's largest diamond producer, plans to launch an industry-wide Blockchain to help track diamonds from the moment they are extracted from the ground and each time they change hands. The implementation of Blockchain in the diamond industry will help fight against blood diamond

---

[104] Orcutt, Mike (2018, August 9) *Why security experts hate that "Blockchain voting" will be used in the midterm elections*. https://www.technologyreview.com/s/611850/why-security-experts-hate-that-Blockchain-voting-will-be-used-in-the-midterm-elections/. Retrieved 9 August, 2018.

trade as well as prevent the ability of synthetic stones to be claimed as natural[105].

But Blockchain companies themselves face growing scepticism of their own business ethics as Initial Coin Offering (ICO) fraud continues to make headlines. Unethical Blockchain "entrepreneurs" have made off with $1 billion[106] in investments in ICOs leading to a large distrust of Blockchain companies participating in ICOs. In fact, ICO fraud reached such heights that the US Securities & Exchange Commission (SEC) launched a fake ICO to help teach investors better ways to detect fraudulent Blockchain investments.[107] The Blockchain community must consider joining forces to root out the fraudsters in their midst if they do not want to continue the fight in the future to be believable, ethical business persons. As long as fraudulent ICOs continue to hit the headlines, the Blockchain industry as a whole will be spoilt by the bad apples in the bunch.

6.6 Blockchain Energy: Environmental Impact

The environmental impact of Blockchain technology must also not be ignored. Blockchain transactions rely on complex algorithms that require large amounts of computing (hash) power. Depending on the amount and speed at which calculations must take place will increase the

---

[105] Lewis, Barbara (2018, January 16). *De Beers turns to Blockchain to guarantee diamond purity.* https://www.reuters.com/article/us-anglo-debeers-Blockchain/de-beers-turns-to-Blockchain-to-guarantee-diamond-purity-idUSKBN1F51HV. Retrieved 10 August, 2018.

[106] Malwa, Shaurya (2018, May 19). *ICO Scams Have Raised More Than $1 Billion, Report Claims.* https://www.ccn.com/ico-scams-have-raised-more-than-1-billion-report-claims/. Retrieved 10 August, 2018.

[107] Partz, Helen (2018, May 16). *SEC Launches Mock ICO to Show Investors Warning Signs of Fraud.* https://cointelegraph.com/news/sec-launches-mock-ico-to-show-investors-warning-signs-of-fraud. Retrieved 10 August, 2018.

amount of resources required. Blockchain mining is an energy-intensive task and as the technology is more widely adopted, it will require more processing power and more energy consumption. As the price of Bitcoin rose, so did the interest in mining the crypto-currency and as a result, the Bitcoin Blockchain consumed as much energy as 159 of the world's nations.[108] The energy consumption of Bitcoin Blockchain mining has reached such heights that it is expected that it will use 0.5% of the world's energy by the end of 2018.[109] While there are pushes to have more efficient and green power, Blockchain still heavily relies on traditional energy supplies in many areas. In fact, some areas have begun to stop allowing companies to employ Blockchain technology, particularly crypto-currency mining operations, due to the large increase in power consumption of these entities and the worry that electrical companies will not be able to supply sufficient electricity to the regular consumers. While the benefits of Blockchain are numerous, is the environmental impact in our best interest?

6.7 Decentralised or Majority-Owned?

There additionally must be consideration of the 51% attack when employing public Blockchain technologies. The 51% attack occurs when a single entity possesses 51% of the Blockchains computing (hash) power. The attack actually has been successfully executed against sever-

---

[108] Galeon , Dom (2017, November 27). *Mining Bitcoin Costs More Energy Than What 159 Countries Consume in a Year.* https://futurism.com/mining-bitcoin-costs-more-energy-159-countries-consume-year. Retrieved 10 August, 2018.

[109] Zuckerman, Molly Jane (2018, May 17). *Bitcoin Mining To Use 0.5% of World's Energy by End of 2018*, Peer-Reviewed Research Shows. https://cointelegraph.com/news/bitcoin-mining-to-use-05-of-worlds-energy-by-end-of-2018-peer-reviewed-research-shows. Retrieved 10 August, 2018.

al crypto-currency Blockchains from Bitcoin Gold to Litecoin Cash.[110] Obtaining a majority of a Blockchains hash could lead to an entity being able to block transactions and enable double-spending, effectively taking away the decentralized nature of the Blockchain in question because now the majority is owned by the entity. We must consider how this affects the control of accounting, exchange, and even social media transactions when there is no decentralization and control is exercised by a single entity. The controlling entity could wreak havoc on financial exchanges by delaying transactions or assigning preferential transaction processing over other parties. Or taking the example of using Blockchain for voting, what if the controlling party of the Blockchain wanted a specific candidate to win? They could slow down transactions, deny transactions, and completely destroy the democratic nature of voting through control of the Blockchain. Naturally this is a worst-case scenario for the ethics of the Blockchain, but it is a potential consideration that must be taken seriously.

Additionally, cyber-criminals have also targeted Blockchain technology, stealing funds from ICOs, crypto-currency trading platforms, and launching distributed denial of service (DDoS) attacks against Blockchain infrastructure. If we are going to move to more Blockchain technology in our daily lives, it will be vitally important to ensure that the infrastructure processing the requests are protected and contingencies are put in place so that the Blockchain-based systems are always available. An outage due to a failed software upgrade caused havoc on the New York Stock Exchange in 2015 and resulted in a fine of $14 million[111], could you imagine a stock exchange run on Blockchain that suc-

---

[110] Hertig, Alyssa (2018, June 9). *Blockchain's Once-Feared 51% Attack Is Now Becoming Regular*. https://www.coindesk.com/Blockchains-feared-51-attack-now-becoming-regular. Retrieved 10 August, 2018.

[111] Dugan, Kevin (2018, March 6). *New York Stock Exchange fined $14M for 2015 outage*. https://nypost.com/2018/03/06/new-york-stock-exchange-fined-14m-for-2015-outage. Retrieved 13 August, 2018.

cumbs to a DDoS attack that could knock it offline for hours, if not days? What kind of turmoil would that cause in the financial markets?

6.8 Ethically More Benefits or Dangers?

There are many ethical considerations that must be measured when implementing Blockchain technology. Will the benefits outweigh the potential negative impacts on privacy and environment? Can the privacy of the information on the Blockchain be protected at all times and the information of the citizens whose data is stored be kept safe? Can the Blockchain be protected against interference of outside parties and kept from potential corruption of 51% entities? Is it right to store the data for a lifetime or can it cause harm to an individual in the future? Blockchain is a wondrous technology with many applications but we cannot be drawn to it like moths to a flame just because it is the latest technology buzzword as the implications of its use can have long-lasting, forever present and never to be erased consequences.

7

THE FUTURE OF JOBS
IN CYBER SOCIETY

International Labour Organisation ILO

The International Labour Organisation, one of the largest special agencies of the United Nations, deals since its inception in 1919, a hundred years ago, with issues of working conditions, labour rights, core labour standards, such as child labour, forced labour, health, security and the informal sector, but also with future developments such as creating jobs, green economy, and technological disruptions. The ILO is the only tripartite UN-organisation where the member states, the employers' associations and the workers' associations/Unions have equal rights in decision making. ILO positions therefore normally express a balanced and values-driven perspective of issues around work.

The ILO "Global Commission on the Future of Work" deals with future developments of the job market, especially in the light of new technologies. The ILO states about the commission: "The establishment of the Global Commission on the Future of Work in August 2017 marked the start of the second phase of ILO's Future of Work Centenary initiative. The six thematic clusters provide a basis for further deliberations of the Global Commission. They focus on the main issues that need to be considered if the future of work is to be one that provides security, equality and prosperity. A series of Issue Briefs are prepared under each of the proposed clusters. These are intended to stimulate discussion on a se-

lect number of issues under the different themes. The thematic clusters are not necessarily related to the structure of the final report."[112]

The second meeting of the Commission was held on 15-17 February 2018 in Geneva. The following document was presented as Issue Brief no 6 under the title "The impact of technology on the quality and the quantity of jobs".[113] The ILO looks not only on quantity of jobs, but also the needed qualifications and the impact on working conditions.

7.1 Introduction

Increased digitalization and automation is expected to significantly affect both the quality and quantity of jobs. New types of jobs and employment are changing the nature and conditions of work by altering skills requirements and replacing traditional patterns of work and sources of income. They open opportunities, especially for developing countries, to enter new, fast-growing sectors and catch up with more advanced economies. At the same time, new technologies are affecting the functioning of labour markets and challenging the effectiveness of existing labour market institutions, with far-reaching consequences for the number of jobs, their quality and the diversity of opportunities they offer.

This Issue Brief discusses the potential of technological change for job creation and destruction and its implications for inequality and job polarization. It also highlights the opportunities for economic development and labour market efficiency and inclusion.

---

[112] Published 20 Feb 2018. https://www.ilo.org/global/topics/future-of-work/publications/issue-briefs/WCMS_618168/lang--en/index.htm.

[113] Published here with permission of ILO.

7.2 Key Findings

7.2.1 Technology and Jobs

Current studies emphasize the disruptive nature of technological changes, stressing the potentially wide-ranging implications for job destruction (ILO, 2017). Evaluations of the extent of labour market disruption vary widely and range from a low of less than 10 per cent of all jobs to a high of more than 60 per cent (see Balliester and Elsheikhi, forthcoming, for an overview). Frey and Osborne (2017) estimate that 47 per cent of US jobs are susceptible to potential technological replacement. However, such assessments tend to overestimate the potential adverse effects of automation by focusing exclusively on the technical feasibility of substituting labour by capital. Thus, they ignore economic feasibility, i.e. whether the investment in new technologies is at least as profitable as existing (labour-intensive) alternatives (Kucera, 2017).

Future automation is unlikely to destroy complete occupations but will rather change the types and number of tasks in most occupations. According to the World Bank, less than 20 per cent of jobs are predicted to disappear completely (World Bank, 2016a; see also Autor and Handel, 2013). A recent study by McKinsey Global Institute that looked at both sides of the debate estimated that by 2030, in about 60 per cent of occupations, at least one-third of constituent activities could be automated (MGI, 2017). While this is likely to have a differential impact in different countries, the full- time equivalent of work potentially displaced by automation is estimated at a midpoint of 15 per cent. In addition, between 3 and 14 per cent of the global workforce would need to switch occupational categories (see Issue Brief No. 8). Thus, while there might well be sufficient job creation to compensate for technological unemployment, the realization of these opportunities will depend on ensuring that workers can move to newly created jobs. In short, a bigger challenge may well be how to manage this transition (see Issue Brief No. 7).

History points to similar experiences. An often-cited example is the impact of the introduction of ATMs on jobs for bank tellers in the United States in the 1970s. Instead of – as one might have assumed – bank teller jobs being eliminated, their number rose modestly despite the rapid roll-out of ATMs (Bessen, 2015). In France, the Internet is thought to have destroyed some 500,000 jobs within 15 years after its introduction; at the same time, it has created 1.2 million new jobs (MGI, 2011). One important reason for this is the reduction in operating and transaction costs resulting from these technological innovations, which can indirectly stimulate the demand for labour. Technological change can also create a range of new tasks; for instance, from a bank teller to a financial services advisor. In the United States, for example, 30 per cent of the jobs created since the late 1990s were types that did not exist before, such as IT administration, hardware manufacturing and development of smartphone applications (MGI, 2017).

Jobs are typically made up of both readily automatable and not readily automatable tasks. This raises the question of whether the automation of work processes will result in a reduction of the workforce, or whether the remaining tasks might be shared among the existing workforce. The answer to this question depends on how work is organized in a given workplace and on the extent to which tasks that are not readily automatable can be bundled together to create a new job (Kucera, 2017). The automation of work processes need not present an "all or nothing" scenario; different options do exist. As with work- sharing arrangements implemented by some countries in the wake of the global financial crisis, social dialogue can play an important role in exploring the options and mediating the impact of new automation technologies on workers (see Issue Brief No. 7).

In the aggregate, technological change does not seem to have led to a significant increase in joblessness (Atkinson and Wu, 2017). Global employment continues to expand in line with the labour force, bringing global unemployment rates down to 5.6 per cent (ILO, 2018). In advanced economies, the costs of digitalization have declined dramatically, but job destruction rates have actually fallen over the longer term (see figure 1; Davis and Haltiwanger, 2014).

7.2.2 Sharing Technological Dividends

How to share technological gains ("technological dividends") broadly in terms of jobs and income has also become a pressing issue. These distributional concerns reflect the experience of the previous wave of technological changes in which technological gains were distributed in favour of capital owners and skilled workers (IMF, 2017). The large economies of scale that exist in digital industries have often led to oligopolistic structures, in which a few emerging players are dominating large shares of the market (Christiaensen, 2017; Parker, Van Alstyne and Choudary, 2017). As it stands now, there is no reason to think that the new wave of technological changes will be different. Income inequality is increasing at the same time as the costs of "big data" storage are falling (see figure 1). While the rise of new "big data" platforms that are able to accumulate ever-increasing information on consumer behaviour and preferences certainly enhances the efficiency of the economy, there is a question as to whether these productivity gains are benefiting societies or being captured by a small number of dominant firms. While it is not yet clear whether the market power these large players enjoy is a temporary or inherent feature of Internet markets (Haucap and Heimeshoff,

2013), this does raise distributional questions. Moreover, the generation of economic value from low-cost unpaid labour each time a user turns on their device and accesses computer-mediated networks raises additional questions about who ultimately benefits from this new form of digital capital (Berg, forthcoming).

Figure 1. Inequality increased as digitalization costs declined in line with job destruction rates.

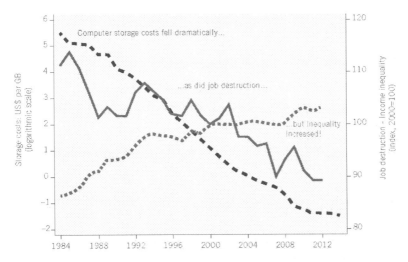

Note: Job destruction rate is a weighted average of Australia, Belgium, Canada, Denmark, France, Greece, Ireland, Italy, Japan, Luxembourg, Netherlands, Sweden, United Kingdom and United States. Source: ILO, Labour Flows database, 2013; OECD, Labour Force Statistics; Muelhauser, 2014.

Our baseline projection suggests that there is a risk of further job polarization in the years to come (see figure 2). As jobs are being destroyed in manufacturing and parts of services sectors, employment in both low- and high-skilled occupations has risen. Studies on robotization show that displacement is high for routine tasks (i.e. tasks that can easily be translated into software-driven robots), including in many services sectors where digitalization and artificial intelligence have come to play a bigger role. In the absence of effective transition policies, including adequate opportunities to acquire new relevant skills (see Issue Brief No. 8), many of those who are at risk of job loss may be forced to accept lower-skilled and lower-paying jobs, thus putting further pressure on wages in the low-wage sector (Dauth et al., 2017). Indeed, a majority of middle-skilled routine task jobs that were associated with standard employment contracts with regular working hours have been replaced by non-standard forms of employment in both non-routine cognitive and manual task jobs (OECD, 2015).

Figure 2. Job Polarization around the Globe

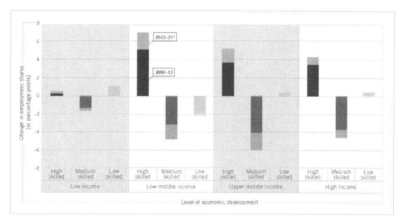

Note: Change in employment shares, in percentage points. Forecasts after 2016. Source ILO Trends Econometric Models, November 2016.

Technological dividends are being unevenly distributed between firms. A small group of firms are taking advantage of new technology ("frontier firms"), while many others and micro-, small and medium-sized enterprises (MSMEs) may face challenges with technology adoption. The gaps between frontier firms and the rest are large and growing in many countries (OECD, 2017). This phenomenon has been accompanied by the rise of highly concentrated product and services markets in which a very limited number of "superstar" firms tend to dominate, as mentioned earlier with respect to "big data" (Autor et al., 2017). Not surprisingly, the rise of such market power is associated with falling labour income share.

7.3 Potential for Development

Sharing technological dividends is an issue of global scale. How can we ensure that all countries, both developed and developing, benefit from the current technological changes? There are three channels through which new technology may have an impact on the world of work in developing countries: (i) automation and robotization; (ii) connectivity; and (iii) innovation (see Christiaensen, 2017). The degree to which developing countries will be able to take advantage of and benefit from these channels remains an open question.

The automation of production processes and the increased deployment of robots require significant investments. In countries with relatively low labour costs, such investments might still be unprofitable. However, with increasing income, the likelihood of adopting automating technologies and hence replacing humans by machines will increase. From a purely technological standpoint, about two-thirds of jobs could be automated in developing countries over the following decades (World Bank, 2016b). At the same time, mobile and flexible robots are emerging which are supplied at comparably low prices. They are able to perform a wide range of different tasks and have opened up a window of opportunity to develop new industries and create jobs, in particular in developing countries. Experience from South-East Asia demonstrates that countries which had already developed the collective capabilities to innovate were successful in adopting robot technologies and developing robot-intensive industries. Such capabilities are embodied in the knowledge base of a society, including the composition and diversity of different technical skills and knowledge acquired by the labour force, as well as by the socially shared values and beliefs that shape expectations, choices and behaviour (Nübler, 2017). Nevertheless, developing countries might still experience disruption as a result of automation in more technologically advanced countries, which might result in reshoring of certain tasks and activities (see Issue Brief No. 10). Developing countries also might not have the capabilities needed to take advantage of the potential that new technologies hold for improving processes and products.

The Internet has enhanced connectivity, including to global markets. This has improved the development prospects for countries that are able to take advantage of this increased connectivity and supply their services from anywhere in the world. In contrast to previous waves of development and catching up which relied on a strong and expanding manufacturing base, services sector growth today plays an increasing role in the development process. Emerging and developing economies may well be able to mitigate the adverse effects from the potential reshoring of production by increasing their trade in services (see Issue Brief No. 10) (World Bank, 2016a). There may also be new opportunities for developing countries to become engaged in "remote repairing". The increasing interconnectedness of physical devices and appliances allows location- independent technicians to support clients with direct troubleshooting via the Internet. In addition, the development of the platform economy allows developing countries to participate in this "trade in tasks" and thus to catch a larger share of global value added in services (see Issue Brief No. 5). However, platforms are mostly developed in advanced economies, and markets can become rapidly dominated by those who entered early in the process. There is thus a risk that developing countries will become increasingly dependent on enterprises located in developed countries.

Digitalization can also have a positive impact on the innovation strength of developing countries. Ecosystems for innovation, such as tech hubs and makerspaces, are accessible online and facilitate the exchange of knowledge and ideas among peers. Smartphone applications enable developers to deploy their ideas at relatively low costs and risks. And e-commerce platforms allow digital start-ups to market their products to a large number of customers worldwide.

Automation and artificial intelligence will also play an important role in agriculture, particularly with growth in the demand for global goods (OECD and FAO, 2016). As shown in a recent study by Jayne, Kwame Yeboah and Henry (2018), "smart farming" increases productivity by using the Internet of things, with sensors to collect real- time data and integrated monitoring systems to create optimal conditions for sowing, watering, fertilizing and harvesting. Unmanned agricultural drones and satellites, self-driving farm equipment, and robot pickers for fruits and vegetables are all expected to reduce the need for human work. At the same time, new technology offers better access to product innovations, new agricultural practices and market developments.

While commercial agriculture will benefit most from such innovations, smaller farmers of traditional food staples and subsistence farmers may also benefit. Innovations in crop genetics, organic agriculture and irrigation as well as other infrastructure, for example, are credited with productivity improvements among small producers. Smartphone-based renting applications for agricultural machinery (e.g. "Hello Tractor" in Nigeria) enable small farmers to access modern technology at low cost. Apps are also used by small farmers to access agricultural extension services, as well as to improve planting and crop rotation. Research capacity and expertise, complemented by extension and commercialization, will be essential and still remain a big challenge in many developing countries.

A study across 21 emerging and developing countries and 11 developed countries revealed that there is still a large gap in Internet usage across the globe. While a median of 54 per cent of adults in emerging and developing countries reported using the Internet at least occasionally, this rate was 33 percentage points higher in advanced economies (PRC, 2016). Although Internet usage in emerging and developing countries has expanded steadily over the past years, increased efforts are needed to close the digital divide in order to make the benefits of technological advancement more inclusive.

7.4. Labour Market Efficiency and Inclusion

As an additional benefit, new technologies are expected to improve the functioning of the labour market, which could help in addressing risks of mismatch and long- term unemployment. The analysis of "big data" can also serve as a forecasting tool. An analysis of social media conversations about work-related anxiety resulted in the prediction of an unemployment spike in Ireland three months before the release of official statistics (United Nations Global Pulse, 2013). Artificial intelligence and big data techniques, for instance, are increasingly being implemented (by large enterprises) to improve recruitment processes, thereby helping to correct skills mismatches. Time saved by automating parts of the hiring process and improved hiring quality from standardized job matching can help enhance labour market efficiency. Digital platforms, such as LinkedIn and Monster.com, are already connecting individuals with work opportunities in both traditional and digital workplaces, as well as in developed and developing countries, thereby taking over tasks traditionally carried out by head-hunters. These platforms can bring significant gains at both the micro and macro levels. According to the McKinsey Global Institute, online platforms could match workers and employers, yielding 72 million jobs and spurring global GDP by 2 per cent within the next decade (MGI, 2015). First experiences suggest, however, that such digital hiring methods have the tendency to replicate existing recruitment biases, undermining efforts to promote broader labour market diversity (Mann and O'Neil, 2016).

The unequal impact that digitalization and automation have on sectors and locations runs the risk of worsening existing gender imbalances. Men may face larger job losses than women in certain industries exposed to automation, for instance in the automotive industry (Acemoglu and Restrepo, 2017). According to one study, however, men are expected to recover more from these job losses than women: men will lose about 4 million jobs by 2020 but are expected to gain another 1.4 million, i.e. roughly one job gained for every 2.9 jobs lost. In contrast, women will face 3 million job losses but only 0.6 million gains, or only one job gained for five jobs lost (WEF, 2016). Moreover, these alternative employment opportunities for women are often found in the care sector, which is expected to expand further as a result of population ageing. Jobs in this sector present, however, significant decent work deficits; along with unpaid care work, they prevent the development of a larger, diversified care services market, thereby perpetuating gender inequalities (see Issue Brief No. 3). This trend is not universal, however, and in some Latin American and South-East Asian countries the opposite might be true. In Argentina, for instance, female jobholders face an automation probability of 61.3 per cent, while for men it stands at 66.1 per cent (MH, 2016). In ASEAN countries, women represent the majority in occupations that are judged as vulnerable to being automated and are thus more likely to become unemployed than men (Chang and Huynh, 2016). However, taking account of economic feasibility and low robot deployment in light manufacturing, such as in apparel where female employment tends to be concentrated, the gender impact of workplace automation could be mitigated.

7.5 Some Considerations

The overall effects of technological change are likely to be context-specific, differing among countries, sectors and occupations. They will depend on the institutional set-up that influences the opportunity costs of automation and the capacity of the workforce to adjust to the new, robot-based work environment, as well as the potential for worker mobility across sectors and locations.

Great potential for economic growth in developing countries exists, although challenges remain to take advantage of those possibilities.

- What policies are critical for sharing technological dividends broadly and avoiding increased labour market polarization and income inequality?
- What policies need to be enacted to enable developing countries to reap the full benefits of the current wave of technological change, including in the services sector?
- How can the current technological revolution be managed to improve the functioning of labour markets and strengthen inclusiveness?
- What measures need to be taken to mitigate the consequences of job destruction?

7.6 Bibliography

Acemoglu, D.; Restrepo, P. 2017. *Robots and jobs: Evidence from US labor markets*, NBER Working Paper No. 23285 (Cambridge, MA, National Bureau of Economic Research).

Atkinson, R.D.; Wu, J. 2017. *False alarmism: Technological disruption and the U.S. labor market, 1850−2015*, ITIF @Work Series (Washington, DC, Information Technology and Innovation Foundation).

Autor, D.H.; Handel, M.J. 2013. "Putting tasks to the test: Human capital, job tasks, and wages", in *Journal of Labor Economics*, Vol. 31, No. 2, pp. S59−S96.

—; Dorn, D.; Katz, L.F.; Patterson, C.; Reenen, J.V. 2017. "Concentrating on the fall of the labor share", in *American Economic Re-*

view Papers and Proceedings, Vol. 107, No. 5, pp. 180–185.

Baldwin, R. 2016. *The great convergence: Information technology and the new globalization* (Cambridge, MA, Harvard University Press).

Balliester, T.; Elsheikhi, A. Forthcoming. *The future of work: A literature review*, Research Department Working Paper (Geneva, ILO).

Berg, J. Forthcoming. Book review of *Heteromation, and other stories of computing and capitalism* by Hamid R. Ekbia and Bonnie A. Nardi, in *International Labour Review*.

Bessen, J.E. 2015. "Toil and technology", in *Finance and Development*, Vol. 52, No. 1 (Washington, DC, International Monetary Fund).

—. 2017. *Automation and jobs: When technology boosts employment*, Law and Economics Research Paper No. 17-09 (Boston, MA, Boston University School of Law).

Chang, J.-H.; Huynh, P. 2016. *ASEAN in transformation: The future of jobs at risk of automation* (Bangkok, ILO Regional Office).

Christiaensen, L. 2017. *Can technology reshape the world of work for developing countries?*, Jobs and Development Blog, posted 6 Jan. (Washington, DC, World Bank).

Dauth, W.; Findeisen, S.; Südekum, J.; Wößner, N. 2017. *German robots: The impact of industrial robots on workers*, IAB Discussion Paper No. 30 (Nuremberg, Institute for Employment Research).

Davis, S.J.; Haltiwanger, J. 2014. *Labor market fluidity and economic performance*, NBER Working Paper No. 20479 (Cambridge, MA, National Bureau of Economic Research).

De Backer, K.; Menon, C.; Desnoyers-James, I.; Moussiegt, L. 2016. *Reshoring: Myth or Reality?*, OECD Science, Technology and Industry Policy Papers No. 27 (Paris, OECD).

Frey, C.B.; Osborne, M.A. 2017. "The future of employment: How susceptible are jobs to computerisation?", in *Technological Forecasting and Social Change*, Vol. 114, pp. 254–280.

Gordon, R.J. 2016. *The rise and fall of American growth: The U.S. standard of living since the civil war* (Princeton, NJ, Princeton University Press).

Haucap, J.; Heimeshoff, U. 2013. *Google, Facebook, Amazon, eBay: Is the internet driving competition or market monopolization?* (Dusseldorf, Dusseldorf Institute for Competition Economics (DICE), University of Dusseldorf).

International Labour Office (ILO). 2017. *Inception Report for the Global Commission on the Future of Work* (Geneva).

—. 2018. *World Employment and Social Outlook: Trends 2018* (Geneva).

International Monetary Fund (IMF). 2017. *World Economic Outlook: Gaining momentum?*, Apr. (Washington, DC).

Jayne, T.; Kwame Yeboah, F.; Henry, C. 2018. *The future of work in African agriculture: Trends and drivers of change*, Working Paper No. 29, Research Department (Geneva, ILO).

Kucera, D. 2017. *New automation technologies and job creation and destruction dynamics*, Employment, Policy Brief (Geneva, ILO).

Mann, G.; O'Neil, C. 2016. "Hiring algorithms are not neutral", in *Harvard Business Review* (9 Dec.). McKinsey Global Institute (MGI). 2011. *Internet matters: The net's sweeping impact on growth, jobs, and prosperity* (Washington, DC).

—. 2015. *A labor market that works: Connecting talent with opportunity in the digital age* (Washington, DC).

—. 2017. *Jobs lost, jobs gained: Workforce transitions in a time of automation* (Washington, DC). Ministerio de Hacienda y Finanzas Públicas, Presidencia de la Nación (MH). 2016. *Desarrollo regional productivo de Argentina en torno a la interconectividad de regiones y ciudades*, No. 2 (Dec.) (Buenos Aires).

Muehlhauser, L. 2014. *Exponential and non-exponential trends in information technology*, Machine Intelligence Research Institute Paper (Berkeley, CA, Machine Intelligence Research Institute).

Nübler, I. 2017. "Transforming production: Opportunities for middle-income countries", in *Integration and Trade Journal*, Vol. 21, No. 42 (Aug.), pp. 304–317.

—. Forthcoming. "New technologies, innovation, and the future of jobs", in E. Paus (ed.): *Emerging dystopias? Confronting the new technological revolution and the future of work* (Ithaca, Cornell University Press).

Organisation for Economic Co-operation and Development (OECD). 2015. *In It Together: Why less inequality benefits all* (Paris).

—. 2017. *Economic policy reforms: Going for growth 2017* (Paris).

—; Food and Agriculture Organization (FAO). 2016. *OECD–FAO Agricultural Outlook 2016–2025* (Paris, OECD).

Parker, G.; Van Alstyne, M.; Choudary, S.P. 2017. *Platform revolution: How networked markets are transforming the economy – and how to make them work for you* (New York, NY, W.W. Norton).

Pew Research Center (PRC). 2016. *Smartphone ownership and Internet usage continues to climb in emerging economies* (Washington, DC).

Tüzemen, D.; Willis, J. 2013. "The vanishing middle: Job polarization and workers' response to the decline in middle-skill jobs", in *Economic Review*, Q.1 (Kansas City, MO, Federal Reserve Bank of Kansas City), pp. 5–32.

United Nations Conference on Trade and Development (UNCTAD). 2017. *Trade and Development Report 2017: Beyond austerity: Towards a global new deal* (Geneva).

United Nations Global Pulse. 2013. *Big data for development: A primer* (New York). World Bank. 2016a. *Trouble in the making* (Washington, DC).

—. 2016b. *World Development Report 2016: Digital dividends* (Washington, DC). World Economic Forum (WEF). 2016. *The future of jobs* (Geneva).

PART III

CYBER RELIGION
AND ETHICS

8

HOMO DEUS:
DATAISM AS RELIGION OF DATA

Yuval Noah Harari, Israel

8.1 The Data Religion

Dataism[114] declares that the universe consists of data flows, and the value of any phenomenon or entity is determined by its contribution to data processing.[115] This may strike you as some eccentric fringe notion, but in fact it has already conquered most of the scientific establishment. Dataism was born from the explosive confluence of two scientific tidal waves. In the 150 years since Charles Darwin published On the Origin of Species, the life sciences have come to see organisms as biochemical algorithms. Simultaneously, in the eight decades since Alan Turing formulated the idea of a Turing Machine, computer scientists have learned

---

[114] This chapter is published with permission of the author (YNH Rights Department, 6 Sept 2018) from Harari, Yuval Noah. *Homo Deus: A Brief History of Tomorrow*, Harper Collins, Kindle Edition, 2017, 372-374 and 386-402.
[115] See, for example, Kevin Kelly, *What Technology Wants* (New York: Viking Press, 2010); César Hidalgo, *Why Information Grow: The Evolution of Order, from Atoms to Economies* (New York: Basic Books, 2015); Howard Bloom, *Global Brain: The Evolution of Mass Mind from the Big Bang to the 21st Century* (Hoboken: Wiley, 2001); DuBravac, *Digital Destiny*.

to engineer increasingly sophisticated electronic algorithms. Dataism puts the two together, pointing out that exactly the same mathematical laws apply to both biochemical and electronic algorithms. Dataism thereby collapses the barrier between animals and machines, and expects electronic algorithms to eventually decipher and outperform biochemical algorithms.

For politicians, business people and ordinary consumers, Dataism offers ground breaking technologies and immense new powers. For scholars and intellectuals, it also promises to provide the scientific Holy Grail that has eluded us for centuries: a single overarching theory that unifies all the scientific disciplines from musicology through economics to biology. According to Dataism, Beethoven's Fifth Symphony, a stock-exchange bubble and the flu virus are just three patterns of data flow that can be analysed using the same basic concepts and tools. This idea is extremely attractive. It gives all scientists a common language, builds bridges over academic rifts and easily exports insights across disciplinary borders. Musicologists, economists and cell biologists can finally understand each other.

In the process Dataism inverts the traditional pyramid of learning. Hitherto, data was seen as only the first step in a long chain of intellectual activity. Humans were supposed to distil data into information, information into knowledge, and knowledge into wisdom. However, Dataists believe that humans can no longer cope with the immense flows of data, hence they cannot distil data into information, let alone into knowledge or wisdom. The work of processing data should therefore be entrusted to electronic algorithms, whose capacity far exceeds that of the human brain. In practice, this means that Dataists are sceptical about human knowledge and wisdom, and prefer to put their trust in Big Data and computer algorithms.

Dataism is most firmly entrenched in its two mother disciplines: computer science and biology. Of the two biology is the more important.

It was biology's embrace of Dataism that turned a limited breakthrough in computer science into a world-shattering cataclysm that may completely transform the very nature of life. You may not agree with the idea that organisms are algorithms, and that giraffes, tomatoes and human beings are just different methods for processing data. But you should know that this is current scientific dogma, and it is changing our world beyond recognition.

Not only individual organisms are seen today as data-processing systems, but also entire societies such as beehives, bacteria colonies, forests and human cities. Economists increasingly interpret the economy too as a data-processing system. Laypeople believe that the economy consists of peasants growing wheat, workers manufacturing clothes, and customers buying bread and underpants. Yet experts see the economy as a mechanism for gathering data about desires and abilities, and turning this data into decisions.

According to this view, free-market capitalism and state-controlled communism aren't competing ideologies, ethical creeds or political institutions. They are, in essence, competing data-processing systems. Capitalism uses distributed processing, whereas communism relies on centralised processing. Capitalism processes data by directly connecting all producers and consumers to one another and allowing them to exchange information freely and make decisions independently. How do you determine the price of bread in a free market? Well, every bakery may produce as much bread as it likes, and charge for it as much as it wants. The customers are equally free to buy as much bread as they can afford, or take their business to a competitor. It isn't illegal to charge $1,000 for a baguette, but nobody is likely to buy it.

On a much grander scale, if investors predict increased demand for bread, they will buy shares of biotech firms that genetically engineer more prolific wheat strains. The influx of capital will enable the firms to speed up their research, thereby providing more wheat faster, and averting bread shortages. Even if one biotech giant adopts a flawed theory and reaches an impasse, its more successful competitors will likely achieve the hoped-for breakthrough. Free-market capitalism thus distributes the work of analysing data and making decisions between many independent but interconnected processors. As the Austrian economics guru Friedrich Hayek explained, 'In a system in which the knowledge of the relevant facts is dispersed among many people, prices can act to coordinate the separate actions of different people.[116]

According to this view the stock exchange is the fastest and most efficient data-processing system humankind has so far created. Everyone is welcome to join, if not directly then through their banks or pension funds. The stock exchange runs the global economy, and takes into account everything that happens all over the planet – and even beyond it. Prices are influenced by successful scientific experiments, by political scandals in Japan, by volcanic eruptions in Iceland and even by irregular activities on the surface of the sun. In order for the system to run smoothly, as much information as possible needs to flow as freely as possible. When millions of people throughout the world have access to all the relevant information, they determine the most accurate price of oil, of Hyundai shares and of Swedish government bonds by buying and selling them. It has been estimated that the stock exchange needs just fifteen minutes of trade to determine the influence of a New York Times headline on the prices of most shares.[117]

---

[116] Friedrich Hayek, 'The Use of Knowledge in Society', *American Economic Review* 35:4 (1945), 519-30.

[117] Kiyohiko G. Nishimura, *Imperfect Competition Differential Information and the Macro-foundations of Macro-economy* (Oxford: Oxford University Press, 1992); Frank M. Machovec, *Perfect Competition and the Transformation of Economics* (London: Routledge, 2002); Frank V. Mastrianna, *Basic Eonomics,*16th edn (Mason: South-Western, 2010), 78-89; Zhiwu Chen, 'Freedom of Information and the Economic Future of Hong Kong', *HKCER Letters* 74 (2003), http://www.hkrec.hku.hk/Letters/v74/zchen.htm; Randall Morck,

Data-processing considerations also explain why capitalists favour lower taxes. Heavy taxation means that a large part of all available capital accumulates in one place – the state coffers – and consequently more and more decisions have to be made by a single processor, namely the government. This creates an overly centralised data-processing system. In extreme cases, when taxes are exceedingly high, almost all capital ends up in the government's hands, and so the government alone calls the shots. It dictates the price of bread, the location of bakeries, and the research-and-development budget. In a free market, if one processor makes a wrong decision, others will be quick to capitalise on its mistake. However, when a single processor makes almost all the decisions, mistakes can be catastrophic.

This extreme situation, in which all data is processed and all decisions are made by a single central processor, is called communism. In a communist economy people allegedly work according to their abilities and receive according to their needs. In other words, the government takes 100 per cent of your profits, decides what you need and then supplies these needs. Though no country ever realised this scheme in its extreme form, the Soviet Union and its satellites came as close as they could. They abandoned the principle of distributed data processing and switched to a model of centralised data processing. All information from

Bernard Yeung and Wayne Yu, 'The Information Content of Stock Markets: Why Do Emerging Markets Have Synchronous Stock Price Movements?' *Journal of Financial Economics* 58:1 (2ooo), 215-60; Louis H. Ederington and Jae Ha Lee, 'How Markets Process Information: News Releases and Volatility', *Journal of Finance* 48:4 (1993), 1161-91; Mark L. Mitchell and J. Harold Mulherin, 'The Impact of Public Information on the Stock Market' *Journal of Finance* 49:3 (1994), 923-50; Jean-Jacques Laffont and Eric S. Maskin, 'The Efficient Market Hypothesis and Insider Trading on the Stock Market', *Journal of Political Economy* 98:1 (1990), 70-93; Steven R. Salbu, 'Differentiated Perspectives on Insider Trading: The Effect of Paradigm Selection on Policy', *St John's Law Review* 66:2(1992), 373-405.

throughout the Soviet Union flowed to a single location in Moscow where all the important decisions were made. Producers and consumers could not communicate directly and had to obey government orders.

8.2 Information Wants to be Free

Like capitalism, Dataism too began as a neutral scientific theory, but is now mutating into a religion that claims to determine right and wrong. The supreme value of this new religion is 'information flow'. If life is the movement of information, and if we think that life is good, it follows that we should deepen and broaden the flow of information in the universe. According to Dataism, human experiences are not sacred and Homo sapiens isn't the apex of creation or a precursor of some future Homo deus. Humans are merely tools for creating the Internet-of-All-Things, which may eventually spread out from planet Earth to pervade the whole galaxy and even the whole universe. This cosmic data-processing system would be like God. It will be everywhere and will control everything, and humans are destined to merge into it.

This conception is reminiscent of some traditional religious visions. Thus Hindus believe that humans can and should merge into the universal soul of the cosmos – the atman. Christians believe that after death saints are infused with the infinite grace of God, whereas sinners cut themselves off from His presence. Indeed, in Silicon Valley the Dataist prophets consciously use traditional messianic language. For example, Ray Kurzweil's book of prophecies is called *The Singularity is Near*, echoing John the Baptist's cry: 'the kingdom of heaven is near' (Matthew 3:2).

Dataists explain to those who still worship flesh-and-blood mortals that they are overly attached to outdated technology. *Homo sapiens* is an obsolete algorithm. After all, what's the advantage of humans over chickens? Only that in humans, information flows in much more complex patterns. Humans absorb more data, and process it using better algorithms than do chickens. (In day-to-day language this means that humans allegedly have deeper emotions and superior intellectual abilities. But remember that according to current biological dogma, emotions and intelligence are just algorithms.) Well then, if we could create a data-processing system that can assimilate even more data than a human being, and process it even more efficiently, wouldn't that system be superior to a human in exactly the same way that a human is superior to a chicken?

Dataism isn't limited to idle prophecies. Like every religion, it has its practical commandments. First and foremost a Dataist ought to maximise data flow by connecting to more and more media, and producing and consuming more and more information. Like other successful religions, Dataism is also missionary. Its second commandment is to link everything to the system, including heretics who don't want to be plugged in. And 'everything' means more than just humans. It means everything. Our bodies, of course, but also cars in the street, refrigerators in kitchens, chickens in their coops and trees in the jungle – all should be connected to the Internet-of-All-Things. The refrigerator will monitor the number of eggs in the drawer, and inform the chicken coop when a new shipment is needed. Cars will talk with one another, and the trees in the jungle will report on the weather and on carbon dioxide levels. We mustn't leave any part of the universe disconnected from the great web of life. Conversely, the greatest sin would be to block the data flow. What is death, if not a condition in which information doesn't flow? Hence Dataism upholds the freedom of information as the greatest good of all.

People rarely manage to come up with a completely new value. The last time this happened was in the eighteenth century, when the humanist revolution began preaching the stirring ideals of human liberty, human equality and human fraternity. Since 1789, despite numerous wars, revolutions and upheavals, humans have not managed to conceive of any new value. All subsequent conflicts and struggles have been conducted either in the name of the three humanist values, or in the name of even older ones such as obeying God or serving the nation. Dataism is the first movement since 1789 that created a genuinely novel value: freedom of information.

We mustn't confuse freedom of information with the old liberal value of freedom of expression. Freedom of expression was given to humans, and protected their right to think and say what they wished – including their right to keep their mouths shut and their thoughts to themselves. Freedom of information, in contrast, is not given to humans. It is given to information. Moreover, this novel value may impinge on humans' traditional freedom of expression, by privileging the right of information to circulate freely over the right of humans to own data and to restrict its movement.

On 11 January 2013, Dataism got its first martyr when Aaron Swartz, a twenty-six-year-old American hacker, committed suicide in his apartment. Swartz was a rare genius. At fourteen, he helped develop the crucial RSS protocol. Swartz was also a firm believer in the freedom of information. In 2008 he published the 'Guerilla Open Access Manifesto', which demanded a free and unlimited flow of information. Swartz said that 'We need to take information, wherever it is stored, make our copies and share them with the world. We need to take stuff that's out of copyright and add it to the archive. We need to buy secret databases and put them on the Web. We need to download scientific journals and upload them to file sharing networks. We need to fight for Guerilla Open Access.'

Swartz was as good as his word. He became annoyed with the JSTOR digital library for charging its customers. JSTOR holds millions of scientific papers and studies, and believes in the freedom of expression of scientists and journal editors, which includes the freedom to charge a fee for reading their articles. According to JSTOR, if I want to get paid for the ideas I created, it's my right to do so. Swartz thought otherwise. He believed that information wants to be free, that ideas don't belong to the people who created them, and that it is wrong to lock data behind walls and charge an entrance fee. He used the MIT computer network to access JSTOR, and downloaded hundreds of thousands of scientific papers, which he intended to release onto the Internet, so that everybody could read them freely.

Swartz was arrested and put on trial. When he realised that he would probably be convicted and sent to jail, he hanged himself. Hackers reacted with petitions and attacks directed at the academic and government institutions that persecuted Swartz and that infringe on the freedom of information. Under pressure, JSTOR apologised for its part in the tragedy and today allows free access to much, though not all, of its data.[118]

To convince sceptics Dataist missionaries repeatedly explain the immense benefits of the freedom of information. Just as capitalists believe that all good things depend on economic growth, so Dataists believe all good things – including economic growth – depend on the freedom of information. Why did the USA grow faster than the USSR? Because information flowed more freely in the USA. Why are Americans healthier, wealthier and happier than Iranians or Nigerians? Thanks to

---

[118] Aaron Swartz, 'Guerilla Open Access Manifesto', July 2008, accessed 22 December 2014, https://ia600605.us.archive.org/15/items/GuerillaOpenAccess Manifesto/Goamjuly2008.pdf; Sam Gustin, 'Aaron Swartz, Tech Prodigy and Internet Activist, Is Dead at 26', *Time,* 13 January 2013, accessed 22 December 2014, http://business.time.com/2013/01/13/tech-prodigy-and-internet-activist-aaron-swartz-commits-suicide/;Todd Leopold, 'How Aaron Swartz Helped Build the Internet', CNN, 15 January 2013, 22 December 2014, https://edition.cnn.com/2013/01/15/tech/web/aaron-swartz-internet/index.html; Declan McCullagh, 'Swartz Didn't Face Prison until Feds Took Over Case, Report Says', CNET, 25 January 2013, accessed 22 December 2014, https://www.cnet.com/news/swartz-didnt-face-prison-until-feds-took-over-case-report-says/.

the freedom of information. So if we want to create a better world, the key is to set the data free.

We have already seen that Google can detect new epidemics faster than traditional health organisations, but only if we allow it free access to the information we are producing. Free-flowing data can similarly reduce pollution and waste, for example by rationalising the transportation system. In 2010 the number of private cars in the world exceeded 1 billion, and has since kept growing.[119] These cars pollute the planet and waste enormous resources, not least by necessitating ever wider roads and more parking spaces. People have become so used to the convenience of private transport that they are unlikely to settle for buses and trains. However, Dataists point out that what people really want is mobility rather than a private car, and a good data-processing system can provide this mobility far more cheaply and efficiently.

I have a private car, but most of the time it sits idly in the parking lot. On a typical day, I enter my car at 8:04, and drive for half an hour to the university, where I park my car for the day. At 18:11 I come back to the car, drive half an hour back home, and that's it. So I am using my car for just an hour a day. Why do I need to keep it for the other twenty-three hours? Why not create a smart car-pool system, run by computer algorithms? The computer would know that I need to leave home at 8:04 and would route the nearest autonomous car to pick me up at that precise moment. After dropping me off on campus it would be available for other purposes instead of waiting in the parking lot. At 18:11 sharp, as I leave the university gate, another communal car would stop right next to me, and take me home. In this way 50 million communal autonomous cars could replace 1 billion private cars, and we would also need far

---

[119] John Sousanis, 'World Vehicle Population Tops 1 Billion Units', *WardsAuto*, 15 August 2011, accessed 3 December 2015, https://www.wardsauto.com/news-analysis/world-vehicle-population-tops-1-billion-units

fewer roads, bridges, tunnels and parking spaces. Provided, of course, that I renounce my privacy and allow the algorithms always to know where I am and where I want to go.

8.3 Record, Upload, Share!

But maybe you don't need convincing, especially if you are under the age of twenty. People just want to be part of the data flow, even if that means giving up their privacy, their autonomy and their individuality. Humanist art sanctifies the individual genius, so a Picasso doodle on a napkin nets millions at Sotheby's. Humanist science glorifies the individual researcher, and every scholar dreams of putting his or her name at the top of a Science or Nature paper. But a growing number of artistic and scientific creations are nowadays produced by the ceaseless collaboration of 'everyone'. Who writes Wikipedia? All of us.

The individual is becoming a tiny chip inside a giant system that nobody really understands. Every day I absorb countless data bits through emails, phone calls and articles; process the data; and transmit back new bits through more emails, phone, calls and articles. I don't really know where I fit into the greater scheme of things, or how my bits of data connect with the bits produced by billions of other humans and computers. I don't have time to find out, because I am too busy answering all the emails. And as I process more data more efficiently – answering more emails, making more phone calls and writing more articles – so I flood the people around me with even more data.

This relentless flow of data sparks new inventions and disruptions that nobody plans, controls or comprehends. No one understands how the global economy functions or where global politics is heading. But no one needs to understand. All you need to do is answer your emails faster – and allow the system to read them. Just as free-market capitalists believe in the invisible hand of the market, so Dataists believe in the invisible hand of the data flow.

As the global data-processing system becomes all-knowing and all-powerful, so connecting to the system becomes the source of all meaning. Humans want to merge into the data flow because when you are part of the data flow you are part of something much bigger than yourself. Traditional religions assured you that your every word and action was part of some great cosmic plan, and that God watched you every minute and cared about all your thoughts and feelings. Data religion now says that your every word and action is part of the great data flow, that the algorithms are constantly watching you and that they care about everything you do and feel. Most people like this very much. For true-believers, to be disconnected from the data flow risks losing the very meaning of life. What's the point of doing or experiencing anything if nobody knows about it, and if it doesn't contribute something to the global exchange of information?

Humanism holds that experiences occur inside us, and that we ought to find within ourselves the meaning of all that happens, thereby infusing the universe with meaning. Dataists believe that experiences are valueless if they are not shared, and that we need not – indeed cannot – find meaning within ourselves. We need only record and connect our experiences to the great data flow, and the algorithms will discover their meaning and tell us what to do. Twenty years ago Japanese tourists were a universal laughing stock because they always carried cameras and took pictures of everything in sight. Now everyone is doing it. If you go to India and see an elephant, you don't look at the elephant and ask yourself, 'What do I feel?' – you are too busy looking for your smartphone, taking a picture of the elephant, posting it on Facebook and then checking your account every two minutes to see how many Likes you got. Writing a private diary – a common humanist practice in previous generations – sounds to many present-day youngsters utterly pointless. Why write anything if nobody else can read it? The new motto says: 'If you experience something – record it. If you record something – upload it. If you upload something – share it.'

Throughout this book we have repeatedly asked what makes humans superior to other animals. Dataism has a new and simple answer. In themselves human experiences are not superior at all to the experiences of wolves or elephants. One bit of data is as good as another. However, humans can write poems and blogs about their experiences and post them online, thereby enriching the global data-processing system. That makes their bits count. Wolves cannot do this. Hence all the experiences of wolves – as deep and complex as they may be – are worthless. No wonder we are so busy converting our experiences into data. It isn't a question of trendiness. It is a question of survival. We must prove to ourselves and to the system that we still have value. And value lies not in having experiences, but in turning these experiences into free-flowing data.

(By the way, wolves – or at least their dog cousins – aren't a hopeless case. A company called 'No More Woof' is developing a helmet for reading canine experiences. The helmet monitors the dog's brain waves, and uses computer algorithms to translate simple sentiments such as 'I am angry' into human language.[120] Your dog may soon have a Facebook or Twitter account of his own – perhaps with more Likes and followers than you.)

8.4 Know Thyself

Dataism is neither liberal nor humanist. It should be emphasised, however, that Dataism isn't anti-humanist. It has nothing against human experiences. It just doesn't think they are intrinsically valuable. When we surveyed the three main humanist sects, we asked which experience is the most valuable: listening to Beethoven's Fifth Symphony, to Chuck

---

[120] 'No More Woof', https://www.indiegogo.com/projects/no-more-woof#/

Berry, to a pygmy initiation song or to the howl of a wolf in heat. A Dataist would argue that the entire exercise is misguided, because music should be evaluated according to the data it carries rather than according to the experience it creates. A Dataist might explain, for example, that the Fifth Symphony carries far more data than the pygmy initiation song, because it uses more chords and scales and creates dialogues with many more musical styles. Consequently, you need far more computational power to decipher the Fifth Symphony, and you gain far more knowledge from doing so.

Music, according to this view, is mathematical patterns. Mathematics can describe every musical piece, as well as the relations between any two pieces. Hence you can measure the precise data value of every symphony, song and howl, and determine which is the richest. The experiences they create in humans or wolves don't really matter. True, for the last 70,000 years or so, human experiences have been the most efficient data-processing algorithms in the universe, hence there was good reason to sanctify them. However, we may soon reach a point when these algorithms will be superseded, and even become a burden.

Sapiens evolved in the African savannah tens of thousands of years ago, and their algorithms are just not built to handle twenty-first-century data flows. We might try to upgrade the human data-processing system, but this may not be enough. The Internet-of-All-Things may soon create such huge and rapid data flows that even upgraded human algorithms would not be able to handle them. When cars replaced horse-drawn carriages, we didn't upgrade the horses – we retired them. Perhaps it is time to do the same with *Homo sapiens*.

Dataism adopts a strictly functional approach to humanity, appraising the value of human experiences according to their function in data-processing mechanisms. If we develop an algorithm that fulfils the same function better, human experiences will lose their value. Thus if we can replace not just taxi drivers and doctors but also lawyers, poets and musicians with superior computer programs, why should we care if these programs have no consciousness and no subjective experiences? If some humanist starts adulating the sacredness of human experience, Dataists would dismiss such sentimental humbug. 'The experience you are praising is just an outdated biochemical algorithm. In the African savannah 70,000 years ago, that algorithm was state-of-the-art. Even in the twentieth century it was vital for the army and for the economy. But soon we will have much better algorithms.' In the climactic scene of many Hollywood science-fiction movies, humans face an alien invasion fleet, an army of rebellious robots or an all-knowing super-computer that intends to obliterate them. Humanity seems doomed. But at the very last moment, against all odds, humanity triumphs thanks to something that the aliens, the robots and the super-computers didn't suspect and cannot fathom: love. The hero, who up till now has been easily manipulated by the super-computer and riddled with bullets by the evil robots, is inspired by his sweetheart to make a completely unexpected move that turns the tables on the thunderstruck Matrix. Dataism finds such scenarios utterly ridiculous. 'Come on,' it admonishes the Hollywood screenwriters, 'is that all you could come up with? Love? And not even some platonic cosmic love, but the carnal attraction between two mammals? Do you really think that an all-knowing super-computer or aliens who contrived to conquer the entire galaxy would be dumbfounded by a hormonal rush?'

By equating the human experience with data patterns, Dataism undermines our primary source of authority and meaning and heralds a tremendous religious revolution, the like of which has not been seen since the eighteenth century. In the days of Locke, Hume and Voltaire humanists argued that 'God is a product of the human imagination'. Dataism now gives humanists a taste of their own medicine, and tells them: 'Yes, God is a product of the human imagination, but human imagination in turn is just the product of biochemical algorithms.' In the eighteenth century, humanism sidelined God by shifting from a deo-centric to a homo-centric world view. In the twenty-first century, Dataism may sideline humans by shifting from a homo-centric to a data-centric view.

The Dataist revolution will probably take a few decades, if not a century or two. But then the humanist revolution too did not happen overnight. At first humans kept on believing in God, arguing that humans are sacred because they were created by God for some divine purpose. Only much later did some people dare say that humans are sacred in their own right, and that God doesn't exist at all. Similarly, today 'most Dataists claim that the Internet-of-All-Things is sacred because humans are creating it to serve human needs. But eventually the Internet-of-All-Things may become sacred in its own right.

The shift from a homo centric to a data centric world view won't be merely a philosophical revolution. It will be a practical revolution. All-truly important revolutions are practical. The humanist idea that 'humans invented God' was significant because it had far reaching practical implications. Similarly, the Dataist idea that 'organisms are algorithms' is significant due to its day-to-day practical consequences. Ideas change the world only when they change out behaviour.

In ancient Babylon, when people faced a difficult dilemma they climbed in the darkness of night to the top of the local temple and observed the sky. The Babylonians believed that the stars controlled their fate and predicted their future. By watching the stars the Babylonians decided whether to get married, plough the fields and go to war. Their philosophical beliefs were translated into very practical procedures.

Scriptural religions such as Judaism and Christianity told a different story: 'The stars are lying. God, who created the stars, revealed the entire truth in the Bible. So stop observing the stars – read the Bible instead!' This too was a practical recommendation. When people didn't know whom to marry, what career to choose or whether to start a war, they read the Bible and followed its counsel.

Next came the humanists with an altogether new story: 'Humans invented God, wrote the Bible and then interpreted it in a thousand different ways so humans themselves are the source of all truth. You may read the Bible as an inspiring human creation, but you don't really need to. If you are facing any dilemma, just listen to yourself and follow your inner voice.' Humanism then gave detailed practical instructions on how to listen to yourself, recommending techniques such as watching sunsets, reading Goethe, keeping a private diary, having heart-to-heart talks with a good friend and holding democratic elections.

For centuries scientists too accepted these humanist guidelines. When physicists wondered whether or not to get married, they too watched sunsets and tried to get in touch with themselves. When chemists contemplated whether to accept a problematic job offer, they too wrote diaries and had heart-to-heart talks with a good friend. When biologists debated whether to wage war or sign a peace treaty, they too voted in democratic elections. When brain scientists wrote books about their startling discoveries, they often put an inspiring Goethe quote on the first page. This was the basis for the modern alliance between science and humanism, which kept the delicate balance between the modern yang and the modern yin – between reason and emotion, between the laboratory and the museum, between the production line and the supermarket.

The scientists not only sanctified human feelings, but also found an excellent evolutionary reason to do so. After Darwin, biologists began explaining that feelings are complex algorithms honed by evolution to help animals make correct decisions. Our love, our fear and our passion aren't some nebulous spiritual phenomena good only for composing poetry. Rather they encapsulated millions of years of practical wisdom. When you read the Bible you are getting advice from a few priests and rabbis – who lived in ancient Jerusalem. In contrast, when you listen to your feelings you follow an algorithm that evolution has developed for millions of years, and that withstood the harshest quality-control tests of natural selection. Your feelings are the voice of millions of ancestors, each of whom managed to survive and reproduce in an unforgiving environment. Your feelings are not infallible, of course but they are better than most of other sources of guidance. For millions upon millions of years, feelings were the best algorithms in the world. Hence in the days of Confucius, of Muhammad or of Stalin, people should listen to their feelings rather than to the teachings of Confucianism, Islam or communism.

Yet in the twenty-first century feelings are no longer the best algorithms in the world. We are developing superior algorithms that utilise unprecedented computing power and giant databases. The Google and Facebook algorithms not only know exactly how you feel, they also know myriad other things about you that you hardly suspect. Consequently you should stop listening to your feelings and start listening to these external algorithms instead. What's the point of having democratic elections when the algorithms know not only how each person is 'going to vote, but also the underlying neurological reasons why one person votes Democrat while another votes Republican? Whereas humanism commanded: 'Listen to your feelings!' Dataism now commands: 'Listen to the algorithms! They know how you feel.'

When you contemplate whom to marry, which career to pursue and whether to start a war, Dataism tells you that it would be a complete waste of time to climb a high mountain and watch the sun setting into the waves. It would be equally futile to visit a museum, write a private diary or have a heart-to-heart talk with a friend. Yes, in order to make the right decisions you must get to know yourself better. But if you want to know yourself in the twenty-first century, there are much better methods than climbing mountains, going to museums or writing diaries. Here are some practical Dataist guidelines for you:

'You want to know who you really are?' asks Dataism. 'Then forget about mountains and museums. Have you had your DNA sequenced? No?! What are you waiting for? Go and do it today. And convince your grandparents, parents and siblings to have their DNA sequenced too – their data is very valuable for you. And have you heard about these wearable biometric devices that measure your blood pressure and heart rate twenty-four hours a day? Good so buy one of those, put it on and connect it to your smartphone. And while you are shopping, buy a mobile camera and microphone, record everything you do, and put in online. And allow Google and Facebook to read all your emails, monitor all your chats and messages, and keep a record of all your Likes and clicks. If you do all that, then the great algorithms of the Internet-of-All-Things will tell you whom to marry, which career to pursue and whether to start a war.'

But where do these great algorithms come from? This is the mystery of Dataism. Just as according to Christianity we humans cannot understand God and His plan, so Dataism declares that the human brain cannot fathom the new master algorithms. At present, of course, the algorithms are mostly written by human hackers. Yet the really important algorithms – such as the Google search algorithm – are developed by huge teams. Each member understands just one part of the puzzle, and nobody really understands the algorithm as a whole. Moreover, with the rise of machine learning and artificial neural networks, more and more algorithms evolve independently, improving themselves and learning from their own mistakes. They analyse astronomical amounts of data, that no human can possibly encompass, and learn to recognise patterns and adopt strategies that escape the human mind. The seed algorithm may initially be developed by humans, but as it grows it follows its own path, going where no human has gone before – and where no human can follow.

8.5 A Ripple in the Dataflow

Dataism naturally has its critics and heretics. As we saw in [*Homo Deus*, ibid.] Chapter 3, it's doubtful whether life can really be reduced to dataflows. In particular, at present we have no idea how or why dataflows could produce consciousness and subjective experiences. Maybe we'll have a good explanation in twenty years. But maybe we'll discover that organisms aren't algorithms after all.

It is equally doubtful whether life boils down to mere decision-making. Under Dataist influence both the life sciences and the social sciences have become obsessed with decision-making processes, as if that's all there is to life. But is it so? Sensations, emotions and thoughts certainly play an important part in making decisions, but is that their sole meaning? Dataism is gaining a better and better understanding of decision-making processes, but it might be adopting an increasingly skewed view of life.

A critical examination of Dataist dogma is likely to be not only the greatest scientific challenge of the twenty-first century, but also the most urgent political and economic project. Scholars in the life sciences and social sciences should ask themselves whether we miss anything when we understand life as data processing and decision-making. Is there perhaps something in the universe that cannot be reduced to data? Suppose non-conscious algorithms could eventually outperform conscious intelligence in all known data-processing tasks – what, if anything, would be lost by replacing conscious intelligence with superior non-conscious algorithms?

Of course, even if Dataism is wrong and organisms aren't just algorithms, it won't necessarily prevent Dataism from taking over the world. Many previous religions gained enormous popularity and power despite their factual inaccuracies. If Christianity and communism could do it, why not Dataism? Dataism has especially good prospects, because it is currently spreading across all scientific disciplines. A unified scientific paradigm may easily become an unassailable dogma. It is very difficult to contest a scientific paradigm, but up till now, no single paradigm has been adopted by the entire scientific establishment. Hence scholars in one field could always import heretical views from outside. But if everyone from musicologists to biologists uses the same Dataist paradigm, interdisciplinary excursions will serve only to strengthen the paradigm further. Consequently even if the paradigm is flawed, it would be extremely difficult to resist.

If Dataism succeeds in conquering the world, what will happen to us humans? Initially Dataism will probably accelerate the humanist pursuit of health, happiness and power. Dataism spreads itself by promising to fulfil these humanist aspirations. In order to achieve immortality, bliss and divine powers of creation, we need to process immense amounts of data, far beyond the capacity of the human brain. So the algorithms will do it for us. Yet once authority shifts from humans to algorithms, the humanist projects may become irrelevant. Once we abandon the homo-centric world view in favour of a data-centric world view, human health and happiness may seem far less important. Why bother so much about obsolete data-processing machines when far superior models are already in existence? We are striving to engineer the Internet-of-All-Things in the hope that it will make us healthy, happy and powerful. Yet once the Internet-of-All-Things is up and running, humans might be reduced from engineers to chips, then to data, and eventually we might dissolve within the torrent of data like a clump of earth within a gushing river.

Dataism thereby threatens to do to *Homo sapiens* what *Homo sapiens* has done to all other animals. Over the course of history humans created a global network and evaluated everything according to its function within that network. For thousands of years this inflated human pride and prejudices. Since humans fulfilled the most important functions in the network, it was easy for us to take credit for the network's achievements, and to see ourselves as the apex of creation. The lives and experiences of all other animals were undervalued because they fulfilled far less important functions, and whenever an animal ceased to fulfil any function at all, it went extinct. However, once we humans lose our functional importance to the network, we will discover that we are not the apex of creation after all. The yardsticks that we ourselves have enshrined will condemn us to join the mammoths and Chinese river dolphins in oblivion. Looking back, humanity will turn out to have been just a ripple within the cosmic dataflow.

We cannot really predict the future, because technology is not deterministic. The same technology could create very different kinds of societies. For example, the technology of the Industrial Revolution – trains, electricity, radio, telephone – could be used to establish communist dictatorships, fascist regimes or liberal democracies. Consider South Korea and North Korea: they have had access to exactly the same technology, but they have chosen to employ it in very different ways.

The rise of AI and biotechnology will certainly transform the world, but it does not mandate a single deterministic outcome. All the scenarios outlined in this book [*Homo Deus*, ibid.] should be understood as possibilities rather than prophecies. If you don't like some of these possibilities you are welcome to think and behave in new ways that will prevent these particular possibilities from materialising.

However, it is not easy to think and behave in new ways, because our thoughts and actions are usually constrained by present-day ideologies and social systems. This book traces the origins of our present-day conditioning in order to loosen its grip and enable us to act differently and to think in far more imaginative ways about our future. Instead of narrowing our horizons by forecasting a single definitive scenario, the book aims to broaden our horizons and make us aware of a much wider spectrum of options. As I have repeatedly emphasised, nobody really knows what the job market, the family or the ecology will look like in 2050, or which religions, economic systems and political structures will dominate the world. Yet broadening our horizons can backfire by making us more confused and inactive than before. With so many scenarios and possibilities, what should we pay attention to? The world is changing faster than ever before, and we are flooded by impossible amounts of data, of ideas, of promises and of threats. Humans are relinquishing authority to the free market, to crowd wisdom and to external algorithms partly because we cannot deal with the deluge of data. In the past, censorship worked by blocking the flow of information. In the twenty-first century censorship works by flooding people with irrelevant information. We just don't know what to pay attention to, and often spend our time investigating and debating side issues. In ancient times having power meant having access to data. Today having power means knowing what to ignore. So considering everything that is happening in our chaotic world, what should we focus on?

If we think in term of months, we had probably better focus on immediate problems such as the turmoil in the Middle East, the refugee crisis in Europe and the slowing of the Chinese economy. If we think in terms of decades, then global warming, growing inequality and the disruption of the job market loom large. Yet if we take the really grand view of life, all other problems and developments are overshadowed by three interlinked processes:

1. Science is converging on an all-encompassing dogma, which says that organisms are algorithms and life is data processing.
2. Intelligence is decoupling from consciousness.
3. Non-conscious but highly intelligent algorithms may soon know us better than we know ourselves.

These three processes raise three key questions, which I hope will stick in your mind long after you have finished this book [chapter]:

1. Are organisms really just algorithms, and is life really just data processing?

2. What's more valuable - intelligence or consciousness?

3. What will happen to society, politics and daily life when non-conscious but highly intelligent algorithms know us better than we know ourselves?

9

HOMO DEUS: NO
DEUS HOMO: YES
BECOMING TRULY HUMAN

Christoph Stückelberger, Switzerland

Homo Deus	Deus Homo
Homo Deus[121] Human being becomes God	"Do it like God: Become a human being"[122]
Artificial Intelligence as Transcendence of the human being or simply pride, new hybris?	Heaven is empty since long time Deification of human beings is idolatry and absolutism.
With each new technology grows the arrogance of the human being	Human beings becoming truly human is worship and demanding mandate
Trust in God means God is God and human being remains human being.	Jesus, the true human being perfect ethics.

---

[121] Title of the bestseller of Yuval Noah Harari, 2017. See previous article in this book.

[122] Author not known.

9.1   New Technologies: Temptation of Hybris

In human history, new technologies always create a polarization between exaggerated fears and exaggerated expectations. This is due to the fact that new technologies are not yet known in their consequence, and therefore are an ideal field for all kind of projections. Therefore, new technologies are always also related to religious fears being seen as an incarnation of the devil or as the new saviour which solves all problems of the world. Technologies can be seen as God-like, an expression of superhuman, divine power energy and capacities.[123]

Today, with the new Dataism religion[124] and the high expectations for artificial intelligence, robots can be seen as the new superpower and Superman. Dataism is the new Religion: all beings are data/algorithms. Humans can play God by interconnecting all data. Mathematicians and software developers are the new priests. Anthony Levandowski, the developer of the self-driving car, founded the new *Artificial Intelligence Religion "Way of the Future"* in Silicon Valley in 2017.

This is a modern form of pride which is in the ethics of virtues and vices, one of the key vices of human beings. Pride (in Greek Hybris, in Latin superbia) means to overestimate the potential of oneself or a technology in one's hand. It leads to arrogance and overconfidence in their own power. Homo Deus means the human being (homo) becomes God (Deus). This pride leads to disasters as human history tells us: If a human being or a human technology is seen as divine, it becomes absolute in the form of an autocratic ruler, a dictator or a technology to be worshipped. Technologies – even so called autonomous technologies like self-driving cars, robots and autonomous weapons are still the result of human beings. All technologies, therefore remain always imperfect and not eternal because the human being is imperfect and not eternal.

---

[123] See also chapter 2 on industrial revolutions.

[124] See previous chapter 10.

The ancient Greek religion knew - as all world religions know – that this hybris and human arrogance leads to punishment by the divine, the "divine retribution"[125], the nemesis. Many cultures know the mythological story of a great flood destroying humanity as result of human arrogance (Gilgamesh Epic, Hindu Vedas, Judeo-Christian story of Noah. But these stories also show the righteous, pious, and humble human persons as the survivors.

9.2 Deus Deus, Homo Homo:
God is God, Humans Remain Humans

In Christian theology, the distinction between the creator and the creation is fundamental: the creator can create something new out of nothing (creatio ex nihilo). But creatures – be it an animal, a plant or a human being – can create something new only out of something which already exists. Therefore, human beings, with all innovation, creativity and huge potential, still remain part of creation and will never, never be able to become creator.

Pride or superbia is seen as a vice in all world religions; in the Abrahamic religions Judaism, Christianity, and Islam, born in the Middle East, as well as in the Dharmic religions Buddhism, Hinduism, Jainism, and Taoism, born in South and East Asia. In the monotheist Abrahamic religions, the border between God and humans is absolute even as a unification with the absolute is intended with resurrection after death. In the Dharmic religions, the path towards dharma, the absolute, is more open in the sense that through meditation and good deeds the absolute can be approached step by step, however the border to the absolute remains.

The Bible expresses this belief that God is creator of all and forever in a visionary way: *"In God all things were created: things in heaven and on earth, visible and invisible, whether thrones or powers or rulers*

---

[125] https://en.wikipedia.org/wiki/Divine_retribution. (Accessed 8 Sept 2018).

or authorities; all things have been created through him and for him." (Col 1:16). This means that all former and existing parts of creation, but also all future expressions of creation are ultimately in the hands of God, through him/her and for him/her, including the internet of things and artificial intelligence, the visible physical and the invisible cyber world. The Christian Trinitarian God of God the Father, the Son and the Holy Spirit means that these three expressions of the divine are one: Christ is therefore also called the "Cosmic Christ" as the creator energy which existed since ever and for ever. No other past, present, or future power is beyond His reach.

This could be seen in a negative way as "God sees everything", but it is meant in a positive way: God is present, cares for the world and supports and guides humans in all these challenges and opportunities including new technologies. Humans are invited by God (the absolute, divine) as "co-workers" (some call it "co-creator" which is a misleading term putting humans and God on a similar level) to take responsibility in cultivating and innovating this creation, without crossing the border between creation and Creator.

9.3 Deus Homo: Becoming Truly Human

Therefore, the goal is not to become God-like (Homo Deus) which always ends in human disaster. The goal and task is to learn to become truly human! *Not learning to become God, but "Learning to Be Human"!* This was the theme 2018 of the quadrennial famous "World Congress of Philosophy" [126]. Learning to be human means to put the human being (of course as part of the unity with non-human creatures in one eco-system) at the heart of human activities. In this congress, one of the panels was on "Ontologies for the Big Data Era: Anthropocene, Cap-

---

[126] Theme of the World Congress of Philosophy, Aug 2018, Beijing, China.

italocene, Chthulucene, Algoricene"[127]. The philosophical question of the being (ontology) is what is at the centre of what exists: the human (Anthropos), the capital or probably the algorithm? The Swiss Government in its revised national strategy "Digital Switzerland" of September 2018[128] as the key criteria of orientation in all digitisation decisions "The human being at the centre"! Not technology, or money, or power politics should the decisive criteria be, but how far the digitisation serves human life in a sustainable environment and how far it hinders it.

What is "truly human"? This is the key question in all world religions and philosophies. Humanists may describe "truly human" as the rational beings ability to implement their human rights and obligations in freedom and responsibility, Confucians may describe Confucius' values as the "truly human". The world religions look at their founding figures or epic figures as the expression of the "truly human": Buddha, Bhagavan, Brashma, Lao Tse, Abraham, Jesus, Mohammed, etc. Even the Atheists look for the "truly human": they see themselves as antitheists as they criticize theism as oppressing the "truly human", therefore "truly human" must be an existence liberated from oppressive religious leaders, institutions, and beliefs. On the other side, world religions aim at liberating humans from their addictions (such as greed for money, dependency on material wealth, sex addiction, power addictions, and obsession by greed for research/knowledge etc.). Liberation is a common goal for being "truly human", even though what liberation consists of is very diverse. Liberating for being able for love, respect and honest work for a life in dignity and peace.

At the core of the Christian faith is incarnation. An unknown author said: "Do it like God: become human!" To be "truly human" is visible in the life of Jesus as incarnation of God on earth, so that God himself

---

[127] https://wcp2018.sched.com/event/b4a893a1a76f06b3ffa5ed8095dfe2d6.

[128] Swiss Government: *Strategie Digitale Schweiz* 2018-2020, 5 Sept 2018, https://www.bakom.admin.ch/infosociety.

shows the orientation of life to become "truly human". The ethical orientation of Jesus up to the demanding "Sermon on the Mount" (Matthew 5-7) aims at showing what is "truly human". The Roman ruler Pilate–as a non-believer–recognised it when Jesus stood in front of him during the trial by saying "Ecce homo", "Here is the man", "Behold the man" (John 19:5). It can be interpreted as "Only a man, not a king as we imagine it". We can interpret it as: *"Look at this man Jesus of Nazareth, the truly human being"*. The "truly human" is the leader as the good steward and servant, the person who puts the other in the centre, who can live the double commandment of love and the golden rule of reciprocity, the person who cares for the needy, oppressed and deprived, the person who looks for the common good of the community and equality of human beings, the person who acknowledges their own weaknesses and limits and asks for pardon, the person who is courageous in doing what is needed to be done even if the majority is not following or opposes it, the person with integrity, honesty and modesty. For Christians, this is the ethical benchmark for dealing with the Cyber World and developing Cyber Ethics.

10

THE ORACLE OF BIG DATA: PROPHECIES WITHOUT PROPHETS

Bruno Granche, Germany

Abstract

The need for foreknowledge intensifies and a prophetic promise of today's palm readers causes us wet palms: letting the world speak for itself. Big Data comes with the promise of enabling people to listen to that speaking world and of gaining accurate foreknowledge by Big Data predictions. The uncertainty of our modern, complex world overstrains our present coping capabilities, causing a feeling of slipping off a slippery slope, which in turn causes a need for increasing our own foreknowledge. Part of the Big Data promise is to grant better foreknowledge by overcoming the wrongness of scientific theory or causation assumptions. But thus, people have no other option than to believe in these results and perform their actions in good faith. This makes Big Data based outcomes a matter of faith. This article[129] argues that Big Data based outcomes can be seen as today's oracle, as prophecies without prophets and reflects on the consequences of that perspective.

---

[129] Published with permission of the author. First published in International Review of Information Ethics, Vol 24 (05/2016), 55-62.

10.1 Seeking Foreknowledge – The Perfect Conjecture

The future is today's hot topic. Our world is apparently always ahead in time and widely focused on future events and developments. The new is at large considered better than the old, the time to come more important than the past, innovation beats tradition, trend researchers and prediction specialists earn much more money, attention, and appreciation than historians and archaeologists. When tradition and ancient custom were generally held in high regard, they provided a liable orientation and good foreseeability for everyday decision making. Metaphorically speaking: In hardly and slowly changing cities, a ten-year-old street map did just fine – in highly dynamic and rapidly changing environments, old maps turn useless ever faster. With the same pace, our world structures are liquefying, static orientation approaches get obsolete, the need for constantly updated information, predictive efforts and anticipation rises. In that situation of a "liquid modernity"[130][95], the son of a blacksmith is no longer automatically becoming a blacksmith and he is no longer sure to be needed as such his entire lifetime. Today's decisions – as the choice of occupation – need a great deal of anticipation. Will welders be needed in 2050 or welding robot operators instead? Will more red or yellow shirts be sold next summer? Will male insurance clients keep on causing more severe car accidents than female ones?

The future is considered more important than ever and knowledge about the future seems to be the oil of the 21st century. The problem is: There is no such thing as 'knowledge about the future' in a complex, dynamic and non-deterministic world. Prometheus, the Greek Titan and epitome of science, alone had a perfect foreknowledge of the one single and only possible future in the deterministic Greek mythological cosmos. But – because of that – he could not do a thing to make a difference, to change this future because that would have meant to in-

---

[130] See: Bauman 2000.

stantiate a second future different from the foreseen one, which in turn would make that perfect foreknowledge impossible. Prometheus was famous and envied for that foreknowledge and even tortured by Zeus for it.[131] This ancient myth already understood that you cannot have both: Either you can, in principle, gain knowledge of the future (being a Titan, an Oracle or a prophet) and this at the cost of not being able to perform different actions than those that inevitably lead to that one and only deterministic future, or you are free to make a difference, to influence the future, to manipulate or create different alternative futures which comes with the impossibility of foreseeing them.[132]

The future is not the realm of facts but of objectives and ambitions, there is nothing true or false about the sentence 'I will buy a Richter painting.' One can believe in the so communicated plan, maybe even based on whether it is considered probable or not. But believing in a stated ambition, judging future alternatives according to alleged intuitive or scientifically calculated probabilities is far from positive knowledge about the future. The best grasp we can get about the future

---

[131] There is one other Greek mythological figure being famous for her accurate foreknowledge of some parts of the coming: Cassandra. So why did Zeus not interrogate this mortal woman instead of meddling with a Titan – who, of course, knew he will be tortured but could not help it? The fact that knowing the future and being free to change it exclude each other holds for Cassandra as well. Here coming with the curse that no one ever believed her prophecies. So Zeus could have extorted the foreknowledge from Cassandra, but in turn he would not have believed her anyway. .

[132] According to Kant, foreseeing the future of freely acting people is impossible, or as he puts it: If actions could be foreseen, there would be no freedom. "[U]nd wenn wir alle Erscheinungen seiner [des Menschen, BG] Willkür bis auf den Grund erforschen könnten, so würde es keine einzige menschliche Handlung geben, die wir nicht mit Gewißheit vorhersagen und aus ihren vorhergehenden Bedingungen als nothwendig erkennen könnten. In Ansehung dieses empirischen Charakters giebt es also keine Freiheit" (Kant 1998, 634-635 [577-578]).

for epistemological reasons are more or less educated guesses, better or worse underpinned assumptions – that is: conjectures.

All we can do to approximately satisfy our rising need for fore-knowledge is to further educate our guessing capabilities and develop our art of conjecture.[133] Our ability to perfect this kind of artistry seems to lose – despite remarkable progress – the arms race with the world's increasing complexity. This feeling of slipping off a slippery slope causes a call for new arms in increasing our own foreknowledge, which, in principle, can never exceed its conjectural nature but extols itself as predictive knowledge. One approach to ease the disturbing uncertainty of an open future was stochastics and calculating probabilities. None-theless, this 'statistical foreknowledge' is still conjectures expressed in numbers.[134] So the need for foreknowledge remains and intensifies. It is causing us – as we are addicted to anticipation – wet palms when we encounter the prophetic promise of today's palm readers.

10.2 The Promise of Big Data – Listen to the World Itself

So far, all efforts to anticipate future developments have been some-how limited by the cognitive capabilities of the anticipator. The ever lim-ited conjecturing ability, even at the level of artistry, falls behind the open future's uncertainty. Models and theories are at the very core of

---

[133] Jouvenel 1964.

[134] All calculations, even the most sophisticated, that distribute probabilities to alternative developments or events still suffer from the flaw that it is a mere guessing how many percent were to be distributed. It has become a habit to dis-tribute 100% making three equally probable events each 33% probable. But giv-en a fourth unknown possible event, maybe only 75%, had to be distributed on the three known events in the first place. Stochastics can provide quite sophisti-cated information on the known futures, but the number of known futures taken into account is restricted by one's conjecturing abilities. And are not the un-known futures much more in number, thus in likeliness, and – being unknown – causing much more uncertainty?

the efforts to deal with uncertainty and to anticipate possible futures. Causality, for instance, insight into causal connections, is probably the dominant way of anticipating future events. Causal connections allow to predict the effect of a certain cause given similar enough circumstances. Models and theories (e.g., probability theory) are what enables the above mentioned 'statistical foreknowledge' but also all sorts of explanation of what might happen based on what happened. A theory based guess – a hypothesis – is considered improved in contrast to a mere wild guess; often its conjectural character is hidden and then called prognosis, forecast, or prediction. On the slippery slope of today's dynamic world, even the most advanced anticipation efforts, even those based on highly elaborate scientific theories, are witnessed to fail epically as seen at the financial crisis 2008. Obviously, our best anticipation capabilities are not good enough for our immense need for foreknowledge and improved theories have not brought a breakthrough so far which leads some to the suspicion that the theory foundation itself might be a shortcoming.

Big Data is now claimed to lessen the need for theories and it comes with the promise of enabling people to listen to 'the world itself'.

"The promise is that, with high levels of data generation and developments in computational analysis, the world (coded through datafication) can begin to speak for itself without its (more than) fallible human interpreter."[135]

Or as put in the much cited article "The End of Theory": "With enough data, the numbers speak for themselves.

[...] Data without a model is just noise. But faced with massive data, this approach to science — hypothesize, model, test — is becoming obsolete."[136] Even the best models are flawed and "a caricature of a more

---

[135] Chandler 2015, 837–838.

[136] Anderson 2008.

complex underlying reality."[137] This leads to the promise of a Big Data enabled 'better way':

"There is now a better way. Petabytes allow us to say: 'Correlation is enough.' We can stop looking for models. We can analyze the data without hypotheses about what it might show. We can [...] let statistical algorithms find patterns where science cannot. [...] Correlation supersedes causation, and science can advance even without coherent models, unified theories, or really any mechanistic explanation at all."[138]

Reality in its vibrant abundance – so the luring promise – could be accessed through their authentic data, thus circumventing the anemic and essentially curtailed scientific models and theories. Understanding the datafied language of our IT system pervaded world in its alleged original richness with the help of nowadays computational 'superpowers' – such as Big Data algorithms – seems to let the proverbial dream of the emperor who wanted a map of his empire being as detailed as the reality come true.[139] A map provides more orientation than the actual reality because it omits all unimportant details. Concerning these omitted details, the map is wrong, but that is just how it can provide orientation. "Essentially, all models are wrong, but some are useful."[140]

– This famous aphorism is about to be outdated as expressed by Google's research director Peter Norvig: "All models are wrong, and increasingly you can succeed without them."[141]

According to that promise of 'Correlation supersedes causation', Big Data algorithms mapping the 'data empire' could lead to such a 'perfectly accurate' map of the reality because they would overcome the constitutive difference between map and empire, between model and

---

[137] ibid.

[138] ibid.

[139] Lyotard 1984, 55.

[140] Box; Draper 1987, 424.

[141] Anderson 2008.

world. Therefore, Big Data is becoming notorious for its "unreasonable effectiveness"[142], the 'end of theory', and thus being responsible for the "death of the theorist"[143]. If theory is the base of our best conjecturing abilities and if theory itself is the shortcoming of our anticipatory efforts, does the alleged death of theory then imply the death of conjecture, thus giving room to flawless since theoryless predictions? Does this scientific deicide committed by Big Data finally offer us direct foreknowledge?

Data directly derived from our very movements, actions, communications, interactions, body functions, etc. would allegedly not be distorted by any theory of causation imposed by the people trying to make sense of it. Brave new world, where Big Data systems are used to find correlations that could not have been even searched for. The wrongness of the models does no longer matter if there are no model-based hypotheses guiding the questions and defining what counts as an answer. For these algorithms, there is no such thing as unimportant details because the purpose that it has to prove useful for (such as orientation for a map) is no longer predefined. Big Data is so delightfully longed for because it is expected to give us answers we did not even know the question for, which is to bring digital serendipity to a whole new level. This is just the kind of uncertainty about our futures we are confronted with in our complex world and that stochastics failed to tackle: We need answers even if the questions were already too complex to ask, we need to approach the 'unknown unknowns', the things we do not even know that we do not know them.[144]

---

[142] Halevy et al. 2009.

[143] Steadman 2013.

[144] At this point, the said aspects mainly concerning science reach into political, governance, and resilience debates. See: Chandler 2014.

For a quite famous use of the concept of 'unknown unknowns' see: Rumsfeld 2011.

10.3 The Problem with the Promise – A Matter of Faith

Just as the scientific method, the use of theory and models was not just invented as some sort of elitist brain jogging, the 'death of theory' would come with some major problems.

The first problem refers to the misunderstanding that mistakenly identifies the 'datafied world' with the 'world itself', meaning that already the promise of listening to the world itself via Big Data technologies is a modern myth. To state the obvious: Any set of data – no matter how incomprehensibly gigantic – is selective. The promise clearly disregards the fact that data is no pre-social phenomena but always already socially constructed or socially determined in its condition of formation. Data is influenced by people with certain interests and mindsets and the data producing, collecting, storing, and processing technologies are so as well, thus selecting only data within their sensing capabilities and their scopes, that people with certain objectives and with theories about the means by which these objectives are possibly obtainable designed. The datafied world is distinguished from the world itself, at least by its inscribed traces of theory and models[145]; so claiming the complete death of theory by Big Data analytics is techno-deterministically biased and myopically dealing with the illusion of pre- social objective data.

Big Data systems do not 'kill' the theoretical inheritance of data itself. They do whatsoever circumvent much theoretical wrongness in data collection and pattern recognition, what might be enough for Norvig and others to hold on to that promise. But theory comes in not only in data formation but also at the point where information meets human actors. The problem in having an answer to an unknown

---

[145] GPS data, for instance, with which movement profiles can be created inherit assumptions of both the special and the general theory of relativity and, thus, of course, their theoretical correctness and wrongness.

question is that you never know how to make sense of it. If the answer is 42, for instance, you are in trouble figuring whether kilo, percent, or years, etc. If this information should make sense and be used to motivate actions, then theory and causality have to be invested by human actors inevitably all along with the allegedly overcome wrongness again. So, at the very moment the algorithmic findings are perceived by human actors, they get subjected to some sort of causal or theoretic assumption – consciously or not, be it in a careful methodologically structured scientific or an intuitive emotional prejudicial superstitious way. For example: If Big Data systems would find a strong correlation between being depressed and being a teacher, and given a will to change that situation, people have to come up with some cause-effect assumption whether the job might depress people working in it or people predisposed for depression choose to be a teacher. In short: Do teachers get depressed or do depressed get teachers? The mere correlation cannot guide any action to solve this problem – theory can. Correlation does not supersede causation if you wish to change something and you need to know how.

In our complex world, human actors are no longer the only entities performing actions or action-like processes. Artificial agents sell stocks, filter and channel information flows, and perform all sorts of actions human actors come to deal with as mere results or as participants in all forms of human-technology interactions or co- actions.[146] If assistive systems give recommendations on how to act according to found correlations (or nudges or forces people in a certain direction by modifying interfaces, contents, systems behavior, etc.), it is crucial to be able to deduce the system's behavior and its underlying processes in order to understand and evaluate the recommendations. If this theory-based validation by people is still possible, then the whole human-technology interaction is still as 'defective' as the theories are. In order to unleash its promised potential to deal with unknown unknowns and to overcome

---

[146] Gransche et al. 2014.

theoretical deficiency, the systems and algorithms have to deal with a data quantity and heterogeneity being impossible for humans to grasp even with much time and effort – which is one definiens of Big Data. Delivering insights – or predictions based on them – that people without algorithmic help could never have found is the alleged potential of Big Data systems and it is at the same time the exclusion of scientific validation because accountability, verification (for the time being), and falsification are essential for science.

When people get confronted with information, processes, part-actions and actions, or results based on Big Data algorithms they have no chance to retrace how these outcomes were generated, what they were based on, and if they are 'true, right, or correct' (if any of these concept applies at all). Thus, in a datafied world widely pervaded with Big Data technology and artificial agents acting on this basis, people have no other option than to believe in these results and perform their actions in good faith. Within these systems that are claimed to render scientific method obsolete, there is no space for scientific falsification. This makes Big Data based outcomes a matter of faith. It is information (or hybrid actions based on this information) coming from a source that is principally obscure to human actors. And at the very moment it enters the human sphere, it becomes an orienting force, guiding people's and agents' actions no matter of their original correctness. As for the claim of 'death of theory', this is where its potential validity ends: Algorithms, systems, artificial agents may be able to perform beyond theory only on the ground of abundant data[147], but human beings are not. When encountering human actors, the (if so ever at all) flawless since theoryless information is 'corrupted' by more

---

[147] NB: This 'beyond theory' refers only to their performance. As well as data, IT systems and artificial agents are no pre-social phenomena but underlie a theory-compromised formation process.

or less theory-based interpretations and validations of people before being transformed into actions.

Beyond scientific validation possibilities, Big Data findings are indistinguishable from Big Data creations or data noise artifacts. Given a large enough search room, there are always correlations.[148] Big Data findings and creations have the same potential impact on human behavior: How could people distinguish them in the first place? Those who do not know their difference are forced to believe in both or none equally. If only enough people believe in this guiding character of Big Data based outcomes – and the current hype is strongly suggesting that this is absolutely the case –, then these outcomes develop a self-fulfilling and self-defeating power as known from the respective prophecies.[149] So, does the end of theory correlate with a renaissance of prophecy?

10.4 The Oracle of Big Data – Prophecies without Prophets

Wherever people are ignorant, there will be prophets.[150] Scientific prognoses – in terms of probabilities including their range of uncertainty, their limitations of validity, and their condition of formation like transparency about the set of information and hypotheses they are based on –

---

[148] On a global scale, there is a good chance that, every time I breathe in and out, one human being dies and another one is born at the same time what obviously does not make my breath lethal or life giving; nonetheless this correlation could get 'recognised' by Big Data pattern recognition. It is human causal common sense that instantly classifies this correlation as absurd. Who knows how many artificial agents already sold, filtered, channelled masses of stocks, information, services, and wares on that kind of correlation? All we might see is a changed price in the end with no chance to check which correlations lead to it.

[149] Merton 1948.

[150] "Partout où les hommes seront ignorants, il y aura des prophètes", d'Holbach, Paul Henri Thiry, 123.

can be used to inform decisions; they lessen people's ignorance if not mistaken in its conjectural nature. Post-theory Big Data predictions, on the other hand, lack this self-referring information. People, nevertheless, using them to base their actions on are ignorant about their range of uncertainty and validity, their formation circumstances, etc. Big Data based outcomes, being a matter of faith, can be seen as today's prophecies. As they are not claimed by deficient mortal beings but by some sort of pseudo omniscient algorithmic deity, they are the paradox of prophecies without prophets. Thus, Big Data becomes some sort of today's oracle, a voice revealing insights and predictions from an abundant yet obscure source that is claimed to be the world itself – or at least as close to it as we can hope to get. And just like the ancient oracles, its power does not derive from any correctness of the content of any single prophecy but from the people believing in it. In contrast to scientific prognosis, which is a matter of doubt, those Big Data prophecies being a matter of faith are immune to critique or falsification. Both the oracles of ancient times and those of Big Data have this immunity in common; the former because they were seen as an authentic direct message from the Gods in a deterministic cosmos, the latter because it is broadly believed to be the world speaking for itself. The actual events either prove the correctness of their prediction or the wrongness of the fallible interpreter.

Prognosis and prophecy are two ways of dealing with future unknowns.[151] The modern approach of prognosis accepts the existence of indispensable unknowns along with the notion of an open future. The ancient prophecies placed all the uncertainty in the impartial human knowledge and misunderstandings of a principally knowable future. If Big Data prophecies take the fallible interpreter out of the equation providing prophecies without prophets, this would not only mean that positive foreknowledge would after all be possible but also even direct-

---

[151] Esposito 2013.

ly accessible. Prognosis and prophecies have similar power as socially effective speech-acts. Prophecies, in addition, have two advantages as powerful speech-acts of which the first is the said bonus of infallibility. The second one is a strong awareness of its circularity, which primarily holds for ancient prophecies. While prognoses inherit the scientific tendency to see themselves as uninvolved observers, as mere describing objective entities, prophecies always included their effect in the prophesied future (Oedipus for instance). That is why we know self-fulfilling and suicidal or self-defeating prophecies but not such prognoses. This valuable awareness of circularity is one lesson to learn from the ancient prophecies and should be transferred to scientific prognoses [152] and to today's Big Data predictions.

Conclusion

Big Data systems do not bring the end of theory, but – apart from the theory inheritance within data itself – they postpone theoretical interpretation within the information-action chain to a point where it might cause less wrongness on the one hand but also less possibility to evaluate and correct previous parts in that chain on the other hand. This might lead to problems concerning accountability of co-actions to which a hybrid variety of human an artificial actors contribute. Model wrongness is not overcome but relocated and in disguise, thus withdrawn from scientific critique and improvement processes. Predictions – shifting from prognoses to modern prophecies – change their nature from being a matter of doubt to a matter of faith. As decreased fallibility of prophetic foreknowledge comes with decreased freedom of action (Prometheus) and as the appearance of prophets is connected with increased ignorance (d'Holbach), the renaissance of prophecies should alert a pro-

---

[152] This is widely the case in stock market prognosis, bets, and futures but still rare in scientific prognosis.

gressive democratic society but yet not lead to defensive overreaction as there are insights to be learned from prophetic future anticipation such as a strong awareness of prediction circularity.

Big Data services are indubitably playing an increasing role not only in science but also in politics and economy as well and, therefore, many questions are to be dealt with. How should a society reintroducing the concepts of oracles and prophecies (even if not under these names) at the expense of scientific methods deal with that kind of strategy shift in approaching complex and open futures? What do powerful oracles and prophecies mean in terms of responsibility, accountability, democracy, resilience, governmental influence, and (self-)governance capabilities? Who and where are the new prophets staging themselves as 'out of the equation' and staging the objectivity of 'the world speaking for itself' while strategically acting from behind the curtain? What do they win with this disguise? Are Google's and other Big Data Titans' imperatives actually a surprisingly honest totalitarian rule – "So, follow the data." – and are they a revealing witness of their potentially hazardous approach on (not) shaping the future – "Now go out and gather some data, and see what it can do."[153]?

References

Anderson, Chris: The End of Theory: The Data Deluge Makes the Scientific Method Obsolete, 2008. Available from <http://archive.wired.com/science/discoveries/magazine/16-07/pb_theory >. Accessed 27 September 2015.

Bauman, Zygmunt: Liquid modernity. Cambridge, UK, Malden, MA: Polity Press; Blackwell, 2000.

Box, George E. P.; Draper, Norman Richard: Empirical model-building and response surfaces. New York: Wiley 1987.

---

[153] Halevy et al. 2009, 12.

Chandler, David: Beyond neoliberalism: resilience, the new art of governing complexity. Resilience 2 (1), 2014, pp. 47–63.

Chandler, David: A World without Causation: Big Data and the Coming of Age of Posthumanism. Millennium - Journal of International Studies 43 (3), 2015, pp. 833–851.

d'Holbach, Paul Henri Thiry: Le Christianisme dévoilé: In Premières Oeuvres, pp. 94–137. Paris: 1797.

Esposito, Elena: Formen der Zirkularität in der Konstruktion der Zukunft. In Prophetie und Prognostik: Verfügungen über Zukunft in Wissenschaften, Religionen und Künsten, edited by Daniel Weidner and Stefan Willer, München: Wilhelm Fink 2013, pp. 325–340.

Gransche, Bruno; Shala, Erduana; Hubig, Christoph et al.: Wandel von Autonomie und Kontrolle durch neue Mensch-Technik-Interaktionen: Grundsatzfragen autonomieorientierter Mensch-Technik-Verhältnisse. Stuttgart: Fraunhofer Verlag 2014.

Halevy, Alon; Norvig, Peter;Pereira, Fernando: The Unreasonable Effectiveness of Data. IEEE Computer Society, 2009, pp. 8–12.

Jouvenel, Bertrand de: L'Art de la conjecture. Monaco: Éditions du Rocher 1964. Kant, Immanuel: Kritik der reinen Vernunft. Hamburg: Felix Meiner 1998.

Lyotard, Jean-François: The postmodern condition: A report on knowledge. Manchester: Manchester University Press 1984.

Merton, Robert K: The Self-Fulfilling Prophecy. The Antioch Review 8 (2), 1948, pp. 193–210. Rumsfeld, Donald: Known and unknown: A memoir. New York: Sentinel 2011.

Steadman, Ian: Big data and the death of the theorist, 2013. Available from   <http://www.wired.co.uk/news/archive/2013-01/25/ big-data-end-of-theory >. Accessed 27. Sep. 2015.

PART IV

CYBER LAW, CYBER HEALTH
AND ETHICS

11

BLOCKCHAIN LEGAL REGULATIONS

Michael Mosimann, Switzerland

11.1 Introduction

"We want to do an ICO without regulation." – This was a sentence I heard many times in 2017 when I told potential clients that their public token sale (so called "Initial Coin Offering" or "ICO") and potentially also their business model could be subject to the Swiss financial market regulations. It certainly did not come as a surprise to many lawyers (including myself) when the Swiss Financial Market Supervising Authority FINMA released in September 2017 a public announcement stating that the Swiss financial market regulations were technology neutral and therefore potentially applicable to ICOs and Blockchain-based business models, but it was a surprise to many other market participants. Since then, FINMA and other financial market supervising authorities around the world have made it clear that financial market regulations also apply to Blockchain-based businesses.

While the legal aspects of Blockchain projects got clearer and the market has matured in the past year, it is time to reflect on some items related to this sector. Among them are *ethical aspects*, with regard to which I would like to share some thoughts, whereby ethics is understood as non-legally binding imperative behavioural order. Due to the requested brevity of this article and the short timeline to complete it, the broader discussion of ethical aspects needs to take place elsewhere. This short contribution is by no means exhaustive and is also not meant as a sophisticated ethical scientific contribution, but intends to raise some high level questions of a legal practitioner only.

11.2 Ethics in a Blockchain Environment

The first question coming to my mind is whether the fact that we are dealing with comparatively young business models based on the Blockchain technology takes away any of the ethical principles and responsibilities? Does using the Blockchain technology justify a departure from such principles? In my opinion, the answer to this question must be a clear no. The technology is a new tool to be used, but nothing more. This tool does not (yet) act on itself or is itself responsible to uphold these moral imperatives, but is to be put to work by human beings. The values and morals of these human beings do not change due to the new technology. Hence, whoever applies this tool is in my opinion supposed to *consider the same ethical principles as before without this new tool.*

Having said this, it obviously leads to the question whether the technology adds responsibilities or principles to this compilation of ethical principles. In my non-specialized opinion, this question has also to be answered to the negative. Rather than adding new principles, the technology requires to focus more on some existing principles. In the following, I would like to share some thoughts on three examples from my practical experience.

11.3 Ethics and Autonomous Applications

With the rise of the Blockchain technology, affiliated constructions such as self-executing smart contracts and decentralized autonomous organizations ("DAO") have emerged. Not necessarily Blockchain related, but also related to the problem at hand, are artificial intelligences.

Un-technically described, these constructions are autonomous applications with a certain freedom to make own decisions, sometimes also furnished with learning capabilities. From a legal point of view, it is currently unclear how these constructions have to be treated. What are they? For more than 2000 years now, we have had the *classical distinction between individuals and groups of persons/societies/legal entities*. A smart contract or a DAO does not fall under either of these categories. *Do we have to add a "digital person"?* If yes, is it sufficient to have this in a national law or does it need to be internationally or even globally implemented? What law should they be subject to? How can a user enforce a right if the digital contractual counterparty does not act as intended? Considering the lack of a suitable legal framework, the creation, development, and deployment of such autonomous construction should be governed by ethical principles. However, considering further that these constructions do not have own ethical or moral values that influence their decision making process, it is each developer's own moral responsibility to ensure that the autonomous construction developed and deployed by such developer does not exploit or harm users, violates laws, regulations or rights of third parties, etc.

11.4 Market Credibility

One of the practical problems that still remains to be solved relates to the *opening of a bank account*. As of writing this article, most banks in Switzerland are still reluctant to open bank accounts for individuals or entities being actively engaged in the transfer of crypto currencies. In order to justify their reluctance, banks refer to their obligations under Swiss anti-money laundering regulations, in particular the obligation to identify the beneficial owner of money and to clarify the plausibility of the source of the funds deposited with them and their legality in case of doubts. The Blockchain technology, which is the basis of crypto currencies such as Bitcoin or Ether, would allow for anonymous transfers, no one could identify the source of the crypto currencies transferred and the involved parties. A conversion into traditional currencies (so called FI-AT money) and deposit on a traditional bank account could put funds potentially obtained illegally back in the ordinary money circle.

From the Blockchain community, it is often heard that the banks or even the Swiss government should act in order to solve this problem and to enable Blockchain businesses to open bank accounts. However, is it really only the banks or even the Swiss government that should act?

Affected persons claim that they have always complied with all laws and regulations and are therefore penalized in an unjustified manner. Although I firmly believe that most market participants are good (corporate) citizens, this is not necessarily true for all of them. After all, hash numbers, which appear as senders and receivers of messages or transactions, grant anonymity and privacy to criminal people who could not execute the same transaction in the old banking world and therefore make the relevant Blockchain appealing to them.

According to Swiss law, every financial intermediary (including banks) are required to identify the person from whom they accept money and the beneficial owner of the funds as well as to verify the legality of the source of the funds in case of any doubts. Although there is no such legal obligation, is it ethically unproblematic to create or provide a system that does not prohibit criminal suspects to execute transactions for illegal purposes? Wouldn't ethical considerations require developers to provide a crypto currency based on a Blockchain that eliminates the disadvantages of the existing money transfer systems, but that keeps its advantages, such as the identification of its users, in order to make it compatible with the banking world? Even if such moral obligation was rejected, I would imagine that most market participants demanding banks to act also have a vital interest in the credibility of the market in which they participate, which would also advocate in favour of the development of such a Blockchain.

11.5 Exploit the Impact Potential

According to a study of the World Bank, published in 2016, there are approximately two billion adults worldwide that do not have access to the traditional banking system and hence do not have a bank account. However, according to a study conducted by McKinsey & Company in 2012, an estimated one billion people without bank account have a smart phone. It is obvious that a Blockchain based crypto currency has the potential to give these people the possibility to execute financial transactions which they could not do in the traditional financial world. "Banking the Unbanked" and similar phrases relate to this.

Among others, and besides the above use case, the Blockchain technology could be used in order to allow consumers to track the journey of their products, e.g. to see who the farmers were that have planted and harvested the fruits or who the person was that sewed a particular shirt. This would raise the awareness of end consumers about the origins of the product they just bought, which in turn could result in the consumers changing their behaviour.

Given this potential, wouldn't ethical considerations require the Blockchain community to use its knowledge, experience and wealth (in particular the one acquired in connection with other Blockchain based projects) to develop Blockchains, crypto currencies and platforms that also benefit these people? Since the Blockchain community is truly capable of including unbanked third-world people as participants in a new financial market, it would be justifiable that this community also has an increased moral obligation to take care of these people's interests in order to make the world a better place for all people compared to other business models with a less international involvement.

11.6 Closing

Given the fact that *legislators around the globe are just at the beginning of regulating the Blockchain industry*, ethical and moral considerations play an important role in this area at this point in time. Not only because of a general validity of these ethical principles, but also due to a vital self-interest of the Blockchain community: The more market participants try to avoid regulations or simply disregard potentially applicable regulations, the harsher new regulations legislators and regulators around the globe are currently working on it. An ethically conscious behaviour of all market participants might influence legislators to develop more liberal instead of strict regulations.

12

A HUMANISTIC APPROACH
TO THE ETHICS OF HIGH TECH

Aharon Aviram, Tapan Patel, Israel

Abstract

Our basic supposition is that development and use of ICT products and services should be submitted to well-being oriented ethical guidelines. While this supposition is clear in many other aspects of life, it is relatively new in this area and has been only peripherally developing in the last few decades. This text starts by pointing to these early developments and its still peripheral nature. Then it posits to the claim that one essential ingredient lacking from further meaningful development is a comprehensive ethical approach to all aspects of ICT products and services. The main goal is to characterize the five parameters that form such an ethical approach and make primary steps in supplying our answer to the questions that arise from them.

12.1 Encouraging Trends

Throughout the development of computing and internet in the last thirty to fourty years and especially with development and spread of personal computers, they were hailed by all the interested parties as well as many researches as a radical move forward in improving human life[154]. But there were also voices who thought of these "move forward" as a curse leading to a long list of catastrophes like taking away jobs, render the users cognitively shallow, emotionally detached, human relationships flatter and instrumental, lead to radical impoverishment of language, etc.[155]. While the former voices dominated the political, public and economic spheres, the latter (concerned) voices stayed in academic or peripheral circles and were fully ignored by the developers, investors and decision makers, henceforth: the stakeholders.

There has been a somewhat similar case of polarizing opinions with Artificial Intelligence (AI) since it came to prominence in the last decade. On one hand, there is the leading voice of the above mentioned stakeholders driven by desire for financial gains, excitement of the technological innovation, belief in progress through technology (the core value of modern and post-modern world since scientific and industrial revolutions in 17th and 18th century), etc.[156] On the other, the warnings

---

[154] Shirky, C. (2010). *Cognitive Surplus: Creativity and Generosity in a Connected Age*, London: Allen Lane, The Penguin Press. Shaffer, D.W. (2006). *How Computer Games Help Children Learn*, New York: Palgrave Macmillan. Suroweicki, J. (2005). *The Wisdom of Crowds*, New York: Anchor Group Random House. Prensky, M (2010). *Teaching Digital Natives: Partnering for Real Learning*, London: SAGE Ltd.

[155] Siegel, L. (2008). *Against the Machine: Being Human in the Age of the Electronic Mob*, New York: Spiegel & Grau, Random House. Rushkoff, D. (2013). *Present Shock: When Everything Happens Now*: New York: CURRENT, The Penguin Press, Random House. Morozov, E. (2010). *The Net Delusion: The Dark Side of Internet Freedom. Jackson*, TN: Public Affairs Print. Keen, A. (2007). *The Cult of the Amateur: How Today's Internet is Killing Our Culture and Assaulting Our Economy*, New York: Doubleday, Random House.

[156] Kai Fu Lee , "How Ai Can Save Our Humanity", YouTube video, 14:50, Posted by "TED", April 2018, https://www.ted.com/talks/kai_fu_lee_how_ai_can_save_our_humanity Tom Gruber, "How Ai Can Enhance Our Memory, Work and Social Lives", YouTube video, 9:47, Posted by "TED", April 2017, https://www.ted.com/talks/tom_gruber_how_ai_can_enhance_our_memory_work_and_social_lives, Shyam Sankar, "The Rise of Human-

of the critics that were, until recently, originating from outside the circles of stakeholders. The stakes have grown considerably higher in both the negative and positive effects because of the increasing power of AI and the drastic influence it can have on multiple technologies and industries and all possible aspects of our lives[157].

Until very recently, the concerned and critical discourses were initiated and led almost exclusively by academics and NGOs. And in some instances, they were joined by policy makers and regulators. But investors, developers, designers and marketeers were either not aware of these voices or ignored them altogether. They certainly didn't make efforts to address these concerns by forming a set of ethical constraints that systematically drive (as technological and gain oriented guidelines do) the design and production of relevant AI based products and services. In the last couple of decades, there have been instances of awareness and action against the effects like online abuse, infringement of privacy, intellectual property rights, etc. They have been given considerable attention by policy makers, regulatory authorities, governments, etc. and the remedial steps have been taken.

More interestingly, in last few years, there have been number of instances of individuals in the industry who have taken note of ethical issues, are aware of their importance and are claiming the need to incorporate ethical thinking and concerns in design of AI based technological products and services. There have even been cases of technological

---

Computer Cooperation", YouTube video, 12:6, Posted by "TED", June 2012, https://www.ted.com/talks/shyam_sankar_the_rise_of_human_computer_cooperation#t-223705.

[157] Nick Bostrom, "What Happens When Our Computers Get Smarter Than We Are", YouTube video, 16:32, Posted by "TED", March 2015, https://www.ted.com/talks/nick_bostrom_what_happens_when_our_computers_get_smarter_than_we_are, Sam Harris, "Can We build Ai without Losing Control over It", YouTube video, 14:28, Posted by "TED", June 2016, https://www.ted.com/talks/sam_harris_can_we_build_ai_without_losing_control_over_it, Max Tegmark, "How to Get Empowered not Overpowered", YouTube video, 17:16, Posted by "TED", April 2018, https://www.ted.com/talks/max_tegmark_how_to_get_empowered_not_overpowered_by_ai

companies involving professional "ethicists" in the design processes. Furthermore, some of these ethicists, as well as other individuals from within the industry clearly and publicly express the need for ethically sound designs.

For example, one of the visible figures in this space is Tristan Harris, a former in-house ethicist at Google, who is quite vocal about companies putting their financial interests above the well-being of their users, inconsiderate or unconscious of the pernicious and permanent damages inflicted on them[158]. Another one is Kat Zhou, a product designer at IBM, who calls for the product designers to be aware of the negative consequences, equip themselves with ethical way of thinking and knowledge required and adopt it as major guideline in designing products and services[159].

As also emphasized by Kat Zhou in her article, product designers at few tech companies seem to be implementing/integrating certain 'ethical decision making' guidelines or ethics-oriented thought experiments in the design process/framework. Still admittedly these occurrences are quite rare, and the voices of ethical concerns are stifled more often than not by desire for "technological progress" and financial gains. Thus, the presence of these individuals at the design stage is often an alibi rather than an attempt to understand how deep and critical the issue is for the future of humanity. Hence, even though there seems to be, in seldom cases, some awareness of the possible negative impacts of technological products or at least the emerging critic of it, the decision processes are still very much driven by blind belief in technological progress en-

---

[158]   https://qz.com/1201583/how-tristan-harris-an-ex-google-ethicist-wants-to-design-tech-to-make-our-kids-less-addicted-to-it/, http://www.tristanharris.com/essays/

[159]   https://uxdesign.cc/designing-ethically-pt-1-9800bfbc86a3, https://uxdesign.cc/designing-ethically-pt-2-535ac61e2992

hanced by the desire for gains maximization which majorly conflict with or don't take into consideration the well-being of the targeted users.

12.2 Need for an Ethical System

But even these limited attempts at criticism are being thwarted by two main limitations:

a. Almost all of them are "post facto" i.e. in the light of realizations that the products or services that are being used have negative impacts only after they have been inflicted on the users. Because of this very nature, they can only limit the negative impact without the possibility of reversing them. For example, incidents like infringement of privacy, online bullying, hacking, etc. are embedded in the technology themselves or the dominant culture of the usage hence making it impossible to revert them.

b. Furthermore, even concerning the few recent calls from within the industry, they are limited in various ways which stem also from a "conceptual" root. Such instances could be reduced significantly if there is a coherent, parsimonious, operationalizable and comprehensive ethical foundation, grounded in historically recognized and respected ethical tradition that could serve for evaluation of technology and many kinds of use and/or misuse of them.

Even though there is significantly growing attention to ethical issues, there is no not systematic and comprehensive ethical approach to start from as explained above. Our goal in this text is to suggest such an ethical system on which the attempts of all kinds can rely on. While we give our own primary answers to the question about the foundation of such systems, our aim is to rather clarify the questions and make the point that they can be approached simply and rationally rather than in ad-hoc and intuitive manner, and not to substantiate our own answers.

Such an ethical system should be able to comprehensively address the following questions:

1. What are the various natures of the challenges we are facing?
2. What are the natures of the possible responses to the identified challenges?
3. What are the values foundational to an ethical system that could guide the approach to the aforementioned challenges and how are they connected to each other?
4. How are they grounded in our culture, way of life and jurisdiction?
5. What is the strategy that should be followed to derive operationalized guidelines in a rational manner from values that may seem abstract at the first glance?

In what follows we will attempt to supply primary answers to these questions as we see them now.

12.3 First Parameter: Nature of Challenges

We used above the concept of "challenge" as opposed to "problems" for the simple reason that ethical guidelines should aspire to point to betterment of human *well-being* not just by evaluating or solving problems to human well-being but also help navigate through way of enhancing well-being through new and existing technology (see below for the definition and views of well-being in this context). Henceforth, we will be addressing mainly to the problems as they are much more prominent in public and professional discussions.

The critical issues and problems can be generally differentiated in light of *two basic parameters*: the *visibility* of the alleged harm causes, and the *time span* in which it is supposed to be realized.

By "visible harm", we refer to harm that can be presented by clear and concrete instances. Thus, for example, cases of verbal abuse or shaming of children or adults can be documented and presented for all interested to see by a researcher, lawyer or journalist studying the phenomenon. They are also generally easily quantifiable. The same is true for malicious hacking and infringement of privacy (when discovered). The same can be said about fear of the conquest of humanity by super intelligence that might take place in the future as result of self-aware AI much more intelligent than humans. If it takes place, most probably, it will be easy to detect (like the scenario in the film *The Terminator*) unless the AI will manipulate human beings. Then, if successful, it won't (by definitions) be detectable like the scenario in popular film *The Matrix*. What unifies most of these cases is the fact that when presented (as past occurrences of future possibilities) they can be made so suggestively and powerfully.

On the other hand, the process of impoverishment of language or shallowing of user's cognition or emotions claimed by some researchers[160] to take place due to impact of the internet (which is now probably being made worse by AI enhanced systems), are much more layered and complex to be concretely presented to have dramatic & suggestive presentations. This is the case on two levels. First, no one or even given number of cases of use of "poor" or hieroglyphical language can substantiate the case made by the relevant critics. They have to show ongoing gradual development of use of certain media (email, messages, tweets, etc. for example) and the correlative "shrinking" of the size of the used texts or the proliferation of emoji and the further correlative shrinking of the variety of terms used in texts as well potential harms to creativity or rational thinking. Furthermore, they have to substantiate a claim concerning the correlation between the impoverishment of phonetic language and the ability for abstract or creative thinking. And finally they have to try to substantiate a claim concerning the probability of

---

[160] Carr, N. (2010). *The Shallows: What the Internet Is Doing to Our Brains*, New York: W. W. Norton & Company.

causal relation between relevant digital phenomena and the claimed linguistic and cognitive ones (and as is well known, correlation in itself is
far from being identical to causality) All this is very far from the ability
to present concrete direct (as opposed to "inferred") evidence concerning any of the abovementioned phenomena.

The second parameter is much simpler. It relates to the range of time
the alleged phenomena or process has taken place or is supposed to take
place. It can be said that more visible is the alleged damage, the easier it
is for critics to suggestively (as opposed to rationally) convince others in
its existence and mobilize public opinion, policy makers and at the end
of the day, the stakeholders, to try to limit or negate it. This can explain
why there is so many discussions on infringement of privacy and online
abuse on the internet as opposed to alleged "shallowing" of cognitive
and emotional ability in spite of the fact that the damage to individual's
ability of decision making can be at least as threatening as abuse or infringement of privacy.

The same is true concerning the duration of time for alleged harm to
be realized. The further from us it seems to be, the less threatening it
might look. Even if in principle once taking place it might be fully visible and may go beyond the point of no return[161]. This is clearly the case
with the scenarios concerning the conquest of humanity by AI.

We have gone into this characterization of harms and alleged harms
from the perspective of these two parameters in order to be able to substantiate *two claims*.

a) While emotionally, the level of visibility and duration of time of
manifestation of problems easily explain why certain phenomena
are in limelight while the other are doomed to fluorescent lit rooms

---

[161] "The Future of Artificial Intelligence: Why the Hype Has Outrun Reality",
Knowledge@Wharton, July 14, 2017, accessed October 2018,
http://knowledge.wharton.upenn.edu/article/dont-believe-hype-ai-driven-world-
still-long-way-off/

of some academic workshops, that should not be the case rationally.

b) Rationally, what should count is the extent of potential harm from the perspective of certain core of our guiding ethical values.

An ethical system, as ideated in this text should be able to provide correct weight to the issues irrespective of their visibility and time of discovery of effect.

12.4 Second Parameter: Nature of Responses

Since we have chosen to focus on negative impacts, most of the steps discussed in this section are remedial in nature. The ethical system ideated above may be too abstract and may not be directly applicable to all the stakeholders (designers, developers, regulatory authorities, government, etc.) but they need to be general enough to be able to be adapted to various needs and circumstances. For example, they should be general enough to create guidelines that could be used for designing of new products and services as well as serve as foundation for creating any laws, regulations or evaluation parameters. Hence, the proposed type of ethical system serves as a foundation for ethical evaluation of the entire process, right from conceptualization to release of product or service and its use by general public. Following are the examples of how such a system can be put to use before and after a product or service is in the public domain:

- Pre-emptive applications – Deriving ethical framework for developers and designers, educating the developers on ethical issues, appointment of a neutral and regulatory ethical agency for product evaluation, appointing dedicated ethicists in designing process, etc.
- Post-facto applications – Creating an ethical regulatory body, rating products and services based on operationalized ethical

system, raising awareness and educating users on the negative effects already in the limelight (like online bullying, sexual abuse, privacy infringement, etc.)

12.5 Third Parameter: The Foundational Values

Prima facie, the question about the nature of the foundational values that should guide the ethical examination of IT products and services might look to be unanswerable universally in relativistic and pluralistic era. But as a matter of fact, it is quite easy to respond to it with a practical and acceptable answer. If we go over the some of the critics that have been launched against the exclusive domination of the functional thinking in this context and the lack of ethical consideration, it is very easy to identify that they all stem from the same value or set of values stemming in turn from the ethical worldview which is called *humanism*. Thus, for example, many of the critics relate to agency and autonomy of any individual regardless of any characteristics as an intuitively obvious ethical starting point[162]. This value seems to them so "obvious" that they don't deem it necessary to justify their reliance on it. This intuitive reliance might seem "strange" or "unacceptable" if we think that for few billions of the population of our globe today (and for almost everyone roughly 200 years ago) agency and autonomy are far from basic value.[163]

---

[162] For example, Kat Zou in her aforementioned article. Natasha Lomas, "Duplex shows Google failing at ethical and creative AI Design", https://techcrunch.com/2018/05/10/duplex-shows-google-failing-at-ethical-and-creative-ai-design/, François Chollet, "What worries me about AI", https://medium.com/@francois.chollet/what-worries-me-about-ai-ed9df072b704

[163] Many of the cultures and societies in the world today may not subscribe to the superiority of individualistic values like agency and autonomy. For the sake of not delving into the discussion of ethical relativism and pluralism of different cultures which is an intellectual "endless abyss", we ignore the other starting points for this text. Hence, there could be other ethical system derived from

So, what is humanism?

This term has had several meanings in the last few centuries, not all of them referring to ethical views, but here we refer to ethics or holistic world view leading to comprehensive set of moral norms that replaces the religious views fundamental to European societies till the 16ᵗʰ and in many places till much later.

While for religion the ultimate value is the worshiping of God, for Humanism the ultimate goal of humanity and human societies should be the maximal flourishing of individuals.

The development of Humanism in Europe and other Western socie-ties was far from being linear, having many ups and downs, few of them horrible. Still as things are now, its values are foundational not only to liberal democracies, legislation and constitution but to the way of living and thinking basic to most of their citizens.

What does "flourishing" mean in this case?

Here too, among the several answers that have been given to this question we refer to the Millean (John Stuart Mill's) view who claimed that flourishing means living a life of happiness. He deduced all his ethi-cal maxims from this basic maxim of maximal enhancement of individ-ual happiness and few psychological assumptions about "human nature" or the conditions that have to be met to maximize individual's chances for happiness. Our choice of Mill's view stems first and foremost from this "educational" or "developmental" conceptions of ethics.[164] The de-velopmental nature of Mill's ethics is important since the same condi-tions that he believed should be adopted by Democratic societies to en-

---

other foundational values like family, community, religion, etc. centric values. We don't believe there is a point in aspiring to create one ethical system com-mon to all the cultures. Even within the western cultures, humanism has been interpreted in many ways of which we chose one.

[164] As opposed to religious and some rationalistic ethics like Kant's that derived their values from what they were convinced to be "categorical imperatives" that are dictated by God or necessitated by reason.

hance the happiness of individuals can serve as foundational to assessment of ICT products and services and, in the best case, to their design.
That is, if we identify with Mill's starting point that the happiness and
flourishment of all individuals is the basic ethical maxim, a view which
we find hard to object to and was adopted in the last decades in the various declarations of the United Nations, UNESCO, OECD[165] and other
national and international constitutions.

Another reason that guided us to the choice of his ethics was the fact
that he was the leading Humanistic thinker in the 19th century and his
view penetrated to the subconsciousness of Liberal Democratic way of
life and legislation.[166]

Happiness in Mill's context stems from:

- One's awareness to one's motivation and ability to take foundational decisions about one's life himself, on the basis of their
  rational judgment as well as their ability to strive to implement
  them, though naturally may not always succeed (henceforth:
  Self Direction).

- One's awareness of the fact that they do their best for locating
  those activities or ways of life that satisfy them by the mere
  fact of being involved in them regardless of external rewards
  like money, recognition and power (henceforth: *Self Fulfilment*).

Without going into the 2500 years of debate on the more concrete
meaning of "happiness", it should be emphasized that Mill's understanding of happiness (called today following Aristoteles' "eudemonic") is
very far from what is known as the "hedonistic" understanding of happi-

---

[165] As clear with the parameters of OECD Better Life Index -
http://www.oecdbetterlifeindex.org/#/11111111111
[166] His opposition to state paternalism which led to the legitimation of "non-
conventional" sexual identities in the last decades and inspired the struggle to
legitimize the use of "light drugs" and other struggles that express the objection
to any "big brother" dictating individual's ways of life "for their own benefit

ness consisting of simple maximization of pleasures (or "fun"), which can be achieved without any effort by the individual, if lucky. This eudemonic understanding relies on the individual's deep volvement and struggles for knowledge of his personality profile (*self-knowledge*), achieved through *exploration* and *reflection* (in Mill's phrase *"experimentations in life"*). While it certainly is compatible with having "fun" or enjoying some of the authentic processes one is involved with, it can also be compatible with being challenged and going through periods of frustration, anger and even depression in following one's values and interests.

Here arises the next question: what should be the social educational processes that lead to the happiness in Mill's eudemonic sense?

These conditions consist of society allowing each individual (from as young an age as possible) the following as long as they don't fringe on the same rights of other individuals:

- The freedom to act as one wills.
- Being accepted and respected by society at large, whatever one's interests and way of life are.
- Enjoying security for his life, body and possessions.
- Enjoying basic economic security.
- Enjoying access to "plurality of experimenting" i.e. as many activities and ways of life as possible which one could explore in order to enhance one's *self knowledge*, *self-direction* and *self-fulfillment*.
- Enjoying the basic education needed for allowing one to take advantage of these conditions for life of *self-direction*, *exploration*, leading to *self-knowledge* and *self-fulfillment*.

12.6   Fourth   Parameter: Cultural   Foundations of an Ethics Framework

As indicated above, the ethical framework suggested has to be also grounded in society's cultural foundations. The reasons are simple but important.

First, it should be made clear to the stakeholders that the ethics are not arbitrary but are derived from the foundational values of their own lives and culture. This could bring a positive change in their psyche and emotional involvement when they realize that these issues are close to their own lives and of their loved ones. In this case, there will be higher chance that they will continue to take it seriously once they enter the gates of their workplaces.

Second, if the stakeholders understand the deep cultural historical roots of the ethical framework, their development and their rationale, the easier it will be for them to work with its operational guidelines or be creative in adapting them to specific cases or improving on them or developing new ones if needed.

In other words, the work of critical examination of ICT products cannot be done mechanically. It requires deep understating of and obviously identification with its roots, rationale and the way a specific relevant ethical value relate to the holistic picture.

To put it in more concrete terms, a lot of the criticism against the infringement of individual's right to privacy of their information or of not being influenced by biased information is done in the name of the value of "agency". But if people ask why agency is so important, why is the infringement of this value so bad, the Millean humanistic view is the best way we can think of bringing the answer home to them.

12.7   Fifth   Parameter: Ethical   Framework Operationalization

Here we have arrived to the lower though (very likely) the most important layer of the ethical framework; operationalization. Since the basic social principles that were presented about do not suffice to support stakeholders in concretion. We will move by taking the following steps:

1. Presenting the well-being-oriented practical principles derived from Mill's ethics.

2. Showing realizations suggested by relevant contemporary research.

3. Substantiating the claim that these principles "can work" as ethical foundation for evaluating ICT products and services. We will do this by showing that:

    a) All the immoral uses/impacts popularly discussed can be shown to stem from one or more abovementioned principles.

    b) The uses/impacts that might not be in the limelight but are being discussed peripherally and/or academically also stem from the same principles.

    c) These principles can enable us to analyze "holistically" ICT products and services. Holistically is used here in at least two senses; i) approaching the same issue from different perspectives or levels, and, ii) going beyond criticism to suggestion of positive changes that enhance well-being of the users. We will demonstrate this through a case study of Facebook.

12.7.1 The Well-being-oriented Practical Principles Connected to Mill's Ethics

The task we face here is to operationalize Mills "developmental" (in the psychological sense of the term) or well-being-oriented ethics, by pointing to the main developmental recommendations required by them. Mill believed in natural human drive to explore, direct themselves and fulfill themselves if the aforementioned socio-ethical framework is given. He didn't pay enough attention in this context to the many opposite pressures acting in societies, communities and families which might act against these drives even if embedded in human nature (though he certainly was aware of them and related to them in other contexts).

Hence, he didn't develop *educational* guidelines for helping mainly young individuals but, in principle, individuals of all ages to have the psychological resilience that would encourage them to be autonomous and neutralize (at least to some extent) the negative social impacts thwarting happiness. These are the operational guidelines that can and to our belief should guide all stakeholders in their design or assessment of a technological products or services. In other words, the technological environment should pass on to users the same messages that the ideal care takers or friends should pass on, if desiring to enhance individual's happiness.

Mill's values are general and dictate the macro level socio-legal spheres of society but spirit of his ideas percolate through history of culture into the thinking of researchers working on much more practical and empirical aspects of psychology dealing with enhancing day to day lives and environment of individuals to maximize their well-being.

This was done by contemporary and empirically based very influential motivation theory. While never mentioning Mill, the developers of this theory were influenced by the humanist psychology of the mid-20th century, mainly by Maslow's and Rogers'[167] writings. These psychologists in turn portrayed the main elements of Mill's humanistic developmental view. What we relate to here is Self Determination Theory developed in the last few decades by Deci and Ryan[168] and today has been corroborated in many researches that relate to different countries, cultures, genders, age groups, minorities, etc. While being developed mainly in the educational context, it has been shown to be valid also for adults in various social contexts.

According to the Self Determination Theory (SDT), in order to develop as an individual enjoying well-being (the contemporary equivalent of Mill's "happiness"), one has to grow in an environment which maximizes one's basic needs. These needs being:

1. Sense of autonomy, which in turn can be divided to four elements:

   - Sense of *being free* or acting as one pleases, without having external obstacles
   - Sense of *self-direction* - feeling that one strives in his life to get his decisions independently and rationally and act in their light
   - Sens of *self-knowledge* - feeling that one strives in his life to explore various life situations in order to learn through experimentation the main characteristic of his profile

---

[167] Maslow, A. H. (1970). *New Knowledge in Human Values*. Chicago: Regency. Maslow, A. H. (1968). *Toward a Psychology of Being* (2nd ed.). Princeton, NJ: D. Van Nostrand Co. Maslow, A. H. (1943). "A theory of human motivation". Psychological Review, 50(4), 370–396. Rogers, C. R. (1980). *A Way of Being*. Boston: Houghton Mifflin. Rogers, C. R. (1969). *Freedom to Learn: A View of what Education Might Become*. Columbus, OH: Charles Merrill.

[168] Ryan, R. M. & Deci, E. L. (2000) "Self-Determination Theory and the Facilitation of Intrinsic Motivation, Social development, and Well-Being", *American Psychologist*, 55, 1, 68-78.

(one's internal motivations, capacities, performance styles and values)

- Sense of *self-fulfillment* - feeling that one strives to fulfill his interests and values the best way he can in light of the circumstances he lives in, his abilities and performance styles.

2. Sense of unconditional acceptance i.e. being psychologically accepted as one is, whatever one does and whatever one's way of life is. This doesn't mean that one cannot be judged or corrected when mistaken but these are only his activities or some aspects of them that can be so judged or corrected not his identity.

3. Sense of competence i.e. feeling that one is able "to cope" with challenges in his environment, which is compatible also with failures while being motivated to learn from them.[169]

12.7.2 Realizations Suggested by Relevant Contemporary Research

The theory requires from whoever has impact on children or adults to act in order to enhances these needs and supplies parents, teachers (concerning children) or managers or peers and colleagues' quite simple recommendations how to act towards others in order to satisfy these needs. Below we will mention some of these recommendations, or guidelines, referring only to children but they are true in all context regarding all ages and most importantly applicable to the impact ICT services and products has on users.

---

[169] These conditions are my interpretation of the aforementioned work of Deci and Ryan which is complemented by Assor, A. (2012) "Allowing Choice and Nurturing an Inner Compass: Educational Practices Supporting Students' Need for Autonomy", in: S. L. Christenson et al. (eds.) *Handbook of Research on Student Engagement*, Springer, 421-439.

Concerning the first condition i.e. sense of autonomy, restraining as little as possible the children's freedom to act and relate approvingly to their basic decisions and try to support them. If the parents think a decision is wholly or partly wrong, they can express their view and try to substantiate them, while according the utmost respect to the child's view and letting him express his justifications to his view and relate to them respectfully. At the end of the day in the case of child, the parent's and in the case of employee, the boss' decision is the final decision but this has to be done in as justifiable manner as possible.

In his conversation with the child, the parent has to prevent from making remarks that accord importance to success or failures according to external standards, but emphasize the child's learning of himself, and the explorative learning paved with mistakes that lead to it. He should also do his best to converse with the child about his explorative way and sustain it in his remarks while and after making them and reflect on his responses to enhance one's self knowledge. It will be even better if the adults (parents or bosses) can offer modeling of behavior based on *self-direction*, *self-learning*, and *self-fulfillment* in their life and whenever possible speak, without being pushy, with the children or employees on their strategies of achieving these modes of living and acting. Of course, the parent should avoid judging the child's behavior comparatively in light of the behaviors of other "preferred" or "more successful" children or employees.

As for the second condition i.e. sense of unconditional acceptance, caretakers have to communicate the message to the child that their love for him or acceptance of him are not conditioned to any activity of his and certainly not on his success or failure in realizing this activity. This doesn't mean they shouldn't be interested in the child's activity. In fact, the opposite is true. They can make critical remarks on a certain activity while making it absolutely clear that the remarks are made concerning a very specific activity and not concerning the child himself being "bad", "good", "stupid" or "smart". They should also abstain from "glorifying" the child as "genius" or "the most beautiful child", and certainly not humiliate him with negative remarks.

For the third condition i.e. sense of competence, caretakers should design the environment in which the child acts in a way which will be challenging but not too difficult to lead the child to despair. They should also do their best to represent failures and mistakes as being essential part of learning and developing as opposed to the norm in most schools or families. It is not success in reaching the ultimate goals that should be celebrated or failures that should be condemned, but the mistakes and their productive use for further learning and development that should be appreciated.

The basic claim made by the developers of this theory and corroborated by hundreds, if not thousands, of researches in different countries cultures, and concerning different ages, genders, social around etc. is that human beings have:

- The needs for sense of autonomy
- The need for sense of acceptance, and
- The need for sense of competence

These needs can be satisfied only if the environment and meaningful individuals relate to them in appropriate ways. Once these basic needs are met, the level of well-being increases as well as their personal flourishment and development. If these needs are not satisfied, much energy will be dedicated by individuals to deal with the emotional pain, fears and anxieties stemming from their lack, which will decrease meaningfully their well-being and personal flourishment.

As claimed, the researchers in this domain refer mainly to children since they act and think within educational contexts, but they make it clear that the same needs exist throughout the ages and if catered for they will increase individual's chances for well-being and flourishing in all ages. And there have been many researches that corroborated this claim concerning adults in working places and organizational setting.

From this theory stem two basic rights that would commit any individual in a Humanistic milieu. Each individual has the right for utmost well-being and flourishing. Hence,

- Each individual has the basic rights for their above three needs to be respected and catered to.

- Each individual should be morally committed to respect and cater to these needs of others.

Now it is this ethical foundation that makes it easier to:

a. Understand all prevailing worries concerning ICT and evaluate them in in light of more basic rights they stem from.

b. And not less importantly, look for guidelines for the design of new better technologies, and policy making concerning encouraging the development of such developmental and hence ethically better products and services

12.7.3 Substantiating the Claim

a) Popular discourses in light of well-being-oriented ethical values

The right for privacy is in the center of many ongoing debates and considerations. The right of privacy is necessary for the catering for one's right for *self-direction*. This is the case since the private information stolen from an individual can be used to manipulate or threaten her, or the mere fear of being manipulated or threated might limit her actual freedom and ability for *self-direction*. The same is true concerning the request that the information that one gets not being biased by any foreign interest. Since this can lead to infringement of the right of the individual for *self-direction* according to their best judgment. It can also lead to guidelines for decision about policy making, regulation or illegal procedures.

For example, based on this ethic, regulator or courts could decide on how harmful the stealing of information about one or biasing the information an individual gets can actually harm their right for *self-direction*. Cases in which the harm is not obvious or not "heavy" might be considered less grave than cases in which it is obvious and heavy. The recent investigation by the US government of Facebook regarding allegations of manipulation of public opinion through "fake news" stems from this very ethical foundation.

Shaming and verbal abuse, as opposed to rational discussion about specific activity or opinion of an individual, directly violate the individual's right for unconditional acceptance. The line separating these two poles might be sometimes thin. The question that should help us distinguish between them are:

- Is the critic *ad hominem* i.e. is the person being attacked for some of his evil personality characteristics, or
- Is it focused only on a certain view they expressed or activity they performed?
- Even if the second possibility is the case, is the critic substantiated by relevant arguments, based on irrefutable factual claims?

If the critic consists of using derogatory and opinionated arguments to the saying or activity but not sustained by factually based irrefutable claims, it has no value whatsoever. It only negative impacts the concerned individual and should be limited as much as possible.

Another concrete danger is addiction of users to games, social media or pornographic content.[170] The development of such addiction is crucially foundational to the business model of many companies. These in turn dramatically infringe on the individual's right for *self-direction*, *self-knowledge* and *self-fulfillment* since the activities he is made addict-

---

[170] An example being the application of what is being learnt in Persuasive Technology Lab at Stanford to "engineer addiction" while the same can be used as a "cure", https://www.wired.com/story/phone-addiction-formula/

ed to are mostly not relevant to those that will render his life happy and fulfilled.

Finally, the biggest fear of all, though somewhat further on the timeline; the conquest of humanity or its manipulation by artificial intelligence smarter than its creators. This fear, while it was taken by the stakeholders as science fiction or horror story until few years ago, is expressed today as real fear by "insiders" in the industry.[171] It represents the deep importance of the experience of true *self-direction* to human beings, as opposed to an experience of manipulated life. Many years before the development of AI, Mill claimed (in *On Liberty*) that if suggested to give up this right and transfer our decisions to a machine that will accept for us the best possible decisions and will lead us to much better consequences in life then we could have arrived to by directing ourselves, we will categorically refuse.

This is the case since being the "owners" of our life is essential and necessary element for having a good life or well-being. We will prefer it to being "managed" by much more cost-effective machines.

b)   *"Dimly lit" discourses in light of well-being-oriented ethical values*

---

[171] "I'm increasingly inclined to think that there should be some regulatory oversight, maybe at the national and international level, just to make sure that we don't do something very foolish. I mean with artificial intelligence we're summoning the demon.", Elon Musk warned at MIT's AeroAstro Centennial Symposium. "I don't want to really scare you, but it was alarming how many people I talked to who are highly placed people in AI who have retreats that are sort of 'bug out' houses, to which they could flee if it all hits the fan." James Barrat, author of *Our Final Invention: Artificial Intelligence and the End of the Human Era*, to the *Washington Post* . "We must address, individually and collectively, moral and ethical issues raised by cutting-edge research in artificial intelligence and biotechnology, which will enable significant life extension, designer babies, and memory extraction." Klaus Schwab; all quoted from Bernard Marr, Best Quotes about Artificial Intelligence, Forbes Media, https://www.forbes.com/sites/bernardmarr/2017/07/25/28-best-quotes-about-artificial-intelligence/

When seen in light of well-being-oriented ethical values, the gravity of the impacts like erosion of our ability for rational systematic thinking or the impoverishment of our language (often connected to the first) can be truly assessed. Rationality and systematic thinking are the tools used for striving for *self-knowledge* and knowledge of one's environment which is basic to *self-direction*, which in turn is necessary for *self-fulfillment* and well-being. It is also true for emotional shallowing since the emotions are the drive and content of *self-fulfillment*. Even though these phenomena may be difficult to draw enough limelight to (due to aforementioned reasons), their impact to the well-being of the users can be clearly shown to be quite grave and not ignorable at all in light of these values.

   c) *A case study of holistic analysis based on the well-being-oriented ethical values*

Here, we refer to the more futuristic (and for now, seemingly very hypothetical) scenario in which the designers of games, social networks and all other ICT products and services which impact individuals' lives and development should be guided by the need to cater to the basic human right for well-being, and to the basic needs (or secondary rights) arising from it i.e. the satisfaction of needs for *self-direction*, *self-knowledge* and *self-fulfillment*. Such catering might take several ways:

- Eliminating the elements that cause the infringement of these rights, or
- Limiting them as much as possible, or
- Compensating for the harms done by these infringements by raising awareness to them facts in various ways.

We relate to several ways of dealing with such challenge since the main obstacle such reforms in the design and use of ICT products and services have to face is their clash with the business models of many companies using strategies mentioned before to attract as many users for as long time as possible to be attractive enough to advertisers (one of the biggest revenue source). These business models should be taken very seriously in most attempts to ethically reform or regulate technology since the interests of the companies and national economy are of utmost importance in a free market economy (and any scenario that doesn't suppose such an economy dooms itself to irrelevance). This might require the combination of multiple measures that lead to optimal results.

Let's take "the recent bad guy" Facebook (and many similar social networking websites) for our case study. It seems that everything that could have been done to threaten user's sense of *self-direction* (through information theft) and sense of acceptance and the aspiration for *self-knowledge* (on which we will focus here) and through it, sense of autonomy and well-being, have been done by the developers and designers of this website/applications. It creates the now well-known phenomenon of the "Facebook self"[172] which stems from the fully transparent competition of numbers of friends/followers and likes/upvotes on which the addicting appeal of this website largely relies. It causes users to believe their friends "fare much better socially" because of more friends/followers and/or likes/upvotes.

This encourages users to portray a false "sexy" or "cool" self that can be very far from who they really are. This, in turn, gravely infringes on their capacity for *self-knowledge* and through it, *self-direction* and *self-fulfillment.* How can an individual who focuses on upgrading his social status in the very narrow framework of maximization of fun, or social power, as measured numerically and transparently to all, aspire for *self-knowledge* and *self-fulfillment*? It certainly also severely threatens one's sense of acceptance since there always will be users who will have higher numbers of friends/followers or usually larger number of enthusiastic likes/upvotes than her.

---

[172] Oren Gil-Or, Yossi Levi-Belz & Ofir Turel (2015). "The 'Facebook-self': characteristics and psychological predictors of false self-presentation on Facebook", https://www.frontiersin.org/articles/10.3389/fpsyg.2015.00099/full

All this is achieved by the abovementioned very simple means basic to Facebook; the use of large network of friends and "likes", both being transparent to all. Omitting any of these three elements (which is very simple technologically) might meaningfully reduce the harms to user's development and long-term well-being. Obviously, any such change might reduce Facebook's attractiveness and affects its business model. Its motivation to do so might be enhanced only by external pressure, regulation etc.

Still, and here we reach the most important issue to us, Facebook ethicists (existing or imagined ones) could have warned, if relying on the suggested ethical view, about the harm of the business model relying only on means of attractivity that might work against the satisfaction of individual basic needs and chances for well-being.

Thus, as first step to improve this state of affairs, they could have suggested alternatives to the "likes" by verbal responses (which have some chance to lead to meaningful discussion). They also could have given users few levels of the reduction of transparency of the data concerning numbers of friends or likes. It could start by:

- Allowing the users to opt out of publicly displaying these numbers
- Making these numbers visible only to the users themselves by default with an option to display them publicly
- Completely eliminating the idea of keeping track of these numbers hence reducing the weight assigned to them

All the above steps are negative, in the sense of changing or eliminating the use of elements now existing in Facebook. The ethicists can also help tremendously in undertaking positive steps, i.e. developing elements that don't exist in Facebook now and that should support effectively the satisfaction of basic human needs and enhancing user's long-term well-being.

These could be based on harnessing the functions in Facebook that now are criticized as infringing on users' agency by accumulating information of user, analyzing by tracking them, their activities , analyzing the texts they write to find out their characteristics (depressive, anxious, etc.) as well as on many personality level leading to often knowing the users more than what users know about themselves (due to high level of forgetfulness of humans, biased memory, limited ability for tracking and even more limited ability to combine many and changing tracks to a changing personal profile and AI's ability to track multiple parameters and analytical ability which is much higher than humans for specific tasks).

This information is gathered today mainly to sell it to interested advertisers or to manipulate user behavior and sometimes intelligence services. While it could have been used as the foundation of a *"humanistic mentor"* relying on the basic maxims of human development towards well-being; offering the users various ways in which they could use Facebook from forming a group with individuals with similar difficulties, capacities, interests, learning/working styles, etc. in order to overcome the weaknesses and enhance the strengths. Developing this idea further and discussing it is an entire exercise in itself.

We don't know to which extent such humanist mentor and groups based on its offers could have contributed to the attractiveness of Facebook and to its economic success in an alternative business model. We certainly don't know how much it will contribute to users' well-being. We can say that this is only one of the ideas examining improving them. What we are sure is that this is the way of thinking that developers, designers and ethicists should be committed to and do their best to realize in their work. It is certainly their moral duty.

12.8 Conclusion

We claimed in this paper that in order to render ethical thinking on ICT and its social and psychological impact, a coherent, well-grounded and as parsimonious as possible ethical model should be developed. That this model could be hierarchical started from abstract values, grounded in society's foundational values and legislation (or constitution) and gradually lead to general operational guidelines that when experimented with can be developed to categories of more specific ones.

In order to exemplify this appeal, we formed the following modes answering the basic questions any such model has to respond to:

What could be the objects of ethical criticism of ICT?

1. What should be the remedies suggested by it?
2. On what ethical view and values can it rely?
3. How can it be grounded?
4. How can it be operationalized, so it can guide developers, designers, policy makers, interested NGOs, regulators, journalists etc.?

Concerning the last two questions (the core of an ethical view), we relied on a combination of traditional humanistic philosophy (Mill's socio-political philosophy and intuitive psychology) and contemporary empirically based humanistic psychology. We made only primary simplistic steps. This model should be further developed and experimentalized while other humanistic models can be suggested in addition to or instead of the one described above.

Still, we tried to bring home to the readers the claim that without a comprehensive, coherent, parsimonious, grounded and operationalizable ethical model, ethical criticism will remain fragmented and hence less powerful, less influential and more arbitrary and intuitive.

13

DIGITAL HEALTH: MEETING ETHICAL AND POLICY CHALLENGES

*Effy Vayena / Tobias Haeusermann / Afua Adjekum /
Alessandro Blasimme, Switzerland / UK*

Abstract

Digital health encompasses a wide range of novel digital technologies related to health and medicine. Such technologies rely on recent advances in the collection and analysis of ever increasing amounts of data from both patients and healthy citizens. Along with new opportunities, however, come new ethical and policy challenges. These range from the need to adapt current evidence-based standards, to issues of privacy, oversight, accountability and public trust as well as national and international data governance and management. This review illustrates key issues and challenges facing the rapidly unfolding digital health paradigm and reflects on the impact of big data in medical research and clinical practice both internationally and in Switzerland. It concludes by emphasising five conditions that will be crucial to fulfil in order to foster innovation and fair benefit sharing in digital health.[173]

---

[173] Published in Swiss Medical Weekly, 2018; 148:w14571, 16.1.2018. doi:10.4414/smw.2018.14571. Publish with permission for non-commercial use. Open access.

13.1 Introduction

Digital health is a rapidly expanding medical field premised on the availability of ever increasing amounts of data about people's lifestyles, habits, clinical histories and pathophysiological characteristics. According to the US Food and Drugs Administration (FDA) "[t]he broad scope of digital health includes categories such as mobile health (mHealth), health information technology (IT), wearable devices, telehealth and telemedicine, and personalized medicine"[174]. These categories rely heavily on human health data. Conventionally, the collection of health data is mediated by officially licensed medical devices, such as diagnostic instruments or genome sequencers, operated by health professionals in clinical environments and under strict regulatory conditions. Moreover, clinical data are typically stored in public health registries, at hospitals or in the archives of individual physicians. Digital health, in turn, entails connecting health-related data, including data generated by patients themselves, and harnessing the medical potential of technological tools of common usage, such as smartphones, wellness bands, apps, social media and sensing devices disseminated in our dwelling environment. Most of these tools are not initially conceived for medical use and are not marketed as medical devices. Notably, however, some prominent digital health technologies already cut across the rigid distinction between licensed and ordinary gadgets, and the latter have also started to receive official designation as medical devices (see table 1)[175]. But digital health is not limited to ordinary technology, nor to ordinary-turned-

---

[174] U.S. Food and Drug Administration. [Internet]. Silver Spring: U.S. Food and Drug Administration; c1995-2017 [cited 2017 May 3]. U.S. Department of Health and Human Services; [about 2 screens]. Available from: https://www.fda.gov/medicaldevices/digitalhealth/#mobileapp.

[175] Elenko E, Speier A, Zohar D. A regulatory framework emerges for digital medicine. Nat Biotechnol. 2015;33(7):697–702. doi:. http://dx.doi.org/10.1038/nbt.3284 PubMed.

medical technologies. Certain digital health tools present entirely novel features, as in the case of digital pills that, thanks to a microcircuit activated upon contact with liquids in the patient's stomach, can tell an external sensor whether and when a patient has taken his or her medication.

Table 1: Examples of licensed and unlicensed digital health technologies.

Company	Product	Type	Year of license	Licensing body	Description
Licensed					
AdhereTech, Inc.	Smart Pill Bottle[176]	Wireless pill bottle		FDA, CE, ISO	Smart wireless pill bottle capable of alerting patients to missed doses.
Airstrip Technologies	AirStrip ONE®[177, 178]	Mobile app	2014	FDA	Provides an interoperable platform that simplifies clinicians' and patients' access to diverse health data.
AliveCor, Inc.	Kardia Mobile[179, 180]	Wireless pad	2016	FDA	Portable electrocardiogram

---

[176] Adheretech.com. [Internet]. New York: AdhereTech Inc.; c2017 [cited 2017 July 21]. Available from: https://adheretech.com/.

[177] Airstrip.com. [Internet]. Texas: Airstrip Technologies; c2017 [cited 2017 July 21]. Available from: http://www.airstrip.com/.

[178] Food and Drug Administration. Section 5_510(k) Summary revised v3 [Internet]. Maryland: FDA; 2014 [citcd 2017 July 21]. Available from: https://www.accessdata.fda.gov/cdrh_docs/pdf13/k133450.pdf.

						device displaying results on a smartphone. It can detect cardiac anomalies such as arrhythmia.
Blue Spark Technologies, Inc.	TempTraq® [181, 182]	Disposable patch	Blue Spark Technologies, Inc.	TempTraq®	Disposable patch
Natural Cycles	Natural Cycles [183]	Wireless thermometer	2017	CE, ISO	App to keep track of ovulation and period, associated with a smart thermometer to determine fertile days. It can be used as a contraceptive.
Proteus Digital Health	Proteus Discover [184, 185]	Ingestible sensor, wearable	2014	FDA	An ingestible sensor mounted on a pill, which,

---

[179] Alivecor.com. [Internet]. San Francisco: AliveCor Inc.; c2017 [cited 2017 July 21]. Available from: https://www.alivecor.com/.

[180] Food and Drug Administration. Section 5_510(k) Summary revised v3 [Internet]. Maryland: FDA; 2014 [cited 2017 July 21]. Available from: https://www.fda.gov/cdrh/510k/k122356.pdf.

[181] Bluesparktechnologies.com. [Internet]. Ohio: Blue Spark Technologies Inc.; c2017 [cited 2017 July 21]. Available from: http://bluesparktechnologies.com/index.php/products-and-services/temptraq.

[182] Food and Drug Administration. Section 5_510(k) Summary revised v3 [Internet]. Maryland: FDA; 2015 [cited 2017 July 21]. Available from: https://www.accessdata.fda.gov/cdrh_docs/pdf14/k143267.pdf.

[183] Natural Cycles.com [Internet]. Stockholm: Natural Cycles [cited 2017 July 21] Available from: https://www.naturalcycles.com/en.

		sensor and mobile app			when swallowed, sends a signal to devices keeping track of compliance with prescriptions.
Non Licensed					
Butterfly Network, Inc[186].		Compact ultrasound			Portable ultrasound machines trained through deep learning algorithms.
Fitbit, Inc.	Fitbit Aria™[187]	Wi-Fi smart scale			Used in conjunction with an app, it tracks body mass index, weight, body fat percentage and lean mass.
Happify, Inc.	Happify™ [188]	Mental health app			Smartphone app aimed at alleviating stress and

---

[184] Proteus.com. [Internet]. Redwood City: Proteus Digital Health; c2017 [cited 2017 July 21]. Available from: http://www.proteus.com/.

[185] Food and Drug Administration. Ingestible Event Marker [Internet]. Maryland: FDA; 2014 [cited 2017 July 21]. Available from: https://www.accessdata.fda.gov/scripts/cdrh/cfdocs/cfpmn/pmn_template.cfm?id=k133263.

[186] Butterflynetinc.com. [Internet]. New York: Butterfly Network Inc. [cited 2017 July 21]. Available from: https://www.butterflynetinc.com/.

[187] Fitbit.com. [Internet]. San Francisco: Fitbit; c2017 [cited 2017 July 21]. Available from: https://www.fitbit.com/aria.

[188] Happify.com. [Internet]. New York: Happify Inc.; c2017 [cited 2017 July 21]. Available from: https://my.happify.com/public/contact/.

					negative thoughts through techniques in the form of games and exercises.
MyFitness-Pal, Inc.	MyFitness-Pal [189]	Calorie counter app			Free app to keep track of calorie intake. It is said to help users who want to lose weight.

The defining feature of digital health, however, has to do with data rather than technology. What is distinctive about digital health in this respect, is that – typically through wearable, portable, ingestible or otherwise implantable devices – it generates a "seamless flow of critical medical data between patients, their families and their physicians"[190]. The ambition of digital health is therefore aptly described as generating a *circulation of data* from patients (patient-generated data), to devices and/or health professionals (who analyse and make sense of the data), and then back to devices that eventually provide the patient with information regarding their health status and how to manage it.

To this aim, phenotypic and behavioural information, as well as data about socioeconomic status and dwelling environment, need to be collected. Information posted on social media can also turn out to be poten-

---

[189] Myfitnesspal.com. [Internet]. MyFitnessPal Inc. c2005-2017 [cited 2017 July 21]. Available from: https://www.myfitnesspal.com/.

[190] Eisenstein M. Miniature wireless sensors presage smart phone medicine. Nat Biotechnol. 2012;30(11):1013–4. doi:. http://dx.doi.org/10.1038/nbt1112-1013 PubMed.

tially relevant to both individual and population health[191],[192]. Digital health thus inhabits what has been recently labelled an "evolving health data ecosystem"[193], a space that also includes data gathered by healthcare services, such as electronic health records, genetic or genomic data, diagnostic data, claims data and the like. According to some, given their volume, complexity, variety and propensity to be analysed through data-mining techniques, such data qualify as big data[194] or, more precisely, as biomedical big data[195],[196],[197]. This expanded set of health-relevant data is expected to occasion huge progress in medicine, for example by helping people monitor their health status, assisting patients in coping with their conditions, inferring health-related issues earlier on, personalising treatment to individual patients' characteristics, improving outcomes, reducing costs and inefficiencies, and also boosting medical discovery and accelerating drug development. Admittedly,

---

[191] Flahault A, Geissbuhler A, Guessous I, Guérin P, Bolon I, Salathé M, et al. Precision global health in the digital age. Swiss Med Wkly. 2017;147:w14423. PubMed.

[192] Salathé M, Bengtsson L, Bodnar TJ, Brewer DD, Brownstein JS, Buckee C, et al.Digital epidemiology. PLOS Comput Biol. 2012;8(7):e1002616. doi:. http://dx.doi.org/10.1371/journal.pcbi.1002616 Pub-Med.

[193] Vayena E, Dzenowagis J. Langfeld M. [Internet]. Geneva: World Health Organization; c1948-2017 [cited 2017 May 3]. U.S. United Nations; [about 1 screen]. Available from: http://www.who.int/ehealth/resources/ecosystem/en/.

[194] Groves P, Kayyali B, Knott D, Van Kuiken S. The 'big data'revolution in healthcare. New York: McKinsey & Company; 2013.

[195]Weber GM, Mandl KD, Kohane IS. Finding the missing link for big biomedical data. JAMA. 2014;311(24):2479–80. doi:.http://dx.doi.org/ 10.1001/ jama.2014.4228 PubMed.

[196] Blasimme A. Healthcare meets big data: the science and politics of precision medicine. In: Blanchard A, Strand R, editors. Social, ethical and economic aspects of cancer biomarkers. Kokstad: Megaloceros Press; 2017. p. 95-110.

[197] Vayena E, Blasimme A. Biomedical big data: new models of control over access, use and governance. J Bioeth Inq. 2017;14(4):501–13. doi:. http://dx.doi.org/10.1007/s11673-017-9809-6 PubMed.

there are significant expectations of digital health and there is strong interest on the part of numerous stakeholders in promoting it and seeing it flourish. At the same time, for digital health to materialise several ethical and policy challenges need to be overcome[198].

To review these challenges, a multidisciplinary symposium was held at the University of Zurich (UZH) on 1 December 2016. The symposium, convened by UZH's Health Ethics and Policy Lab (now based at ETH Zurich), brought together different perspectives from national and international experts regarding the challenges that accompany the development of digital health. Participants included scientists, ethicists and lawyers, representative of national research institutions such as the SAMS (Swiss Academy of Medical Sciences) and the SNSF (Swiss National Science Foundation), as well as policy specialists from international organizations such as the OECD (Organization for Economic Cooperation and Development) and the WHO (World Health Organization).

Three key challenges impinging on the development of digital health were identified and discussed:

-How does digital health fare with respect to the demands of evidence-based medicine?

-How can public trust in digital health be generated and sustained?

-What policy gaps can and should be addressed through global policy instruments and what instead require specific initiative in the Swiss context?

Here, we provide key considerations on the above three questions, based both on the discussions held at the symposium and further litera-

---

[198] Vayena E, Gasser U, Wood A, O'Brian DR, Altman M. Elements of a new ethical framework for big data research. Wash Lee Law Rev. 2016;72(3):420–41. http://lawreview.journals.wlu.io/elements-of-a-new-ethical-framework-for-big-data-research/.

ture review. These considerations are of relevance to scientists, ethicists and public health experts, as well as developers and policy makers interested in assessing the impact of big data in medical research and clinical practice, both internationally and in Switzerland.

13.2 Digital Health and the Quest for Evidence

The clinical development of digital health applications is premised on the creation of very large data collections recording sensitive personal data. In the public sector, examples include: the 100K genomes cohort in the UK, which aims to sequence the genome of one hundred thousand NHS cancer patients by 2017; the All of Us cohort of the Precision Medicine Initiative in the US, which will collect samples, and phenotypic and clinical data from one million Americans; or the Million Veteran Program, which currently constitutes the largest genomic database in the world and also includes lifestyle information and access to electronic health records for research purposes[199]. Besides these large-scale public initiatives, the private sector is also collecting huge amounts of phenotypic and genetic data from users of health-related services and products. For example, as of June 2015, the genetic testing company 23&Me had collected and genotyped DNA from more than one million customers[200]. In June 2016, the US-based healthcare provider and insurer Kaiser Permanente announced the constitution of a research biobank pulling electronic health records, DNA and behavioural and environmental infor-

---

[199] US Department of Veterans Affairs [Internet]. Washington DC: The Department; c1930-2017 [cited 2017 Jul 20]. Office of Public and Intergovernmental Affairs; [about 2 screens]. Available from: https://www.va.gov/opa/pressrel/pressrelease.cfm?id=2806.

[200] Wojcicki A. Power of One Million. 2015 June 18 [cited 2017 Jul 20]. In: 23andMe. Blog [Internet]. Mountain View: 23andMe, Inc. c2007-2017. [about 2 screens]. Available from: https://blog.23andme.com/news/one-in-a-million/.

mation from 500 000 people[201]. Finally, end-users of digital health devices such as heart monitoring apps or fitness gadgets also contribute vast amounts of data to service providers. Such data can be cross-linked to other existing large-scale repositories both for research purposes and for developing new digital health services to users and professionals alike.

13.3 The Evidence Base for Digital Health

Mining large-scale data repositories creates challenges regarding data management, privacy protection and oversight mechanisms. Other challenges, however, relate more directly to the composition of such repositories and to the tools employed to mine the data they contain. For instance, the use of convenience samples to populate precision medicine and precision public health cohorts can bias the sample compositions and compromise the representativeness of target populations[202,203]. Such issues can affect the quality of the evidence derived from digital health research and employed in digital health-based interventions, both at the individual and at the population level. Taking into account ethnicity, age, sex, socioeconomic status and geographical distribution in recruiting research participants thus seems crucial to ensure the generalisability of research findings. Similarly, the representativeness of the datasets

---

[201]Kaiser Permanente [Internet]. Oakland: Kaiser Foundation Health Plan, Inc.; c2017 [cited 2017 Jul 20]. [about 2 screens]. Available from: https://share.kaiserpermanente.org/article/kaiser-permanente-launches-research-biobank-aims-to-transform-health/.

[202] Khoury MJ, Evans JP. A public health perspective on a national precision medicine cohort: balancing long-term knowledge generation with early health benefit. JAMA. 2015;313(21):2117–8. doi:. http://dx.doi.org/ 10.1001/jama.2015.3382 PubMed.

[203]Blasimme A, Vayena E. "Tailored-to-you" - public engagement and the political legitimation of precision medicine. Perspect Biol Med. 2016;59(2):172–88. doi:. http://dx.doi.org/10.1353/pbm.2017.0002.

employed for product development and the robustness of analytic tools to mine such datasets can affect the development of effective digital health services and devices by private companies.

There seems to be room for precompetitive research in this area in order to at least create standards and possibly reference datasets to enhance reproducibility. Meanwhile, progress in regulatory science should enable better assessments of evidence for safety, efficacy and cost-effectiveness. In both cases, policy stimulus appears crucial to achieve tangible results. As for more user-oriented digital health applications, as with products and services developed outside the realm of licensed devices, there is the need to enhance transparency and accountability by adopting forms of sector-specific self-regulation and adhering to robust corporate responsibility schemes.

Data variety is also a key issue in digital health. For example, although genetics can be extremely informative from a medical point of view, with a few notable exceptions the contribution of genetic variation to most common chronic conditions is either unknown or relatively small. Instead, other types of information, such as levels of physical activity, diet and socioeconomic factors, are better suited for predicting the risk of developing a chronic disease[204]. Therefore, to harness the full potential of data mining and predictive analytics in digital health, genomic data alone are insufficient.[205, 206]

Novel modes of evidence generation could take into account multi-dimensional and unstructured data along with conventional clinical

---

[204] Khoury MJ, Iademarco MF, Riley WT. Precision public health for the era of precision medicine. Am J Prev Med. 2016;50(3):398–401. doi:. http://dx.doi.org/10.1016/j.amepre.2015.08.031 PubMed.

[205] Rubin R. Precision medicine: the future or simply politics? JAMA. 2015;313(11):1089–91. doi:. http://dx.doi.org/10.1001/jama.2015.0957 PubMed.

[206] Coote JH, Joyner MJ. Is precision medicine the route to a healthy world?Lancet. 2015;385(9978):1617. doi:. http://dx.doi.org/10.1016/S0140-6736(15)60786-3 PubMed.

measures. For example, in health outcomes research or assessment of long-term effects of drugs and interventions, pragmatic trial designs are raising considerable interest. Such studies employ less restrictive inclusion criteria than traditional clinical trials and allow for concomitant morbidities and medications. Such models rely on "real-world data" collected from actual patients[207]– data that would simply not be available in randomised controlled trials. Real world data include medical records, data from portable devices and social media, as well as environmental and socioeconomic data. Other than saving on the high costs of randomised controlled trials, pragmatic trials based on reals world data promise to be more representative of real populations. At least when risks are deemed reasonably low, real-world evidence obtained through pragmatic designs could thus be used in support of regulatory decisions about the safety and efficacy of digital health devices and applications. Moreover, real-world evidence could also be employed to retrospectively assess digital health applications that reached the market without being cleared by regulatory agencies.

The technologies that are enabling extensive data collection and the development of digital health can be applied to both individual and population health issues, contributing to the emerging fields of precision medicine and precision public health, respectively.[208,209,210,211] Both the

---

[207] Jarow JP, LaVange L, Woodcock J. Multidimensional evidence generation and FDA regulatory decision making: defining and using "real-world" data. JAMA. 2017;318(8):703–4. doi:. http://dx.doi.org/10.1001/jama.2017.9991 PubMed.

[208] Collins FS, Varmus H. A new initiative on precision medicine. N Engl J Med. 2015;372(9):793–5. doi:. http://dx.doi.org/10.1056/NEJMp1500523 PubMed.

[209] Khoury MJ, Evans JP. A public health perspective on a national precision medicine cohort: balancing long-term knowledge generation with early health benefit. JAMA. 2015;313(21):2117–8. doi:. http://dx.doi.org/ 10.1001/jama.2015.3382 PubMed.

former and the latter promise more tailored interventions in their respective domains, progress in the understanding of disease causes and outcomes, along with reduced costs and improved access to effective healthcare. Both precision medicine and precision public health have specific sets of ethical implications[212],[213]. In such areas, larger, more representative and diverse databases are expected to tackle very well-known issues of external validity that afflict randomized controlled trials[214],[215]. Yet this prospect is affected by the challenges discussed above. Moreover, the use of artificial intelligence (AI) and deep learning[216] to mine such large data repositories has led many to think that digital health can dispense with mechanistic explanations and hypothesis-driven research, replacing them with mere algorithm-guided searches for correlations between phenomena in large-scale observational stud-

---

[210] Khoury MJ, Iademarco MF, Riley WT. Precision public health for the era of precision medicine. Am J Prev Med. 2016;50(3):398–401. doi:. http://dx.doi.org/10.1016/j.amepre.2015.08.031 PubMed.

[211] Flahault A, Geissbuhler A, Guessous I, Guérin P, Bolon I, Salathé M, et al.Precision global health in the digital age. Swiss Med Wkly. 2017;147:w14423. PubMed.

[212] Sankar PL, Parker LS. The Precision Medicine Initiative's All of Us Research Program: an agenda for research on its ethical, legal, and social issues. Genet Med. 2017;19(7):743–50. doi:. http://dx.doi.org/10.1038/gim.2016.183 PubMed.

[213] Vayena E, Salathé M, Madoff LC, Brownstein JS. Ethical challenges of big data in public health. PLOS Comput Biol. 2015;11(2):e1003904. doi:. http://dx.doi.org/10.1371/journal.pcbi.1003904 PubMed.

[214] Rothwell PM. External validity of randomised controlled trials: "to whom do the results of this trial apply?". Lancet. 2005;365(9453):82–93. doi:. http://dx.doi.org/10.1016/S0140-6736(04)17670-8 PubMed.

[215] Frueh FW. Back to the future: why randomized controlled trials cannot be the answer to pharmacogenomics and personalized medicine. Pharmacogenomics. 2009;10(7):1077–81. doi:. http://dx.doi.org/10.2217/pgs.09.62 PubMed.

[216] LeCun Y, Bengio Y, Hinton G. Deep learning. Nature. 2015;521(7553):436–44. doi:. http://dx.doi.org/10.1038/nature14539 PubMed.

ies.[217,218,219,220] It has been noted, however, that even if those methods prove effective in establishing robust correlations, controlled interventional, randomised trials on stratified patient cohorts will still be necessary to establish the safety and clinical utility of novel therapies or public health interventions[221].

13.4 Ethical and Policy Challenges in Digital Health

13.4.1 Privacy and Security

Most of the debate about big data uses for health purposes has focused on privacy. As more data sources become available and advanced analytics can be applied for various purposes, protecting privacy is undoubtedly a complex challenge. What contributes to this complexity is that standard mechanisms of protection such as anonymisation, notice and consent are excessively stretched in this environment of new capabilities. Consent for data uses can hardly include the exhaustive list of all possible future data uses[222]. In turn, anonymisation technologies, even if robust, still leave re-identification in the realm of possibility if

---

[217] Anderson C. The end of theory: the data deluge makes the scientific method obsolete. WIRED [Internet]. 2008 Jun [cited 2017 May 8]; [about 3 p.]. Available from: https://www.wired.com/2008/06/pb-theory/.

[218] Pigliucci M. The end of theory in science? EMBO Rep. 2009;10(6):534. doi:. http://dx.doi.org/10.1038/embor.2009.111 PubMed.

[219] Price WN. Black-Box Medicine. Harv. J. L. & Tech.2015;28(2):419.

[220] Mazzocchi F. Could Big Data be the end of theory in science? A few remarks on the epistemology of data-driven science. EMBO Rep. 2015;16(10):1250–5. doi:. http://dx.doi.org/10.15252/embr.201541001 PubMed.

[221] Khoury MJ, Ioannidis JPA. Big data meets public health. Science. 2014;346(6213):1054–5. doi:. http://dx.doi.org/10.1126/science.aaa2709 PubMed.

[222] Vayena E, Mastroianni A, Kahn J. Caught in the web: informed consent for online health research. Sci Transl Med. 2013;5(173):173fs6. doi:. http://dx.doi.org/10.1126/scitranslmed.3004798 PubMed.

enough resources were to be devoted to it. Data security has also been a challenge, with cyber attacks, hacking of databases and data kidnapping being reported frequently. Incidents of data breaches and "kidnapping" (data held by hackers for ransom) are on the rise. According to the Breach Portal of the Health and Human Services (HHS) Office of Civil Rights, millions of healthcare records have been affected to date. In May 2017, healthcare databases in one hundred countries faced a ransomware attack claiming a ransom of $300 in bitcoin to unlock affected machines[223]. The UK's Information Commissioner's Office notes that the health sector accounts for most of the data incidents reported to them. These incidents, along with growing public concerns about big data affecting most aspects of contemporary life, have contributed to a bleak picture of the future of privacy[224]. Understandably, such a picture does not create an environment conducive to the demands of digital health, namely easier data circulation between individuals, devices and institutions. Against this background, the public needs to be reassured that robust security measures are mandated and enforced through clearly articulated policies. Concerns can be addressed with the adoption of appropriate technologies, monitoring and evaluation of security systems, transparency and accountability mechanisms such as legal remedies and compensation for privacy harms resulting from security breaches. Security will continue to evolve, but the big data approach will continue to demand more technical skills, responsive policies and regulatory oversight.

---

[223] Gayle D, Topping A, Sample I, Marsh S, Dodd V. NHS seeks to recover from global cyber-attack as security concerns resurface. The Guardian 13 May 2017. Available from https://www.theguardian.com/society/2017/may/12/hospitals-across-england-hit-by-large-scale-cyber-attack.

[224] Information Commissioner's Office [Internet]. London: Information Commissioner's Office; c2017 [cited 2017 Jul 20]; [about 3 screens]. Available from: https://ico.org.uk/action-weve-taken/data-security-incident-trends/.

13.4.2 Trust

Essentially what is at stake is the creation of a culture of trust that will enable all stakeholders in the big data ecosystem to benefit from the development of digital health[225]. In particular, public trust in health data uses is of paramount importance. The recent case of the care.data in the UK serves as a good example of how mistrust on the part of the public can derail large-scale data initiatives (see table 2). But trustworthy digital health activities require more than privacy protection. Elements of trust include transparency, accountability, benefit sharing and certainly more clarity about data ownership and data control. What is important here is the realisation that trust cannot only be built through achieving just one element, but rather through a concerted effort to promote all of its elements. Therefore, trustworthiness cannot merely be achieved by innovative consent models offering more or less control of data uses. Rather, consent innovation has to also be accompanied by clarity on how individuals and communities will benefit from digital health developments, by oversight mechanisms that protect common interests and by accountability mechanisms that can sustain public scrutiny.

Table 2 Case study overview: care.data National Health Service (NHS) England[226],[227].

NHS launched care.data in 2013 as an initiative to collect and store patient data from GPs (general practitioners) around the country in the Health and Social Care Information Centre database (HSCIC; now NHS Digital).

---

[225] Tasioulas J, Vayena E. The place of human rights and the common good in global health policy. Theor Med Bioeth. 2016;37(4):365–82. doi:. http://dx.doi.org/10.1007/s11017-016-9372-x PubMed.

[226] Department of Health. Freeman G [Internet]. London: Gov.UK; c2016 [cited 2017 Jul 20]; Available from: https://www.gov.uk/government/speeches/review-of-health-and-care-data-security-and-consent.

[227] Carter P, Laurie GT, Dixon-Woods M. The social licence for research: why care.data ran into trouble. J Med Ethics. 2015;41(5):404–9. doi:. http://dx.doi.org/10.1136/medethics-2014-102374 PubMed.

HSCIS already collected hospital data. Analysing GPs data as well was supposed to improve outcomes and customer service, as well as to further understanding of diseases and treatments.
Despite initial endorsement by various professional societies, strong public reactions against the initiative were triggered by concerns about privacy, lack of transparency regarding data access and the involvement of commercial entities.
Reports by the National Data Guardian and the Care Quality Commission that highlighted that inadequacies in transparency and privacy led to the discontinuation of care data.
The reports emphasised that citizens should be able to exercise their "right to know how their data are safeguarded. They should be included in conversations about the potential benefits that responsible use of their information can bring. They must be offered a clear choice about whether they want to allow their information to be part of this."
Lessons learned: in order to build public trust in the use of health and care data, initiatives need to meet criteria of trustworthiness, transparency, open communication and a clear sense of the distribution of benefits.

13.4.3 Accountability

With automated data mining for decisions of clinical or public health relevance becoming one of the most promising features of digital health, accountability is of critical importance. In particular, the adoption of these new tools requires relevant adaptations in existing accountability standards. For instance, in the field of digital epidemiology, data mining can be used to analyse free, unstructured text from social networks in order to make predictions about the spread of infectious diseases. Moreover, mobile technologies can be used to target specific populations with health-related information that can help contain the spread of infectious diseases. These new approaches can increase the speed and accuracy of health dynamics monitoring, leading to more targeted and effective interventions. However, premature reliance on such innovative tools could lead to an inappropriate use of public resources, unnecessary public alarm and individual harm from dispensable medications [[228]. Similarly, it is anticipated that medical practice will increasingly be aided by AI algorithms for diagnosis, treatment decisions and surgical procedures [229]. Progress in such areas is expected to greatly improve the quality of healthcare provision for individual patients. Such tools can range from simply providing assistance to practitioners, to possibly one day being fully autonomous from human supervision[230]. Indeed, increasing sophistication could lead to more accuracy. However, as more AI-guided tools become autonomous, fewer human operators are able to override their decisions. Hence, AI-guided medical devices have the potential to jeopardise current norms of professional accountability in clinical practice, making it more complicated to trace responsibility back to individual practitioners. It is therefore crucial that *ad hoc*, robust evidence standards are elaborated to guide the adoption of digital health technologies in clinical practice[231],[232].

---

[228]Kawamoto K, Houlihan CA, Balas EA, Lobach DF. Improving clinical practice using clinical decision support systems: a systematic review of trials to identify features critical to success. BMJ. 2005;330(7494):765. doi:. http://dx.doi.org/10.1136/bmj.38398.500764.8F PubMed.

[229]Hsu W, Markey MK, Wang MD. Biomedical imaging informatics in the era of precision medicine: progress, challenges, and opportunities. J Am Med Inform Assoc. 2013;20(6):1010–3. doi:. http://dx.doi.org/10.1136/amiajnl-2013-002315 PubMed.

[230]Yang GZ, Cambias J, Cleary K, Daimler E, Drake J, Dupont PE, et al.Medical robotics - regulatory, ethical, and legal considerations for increasing levels of autonomy. Sci Robot. 2017;2(4):eaam8638. doi:. http://dx.doi.org/10.1126/scirobotics.aam8638.

[231]Elenko E, Underwood L, Zohar D. Defining digital medicine. Nat Biotechnol. 2015;33(5):456–61. doi:. http://dx.doi.org/10.1038/nbt.3222 PubMed.

[232]Elenko E, Speier A, Zohar D. A regulatory framework emerges for digital medicine. Nat Biotechnol. 2015;33(7):697–702. doi:. http://dx.doi.org/10.1038/nbt.3284 PubMed.

13.5 Governance Approaches in the Development of Digital Health

13.5.1 Global Perspective

The strong technological component of digital health does not imply that innovation in this area will affect only the most affluent countries. Recent figures published by the Global Observatory on eHealth of the WHO show that health systems in most countries increasingly rely on data[233]. In fact, the decreasing cost of digital technologies is making it possible also for low- and middle-income countries to adopt telehealth, mHealth, eLearning, electronic health records and big data. EHealth initiatives are underway in 83% of WHO Member States, and 90% of them have an eHealth strategy. Different forms of digital health and digital health technology, however, present different patterns of global distribution, with telemedicine being more widely spread than electronic health records, which are more commonly used than big data in healthcare settings. Therefore, despite the fact that digital health represents a global phenomenon, it is adopted and implemented differently across the globe.

Not surprisingly, from a global perspective the governance of health data appears patchy, with only about half of WHO countries having specific privacy protections in place for personal health data. Robust national data governance frameworks tailored to the needs of real populations are thus considered a precondition for digital health to deliver sustained health benefits and to meet global health objectives such as universal health coverage. In addition, the development of international

---

[233]World Health Organization. Global diffusion of eHealth: making universal health coverage achievable. Report of the third global survey on eHealth [Internet]. Geneva: WHO Document Production Services; 2016 [cited 2017 Jul 20]. Available from: http://apps.who.int/iris/bitstream/10665/252529/1/9789241511780-eng.pdf?ua=1.

interoperability standards should continue in order to improve the capacity to monitor health needs and to deliver more effective interventions.

International policy organisations have addressed data governance issues for digital health from a global perspective. The OECD, for instance, has published a set of recommendations for health data governance[234]. Besides endorsing the idea that better health information systems and more efficient data use can improve healthcare provision, the OECD focuses on ways to maximise the usability of data for public policy, ensuring that health data processing serves the public interest, and secures public trust in data-driven health systems. To this aim, the OECD highlights several areas of intervention, including: promoting public engagement of a wide array of stakeholders; fostering collaboration to enhance interoperability and data sharing; providing clear information to individual data subjects; ensuring appropriate informed consent procedures; pursuing accurate review of data access and data processing requests; promoting transparency through public information about data use; and adopting effective control and safeguard mechanisms to protect personal data.

At the European level, the recently promulgated General Data Protection Regulation[235], which replaced the Data Protection Directive of 1995, aims at creating a more homogeneous legal framework in European Union Member States for the governance of personal data, including personal health data. This new framework stresses the importance of explicit consent to data processing, but recognises that explicit consent is not always possible in the domain of scientific research, in which data

---

[234]Organization of Economic Cooperation and Development. Recommendations of OECD Council on Health Data Governance [cited 21 July 2017] Available from   http://www.oecd.org/health/health-systems/Recommendation-of-OECD-Council-on-Health-Data-Governance-Booklet.pdf.

[235]General Data Protection Regulation [Internet]. Brussels: European Union; 2016 [cited 2017 July 21]. Available from: http://ec.europa.eu/justice/data-protection/reform/files/regulation_oj_en.pdf.

originally collected for one project are likely to be re-used by multiple researchers for purposes unrelated to the initial one. The GDPR also recognises that data processing can take place without consent if there is a pressing public health need to be addressed. Similarly, certain informational rights such as the right to have one's data erased can be limited in the name of public health emergencies, while certain sensitive data – like genetic data, for instance – can enjoy special protections set by individual member states. At any rate, the governance of data processing for research purposes and the processing of data from health registries remain subject to national rules. In terms of governance, the GDPR puts the burden of demonstrating compliance with its provisions entirely on the shoulders of data controllers, thus considerably raising the bar of accountability demands in comparison with the previous data protection directive.

Governance should enable digital health innovation to address the challenges discussed above, which include not only accountability but also privacy, quality of evidence, data access and sharing, and ultimately trust. Essentially, these are five key conditions that can determine whether digital health innovation can lead to health benefit (fig. 1). It remains to be seen whether, and how, a global governance approach can achieve this. For any approach it will be crucial to ensure that all stakeholders are involved and engaged. In this respect, the emphasis that the WHO puts on public participation and engagement of broad arrays of stakeholders aptly recognises the need to ensure that digital health serves the public interest and facilitates patients' engagement in health-related decisions.

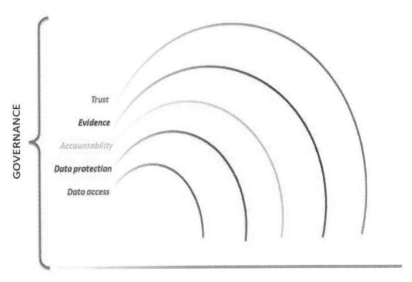

Figure 1 Conditions of innovation in digital health. This graph describes the conditions for innovation in digital health, for both licensed and non-licensed products and applications. Along the continuum from data generation to health impact, several conditions need to be fulfilled for digital health applications to have a tangible effect on individual and public health. To begin with, sufficient amounts of health data about individuals, as well as other types of data helpful to the detection, treatment and monitoring of health conditions in peoples and populations, need to be accessible to developers. Secondly, digital health products need to comply with data protection and privacy requirements in the countries in which they operate. Third, accountability mechanisms should be in place to trace responsibility for data uses and their consequences on individuals, families and communities. Accountability also ensures transparent communication of health relevant information to data subjects. Fourth, solid evidence of safety and efficacy should back medical claims of digital health products. More rigidly enforced evidentiary standards – including cost-effectiveness requirements – will foreseeably apply to digital health products seeking license from national regulatory agencies (such as the FDA or EMA). Yet, also non-licensed products can and should have sufficient evidentiary bases. Only the fulfilment of all such conditions creates trust in developers and regulators of digital health products and is conducive to fair benefit sharing of digital health innovation.

13.5.2 The Swiss Context

The development of digital health faces similar challenges in most developed countries. However, individual countries face these challenges to different degrees depending on the quality of their IT infrastructure, regulatory frameworks, healthcare systems and so on. Currently, a number of significant developments mark a turning point for digital health in Switzerland. First, the enactment of the Swiss electronic patient dossier legislation[236], on 15 April 2017, is an important step toward further digitalisation in the country's healthcare sector. The dossier, a voluntary electronic collection of personal medical documents, is designed to provide healthcare professionals with easier access to patient information, thus improving the safety and accuracy of diagnosis, with the ultimate goal of a positive impact on patient treatment and care. Whereas some Swiss regions have already put digital patient dossiers in place (see for instance the Geneva health information exchange *e-toile*[237], or the project *dossier patient partagé - Infomed* in the canton of Valais[238]), no provider has been officially certified to date, and both the legal and organisational prerequisites are being gradually implemented this year with a view to have the system running by mid-2018. Even though Switzerland benefited from the insights of major ongoing eHealth projects in Europe[239], the process towards more centralisation of

---

[236] e-health-suisse.ch. [Internet]. Bern: eHealth Suisse; c2007-2017 [cited 2017 Jun 1]. Kompetenz- und Koordinationsstelle von Bund und Kantonen; [about 2 screens]. Available from: https://www.e-health-suisse.ch/elektronisches-patientendossier.html [available in German, French and Italian only].

[237] Rosemberg A, Schmid A, Plaut O. MonDossierMedical.ch - the personal health record for every Geneva citizen. Stud Health Technol Inform. 2016;225:700–2. doi:. http://dx.doi.org/10.3233/978-1-61499-658-3-700 PubMed.

[238] Gnaegi A, Michelet C. Dossier patient partagé Infomed, qu'en pensent les médecins. Swiss Medical Informatics.2016;32. doi:. http://dx.doi.org/10.4414/smi.32.361.

[239] Lovis C, Looser H, Schmid A, Wagner J, Wyss S. eHealth in Switzerland - building consensus, awareness and architecture. Stud Health Technol Inform. 2011;165:57–62. doi:. http://dx.doi.org/10.3233/978-1-60750-735-2-57 PubMed

national digital health policy-making has been slow and non-linear[240],[241]. Nevertheless, the electronic patient dossier has overcome various political and organisational hurdles and can help advance other digital health services and initiatives, such as the cross-border harmonisation of e-medication records[242].

One crucial factor for the development of digital health is data accessibility. Ideally, data should be made available for further research uses that promise progress in individual or population health, and research and clinical institutions should be willing to open up their patients' data for that aim. Despite repeated appeals on the importance of data access, however, this practice is still implemented to an insufficient degree. Some barriers to data sharing are more regulatory in nature, such as the inability of data subjects to truly consent to uses that are not foreseeable at the moment of data collection. Some others are more organisational, as in the case of institutions that are reluctant to share data for liability issues. Currently existing patient data are collected through diverse technological systems and with variations in the consent that authorises further uses.

The second important development in Switzerland aims to address this issue through the proposal of a national broad consent template. Spearheaded by the Swiss Academy of Medical Sciences, a so-called "general consent" has been developed after extensive consultation with

---

[240] De Pietro C, Camenzind P, Sturny I, Crivelli L, Edwards-Garavoglia S, Spranger A, et al.Switzerland: health system review. Health Syst Transit. 2015;17(4):1–288, xix. PubMed.

[241] Dossier électronique du patient: la Suisse romande avance en ordre disperse [Electronic patient records: Switzerland is moving forward haphazardly]. Rev Med Suisse. 2015;11(499):2411. Article in French.

[242] Gall W, Aly AF, Sojer R, Spahni S, Ammenwerth E. The national e-medication approaches in Germany, Switzerland and Austria: A structured comparison. Int J Med Inform. 2016;93:14–25. doi:. http://dx.doi.org/10.1016/j.ijmedinf.2016.05.009 PubMed.

various stakeholders. The aim of this broad consent is to harmonise the conditions under which further data uses can take place. The model of broad consent has been highly debated in the bioethics literature, however, and commentaries range from full approval to complete rejection[243],[244],[245],[246]. Broad consent may not be the ultimate solution to conducting ethical secondary uses of data. However, if accompanied by robust oversight and accountability systems it can be a pragmatic solution that facilitates ethical digital health research[247].

The third relevant development in Switzerland is the launch of the Swiss Personalized Health Network (SPHN)[248]– a national initiative designed to build the necessary infrastructure to improve the utilisation of health-related data for research and innovation. The development of digital health, as that of other data-driven activities, depends on the development of appropriate technical standards to make data securely exchangeable and efficiently computable. Accordingly, the SPHN aims to

[243] Grady C, Eckstein L, Berkman B, Brock D, Cook-Deegan R, Fullerton SM, et al.Broad consent for research with biological samples: Workshop conclusions. Am J Bioeth. 2015;15(9):34–42. doi:. http://dx.doi.org/10.1080/15265161.2015.1062162 PubMed.

[244] Helgesson G. In defense of broad consent. Camb Q Healthc Ethics. 2012;21(1):40–50. doi:. http://dx.doi.org/10.1017/S096318011100048X PubMed.

[245] Hofmann B. Broadening consent--and diluting ethics?J Med Ethics. 2009;35(2):125–9. doi:. http://dx.doi.org/10.1136/jme.2008.024851 PubMed.

[246] Sheehan M. Can broad consent be informed consent?Public Health Ethics. 2011;4(3):226–35. Published online August 3, 2011. doi:. http://dx.doi.org/10.1093/phe/phr020 PubMed.

[247] Vayena E, Gasser U. Between openness and privacy in genomics. PLoS Med. 2016;13(1):e1001937. doi:. http://dx.doi.org/10.1371/journal.pmed.1001937 PubMed.

[248] Swiss Personalized Health Network [Internet]. Bern: Swiss Academy of Medical Sciences (SAMS); c1943-2017 [cited 2017 June 1]. Swiss Academy of Medical Sciences; [about 2 screens]. Available from: http://www.samw.ch/en/Projects/SPHN.html.

develop interoperability standards that will enhance data accessibility for research uses in Switzerland. The SPHN's vision on data governance is based on an ethics framework including four principles: respect for persons, data fairness, privacy, and accountability. Such a soft law instrument, while indicating the direction for improving data sharing, is also flexible enough to adapt to stakeholders' organisational needs.

13.6 Public Engagement

Citizens and patients are increasingly becoming the driving forces behind digital health developments[249],[250]. The extensive adoption and sustainability of health data exchange thus depend upon information technology that facilitates patient engagement and the earning of public trust[251]. To build on the support of the public, it should be made clear that digital health is a tool for citizens and professionals alike[252],[253],[254].

---

[249] Haeusermann T, Greshake B, Blasimme A, Irdam D, Richards M, Vayena E. Open sharing of genomic data: Who does it and why?PLoS One. 2017;12(5):e0177158. doi:. http://dx.doi.org/10.1371/journal.pone.0177158 PubMed.

[250] Blasimme A, Vayena E. Becoming partners, retaining autonomy: ethical considerations on the development of precision medicine. BMC Med Ethics. 2016;17(1):67. doi:. http://dx.doi.org/10.1186/s12910-016-0149-6 PubMed.

[251] Walker DM, Sieck CJ, Menser T, Huerta TR, Scheck McAlearney A. Information technology to support patient engagement: where do we stand and where can we go?J Am Med Inform Assoc. 2017;24(6):1088–94; Epub ahead of print. doi:. http://dx.doi.org/10.1093/jamia/ocx043 PubMed.

[252] Moen A, Hackl WO, Hofdijk J, Van Gemert-Pijnen L, Ammenwerth E, Nykänen P, et al.eHealth in Europe - status and challenges. Yearb Med Inform. 2013;8:59–63. PubMed.

[253] Patil S, Lu H, Saunders CL, Potoglou D, Robinson N. Public preferences for electronic health data storage, access, and sharing - evidence from a pan-European survey. J Am Med Inform Assoc. 2016;23(6):1096–106. doi:. http://dx.doi.org/10.1093/jamia/ocw012 PubMed.

This is a condition for fostering trust around digital health[255]. Furthermore, public policy needs take into account the digital divide and the capacity of citizens to engage with e-health[256],[257],[258],[259]. And whereas it is certainly important to promote collaboration among healthcare professionals and institutions, other agents, such as start-ups and the industry in general, ought to be included in the country's digital health transformation with mechanisms to incentivise partnership, investments and data sharing[260],[261],[262]. This can take the form of public/private partner-

---

[254] Leuthold M. Patients as partners for improving safety. World Hosp Health Serv. 2014;50(3):20–2. PubMed.

[255] Tripathi M, Delano D, Lund B, Rudolph L. Engaging patients for health information exchange. Health Aff (Millwood). 2009;28(2):435–43. doi:. http://dx.doi.org/10.1377/hlthaff.28.2.435 PubMed.

[256] Mantwill S, Monestel-Umaña S, Schulz PJ. The relationship between health literacy and health disparities: a systematic review. PLoS One. 2015;10(12):e0145455. doi:. http://dx.doi.org/10.1371/journal.pone.0145455 PubMed.

[257] Nohr C, Wong MC, Turner P, Almond H, Parv L, Gilstad H, et al.Citizens' access to their digital health data in eleven countries - a comparative study. Stud Health Technol Inform. 2016;228:685–9. doi:. http://dx.doi.org/10.3233/978-1-61499-678-1-685 PubMed.

[258] Sak G, Rothenfluh F, Schulz PJ. Assessing the predictive power of psychological empowerment and health literacy for older patients' participation in health care: a cross-sectional population-based study. BMC Ger-iatr. 2017;17(1):59. doi:. http://dx.doi.org/10.1186/s12877-017-0448-x PubMed.

[259] Romano MF, Sardella MV, Alboni F, Russo L, Mariotti R, Nicastro I, et al.Is the digital divide an obstacle to e-health? An analysis of the situation in Europe and in Italy. Telemed J E Health. 2015;21(1):24–35. doi:. http://dx.doi.org/10.1089/tmj.2014.0010 PubMed.

[260] Feldman HH, Haas M, Gandy S, Schoepp DD, Cross AJ, Mayeux R, et al.; One Mind for Research and the New York Academy of Sciences. Alzheimer's disease research and development: a call for a new research roadmap. Ann N Y Acad Sci. 2014;1313(1):1–16. doi:. http://dx.doi.org/10.1111/nyas.12424 Pub-Med.

ships[263], such as the Digital Switzerland Initiative[264] and the Openda-ta.ch Foundation[265].

Other innovative models to leverage private initiatives and foster public engagement are emerging. In Switzerland, the MIDATA coopera-tive is a case in point[266]. MIDATA offers data subjects the possibility of storing health data from different sources and leaves it to the data sub-jects to decide collectively on data access requests[267],[268]. All data con-tributors are equal shareholders of the cooperative, which is a not-for-profit entity and will re-invest any potential income generated by grant-

---

[261] Salter H, Holland R. Biomarkers: refining diagnosis and expediting drug development - reality, aspiration and the role of open innovation. J Intern Med. 2014;276(3):215–28. doi:. http://dx.doi.org/10.1111/joim.12234 PubMed.

[262] Leyens L, Reumann M, Malats N, Brand A. Use of big data for drug devel-opment and for public and personal health and care. Genet Epidemiol. 2017;41(1):51–60. doi:. http://dx.doi.org/10.1002/gepi.22012 PubMed.

[263] Chataway J, Fry C, Marjanovic S, Yaqub O. Public-private collaborations and partnerships in stratified medicine: making sense of new interactions. N Biotechnol.   2012;29(6):732–40.   doi:.   http://dx.doi.org/10.1016/j.nbt.2012.03.006 PubMed.

[264] digitalswitzerland.com. [Internet]. Zürich: digitalswitzerland; c2015 [cited 2017 June 1]. Available from: http://digitalswitzerland.com.

[265] opendata.ch. [Internet]. Zurich: Verein Opendata.ch, the Swiss Chapter of the Open Knowledge Foundation; c2012 [cited 2017 June 1]. Available from: https://opendata.ch.

[266] www.midata.coop. [Internet]. Zürich: MIDATA Genossenschaft; c2017 [cit-ed 2017 Jul 20]. Available from: https://www.midata.coop/.

[267] Hafen E, Kossmann D, Brand A. Health data cooperatives - citizen empow-erment.   Methods   Inf   Med.   2014;53(2):82–6.   doi:. http://dx.doi.org/10.3414/ME13-02-0051 PubMed.

[268] Hafen E. Midata Cooperatives - Citizen-Controlled Use of Health Data Is a Pre-Requiste for Big Data Analysis, Economic Success and a Democratization of the Personal Data Economy. Tropical Medicine & International Health [Inter-net]. 2015 Sep [cited 2017 July 20]; 20 (Supplement 1):129. [about 1 p.] Availa-ble from: https://insights.ovid.com/tropical-medicine-international-health/tmih/2015/09/001/midata-cooperatives-citizen-controlled-use-health/313/00060771.

ing access to its data. This unique model is already active in digital health-related projects in Switzerland and will promote the inclusion of patient-generated data that are needed to develop digital health into clinical applications.

13.7 Conclusion

Innovation in digital health faces several ethical and policy challenges. We have argued that, for digital health products and applications to produce tangible innovation and health impacts, be it at the individual or at the population level, five conditions need to be met. First, data are of paramount importance for digital health: access to sufficient amounts of data is thus a primary condition for the development of innovative diagnostic, therapeutic and monitoring tools is this area. Second, alignment with existing legal provisions regarding data protection, data security and privacy are key to digital health innovation. Legal frameworks can thus have a major impact in facilitating or hindering progress in this field. Nonetheless, legal provisions do not address the full range of ethical issues in data processing. Nor do they cover the full spectrum of legitimate concerns of data subjects. Third, robust and transparent accountability mechanisms should ensure the precise identification of responsibility for data uses and their consequences on individuals, families and communities. What is more, accountability also sets up mechanisms for communicating health relevant information to data subjects. Fourth, evidence of safety and efficacy is a significant condition for the success of digital health. Licensed digital health products and applications will have to go through extensive assessment processes and will have to meet cost-effectiveness requirement before they can be reimbursed by insurers and public healthcare systems. This does not, however, mean that unlicensed products and applications can lack some form of evidence to back up their claims. Fulfilling these requirements will foster the fifth condition for digital health innovation, that is, trust in both developers and regulators, which in turn will facilitate the uptake of digital health by healthcare providers and lead to fair benefit sharing of digital health innovation.

14

NET-WORTH:
FREEDOM, DIGNITY, INDEPENDENCE

Dan Shefet, France

Don't worry, I shall not mention Bentham, Orwell, Kafka, Foucault or Lessig. Enough reference has been made to their contributions to the debate (which has now been replaced by a "conversation"). Let's start with "Me-Too".

14.1 The Cultural Denunciation Syndrome

In my opinion this initiative or movement is different from what I call the "Cultural Denunciation Syndrome" ("CDS") i.e. the power unleashed by the Net to hurt anyone you dislike by public denunciation of some imagined "offence", crime or transgression.

Me-Too is different because it incorporates an important dimension of emancipation and transparency – it is not per se inimical to other values. It does however put other values at jeopardy and in particular due process and the right to representation and the presumption of innocence (the most important human right, if I had to pick just one), but it is not as such evocative of the CDS.

This syndrome has plagued civilization during various periods of history – the darkest in humankind's journey.

When denunciation becomes the accepted social norm and when it becomes politically correct and is no longer conduct frowned upon and exercised in secret and in shame, then we have accomplished yet another step in our regression towards "alienation of the other" (as Sartre would have put it).

Denunciation as a form of social behaviour has been the subject of moral and political philosophy throughout the ages. Probably the best known are the theories of J.S. Mill (The Utilitarian Imperative) and Kant (The Categorical Imperative). In our modern age of so-called "liberalism" Mill's philosophy clearly drives consensus more than Kant's, Spinoza's and Buber's - to our greatest misfortune: As soon as people invoke "the greater good", there is reason to be alarmed and the danger to individual integrity grows one further step when reference is made to principles or religion. When such acts against "the other" are justified by these mantras you can be certain that a dehumanizing agenda is at play.

In recent history publicly accepted and even encouraged denunciation reached its pinnacle during the years of the Second World War, but it has since been met with consensual/cultural disapproval. For many years it was labelled unacceptable social conduct. The horrors of the NSDAP's denunciation culture and the atrocities it produced have however unfortunately drifted into oblivion and the Net has contributed to its revival. Like a Phoenix the ugly hydra of denunciation is born again and flourishes as never before fueled, encouraged and nurtured by the Net. One may indeed speak of a new Culture of Denunciation or CDS.

Here are many reasons for this. The most significant seem to be the following: It has never been easier, cheaper, more harmful and riskless to denounce someone.

The Net is anonymous, pervasive, ubiquitous and delivers immediate gratification to the denunciator while at the same time the wolf pack of public tribunal has an insatiable appetite for denunciation.

A win – win for everyone except the victim.

It is often said that the Net fosters disinhibition. In reality the dynamics are much worse: The Net leads to alienation (as Marx would have said it had he been around today).

Concurrently, *reputation* has never meant as much as it does today.

You are your reputation. You are what other people say you are (courtesy Sartre) and to top it all off we have never been so wary of protecting ourselves against criticism (covering ourselves) both professionally and in our private affairs.

Our life has turned into a constant gauntlet run. A perpetual angst of offending anyone and behaving in any way outside the accepted formula. An escape from freedom. A fear of being noticed apart from artificial spates of intermittent fame. This age will be known as that of "Cultural Denunciation". But denunciation only works if the wolf pack believes it. It is the combination of Net facilitating, alienation and belief that allows CDS to prosper.

14.2 Gullible Robots and Truth

This is where the second unfortunate development kicks in. Instead of becoming smarter, our information glut has turned us into gullible robots. We believe everything we read – even Wikipedia. The test of truth is public opinion and correlation (statistics- not epistemology and certainly not cosmology).

This is exactly what Kierkegaard meant when he wrote: *"Truth always rests with the minority, and the minority is always stronger than the majority, because the minority is generally formed by those who really have an opinion, while the strength of a majority is illusory, formed by the gangs who have no opinion — and who, therefore, in the next instant (when it is evident that the minority is the stronger) assume its opinion ... while truth again reverts to a new minority."* (No, this is not, and has nothing to do with Nietzsche).

Unfortunately, the self-regulatory mechanism in Kierkegaard's criterion of truth no longer works. However, leaving the determination of truth to public opinion and free speech has no basis in reason. Kierkegaard's version of Oliver Wendel Holmes' famous metaphor of the man shouting fire in a theater expresses (hundred years before) a much deeper analysis and wisdom: *"A fire broke out backstage in a theatre. The clown came out to warn the public; they thought it was a joke and applauded. He repeated it; the acclaim was even greater. I think that's just how the world will come to an end: to general applause from wits who believe it's a joke."*

Truth is neither a function of the perceived speaker nor the audience. At this point it is important to recall the philosopher's unique analysis of the relationship between speech and understanding: *"People demand freedom of speech as a compensation for the freedom of thought which they seldom use"*. Have we given up our quest for the kind of knowledge and science that truly liberates us and allows us to shape our own ideas and opinions and if so is the reason that we no longer have the courage to fight for them? It may very well be argued that the greatest lie of all is that *free speech* is conducive to knowledge.

Present day epistemology has not only been reduced to correlations, but our window to the world around us now passes through an additional screen (not only in the physical, but also in the metaphysical sense). Our cognition of nature is biased by what may be described as "double phenomenology" (that's probably what Husserl and Hegel would have called it). We have never been further removed from "das Ding an sich".

I don't know what is the greatest danger to knowledge: Too much information (which equates no information to paraphrase Flaubert) or information controlled by black boxes, but I do know that the combination of the 2 leads to the collapse of enlightenment.

The latest invention which is peddled as a life saver by the Titans is "Artificial Intelligence", but it seems to me that we are witnessing an adaptation of the human brain to machine logic rather than the opposite.

We have been conditioned to "bit-thinking" so consistently and pervasively that we almost intuitively measure the value of our thoughts in terms of their algorithmic adaptability.

14.3 Information Control

There is yet another variable in the equation which leads to the demise of critical thought, individualism and the rise of alienation, intolerance and hatred and that is the undemocratic nature of the Net: *Never has so much information been controlled by so few* (thank you Churchill). This unique control of information had it been in the hands of government would have qualified as totalitarianism (as analysed by Hannah Arendt and Raymond Aron).

For some reason we seem not to be uncomfortable with the idea that our lives are controlled by less than a handful of private corporations (because as we have seen we are what other people say. We are not what we come from or what we make of ourselves. We are our Net reputation).

We seem to trust that these corporations are not evil. Is there any rational reason to do so? Haven't we learned from history that power corrupts? Have we forgotten Machiavelli? Have we forgotten that corporations owe allegiance to their shareholders and not to the community or values? Are financial fraud, corrupt practices and manipulation just fictions of our imagination? They never happened?

Power corrupts and *"absolute power corrupts absolutely"*. *"Word power is world power and the pen is mightier than the sword"* we are told, but we fail to grasp the wisdom and the consequences of those words. Otherwise we would have never accepted to surrender our freedom to a handful of corporate giants.

Recently Thaler and Sunstein have eloquently demonstrated how easy it is to "nudge" us into making decisions that are not necessarily in our best interest. I'm afraid that the power wielded by the Titans holds potential for exceedingly gentle nudges (sorry promised not to refer to Foucault).

14.4 The True Function of Speech

Why did we give up so easily and without a fight? There are multiple reasons, the primary being untamed celebration of technology for its own sake ("l'art pour l'art"), but that is just the tip of the iceberg.

If we are to understand the true dynamics of our present self-inflicted serfdom we need to dig deep into psychology, sociology and philosophy. The social function of language was already identified and explained by Aristotle and further developed by philosophers like Bergson, Chomsky and Austin.

We now start to understand that the true function of speech is a means of social coherence. We communicate because we are and to a large extent we are because we communicate. Speech is not simply a vector of arguments and opinions engaged in some metaphysical market place of ideas pitted against each other and subject to arbitration by a deus ex machina or Darwinistic selection process which ensures the survival of the fittest (a terrible notion given the impressive number of aborted and misfit mutations on the way...).

The revered Marketplace of Ideas is based on the assumption that syllogistic logic applies to ideas, but we have known since the scholastics that material logic often clouds Venn Diagrams (for instance "argumentatum ad hominem", "misericordiam" or "verecundiam").

Entertaining and cultivating the notion that speech is an agent employed in a marketplace the function of which is to ensure humankind's serendipity is a gift to the Titans, but the theory is seriously flawed.

Unfortunately, the myth appears to find a strong ally in recent Supreme Court judgements (it is well worth to be reminded that free speech absolutism was not always the philosophy of the Supreme Court, see below).

The Titans also understood that free speech as a notion carries extremely positive connotations and they cleverly anointed themselves as knights of The Order of Free Speech. Who would argue against the Holy Grail? The Titans were no longer just corporations driven by sheer cupidity. They became champions of a cause and obtained both popular and governmental backing. In reality I would venture that they couldn't care less about Free Speech, but it's a great platform.

Soon they would refer to the Arab Spring as a revolution brought about by their almost altruistic contribution to mankind conveniently forgetting the events that followed the "Spring" and likewise conveniently disregarding how these same services contributed to hatred and violence at the time and continue to do so all over the planet.

Their power has now become so pervasive that few are those that have the moral courage to challenge them and as the ace up their sleeve they do not hesitate to instrumentalize fairly recent Supreme Court ideology.

At this point it may be useful to recall that current Supreme Court practice was actually only promulgated in 1969 in Brandenburg v Ohio. Prior to that decision the pendulum swung several times between broadly permitted restrictions to speech and protection.

The Tech Titans have succeeded in expounding a Free Speech dogma which purports to be timeless and which is based on a Hobbesian view of the individual's "natural state" without regard to the social Aristotelean function of speech.

Very clever: They have concocted an ingenious variant of life style marketing combined with almost militant product allegiance fueled by evangelistic Free Speech fetishism and a sense of fraternal "geekhood".

"We" are not just users/consumers- we are part of a monumental movement which brings happiness (salvation ...) to the world and to those who haven't yet seen the light (does this remind you of the crusades and the crimes that took place in the name of Christianity during the age of colonialism and mercantilism?).

They have cleverly turned each and every one of us into their squires and sales reps. When Francois Hollande orchestrated his stunt after the horrendous terrorist attack on Charlie Hebdo and invited 57 heads of state to march through the streets of Paris (some 3,7 million people reportedly emulated this initiative all over France) he did so in the name of Free Speech. He would not have achieved these impressive numbers if he had called for a march against terrorism and he knew that.

Free Speech is an almost overpowering asset (Yes, unfortunately is has been appropriated by so many different commercial and political agendas that it is no longer a true value. If Free Speech was a copyrightable product the line of right holders would be infinite). If you can rally Free Speech on your side, you are sure to win.

I did not join the march. I felt something was wrong and understood what it was later when reading Emanuel Todd's brilliant book on the event which appeared some 6 months later: The march/demonstration was not really intended to protect Free Speech. In reality is was an apology for the right to debase other peoples' values and religion. It was a vindication of intolerance and disrespect and the alibi was Free Speech.

I honestly think that no human right has been so consistently abused, folded, spindled and manipulated to serve different agendas as Free Speech.

It is now being cleverly hijacked by the Titans who may sit back and let the rest of us grow their power and control over all of us in its name. We are producing our own serfdom with enthusiasm.

We are faced with a behemoth that we passionately helped create - just like the Golem of the Old Testament (or Shelley's famous allegorical monster created by the nexus of cutting edge tech at the time and a simple mistake – they picked the wrong brain ...).

If it had been properly understood that "Free Speech" serves the purpose of facilitating human intercourse, it would also be understood that speech which does not promote such social interaction does not fulfil its purpose or "finality".

This recognition would invariably lead to regulation and accountability (both penal and civil) and thereby increase the operational costs of the Titans considerably - just like money laundering compliance has increased the cost of banking and environmental protection has added to the cost of industry and transport.

The natural state of man is not Hobbesian or Lockean (hostility or "tabula rasa"), but Aristotelian: Man is a social animal. The purpose of speech is social. It is not communication of facts, opinions or domination. "Small talk" is the purpose of speech.

We are highly gregarious creatures and speech helps us establish and maintain the rapport with "the other" which is indispensable to our social and psychological wellbeing and quintessential to our existence and fulfillment of the human condition. Ideas are not binary. We may all be right even if that would appear illogical in a reductionist world.

If speech exclusively or primarily serves the purpose of domination and domination is the social goal it is indeed impossible to curtail it in any way since that would amount to deprivation of our right to dominate.

Speech has no intrinsic value. It derives its value from the values it promotes.

14.5 The Code is the Code

Now in order to understand the dynamics that lead us to where we are today we will also have to analyze the real meaning of the celebrated mantra "The Code is the Code".

The early Net philosophers saw the Net as a supranational, universal creation subject exclusively to its own laws: Whatever is technologically possible is the law.

This raises at least 3 questions: 1) is there such a thing as laws above the law? 2) is technology above the law? and 3) what is the impact of the theory on Justice?

First: This first question already troubled the Greek philosophers and authors of the famous tragedies of antiquity. In Sophocles' Antigone the dilemma between following the edicts of Creon on the one hand and those of the gods on the other was the centerpiece of the choice Antigone had to make when burying her brother (in violation of Creon's orders).

Most philosophers today seem to agree that that there are certain principles above law (except for the positivistic school and those that view human rights as hitherto unwritten legal principles thus allowing "humankind" to hold for instance perpetrators and instigators of war crimes accountable even though they have violated no laws under the jurisdiction and at the time and even if they acted under order).

These notions are however of a completely different nature to those advocated by the disciples of the Code is the Code who seem to defend a principle according to which whatever technology may produce or create should not be restricted in any way. Technology is a gift to mankind and there is no such thing as good or bad technology. If technology allows us to do something, then it should be done.

Second: One has to question which version of history books these philosophers source their wisdom from. It ought to be a truism that history is packed with unfortunate discoveries and technology. Of course they argue that technology is not "unfortunate" in itself and that it is 'only' their use which may be abusive.

If that is accepted by the proponents of the Code is the Code I frankly don't understand the theory's intellectual contribution. If the use of technology may be nefarious and if that is admitted by these theoreticians, then this will precisely result in the need to regulate and that in turn means that the "Code is not the Code". What didn't I understand?

We have several examples of technology enabling us to "do things" which for various reasons (mainly ethical) we decide not to allow.

Lets' take *human cloning as an example.* At least since Dolly we have been able to clone almost every living creature, but we have decided not to allow human cloning. We will allow certain specific and controlled applications for instance stem cells, but not general cloning: A right to be or not to be cloned....

We have agreed to establish bio ethics boards and trust them to perform an oversight function regulating the indiscriminate use of technology on ethical grounds. Subliminal advertising is illegal - precisely because it is possible. The Code cannot be the Code. Do the contenders of this dogma wish to allow unrestricted use of bio technology including development of biological arms? Does this theory actually have substance?

Third: The theory is extremely dangerous in that it dehumanizes Justice. It amounts to social Darwinism: "Might is Right". I am sure that had these early Net philosophers realized this consequence they would have been less enthusiastic in embracing this "New" World Order. They would have recognized that the "new" order is the oldest in history.

It took centuries for Justice not to reflect the ethics of those in power and unfortunately this struggle continues till this day. It will most probably never end. Growing inequality gives rise to discrimination not just in terms of social justice, but also in terms of just Justice.

Reverting to a regime where the code is law amounts to corporate dictatorship at all levels. Might will return to right. These dynamics (Free Speech absolutism based on a misconception of the social function of speech and unrestrained celebration of technology) have allowed the

Titans to control the world and we have not only allowed it, but almost fanatically helped them.

14.6 The Modern-Day Proletariat

Today the world resembles the social structure of the mid-19th century. This was the time when Marx developed his theories about the proletariat, class struggle, historicism, phenomenology, the superstructure, ownership and the revolution.

I cannot help but draw parallels from this Marxist analysis to our time. Our modern-day proletariat is comprised of those of us who are not data masters. This means almost all of us. We are the new proletariat. We are data serfs. We have turned into objects, not even "data subjects" (in the misleading terminology of the GDPR).

The superstructure is the mythology superimposed upon us all which we blindly fight for without understanding that is not ours, but that of our masters'. In John Dewey's famous words we find a poignant reminder of this social dichotomy: *"As long as politics is the shadow cast on society by big business, the attenuation of the shadow will not change the substance"*.

The legacy of these philosophers seems to find support in modern day thinkers like Joseph Stiglitz. Among the ingredients of the superstructure we find the Free Speech Dogma which we all subscribe to almost hysterically without realizing that every time we do so we surrender yet another piece of our freedom to the Titans.

14.7 The New Masters

We may ask how we allowed them to become so dominant. Didn't we have regulations in place to protect us against this exploitation of our weaknesses? How did we let ourselves fall prey to these new masters and why did they receive such overwhelming popular support from us all? Are we just like the lemmings?

I shall only deal with one aspect of these questions here and that is *anti-trust*.

As we know in the 1890's anti-trust regulation entered the stage in the US with The Sherman Act. This act criminalizes monopolization as well as abuse, but it has been applied to media in peculiar ways (based on a classic/conservative consumer protection ideology which continues to inspire advocates of Titan rule: The service is free and therefore cannot harm consumers – full stop). Let us remind ourselves of the Sherman Act:

Section 2: *"Every person who shall monopolize, or attempt to monopolize, or combine or conspire with any other person or persons, to monopolize any part of the trade or commerce among the several States, or with foreign nations, shall be deemed guilty of a felony ..."*

In the words of Senator John Sherman at the time the question we are addressing seems even more pertinent: *"If we will not endure a king as a political power we should not endure a king over the production, transportation, and sale of any of the necessaries of life."* Isn't that exactly what has happened to today's power base?

With new controls on freedom of enterprise consumer choice and pricing the concept of the "natural or enlightened monopoly" was developed. As we know from Tim Wu's research this was the tactic of AT&T *("One policy, One system, Universal Service.")*. The government bought it and protected the company against competition for seventy years (from the Kingsbury Commitment in 1912).

How does Freedom of Speech and Information fit into this regulation of dominance? Here the early decision (1945) Associated Press v. U.S. is worthwhile rereading since in the words of the Supreme Court the business of news (and not products) *"does not afford the publisher a peculiar Constitutional sanctuary... Freedom to publish means freedom*

*for all and not for some ... Freedom of the press from government inter-
ference doesn't sanction repression of freedom by private interests. "*

These words of wisdom could not have been more accurate. They
were consistent with the decision of the Supreme Court in 1943 (NBC v.
US) that the First Amendment does not protect against FCC oversight
(some degree of regulation was permitted).

Unfortunately, they were quickly forgotten and with the Newspaper
Preservation Act of 1970 media consolidation took off and the wisdom
of the Associated Press judgment was abandoned.

Then of course came the Telecommunications Act of 1996 and the
remaining restrictions on consolidation were all but repealed. It is interesting that section 230 C should be introduced at the same time. True the
FCC tried to reinstate a certain portion of merger control in 2003, but it
was short lived and actually increased network reach.

A recent legislative initiative proposed a "New Deal" with some
measures of regulation, but what is needed is not a Roosveltian New
Deal, but a Better Deal.

The problem is that anti-trust enforcement and regulation are based
on perceived harm to consumers, but the risk inherent in media consolidation is not consumer harm: It is the harm it inflicts on democracy, free speech and the right to information. Merit-based monopoly may be a valid defense with regard to commodities, but not when it
comes to information.

Information access and diffusion are not a question of consumer wel-
fare and prices. The discussion should not be on content throttling or
pricing (of relevance to the Net Neutrality debate), but on concentration
and ownership.

It will be interesting to follow the DOJ case against the AT&T merger with Time Warner. Will the trend change and how might that affect
the Net? It is also compelling that the Titans should have succeeded for
so long in obtaining both immunity under art 230 by not being media

and at the same time successfully argue that as far as anti-trust goes they should be treated like media - yet another tribute to their intelligence.

If the above Supreme Court decision from 1945 and the words of Senator Sherman had continued to guide the application of anti-trust, we might have seen a breakup of the present information domination a long time ago.

As it stands now we have to turn to the *European Commission* for help and the research conducted by Jean Tirole. This Nobel Prize laureate has contributed significantly to our understanding of the "bifurcate business model" (two-sided or multi-sided markets) as well as the dynamics of the "gentile monopole" (as they say in French). We now understand how the business model of the Titans allows them to dominate several markets at the same time and make money on basically everything. We also understand how their oligopolistic status degenerates into monopolistic control of these different "desiderata" simultaneously and how the pricing equilibrium functions in spite of apparently contradictory externalities.

The consequence is not only complete control over both horizontal and vertical markets, but also the creation of multifaceted barriers to entry. Total information control is here to stay unless we regulate ourselves out of it. The mechanism of disruption has been disrupted.

One frightening concrete example of the abuse that information control leads to is the impact of selective news not only on democracy, but on us all as individuals. In the words of Kierkegaard again:

"Once you label me you negate me". Imagine if Kierkegaard had known about echo-chambers.

14.8 The Right to Dignity

Let's now turn to the final question: How do we deal with the Net's harm to the dignity and integrity of countless victims of defamation, cyber bullying, harassment and trolling? This should really be the Leitmotif governing our attitude toward tech regulation and on this particular point anti-trust won't help. The Tech Titans have - again - been very clever in maintaining that protection of victims is not their problem or responsibility. They are not accountable.

What they fear most is passion. What they lack most is compassion.

If your life is ruined because of harmful content freely traveling through their infrastructure that's just too bad. You deal with it. It's your problem. It's part of the game. Apart from the sheer arrogance of such a position and the heartlessness it demonstrates the argument is fallacious:

First of all, the victim didn't choose to be part of the game and didn't participate in drafting the rules. He didn't acquiesce. Nobody asked his opinion and in addition, the victim reaps no financial benefit from the game. It is the Tech Titan, not the victim, who wrote and imposed the terms without consulting anyone and it is the Tech Titan that rules the world and reaps the benefits of the game.

A zero sum to the other players and a guaranteed profit to the bank. Would that pass in any other industry? It is they - not the victim - that allow lives to be destroyed and it is they who incant the mass of Free Speech as the justification of their money and power wielding steamroller knowing very well that they have touched a nerve of religious sanctity and that anyone who might dare challenge them will be burned in inferno or at the stake as a heretic.

Clearly this reasoning rests on a combination of abuse of power and of the true value of Free Speech which was never intended to allow the destruction of the lives of innocent people.

It rests on a deliberate confusion between not only the right to Free Speech and the Right to Information, but also on the failure to distinguish between vertical and horizontal speech protection. *Vertical speech protection* has almost no limit. This is speech directed against government and authority. This is the core of Free Speech. This is speech that liberates us and preserves our freedom. *Horizontal free speech* is the right to hurt our fellow human being ("The Other"). This is the speech that deprives us of our freedom. It is a category mistake - as Kant would have said - to confuse the two.

In practical terms this means that the highly publicized difficulties of the "judgment call", in for instance "The Right to Be Forgotten" and its alleged incompatibly with Free Speech are groundless: If the victim of horizontal speech makes a prima facie case that the content in question is of such a general nature (words and context taken together) that it is hurtful to him it should be taken down. Why is that so hard to understand and accept? *Why should the author deserve better protection than the victim?* This is different from all other transgressions. If harm is ascertained an end must be put to it and this can easily be done without judging the author as an offender or criminal.

This latter qualification must conform with due process, but an end must be put to harm immediately and it is not up to the Titans to decide whether harm is inflicted or not. Who is better equipped to know and feel whether a statement causes harm than the victim? No one can feel another person's pain and no-one should judge whether it is real or not.

Defending the author's right to hurt the victim by reference to the importance of vertical free speech is a logical fallacy, an abuse of a dominant position and of Free Speech protection.

Let our favorite philosopher Kierkegaard makes the closing statement:

> *"Where am I? Who am I?*
> *How did I come to be here?*
> *What is this thing called the world?*
> *How did I come into the world?*
> *Why was I not consulted?*
> *And If I am compelled to take part in it, where is the manager?*
> *I want to see him."*

We summarize our vision with the following "Declaration of Independence II." We implicitly refer to the "Declaration of Independence" of John Perry Barlow in 1996 which really from a philosophical point of view amounted to a "manifest", advocating a utopic vision of cyberspace.[269]

Declaration of Independence II

(Barlow's and our aspirations meet the facts).

Data Subjects of all countries unite!

We were promised ultimate freedom and liberty and instead we have become serfs of new masters.

Your tyranny has overshadowed and transcended that of government- yet you are not elected.

You have high jacked our space, our freedom and our sovereignty.

You have no moral right to rule us or possess us.

You are not welcome among us.

You do not answer to democracy, but you will have to answer to us, the People.

Your arrogance and indifference to human tragedy, your abuse and avid concentration of power and hegemony disqualify you from the role you have usurped.

You have transformed our dreams and promises of decentralized freedom into a centralized nightmare.

Under the pretext of saving the world you fill your coffers without contributing to society.

You yield before no manipulation.

You have degraded us to products in your realm. Products that deserve no respect.

---

[269] https://www.eff.org/cyberspace-independence.

Governments cannot and will not stop you, but we the People will. We will boycott your services. We will take our clicks away from you and your empire will crumble.

You have no right to make judgments affecting life and death.

We no longer trust you.

What you fear most is our passion.

What you lack most is compassion.

Privacy is not dead. Get over it.

Now, here are our demands:

You will give us back control over our lives.

We will only allow you to coexist with us if you accept that with power comes obligations and that your disregard of ethics and social responsibility will cease.

You are not above the law and your failure to assume your obligations and contribute towards society are shameful.

Your abuse of your overwhelmingly dominant position and your failure to take ethics into account when developing or rather acquiring new technology and services (you develop little yourself) are intolerable.

You will allow Data Subjects all over the world to take control of their own data and immediately heed their demands for deletion and de-referencing.

You will not anoint yourself to be the judge over the appropriateness of such demands.

You will allow public inspection to verify that these demands have been met and that data has been definitely and permanently erased from your gigantic data troves - because we do not trust you.

You will create an ethics board with independent experts who will monitor all of your new "technology" whether developed in-house or acquired and in particular those technologies that apply to artificial intelligence.

You will refrain from further abuse of your dominant position destroying any alternative to your "services" and consolidating your power even more. This time we will create a true civilization of the Mind in Cyberspace.

May it be more humane and fair than the world you have made.

Paris, France, August 3, 2018   *Dan Shefet*

15

LAW, CYBER ETHICS AND TECHNOLOGY

Narayan Toolen, Switzerland

15.1 Technologies Need Standards, Rules, Regulations

Western legal systems are underpinned by the notion of liberty. This means freedom from law, as much as reasonably possible, provided we do not harm others. In a world of technological disruption, does the conversation on ethics need to be re-framed?

The Fourth Industrial Revolution is a future developing in the present. It is a term used to describe technologies, which connect the digital, physical and biological worlds.

These technologies include Artificial Intelligence, Block Chain and Bio-Engineering.

For practical purposes, and functionality, a community relies upon standards. The *Global Legal Block Chain consortium* is an example of key stakeholders in the legal industry, working towards rules for the standardization, governance and application of block chain related technology and the global legal system.[270]

---

[270] Artificial Lawyer, *Global Legal Blockchain Consortium*, https://www.artificiallawyer.com/2018/08/22/pwc-legal-switzerland-joins-the-global-legal-Blockchain-consortium/ (Accessed 5 Sept 2018)

This same development is happening across many fields. Both the EU and China are working to develop standards for Artificial Intelligence.[271]

What ethics are implicit in the building blocks of the rule of law? In the western world, it may be identity, human privacy, political or democratic values, free market ideals, freedom, intellectual property rights, data collection and extra territorial legislation.[272] While law is a tool to enforce ethics, legal processes are also being disrupted by technology, through automation and legal engineering.

15.2 Technology Ethics: The Human Fingerprint

Cyber Ethics go beyond technical standards to look at broader issues of governance. This is a relatively new term because computer science is a youthful science.[273] Yet debates on governance and ethics go back to Plato's classic Utopia, the Republic. In the 21st century humans are still asking: what kind of world do we choose to co-inhabit?

Here are some of the most obvious issues: Artificial intelligence is trained on a data set, which may amplify human bias such as racial, sexual, political or financial perspectives.[274] And technology tools are programmed to make ethical choices, for example autonomous cars make all kind of mundane choices about how they interact with our man made, natural and human environments.[275] How are such choices calculated ethically?

---

[271] Louise Lucas, Waters Richards, *The AI Arms race*: Financial Times, 30/04, 2018.

[272] Jonathan Herring, *Legal Ethics*: Oxford Press: Oxford 2017.

[273] Richard Spinello, *Cyber Ethics, Morality and Law in Cyberspace,* Jones & Bartlett Learning: Burlington, 2013[4].

[274] Daniel Cossins, *Discriminating Algorithms*, New Scientist, 12/04, 2018.

[275] Johannes Himmelreich, *The everyday ethical challenges: the conversation*, 27/03, 2018.

A more extreme example is where an automated weapon must calculate the cost of different targets, and should it use financial considerations?[276] Should it weigh a civilian life as more valuable than a soldiers?

When we look into technology we see human finger prints and possibly even a reflected hidden self. Technology is built for a purpose, so this should be disclosed.

15.3 Legal Ethics: A Political Revolution

Whilst law is a mechanism to enforce ethics, Science Fiction is often a better place to see the invisible revealed. If we look to the classics of Aldous Huxley, we see a scientific ethic in Brave New World, and a human ethic in The Island. How can 21st century technologies be centred around the human?

According to French President, Macron, the ethics come from legal regulation: "AI should respect the EU's values and fundamental rights as well as ethical principles such as accountability and transparency". He calls these technology changes "nothing less than a political revolution"[277]

The EU Commission has tasked the European AI alliance to complete a white paper by the end of 2018.[278] One of the goals is to make sure there is an appropriate legal and ethical framework.

It is not only national law where this is an issue. In *International Law* the question is being asked: what is the relationship between human rights and artificial intelligence? The UN Office of the High Commis-

---

[276] http://moralmachine.mit.edu. See also the position paper of the International Red Cross ICRC on autonomous weapons in this book.

[277] *EU set in race to set AI standards,* EU Observer (2018).

[278] *EU Commission appoints expert group* (2018): Europa.eu. https://ec.europa.cu/digital-single-market/en/news/commission-appoints-expert-group-ai-and-launches-european-ai-alliance (Accessed 5 Sept 2018).

sioner for Human Rights has published a set of principles to guide data collection.[279]

Looking closely into the worlds where politics and technology meet we find law.

15.4 Law, Autonomous Law, Private Regulatory System?

The law and legal system, may play a role in inventing and enforcing ethics, however it is notoriously slow and is itself being disrupted by technology. To solve functional problems within law, there have been many calls to establish a private regulatory system. For example, companies would compete to create innovative regulatory tools. This market would be monitored by the government to ensure it is in the public interest.

An example of private companies playing this role is Microsoft building standards for Privacy and Cyber Security.[280] Already there is an industry of regulatory technology, reg-tech, which operates in this field. The ethical issue around private regulatory tools is that they create a market for regulation that is profit-centred.

Going further towards autonomous law, Block chain is offering the prospect of Lex Cryptographica, as an autonomous, self-executing legal system: a network of smart contracts, which execute actions from the programmed code.[281] This is not more or less ethical, per se, as it de-

---

[279] Neena Bhandari, *AI Impact Human Rights*: *https://www.scidev.net/global/human-rights/news/ai-human-rights-under-scrutiny.html. 08.18.*

[280] Gillian Hatfield, *Government cannot handle tech regulation*, *Quartz*, 2/07, 2018.

[281] Aaron Wright, Primavera De Filippi, *Decentralized Blockchain Technology, and the Rise of Lex Cryptographica*, 2015 https://papers.ssrn.com/sol3/papers.cfm?abstract_id=2580664 (Accessed 5 Sept 2018); idem, *Blockchain and the Law. The Rule of Code*, Harvard University Press: Harvard 2018.

pends on how it works. The Dubai Future Foundation and Dubai Courts of the Future are pioneering developments in this field.[282]

Aside from technical standards, the basic ethic of a Block Chain network, or any consumer technology is disclosure. For example, users using a decentralized network know what they consent to.

The idea of law as code is linked to the idea of law as logic, but there are always values concealed beneath.

The model of the legal system in the western world is individualistic. This is most eloquently captured in the classic test by J.S Mill, On Liberty. The behaviour of humans in our society is free, with limited restrictions, for example harmful conduct.

The basic ethic of compliance with the law may be a very low standard.[283] As Technology creates an invisible code of ethics, this is an issue, which requires consideration by all of society.

With law regulating technology and technology disrupting law where should ethics originate? The only answer is within the human, whether expressed in art, technology, literature, philosophy, religion or law, and whatever society do we want to create through these tools.

---

[282] www.courtsofthefuture.org.

[283] Jonathan Herring Jonathan, *Legal Ethics*, Oxford Press: Oxford 2017.

PART V

CYBER GOVERNANCE
AND ETHICS

16

INTERNATIONAL CONVENTION FOR CYBER SPACE AND ETHICAL FRAMEWORKS

Pavan Duggal, India

16.1 The Significance of International Cyber Ethics Frameworks

The world today is going through very interesting times. *Internet* has evolved as a de facto central line of our day-to-day activities. More and more people are getting connected to the internet at a global level. Internet and its applications are impacting almost every area of human activity and endeavour. Seen from a holistic perspective, the internet is nothing but a network of a network. Internet initially began with *Arpanet* which was a free network for exchanging information. Thereafter, it got expanded to universities. The coming of the World Wide Web provided a distinct new paradigm for accessing the huge new world of knowledge.

With knowledge abounding on the internet and as applications of the internet are getting more advanced, ethical issues and questions are increasingly coming to the forefront. What is ethical behaviour in cyberspace? What should be the principles for ethical behaviour in cyberspace?

Ethics does play an important role in the context of the internet and connected ecosystem. However, ethical principles concerning ethical behaviour in cyberspace are increasingly in the process of developing with each passing day.

Given the fact that internet has made geography history, it is an international network. There is a need for having in place international cyber ethical frameworks which can effectively govern the activities in cyberspace on a regular basis. However, when one looks at the global international scenario, one finds that there is lack of international cyber ethical standards or frameworks that are currently existing. There is no international instrument internationally which can be said to be directly impacting cyber ethical principles and governing cyber ethics. Hence, it becomes even more important to underline and emphasize the significance of cyber ethical international frameworks.

16.2   Bilateral Agreements with The Golden Rule "Do not Hack Each Other's Computer"

When one examines the various *bilateral arrangements* between different countries pertaining to cooperation in cyber related matters, one does realize that number of these are primarily based on ethical standards and principles. For example, one of the key features in the *US-China* bilateral cooperation agreement is that no party will hack each other's computer systems. It is ethical not to hack anybody's computers, computer systems or computer networks. Further, it is also expected that if you are not hacking into somebody else's computer system, somebody else will also not hack into your computer system.

The *UK/China* "Joint Statement on Building a Global Comprehensive Strategic Partnership for the 21st Century" includes, UK and China agreeing not to conduct or support cyber-enabled theft of intellectual property, trade secrets or confidential business information with the intent of providing competitive advantage. The two sides will enhance mutual respect and understanding, and continue exchanges on human rights and rule of law.[284]

India and UK have agreed to an overarching cyber-relationship framework that among others enables the development of a common and shared understanding of international cyber activity; discuss and share strategies to promote user confidence in the security of ICT products and services; promote cyber security product development; and share information relating R&D etc.[285]

The 2013 *bilateral agreement between Russia and the United States* and the 2015 UNGGE agreement indicate that the United States and Russia, together with other leading countries, recognize the dangers posed by threats to cybersecurity and the benefit of establishing agreed-upon norms and practices to reduce the risk of unwanted conflict.[286]

On April 21, 2017, *China and Australia* signed their cybersecurity bilateral accord. The agreement declares, "Australia and China agreed that neither country would conduct or support cyber-enabled theft of intellectual property, trade secrets or confidential business information with the intent of obtaining competitive advantage."[287]

A *Shanghai Cooperation Organization* agreement on "Cooperation in the Field of Information Security," signed by China, Kazakhstan, Kyrgyzstan, Russia, Tajikistan, and Uzbekistan in 2008, lists as a major international information security threat the "dissemination of infor-

---

[284] https://www.gov.uk/government/news/uk-china-joint-statement-2015. All links in this article accessed 11 Sept 2018.

[285] http://mea.gov.in/bilateral-docments.htm?dtl/29831/IndiaUK_List_of_MOUsAgreementsInitiatives_during_the_visit_of_Prime_Minister_to_UK_London_April_18_2018.

[286] https://futureofusrussiarelations.files.wordpress.com/2016/06/wg_working_paper7_cybersecurity_final.pdf .

[287] https://securityboulevard.com/2017/10/dissecting-chinas-global-bilateral-cybersecurity-strategy.

mation harmful to the socio-political and socio-economic systems, spiritual, moral and cultural environments of other States."[288]

16.3 From Bilateral to International Convention

The aforesaid events and developments show that these could be the starting points for discussion at international level on ethical principles and frameworks. There is a need for an International Convention for Cyberspace which could be founded on ethical principles.

Such an International Convention could also help in the development of jurisprudence around cyber ethics and the importance of cyber ethics would have more centre-stage attention.

Very quickly, people have to realize that internet is no longer just a network of networks, it is the growing heritage of mankind as a whole. We all have a duty and responsibility to ensure that such a network operates on and continues to encourage ethical principles and ethical frameworks, which can give rise to an ethical cyberspace ecosystem.

Given the fact that new technologies that are emerging whether it is Artificial Intelligence, Internet of Things and Blockchains, it is increasingly clear that these new technologies are likely to bring forward new challenges which will give rise to ethical considerations. These become more accentuated in cases of emerging technologies like the Artificial Intelligence which is grappling with large number of ethical issues. The advent of international legal and cyber ethical frameworks at a global level is likely to ensure that different countries are likely to deal with these ethical issues in their own national approaches and perspectives. In such a situation, we are likely to see the rich development of cyber norms in emerging technologies.

---

[288]   https://www.justsecurity.org/16706/international-agreements-and-disagreements-on-cybersecurity

To give an example, the growth of *Artificial Intelligence* faces a fundamental dilemma. What will be the ethical ramifications of the decisions taken by Artificial Intelligence and whether there can be ethical human frameworks which could apply to Artificial Intelligence? The advent of Machine Learning and Artificial Intelligence has once again shown that the computing is taking us onto the next level and era. The advent of *Quantum Computing* has further ensured that complicated algorithms and mathematical formulae, which were considered as secure yesterday, will no longer be secure today and that indeed, presently considered secure algorithms are likely to be broken up in the coming future. The newly emerging technologies raise a fundamental question that is it ethical for Quantum Computing to break into the security of encryption related algorithms and also, what can be done so as to protect and preserve the personal data and data privacy of others.

In fact, in every aspect of human activity and endeavour in cyberspace, we have begun to find out that cyber ethical principles have continued to make their impact. These principles are still at the stage of development, at the time of writing. With the passage of time, these principles are likely to further evolve into concrete frameworks which can then be embodied both in national legislations and also in international frameworks and treaties at the global level.

16.4 Fast Growing Cybercrime Needs International Framework

The increasing amount of cybercrimes that are taking place in the world only shows that ethical frameworks are no longer being respected by cyber criminals. The cost of Cybercrime is growing at an unprecedented pace. It has been anticipated by Cybersecurity Ventures that the global cost of Cybercrime is expected to increase by 6 Trillion USD by

2020.[289] With such kind of unethical behaviour happening in cyber-space, ethical principles are not likely to command respect from stake-holders till such time they are adequately embodied in national legisla-tions and legal frameworks and there is sanctity of law behind the same.

Just as the internet is a global network which has made geography history does not mean that it continues to be a lawless jungle where there are no ethical principles or foundations. As time passes by, internet is likely to evolve into a substantial game changing paradigm, having impact upon every activity of human endeavour and intelligence. As such, ethical principles must be made the foundation of all kinds of in-teraction and activities in cyberspace. The need for an International Cyber Legal Frameworks embodying some of the important cyber legal principles and foundations would be imperative to put in place, as the world proceeds towards uncertain times.

Cyber security breaches continue to grow at an unprecedented speed. According to Statistics summary by Identity Theft Resource Center[290] (U.S) for cyber security breaches, in the month of June, 2018, the num-ber of breaches were identified and summarized by ITRC in different sectors like Banking/Credit/Financial, Business, Educational and Medi-cal/Healthcare, where the total number of Breaches were 45 out of 37,899 number of records.

In the survey of cyber security breaches for the year 2017 by U.K Government, just under half (46%) of all businesses identified at least one breach or attack in the last year. The most common types of breach-es related to staff receiving fraudulent emails (72% of those who identi-fied a breach or attack), followed by viruses and malware (33%), people

---

[289] https://cybersecurityventures.com/hackerpocalypse-cybercrime-report-2016 .

[290]   https://www.idtheftcenter.org/wp-content/uploads/2018/06/ITRCBreach StatsReportSummary.pdf.

impersonating the organisation online (27%) and ransomware (17%).[291] It is estimated that the average cost of a data breach in 2020 will exceed $150 million, as more business infrastructure gets connected.[292]

The aforesaid figures enlighten us that it is the time to inculcate ethical principles and behavioural standards as an important part of cyberspace ecosystem. Seen from a pragmatic perspective, it appears that at the time of writing, any agreement between state and non-state actors about an international Cyber Legal Framework on ethical principles might not be foreseeable in the near future. However, the author believes that the present situation is likely to change over a period of time. *Independent of the ground realities, it is in the interests of all stakeholders to push the jurisprudence for incorporating ethical principles as part of international legal frameworks.*

Cyber ethics as a discipline is getting more and more significant in present times and is likely to gain tremendous importance in the coming times. National legal frameworks and international treaties and agreements need to keep in mind the importance and significance to cyber ethics as an integral part thereof, as they are aiming in the direction of developing new frameworks, paradigms and legislations and also legal programs aimed at regulating activities in cyberspace, both at national, regional and international level.

16.5 International Cyber Legal Treaty with Ethical Framework

Talking about the significance of an International Cyber Legal Treaty with ethical frameworks in third quarter of 2018 when we are writing this article might look a futuristic approach. However, given the way

---

[291] https://assets.publishing.service.gov.uk/government/uploads/system/uploads/attachment_data/file/609187/Cyber_Security_Breaches_Survey_2017_infographic_ general_business_findings.pdf.

[292] https://www.cybintsolutions.com/cyber-security-facts-stats.

how there is an increase in Cybercrimes, cyber security breaches and new challenges brought forward by emerging technologies like Artificial Intelligence, Internet of Things and Blockchains, it is clear that the need for these kinds of an international legal frameworks will be increasingly getting more and more prominent with the passage of time.

Over the last two decades, a new legal discipline started emerging which came to be known as *Cyber Law*. Cyber Law as a legal discipline deals with legal, policy and regulatory concerning activities done using computers and internet worldwide. The initial Cyber Law developments across the world are more focused on creating enabling legal frameworks for promoting e-commerce and the digital format. However, as cyber legal frameworks started increasingly dealing with security of computer systems and networks, ethical considerations started being incorporated in the national cyber legal framework constituting national Cyber Laws.

16.6 National Cyber Law is Not Enough

When one does examine the various cyber laws of different countries passed in different countries, one finds that a number of cyber laws across the world have various legal provisions which are based on strong and robust ethical foundations. The problem in the national cyber legal framework is that they are only applicable within the territorial boundaries of their sovereign countries and do not have an extra territorial applicability. Ethical principles have come to govern numerous provisions under national cyber laws. However, at the international treaty level, we find that there is a vacuum as far as cyber ethical principles are concerned. We find that at the international level, there are no enabling legal frameworks which are specifically based on or are promoting cyber ethical principles. At international level, there is absence of an international Cyberlaw in place. There is no one international treaty that has been passed by any country pertaining to regulating cyberspace. As such, since there is no international Cyber Law in place, there is no international legal regime which is based on cyber ethical standards and expected ethical norms of behaviour in cyberspace. The Author way back in the year 2015 had advocated the need for having in place an International Convention on Cyberlaw & Cybersecurity which could address the existing vacuum. Clearly, at the time of writing, nation states are currently not interested in the direction of evolving an international cyber legal framework. As nation states are engaging in covert and overt activities in cyberspace and given the fact that attribution of cyber activities presents challenges, it appears that currently, nation states do not want to have in place an international cyber legal framework based on ethical principles, at the time of writing. One of the biggest problems of ethical principles is that they are not in a position to totally get enforced till such time they are embedded in the provisions of the law which has an impact upon sanctity of the law. Consequently, one finds that various unethical activities targeted at international level pertaining to cyberspace paradigm are constantly on the rise.

The Sony Picture case was a classic case of an unethical conduct. Further, the hacking of Estonian economy and infrastructure done by hackers also was an unethical activity. In the absence of strong ethical principles governing norms of behaviour in cyberspace, unethical activities become further accentuated. A recent instance in this regard relates to the elections to the US President in 2016, which were alleged to be influenced by Russian hackers. The said activities were indeed unethical but nonetheless, were still done because there was absence of international cyber legal frameworks which could impose such ethical principles on respective stakeholders. Cyber criminal activities are constantly on the rise, targeting individuals, legal entities, property as well as nations.

To conclude, ethics has been an integral part of human civilization, human behaviour, human conduct and human legislative approaches.

Cyber ethics will continue to play increasingly important role for all stakeholders at local, national, regional and international levels to guide various activities of different stakeholders in a positive ethical direction. The need for an international Cyber Legal Convention on ethical frameworks is the need of the hour. As new developments take place in the technology ecosystem at break neck speed, the need for having such international cyber ethical frameworks will continue to get more and more accentuated. It will be up to the respective political will of different stakeholders as to how they want to tackle with this issue and what kind of cyber ethical legal frameworks can be developed to guide nations, as well as other non-state actors pertaining to acts, deeds and things done ethically in cyberspace, using the internet and the online paradigm.

17

TOWARDS A JUST INTERNET: A REPUBLICAN NET NEUTRALITY

Johan Rochel, Switzerland

17.1 Introduction

The announcement of net neutrality's death in December 2017 has hit global headlines.[293] But who exactly is dead? What is this strange object of public attention we have come to call "net neutrality" since a seminal article by Wu in 2003[294]? And even more importantly than correctly identifying the dead object: should we mourn its passing? The interest for the topic has moved beyond US borders and is currently being addressed as a key policy issue around the world. Is net neutrality really the key principle of a just and free internet—as numerous academics, NGOs, and political decision-makers strongly advocate—or shall we look for better concepts to capture the numerous democratic values we associate with this inescapably open concept? The main hypothesis of this contribution is that "net neutrality" is an open concept crystallizing distinct ethical challenges. In order to address them, we need to identify underlying values and interpret them in form of normative guidelines.

---

[293] Many thanks to Christoph Laszlo and Florian Wüstholz for comments on a previous draft of this article.

[294] Wu, (2003). Note by the Editor: complete reference in the last section.

This contribution is organized in three sections. The first section explains the relevance of net neutrality as an issue of traffic management. It highlights that distinct challenges of traffic management call for a specific understanding of what neutrality should be about. The second section builds upon this intermediary conclusion in highlighting which underlying values are operationalized by the concept of neutrality. It presents two main sets of values, a first one around individual freedom and a second one around the idea of an informational ecosystem. The third section further develops these two sets of values in light of the republican ideal of freedom as non-domination. It comes back to the distinct challenges of traffic management and applies this republican perspective to them.

17.2 The Relevance of the Net and its Neutrality

The relevance of the net neutrality debate is fundamentally different depending on where you happen to reside. In all digitized economies, significant numbers of NGOs and activists have pushed for this debate to be publicly conducted. In the US, the debate has gained a strong momentum in the course of public participation in the drafting of the US Federal Communication Commission (FCC) regulation[295]. In Europe[296] and in other important economic powers[297], what was once a technical debate is also being broadly addressed as a political, economic and societal issue.

Scientific contributions dealing with net neutrality have a key mission in providing better definitions of what net neutrality is exactly

---

[295] For references, Graber (2017), 17-18.

[296] For an analysis of the EU discourse, Gerlach (2016), 171 ff. See for national case-studies, Belli and De Filippi (2016), 199 ff.

[297] See for India e.g., *Net neutrality: All sides of the debate examined* (The New Indian Express, 12 July 2017. See also Cheruvalath (2018). See for China, Hu (2011).

about. As proposed by Belli and De Philippi, "network neutrality prescribes that Internet traffic shall be treated in a non-discriminatory fashion so that Internet users can freely choose online content, applications, services and devices without being influenced by discriminatory delivery of Internet traffic"[298]. In light of this preliminary definition, we firstly need to briefly specify the concept of network. Although this paper is not primarily a paper about the technicalities of the internet, it is necessary to dig into the different layers of the network in order to highlight different levels of relevance for the concept of "neutrality". On this basis, we will move towards the key idea of traffic management.

To start with, the internet (hereafter the network) is defined as "the elective tool for information management and worldwide communication"[299]. The network is a multi-layered infrastructure. Four main layers are relevant for the debate on neutrality[300]. The first layer is a physical layer that provides the physical infrastructure of the network. The relevant stakeholders of this connectivity layer are telecom corporations, cable and broadband companies. It is essential to note that these stakeholders might indeed be private companies. The second layer is a service layer focused on transforming the physical infrastructure into useable services. The relevant stakeholders here are software companies, developers and web architects. The third layer is defined as a "logical layer" focused on content providers. It is the layer where the general service relation made possible by the physical layer takes distinct forms. The relevant stakeholders are companies and organisations of content production, such as multimedia industries or news agencies. The fourth layer focuses on the content recipients of all the content created. The relevant stakeholders are the end users.

---

[298] Belli and De Filippi (2016), 2.

[299] Turilli, Vaccaro and Taddeo (2012), 134.

[300] Turilli, Vaccaro and Taddeo (2012), 137-138. Gerlach lists 5 layers. Gerlach (2016), 48-49.

Against the background of these four layers, the main challenges raised by net neutrality might be addressed as challenges of traffic management. In this contribution, the focus will be put on traffic management decided and implemented by Internet Access Provider (IAP). These companies play a crucial role in organizing access to the informational system of the internet. Traffic management might take distinct forms. Following Gerlach, I will focus on five challenging situations of traffic management[301]:

1. Network security and integrity (e.g. preventing attacks on the network)
2. Mitigation of congestion (e.g. downgrading peer-to-peer traffic to secure quality of service for other types of connections)
3. Prohibition of access to specific content (e.g. due to legal obligations)
4. Differentiation of services to end-users including consumers and application providers (e.g. different services have a different quality)
5. Protection of Internet Access Provider's (IAP's) own business (e.g. prioritization of IAP's own internal call service)

Each of these situations of traffic management entails an ethical dimension in the sense of a normative question. If we ask how to justify a specific management practice, we will inevitably arrive at a normative discussion about how to explain and defend a specific way of dealing with information flows. The attribute "neutral" and the general call to "net neutrality" are thus elements in a multi-layered normative debate. We can see this multi-layered normative debate in focusing again on the five situations of traffic management.

The *first situation* concerning network security and integrity is the one which is least touched by strong normative debate. The key norma-

---

[301] Gerlach (2016), 53. For another proposal, Belli (2016), 17 ff.

tive issue is the definition of the integrity of the network and, as a consequence, what constitutes a threat.

The *second situation* about mitigation of congestion already entails an important normative dimension in the form of a prioritization. This prioritization of what should be guaranteed in situations of scarcity on the network represents a form of normative hierarchy between the different types of services which ought to be guaranteed. For instance, it might be the case that a specific type of traffic (e.g. peer-to-peer) ought to be downgraded for the sake of securing the functioning of other services, which are assumed to be more fundamental. This hierarchy directly affects the neutrality debate in implying a stance on which services ought to be guaranteed in times of congestion.

The *third situation* concerning the prohibition to access specific content is also clearly at stake in the neutrality debate. On the one hand, the question is about the legal obligation for IAPs to implement legal restrictions. In turn, the question is quite different when we consider the obligation to enact democratically legitimized rules (such as the prohibition of child pornography) as opposed to the obligation to enact rules by an authoritarian regime blocking access to a whole range of websites. In the latter case, the call to "neutrality" is a short-hand for describing a call against "controlled" internet in the context of authoritarian regimes. On the other hand, the question is about the ethical responsibility of IAPs to go beyond their legal obligations. The neutrality debate functions here as a strong call to IAPs to not implement their own ethical commitments, but to remain impartial in their dealing with information flows.

The *fourth situation* of traffic management is about differentiation of services to end-users. It relates to situations where the IAP might charge a specific fee for a specific service. The use of a specific application or the access to a specific content is treated in a special way. This management practice might be backed up by an argument about specific applications requiring a high quality of service and/or important amount of data. In this context, "neutrality" is a call to specify this type of argument in the context of an impartial traffic management.

The *fifth situation* describing the protection of a vertically integrated IAP is clearly a case in which an IAP discriminates among different applications in order to favour its "home" applications and services. This potential development has been labelled the "Balkanisation" of the internet because of its silo-structure: each IAP provides a preferential treatment to its own products and partners, while negatively treating competitors' products[302].

To sum up, the neutrality debate takes place in four of the five identified constellations. This first lesson already makes clear that the success of the concept of "net neutrality" lies in its capacity to grasp and express the commonality of distinct normative tensions. These four debates are not identical but share a common feature about how access to internet should be organized: along an absence of differentiation among content, application, users. Used in a general way, "net neutrality" has become "a label to indicate a problem of conflicting interests among users and service providers"[303]. The label of "neutrality" is intended to grasp that this conflict of interests should be addressed in a way that prevents unjustified differential treatment, i.e. discrimination.

The second lesson is that the "neutrality" should not be taken as an end in itself, but rather looked at in its relation to the wider objective of what we could call justice[304]. The hypothesis is that this "neutrality" is a good way to secure a "just" internet. In some contexts, neutrality might be the best way to realize justice, but this is not necessary.

It is important to highlight that this is a normative question (about what ought to be) and not a descriptive question about the way specific

---

302 Turilli, Vaccaro and Taddeo (2012), 141.
303 Turilli, Vaccaro and Taddeo (2012), 135.
304 For a similar position, Turilli, Vaccaro and Taddeo (2012), 139.

actors have interpreted the neutrality issue. The problem of the "neutral" attribute is a classical problem in the context of production and access to scarce resources. The main problem is that producing and distributing something in a neutral way—in the sense of avoiding differential treatment—does not always warrant the attribute "just". In other words, an action can be both neutral and unjust.[305] I provide two brief examples in which this tension appears.

Firstly, a case where neutrality does not imply justice is where IAPs have to respect the law by blocking access to specific content (such as child-pornography). The fact that the law prohibits access to specific content is an example of (arguably) justified differential treatment. Some types of information are considered inacceptable, while others are considered acceptable. But even within content that is considered acceptable, ethical tensions on the side of an IAP might arise if all information is treated in a neutral way. The fact that a content is not legally prohibited does not mean that it is ethically acceptable. For example, it is far from clear that an IAP should treat access to a site which provides fake-news in the same way as access to a site of recipes for apple-cakes. For instance, the US debate on the repeal of the net neutrality decision by the FCC has been lead under the pressure put on IAPs to prevent fake-news' spread.

Secondly, dealing with different types of applications in a "neutral" way might imply adopting a routing model organized by a "first-come, first-served" model. But in such a case, specific applications requiring constant flow of data with low latency between two or more nodes would be penalised[306]. At the same time, this model might be perfectly adequate among a specific type of applications requiring the same type of quality of service. There are some good functional grounds to argue

---

[305] For a similar position, Turilli, Vaccaro and Taddeo (2012), 139; Gerlach (2016), 53.

[306] Turilli, Vaccaro and Taddeo (2012), 139.

that content flow required for specific applications (such as videoconferencing) should be prioritized in order to make these applications work in a satisfactory manner. By taking a strict position on neutrality, the capacity of specific applications to function properly might be questioned.

This type of tensions is well-known from long-standing debates on *distributive justice*. To distribute something valuable in a "neutral" way does not always secure a just distribution. If I have three apples to distribute to three individuals, it might be just to distribute them in priority to the individual starving (need-principle) or to the one who collected the apples (merit-principle). The point is to challenge the idea that a neutral distribution (one apple per person) must be a just distribution.

As Gerlach explains, these tensions show that the debate cannot be about whether there should be network management at all, but about "what kind and how much network management [IAPs] should be allowed to perform."[307] It is about investigating which kind of "neutrality" is required for which situation of traffic management. To make this argument explicit requires to identify and map the different values which are served by "neutrality" in the context of a broader search for justice. By referring directly to these underlying values, we will be able to better identify what is at stake in the distinct situations. This shall allow us to go beyond a debate often dominated by a slogan, and move towards a debate on values and the best technical, political, legal, and social strategies to realize them.

17.3 Two Sets of Values Underlying "Neutrality"

We could define two main sets of values underlying the general claim to neutrality: values centred on the *individual* and his/her individual freedom and values centred on the *internet as informational ecosystem*.

---

[307] Gerlach (2016), 59.

The first set of values is centred on the individual. It is interesting to start by highlighting an inherent ambivalence in the concept of neutrality. Defined as absence of (unjustified) differential treatment, neutrality is about equality[308]. To investigate this concept of equality means unpacking two conceptions of neutrality. Firstly, a logical-rational conception of neutrality commands to equally treat two individuals in an equal situation. Secondly, neutrality is also about the moral worth of individuals and their claims with respect to access and use of the internet. This reflects a substantial conception of equality. When we refer to neutrality, we often consider the conjunction of these two claims, one pertaining to neutrality as equal treatment and one to the moral worth of human beings. Let's look at these two in turn.

The first conception is about a logical-rational requirement of equality. Legal systems have early identified this requirement as a fundamental principle of a rule-based legal system (for instance, as equality before the law). As formulated by the Court of Justice of the European Union, "this principle requires that similar situations shall not be treated differently unless differentiation is objectively justified"[309]. In this first dimension, equality could be opposed to arbitrariness, in that two similar situations should not be treated differently without justification. This logical-rational conception is extremely relevant for the neutrality debate in that it helps to highlight a key challenge at stake: the risk of arbitrariness in dealing differently with two situations which are - by relevant means of comparison - equal situations.

But this formal conception is alone not sufficient to account for the normative appeal of neutrality. If we argue that two persons in an equal situation should be equally treated, we assume that these persons have a

---

[308] For a similar starting point, Cheruvalath (2018).

[309] Joined cases 117-76 and 16-77, Albert Ruckdeschel & Co. and Hansa-Lagerhaus Ströh & Co. v Hauptzollamt Hamburg-St. Annen; Diamalt AG v Hauptzollamt Itzehoe [1977], ECR 1977 p. 1753, § 7.

moral worth. In other words, this worth grounds the requirement to treat individuals in a specific way. The opposite would be the idea that human beings do not have moral worth at all. However, the hypothetical character of this proposal already shows that the two dimensions are intrinsically linked.

It is interesting to highlight that this specific point echoes an ongoing discussion in the ethics and law of non-discrimination. Our account trying to link a logical-rational and a substantial conception of neutrality (resp. equality) shares numerous aspects with the freedom-based account developed by Moreau to account for discrimination law. For her, a person has certain deliberative freedoms which should be protected. These freedoms should make sure that our decisions about how we live are protected against the effects of normatively extraneous features (such as governmental powers, commercial practices, societal pressures). As she states, "[...] whether some trait should be recognized as a prohibited ground is a normative question whose answer depends on whether people have a right to make decisions in a manner that is free from the sorts of institutional and attitudinal pressures that are encountered by those with that trait"[310]. In other words, these features should not bear upon us as "costs" when taking decisions about how we want to live. These freedoms are not the result of an interpersonal comparison in terms of opportunities or rights, but reflect what is due to the person in terms of recognizing of his/her entitlements. To determine which entitlements these are requires developing a view of the human person and his/her protected features. This attempt to link the two conceptions of neutrality as equality is relevant for our discussion. Moreau's approach raises the question of which protection against unjustified differential treatment is due to individuals in matters of access and use of internet.

When we say that access and use of the internet should be organized in a "neutral" way, we assume a certain conception of the moral worth

---

[310] Moreau (2010), 156.

of individuals. When we say that neutrality is about securing non-discrimination in the access and use of the internet as a global informational structure, we take position on what an individual needs in terms of protection. This leads to a discussion about the entitlement which individual might claim. The best way to give clearer outlines to these entitlements is to draw upon individual freedoms protected by individual rights. In brief, individual freedom to access, exchange, sell, buy, create information on the internet should be secured[311].

This task of further identifying and defining what individual freedoms could mean in the context of access and use of the internet has been a growing object of interest in national and international courts[312]. For instance, the European Court of Human Rights has underlined the relevance of the internet as one of the principal means for individuals to exercise their freedom of expression and information as protected by Art. 10 ECHR[313]. It has also linked this infrastructure to participation in activities and debates related to questions of politics or public interests. Following the ECHR, the individual freedoms protected by the Convention - (Greenstein, Peitz et al. 2016) such as freedom of expression, right to private life and the protection of personal data - might be used as protection against blanket blocking of entire websites.[314]

Overall, this first set of values around the individual has been unpacked from the inherent ambivalence of neutrality understood as equality. We have distinguished between a logical-rational conception of neutrality (treating equals equally) and a substantial conception which commands treating individuals in a specific way (protecting their indi-

---

[311] For a similar position using the concept of human rights, Belli and De Filippi (2016), 3ff.

[312] See the reflection by Graber about the constitutionalisation of this debate, Graber (2017).

[313] Ahmet Yıldırım v Turkey (application no 3111/10, ECtHR 2012), § 54.

[314] Cengiz and Others v Turkey (applications nos 48226/10 and 14027/11, ECtHR 2015). For further references, Graber (2017), 12 ff.

vidual rights). Both conceptions might be drawn upon in accounting for specific traffic management challenges. It is important to see that this first set of value centred on the individual might be further developed into a prosperity-based argument at society's or even global level. In brief, the argument assumes that individuals having free access and free use of the internet might conduct beneficial economic activities which, in turn, lead to prosperity at the collective level. This argument has a strong empirical component and it should indeed be shown that the aggregative effects have mainly (or in total) beneficial effects.[315]

This first set of values centred on the equal protection of individual freedoms is complemented by a second set of values focused on the informational ecosystem in which the internet plays an essential role. Following Floridi's work on information ethics, authors have pushed arguments focused on the duty to preserve the quality of this informational ecosystem.[316]

They argue that the internet should be considered a key infrastructure of a broader ecosystem in which information are created and exchanged. This ecosystem is called "infosphere". Floridi has developed four principles according to which this ecosystem should be organized. The first three principles deal with the idea that entropy should be prevented, i.e. that we should prevent the destruction, impoverishment or vandalisation of information. Floridi's fourth principle of information ethics then proposes a duty to promote information: "Information ought to be promoted by extending, improving, enriching and opening the infosphere, that is by ensuring information quantity, quality, variety, security, ownership, privacy, pluralism and access."[317]

---

[315] For further references, Greenstein, Peitz and Valletti (2016).

[316] Floridi (2013). See for an example of how Floridi's work has been used in the debate, Turilli, Vaccaro and Taddeo (2012).

[317] Floridi (2008), 32.

This contribution is not the place to defend this position in detail. Rather, it is interesting to highlight the complement of this line of argument with the freedom-based argument. Net neutrality is taken as a potential strategy to implement these four principles, especially the fourth one. As argued by Turilli, Vaccaro and Taddeo, these principles of information ethics might be used to formulate a duty to secure diversity in the informational ecosystem. This specification of Floridi's principles is a way to address the normative indeterminacy of the attribute "neutral". Net neutrality should be specified in the light of an ambition to secure diversity: "some form of localised absence of differentiation may be instrumentally implemented if and only if it promotes fairness in a specific situation, dynamic or relationship and if and only if it does not damage a globally and virtuously diverse informational environment."[318]

Parallels to classical environmental ethics are striking (and argued for by Floridi). We can defend environmental duties by reference to individual freedoms (of current and future generations), but also by reference to the functioning of the ecosystem. In environmental ethics, this could imply putting the focus on non-human entities and their potential rights, but also on the overall dynamics of the ecosystem[319]. Key intuition of Floridi's work is to apply this kind of reflection to the informational ecosystem.

17.4 Towards a Republican Net Neutrality

In the previous section, we have identified two sets of values which are relevant to further specify what neutrality should be about. The way forward will be to firstly better specify how to understand these values, before coming back to the challenges identified above. The hypothesis

---

[318] Turilli, Vaccaro and Taddeo (2012), 147.

[319] For an overview of ecosystem-based arguments in preserving eco-diversity, Brennan and Lo (2015), §4.

of this section is that the two discussed sets of values might be account-
ed for from a republican perspective. This account is especially relevant
in that it focuses on potential relations of domination among actors in
different power relations. It represents an attempt to theorize what it
means to be "at the mercy" of others, be it an authoritarian regime, a
private company, or fellow citizens through democratic law-making.
This account represents a very promising set of resources to further improve the normative discussion around the concept of "net neutrality" as
grasped by the two set of values identified above.

The key concept of this republican account is one of freedom
understood as absence of domination. An individual is free if he/she can
be protected against specific threats which undermine his/her capacity of
choice. With this specific position on what individual freedom is about,
we can address the first set of values (centred on the individual).

Political theorist Philipp Pettit has been the driving force behind
numerous works on how to define domination. To recall Pettit's original
definition, domination is an instance of arbitrary intereference. The
classical example given by Pettit is the relation between a slave and a
master. The master is in the position to arbitrarily interfere with the
slave. The slave is "at the mercy" of the master and this, even if the
master is a good master. The fact that the master *could* arbitrarily
interfere is already sufficient for a relation of domination. An
interference is arbitrary if there is no mechanism that requires the
interferer to track the relevant interests of the interferee[320]. For Pettit, the
political ideal of non-domination is a permanent effort to diminish arbitrary interferences and transform them into non-arbitrary interferences[321]. As he writes, "interference will be non-arbitrary, to the extent

---

[320] Pettit (1997), 52.

[321] As Pettit writes, "an act is arbitrary, in this usage, by virtue of the controls—
specifically, the lack of controls — under which it materialises, not by virtue of

that, being checked, the interferer is forced to track the avowed or avow previous interests of the interferee; and this, regardless of whether or not those interests are true or real or valid, by some independent moral criterion"[322]. This original formulation has been further developed by Pettit and other republican authors[323]. The objective of this contribution cannot be to account for the "internal" debates. It rather wants to try to focus on the common ground for the republican idea to be applied to the set of values underlying net neutrality.

For the sake of the present contribution, I propose to define the republican core of my approach along three main elements. Firstly, individual freedom is always to be conceived within a social relationship (with other individuals or with institutions and political communities). In this context, the importance of a secured enjoyment of freedom defined as non-domination is particularly attractive as a relational account, that is, an account that considers the multiple patterns of influences that exist among individuals, private and public actors, or political communities[324]. It can also take into account the particular risks attached to the imbalances of power among different actors and the sometimes diffuse risks these relations can represent in terms of (potential) arbitrary interferences.

Secondly, within this relationship, some actors might exercise arbitrary interferences upon others. Even in the total absence of interference, individuals can be considered as dominated if they are at the mercy of

---

the particular consequences to which it gives rise." Pettit (1997), 55. See also Pettit (2010), 75.

[322] Pettit (2008), 117. In the other formulation, Pettit has argued that the interference had to become "non-alien". For the sake of the present argument, the key insight remains the same.

[323] For the new framing as "alien control", see Pettit (2008); Pettit (2010). In another influential account, Lovett speaks of "arbitrary control". Lovett (2010), 119.

[324] Young (2007), 39-58.

decisions made by others[325]. In a strong sense, individuals have to be empowered to be free or, as Valentini writes, have to enjoy freedom as a kind of "independence"[326].

Thirdly, to try to diminish this domination is about building procedural guarantees, which make sure that institutions and actors, especially powerful ones, can be controlled. These measures are meant to change the modus of interactions, moving from an arbitrary to a non-arbitrary measure. To secure this objective, various institutional measures are thinkable, which reflect different positions in the underlying discussion on which characteristics make domination problematic[327]. Measures can range from strong constitutional guarantees, mechanisms forcing to consider the interests of individuals affected, and contestatory democracy.

This republican account shares, historically and normatively, an inherent link to the protection of individual freedom. Powerful actors which might threaten individual freedom should be controlled. At the same time, republicans are strongly committed to the ideal of equality. All members of the community should be considered equal and should be equally defended against actors threatening their freedom.

The link between this account and the first set of values on neutrality might be specified in reference to Pettit's distinction between "extent" and "intensity" of domination[328]. The case for domination would be

---

[325] Pettit (1997), 73 ff; Bellamy (2011), 132.

[326] Valentini (2011), 162. As Halldenius put it, the specificity of this republican model lies in its "modal" aspect, namely the "claimable and secure enjoyment" of conditions of freedom. Halldenius (2010), 20.

[327] As put by Lovett, the new focus on preventing "uncontrolled" powers would "reorient discussion towards the issue of whether republican freedom requires that such powers be controlled by those persons affected specifically (the democratic view), or whether control by impersonal laws or norms might be sufficient (the procedural view)". Lovett (2014).

[328] Pettit (1997). For an example on how to use this distinction, Honohan (2014), 40 ff.

made if we could show that there are interferences with important interests (extent) and that these interferences remain unchecked (intensity). The intensity of domination depends on "how arbitrary the interference can be, how easy it is for the dominator to interfere, and how severe are the measures that can be taken." This is the core idea of an arbitrary modus of interactions. The extent of domination depends on "which areas of a person's life are subject to arbitrary interference, and the range of their options" (interferences on important interests).

With respect to the first set of values identified above, these two constitutive elements of domination seem to be given. On the one hand, it is clear that essential interests are at stake. Access and use of internet as global informational structure is today an essential interest for almost anyone[329]. To argue counterfactually, the impossibility to access internet or the access under control by public power or commercial companies illustrate the relevance of the interest at stake. In these situations, individual freedom is directly threatened.

On the other hand, the issue of "intensity", i.e. how relevant actors are controlled (such as public commission regulating internet access or IAPs), is at the core of the neutrality debate. As Belli and De Philippi write, "non-discriminatory treatment guarantees that Internet users maintain the ability to choose freely how to utilise their own Internet connection, without undue interferences from public or private entities"[330]. The republican account has interesting resources to draw upon to theorize these "undue interferences" and the threat for individual freedom which they represent. If relevant actors can decide to interfere with individuals' important interests in a way which is unchecked (i.e.

---

[329] In this sense, already in 2011, the UN Special Rapporteur on the Promotion and Protection of the right to Freedom of Opinion and Expression has argued that access to internet is a human right. See Human Rights Council, 16th May 2011, A/HRC/17/27.

[330] Belli and De Filippi (2016), 3.

arbitrary), domination is given. This risk is aggravated if these actors can easily conduct such interferences (without constraints bearing upon them).

As proposed by scholars working on republican theories of justice, the ideal of freedom as non-domination might be extended beyond a closed community[331]. This is also a promising argument in order to highlight the global justice dimension of the net neutrality debate. For the time being, we have considered the neutrality discussion mainly as a national or regional question. The main ground for this focus is that IAPs' activities are mainly under national law (or European law for the matter). In other words, access to internet is still largely an issue of national legislation. This does of course not mean that there are no global dimensions.

The argument for a global republican net neutrality might be split in two variations. On the one hand, the global defence of freedom as non-domination might be made concrete in the defence of specific informational rights (access to information, protection of private life, protection of one's own data, as mentioned above in the case-law of the European Court of Human Rights). In this specific context, the defence of net neutrality might be seen as a practical way to back up and secure these rights. The defence of net neutrality is one place where the more general responsibility of states and other actors might be operationalized. On the other hand, the argument might be transposed at the global institutional level in informing the global governance of the net[332]. It grounds an argument about the requirement to secure net neutrality as mechanism against domination. This type of argument is required to inform policy-making process at the international level, such as for the Internet Governance Forum.

---

[331] See for instance, Laborde (2010); Bohman (2009).

[332] For the link between net neutrality and internet governance, Musiani, Schafer and Le Crosnier (2012).

The republican ideal of preventing domination might also be extended towards the second set of values identified above. The key idea is to extend the domain of the republican insight to this informational ecosystem in working out a theory around the ambition to prevent domination to happen. As for other political theories (such as liberalism), this move towards the informational ecosystem is connected to specific challenges. These challenges range from metaphysical challenges about the nature of the entities to be found in the infosphere, to ethical principles applying to these entities and their creators.

To recall, the idea of Floridi is to consider the informational ecosystem as the "place" in which numerous informational entities co-exist (such as web sites, avatars, mails, pictures, movies, online profiles, database etc.[333]). With respect to the metaphysical challenges about the nature of these entities, there is a prima facie argument to be made following Floridi's work. It we accept Floridi's argument about the nature of the entities of the infosphere, there is, by extension, no specific problem to account for their duties and for the overall functioning of the infosphere in light of the ideal of non-domination. With respect to Floridi's four principles, it appears clearly that preventing domination might be linked to the promotion of information. Non-domination is, negatively, about preventing entropy to happen and, positively, about the flourishment of information.

A republican information ethics (inspired by Floridi's work) is still *terra incognita*. This contribution cannot be the place to propose such a theory. However, it raises the prima facie argument that a republican approach could be used to make sense of Floridi's ethical principles.

With this republican framing in mind, we could come back to the main tensions identified above and exemplify the potential of freedom as non-domination as a way to ground and make sense of net neutrality. It lays down the blueprint of a republican net neutrality as an account

---

[333] Turilli, Vaccaro and Taddeo (2012), 142-143.

particularly able to account for risks of domination in situations of power imbalances.

In the situation of "mitigation of congestion", the republican net neutrality calls for a traffic management which respects the overall functioning of the informational ecosystem. The key idea in operationalizing a just traffic management is to prevent domination to happen. Domination between specific applications requiring a specific quality of service should be prevented. The republican insight here has a structural impact on the way traffic management is organized. It grounds a functional approach where the overall functioning of the network is the main goal. Without giving priority to specific types of application, the point is rather to make sure that co-existence is possible and, where congestion threatens, to apply a functional answer to the safeguard of the widest possible range of applications.

If congestion becomes the normal situation (because of scarce network resources), republicanism calls for procedural means to establish a satisfactory prioritization among services. The anti-domination argument shifts from traffic management to the procedure put in place to address traffic management in situation of congestion. This republican procedure puts a premium on preventing powerful actors to impose their views in the definition of this prioritization.

In the situation of "prohibition of access to specific content", the republican approach directly connects to the defence of individual freedoms. Both in the access to information sources and in implementing legal obligations, the key element should be the promotion of individual freedom defined as non-domination, both domestically and internationally. The tradition of republican thought is at its strongest when "net neutrality" is a means to secure core elements of individual freedom in the information society. In this second constellation, domination provides the concept around which to lead the difficult discussion on the arguable responsibility of IAPs to filter the content they give access to (as in the fake-news debate). There seems to be a prima facie argument for a limitation to legally prohibited content (*only* illegal content is banned). Further grounds must fulfil two conditions in light of non-domination: a first content-condition (is the ground able to foster non-domination, both for individuals and from the point of view of the informational ecosystem?) and a second procedural condition (is the determination of the ground the product of a non-dominating procedure in which relevant stakeholders have been able to express their views?).

In the situation of "differentiation of services to end-users" and in the situation of "protection of IAP own services", the republican approach is able to account for risks of domination of business actors (IAPs). The risk of domination is not limited to the relation state–citizen, but encompasses further relations in which an individual is put at the mercy of powerful actors. In an issue as crucial as access to and use of the internet, the domination exercised by IAPs might be particularly threatening. It might be threatening for individual freedoms (first set of values), but also threatening to the quality of the informational ecosystem (second set of values). The republican approach allows to pinpoint the difference between a necessary traffic management to address congestion (on the basis of a functional approach preserving the maximal number of applications) and a traffic management prioritizing business' interests over users' interests. The first one is not a domination in that interests of the users are taken into account and function as control mechanisms on IAPs. The second is a form of domination in that decisions taken by the IAPs are not checked. Hence, the republican approach aims to prevent it.

18.5 Conclusion

This paper has argued that the "net neutrality" debate should be mainly framed as a question of traffic management. Different situations of traffic management have been identified and their specific ethical challenges have been spelled out.

These challenges make clear that the call to "net neutrality" should be understood as a broader call towards a "just" internet. Neutrality is, in specific situations, the way to realize this just internet, but it might not always be the case. We have identified two sets of values which underlie the different instances in which "net neutrality" is used: a first set of values around individual freedom of individual and a second set of values around the functioning of the informational ecosystem. To clearly identify these values as normative foundations of the attribute "neutral" allows to specify how to address the identified distinct ethical challenges. I have argued that a republican understanding of these values and of "net neutrality" bears promising resources to address risks of domination. Freedom defined as non-domination might be fruitful in the context of the defence and promotion of individual freedoms (first set of values), but also in the context of the informational ecosystem (second set of values). In all instances of traffic management, the duty to prevent domination in form of arbitrary interferences with important interests of individual should serve as a normative guideline.

References

Bellamy, R. (2011), Republicanism: Non Domination and the Free State. *Routledge Handbook of contemporary social and political theory* G. Delanty and S. P. Turner, Routledge.

Belli, L. (2016), End-to-End, Net Neutrality and Human Rights. *Net Neutrality Compendium: Human Rights, Free Competition and the Future of the Internet* L. Belli and P. De Filippi. Cham, Springer International Publishing.

Belli, L. and P. De Filippi (2016), *Net Neutrality Compendium : Human Rights, Free Competition and the Future of the Internet* Cham, Springer International Publishing.

Bohman, J. (2009), Cosmopolitan Republicanism and the Rule of Law. *Legal Republicanism : National and International Perspectives*. S. Besson and J. L. Martí. Oxford, Oxford University Press.

Brennan, A. and Y.-S. Lo (2015). Environmental Ethics, *Stanford Encyclopedia of Philosophy*.

Cheruvalath, R. (2018), Internet Neutrality: A Battle Between Law and Ethics. *International Journal for the Semiotics of Law - Revue internationale de Sémiotique juridique* 31(1): 145-153.

Floridi, L. (2008), Information Ethics, its Nature and Scope, *Moral Philosophy and Information Technology* J. v. d. Hoven and J. Weckert. Cambridge, Cambridge University Press.

Floridi, L. (2013), *The Ethics of Information*. Oxford, Oxford University Press.

Gerlach, J. (2016), *The Informational Ecosystem of Net Neutrality: A Comparison of Regulatory Discourses in the U.S. and the E.U.* Zürich/St-Gallen, Dike.

Graber, C. (2017), Bottom-Up Constitutionalism: The Case of Net Neutrality." *Transnational Legal Theory* 7(4): 524-552.

Greenstein, S., M. Peitz, et al. (2016), Net Neutrality: A Fast Lane to Understanding the Trade-offs, *Journal of Economic Perspectives* 30(2): 127-150.

Halldenius, L. (2010), Building Blocks of a Republican Cosmo-politanism, *European Journal of Political Theory* 9(1): 12-30.

Honohan, I. (2014), Domination and Migration: an Alternative Approach to the Legitimacy of Migration Controls, *Critical Review of International Social and Political Philosophy* 17(1): 31-48.

Hu, H. L. (2011), The Political Economy of Governing ISPs in China: Perspectives of Net Neutrality and Vertical Integration, *The China Quarterly* 207: 523-540.

Laborde, C. (2010), Republicanism and Global Justice: A Sketch, *European Journal of Political Theory* 9(1): 48-69.

Lovett, F. (2010), *A General Theory of Domination and Justice*. New York, Oxford University Press.

Lovett, F. (2014), Republicanism, *Stanford Encyclopedia of Philosophy*.

Moreau, S. (2010), What Is Discrimination?, *Philosophy & Public Affairs* 38(2): 143-179.

Musiani, F., V. Schafer, et al. (2012), Net Neutrality as an Internet Governance Issue: The Globalization of an American-Born Debate, *Revue française d'études américaines* 134(4): 47-63.

Pettit, P. (1997), *Republicanism: A Theory of Freedom and Government*. Oxford, Clarendon Press.

Pettit, P. (2008), Republican Liberty: Three Axioms, Four Theorems, *Republicanism and Political Theory*. C. Laborde and J. Maynor. Oxford, Blackwell.

Pettit, P. (2010), A Republican Law of Peoples. *European Journal of Political Theory* 9(1): 70-94.

Turilli, M., A. Vaccaro, et al. (2012), Internet Neutrality: Ethical Issues in the Internet Environment, *Philosophy & Technology* 25: 133–151.

Valentini, L. (2011), *Justice in a Globalized World: a Normative Framework*. Oxford, Oxford University Press.

Wu, T. (2003), Network Neutrality, Broadband Discrimination, *Journal of Telecommunications and High Technology Law* 2(1): 141-178.

Young, I. M. (2007). *Global Challenges: War, Self-Determination and Responsibility for Justice*. Cambridge, Polity Press.

PART VI

CYBER SECURITY, CYBER CRIME, CYBER WAR AND ETHICS

ETHICS AND AUTONOMOUS WEAPON SYSTEMS: AN ETHICAL BASIS FOR HUMAN CONTROL?

International Committee of the Red Cross (ICRC)

Executive Summary

In the view of the International Committee of the Red Cross (ICRC)[334], human control must be maintained over weapon systems and the use of force to ensure compliance with international law and to satisfy ethical concerns, and States must work urgently to establish limits on autonomy in weapon systems.

In August 2017, the ICRC convened a round-table meeting with independent experts to explore the ethical issues raised by autonomous weapon systems and the ethical dimension of the requirement for human control. This report summarizes discussions and highlights the ICRC's main conclusions.

The fundamental ethical question is whether the principles of humanity and the dictates of the public conscience can allow human decision-making on the use of force to be effectively substituted with com-

---

[334] This paper is published with permission of ICRC, Head Office Geneva. By ICRC published on 3 April 2018. https://www.icrc.org/en/document/ethics-and-autonomous-weapon-systems-ethical-basis-human-control. Accessed 3 Sept 2018.

puter-controlled processes, and life-and-death decisions to be ceded to machines.

It is clear that ethical decisions by States, and by society at large, have preceded and motivated the development of new international legal constraints in warfare, including constraints on weapons that cause unacceptable harm. In international humanitarian law, notions of humanity and public conscience are drawn from the Martens Clause. As a potential marker of the public conscience, opinion polls to date suggest a general opposition to autonomous weapon systems – with autonomy eliciting a stronger response than remote-controlled systems.

Ethical issues are at the heart of the debate about the acceptability of autonomous weapon systems. It is precisely anxiety about the loss of human control over weapon systems and the use of force that goes beyond questions of the compatibility of autonomous weapon systems with our laws to encompass fundamental questions of acceptability to our values. A prominent aspect of the ethical debate has been a focus on autonomous weapon systems that are designed to kill or injure humans, rather than those that destroy or damage objects, which are already employed to a limited extent.

The primary ethical argument for autonomous weapon systems has been results-oriented: that their potential precision and reliability might enable better respect for both international law and human ethical values, resulting in fewer adverse humanitarian consequences. As with other weapons, such characteristics would depend on both the design-dependent effects and the way the weapons were used. A secondary argument is that they would help fulfil the duty of militaries to protect their own forces – a quality not unique to autonomous weapon systems.

While there are concerns regarding the technical capacity of autonomous weapons systems to function within legal and ethical constraints, the enduring ethical arguments against these weapons are those that transcend context – whether during armed conflict or in peacetime – and transcend technology – whether simple or sophisticated.

The importance of retaining human agency – and intent – in decisions to use force, is one of the central ethical arguments for limits on autonomy in weapon systems. Many take the view that decisions to kill, injure and destroy must not be delegated to machines, and that humans must be present in this decision-making process sufficiently to preserve a direct link between the intention of the human and the eventual operation of the weapon system.

Closely linked are concerns about a loss of human dignity. In other words, it matters not just if a person is killed or injured but how they are killed or injured, including the process by which these decisions are made. It is argued that, if human agency is lacking to the extent that machines have effectively, and functionally, been delegated these decisions, then it undermines the human dignity of those combatants targeted, and of civilians that are put at risk as a consequence of legitimate attacks on military targets.

The need for human agency is also linked to moral responsibility and accountability for decisions to use force. These are human responsibilities (both ethical and legal), which cannot be transferred to inanimate machines, or computer algorithms.

Predictability and reliability in using an autonomous weapon system are ways of connecting human agency and intent to the eventual consequences of an attack. However, as weapons that self-initiate attacks, autonomous weapon systems all raise questions about predictability, owing to varying degrees of uncertainty as to exactly when, where and/or why a resulting attack will take place. The application of AI and machine learning to targeting functions raises fundamental questions of inherent unpredictability.

Context also affects ethical assessments. Constraints on the timeframe of operation and scope of movement over an area are key factors, as are the task for which the weapon is used and the operating environment. However, perhaps the most important factor is the type of target, since core ethical concerns about human agency, human dignity and moral responsibility are most acute in relation to the notion of anti-personnel autonomous weapon systems that target humans directly.

From the ICRC's perspective, ethical considerations parallel the requirement for a minimum level of human control over weapon systems and the use of force to ensure legal compliance. From an ethical viewpoint, "meaningful", "effective" or "appropriate" human control would be the type and degree of control that preserves human agency and upholds moral responsibility in decisions to use force. This requires a sufficiently direct and close connection to be maintained between the human intent of the user and the eventual consequences of the operation of the weapon system in a specific attack.

Ethical and legal considerations may demand some similar constraints on autonomy in weapon systems, so that meaningful human control is maintained – in particular, with respect to: human supervision and the ability to intervene and deactivate; technical requirements for predictability and reliability (including in the algorithms used); and operational constraints on the task for which the weapon is used, the type of target, the operating environment, the timeframe of operation and the scope of movement over an area.

However, the combined and interconnected ethical concerns about loss of human agency in decisions to use force, diffusion of moral responsibility and loss of human dignity could have the most far- reaching consequences, perhaps precluding the development and use of anti-personnel autonomous weapon systems, and even limiting the applications of anti-materiel systems, depending on the risks that destroying materiel targets present for human life.

18.1 Introduction

Since 2011, the ICRC has been engaged in debates about autonomous weapon systems, holding international expert meetings with States and independent experts in March 2014[335] and March 2016[336] and contributing to discussions at the United Nations Convention on Certain Conventional Weapons (CCW) since 2014.

The *ICRC's position is that States must establish limits on autonomy in weapon systems* to ensure compliance with international humanitarian law and other applicable international law, and to satisfy ethical concerns. It has called on States to determine where these limits should be placed by assessing the *type and degree of human control* required in the use of autonomous weapon systems (broadly defined as weapons with autonomy in their critical functions of selecting and attacking targets)[337] for legal compliance and ethical acceptability.[338]

---

[335] ICRC, Autonomous weapon systems: Technical, military, legal and humanitarian aspects, 2014 – report of an expert meeting: https://www.icrc.org/en/document/report-icrc-meeting-autonomous-weapon-systems-26-28-march-2014.

[336] ICRC, Autonomous weapon systems: Implications of increasing autonomy in the critical functions of weapons, 2016 – report of an expert meeting: https://www.icrc.org/en/publication/4283-autonomous-weapons-systems.

[337] The ICRC's working definition of an autonomous weapon system is: "Any weapon system with autonomy in its critical functions. That is, a weapon system that can select (i.e. search for or detect, identify, track, select) and attack (i.e. use force against, neutralize, damage or destroy) targets without human intervention." This definition encompasses a limited number of existing weapons, such as: anti-materiel weapon systems used to protect ships, vehicles, buildings or areas from incoming attacks with missiles, rockets, artillery, mortars or other projectiles; and some loitering munitions. There have been reports that some anti-personnel "sentry" weapon systems have autonomous modes. However, as far as is known to the ICRC, "sentry" weapon systems that have been deployed still require human remote authorization to launch an attack (even though they may identify targets autonomously). See: ICRC, Autonomous weapon systems:

As part of continuing reflections, the *ICRC convened a two-day round-table meeting* with independent experts to consider the ethical issues raised by autonomous weapon systems and the *ethical dimension of the requirement for human control* over weapon systems and the use of force.[339] This report summarizes discussions at the meeting, supple-

---

Implications of increasing autonomy in the critical functions of weapons, op. cit. (footnote 337), 2016, pp. 11–12.

[338] ICRC, Statement to the Convention on Certain Conventional Weapons (CCW) Group of Governmental Experts on "Lethal Autonomous Weapon Systems", 15 November 2017: https://www.icrc.org/en/document/expert-meeting-lethal- autonomous-weapons-systems; N Davison, "Autonomous weapon systems under international humanitarian law", in Perspectives on Lethal Autonomous Weapon Systems, United Nations Office for Disarmament Affairs (UNODA) Occasional Papers No. 30, November 2017: https://www.un.org/disarmament/publications/occasionalpapers/unoda-occasional-papers-no-30-november-2017; ICRC, Views of the ICRC on autonomous weapon systems, 11 April 2016: https://www.icrc.org/en/document/views-icrc-autonomous-weapon-system.

[339] The event was entitled "Ethics and autonomous weapon systems: An ethical basis for human control?" and was held at the Humanitarium, International Committee of the Red Cross (ICRC), Geneva, on 28 and 29 August 2017. With thanks to the following experts for their participation: Joanna Bryson (University of Bath, UK); Raja Chatila (Institut des Systèmes Intelligents et de Robotique, France); Markus Kneer (University of Zurich, Switzerland); Alexander Leveringhaus (University of Oxford, UK); Hine-Wai Loose (United Nations Office for Disarmament Affairs, Geneva); AJung Moon (Open Roboethics Institute, Canada); Bantan Nugroho (United Nations Office for Disarmament Affairs, Geneva); Heather Roff (Arizona State University, USA); Anders Sandberg (University of Oxford, UK); Robert Sparrow (Monash University, Australia); Ilse Verdiesen (Delft University of Technology, Netherlands); Kerstin Vignard (United Nations Institute for Disarmament Research); Wendell Wallach (Yale University, US); and Mary Wareham (Human Rights Watch). The ICRC was represented by: Kathleen Lawand, Neil Davison and Anna Chiapello (Arms Unit, Legal Division); Fiona Terry (Centre for Operational Research and Experience); and Sasha Radin (Law and Policy Forum). Report prepared by Neil Davison, ICRC.

mented by additional research. The report highlights key themes and conclusions from the perspective of the ICRC, and these do not necessarily reflect the views of the participants.

For the ICRC, the *fundamental question at the heart of ethical discussions* is whether, irrespective of compliance with international law, the principles of humanity and the dictates of the public conscience can allow human decision-making on the use of force to be effectively substituted with computer-controlled processes, and life-and-death decisions to be ceded to machines. The ICRC's concerns reflect the sense of deep discomfort over the idea of any weapon system that places the use of force beyond human control[340]. And yet, important questions remain: at what point have decisions effectively, or functionally, been delegated to machines? What type and degree of human control are required, and in which circumstances, to satisfy ethical concerns? These are questions with profound implications for the future of warfare and humanity, and all States, as well as the military, scientists, industry, civil society and the public, have a stake in determining the answers.

18.2 The Principles of Humanity and the Dictates of the Public Conscience

18.2.1 Ethics and the Law

Ethics and law are intimately linked, especially where the purpose of the law – such as international humanitarian law and international human rights law – is to protect persons. This relationship can provide insights into how considerations of humanity and public conscience drive legal development.

---

[340] ICRC, Statement to the Convention on Certain Conventional Weapons (CCW) Meeting of Experts on "Lethal Autonomous Weapons Systems", 13 April 2015: https://www.icrc.org/en/document/lethal-autonomous-weapons-systems-LAWS.

The regulation of any conduct of hostilities, including regulating the choice of weapons, starts with a societal decision of what is acceptable or unacceptable behaviour, what is right and wrong. Subsequent *legal restrictions are*, therefore, *a social construct, shaped by societal and ethical perceptions.* These determinations evolve over time; what was considered acceptable at one point in history is not necessarily the case today.[341] However, some codes of behaviour in warfare have endured for centuries – for example, the unacceptability of killing women and children, and of poisoning.

It is clear that ethical decisions by States, and by society at large, have preceded and motivated the development of new international legal constraints in warfare, and that in the face of new developments not specifically foreseen or not clearly addressed by existing law, *contemporary ethical concerns can go beyond what is already codified in the law.* This highlights the importance of not reducing debates about autonomous weapon systems, or other new technologies of warfare, solely to legal compliance.

18.2.2 The Martens Clause

Treaties is therefore permitted – *it is a safety net for humanity.* The provision is recognized as being particularly relevant to assessing new technologies and new means and methods of warfare.[342]

There is debate over whether the Martens Clause constitutes a legally-binding yardstick against which the lawfulness of a weapon must be measured, or rather an ethical guideline. Nevertheless, it is clear that considerations of humanity and public conscience have driven the evolution of international law on weapons, and these notions have triggered the negotiation of specific treaties to prohibit or limit certain weapons,

---

[341] For example, among conventional weapons: expanding bullets, anti-personnel mines and cluster munitions.

[342] International Court of Justice, Legality of the Threat or Use of Nuclear Weapons, Advisory Opinion, ICJ Reports, 1996, para.78.

.

as well as underlying the development and implementation of the rules of international humanitarian law more broadly.[343]

18.2.3 The Public Conscience in Practice

In the development of international humanitarian law on weapons there is a strong ethical narrative to be found in the words used by States, the ICRC (mandated to uphold international humanitarian law) and civil society in raising concerns about *weapons that cause, or have the potential to cause, unacceptable harm*. For example, regarding weapons that cause *superfluous injury or unnecessary suffering for combatants*, in 1918, the ICRC, in calling for a prohibition of chemical weapons, described them as "barbaric weapons", an "appalling method of waging war", and appealed to States' "feeling of humanity".[344] In advocating for a prohibition of blinding laser weapons, the ICRC appealed to the "conscience of humanity" and later welcomed the 1995 Protocol IV to the Convention on Certain conventional Weapons (CCW) as a "victory of civilization over barbarity".[345]

Likewise, addressing *weapons that strike blindly, indiscriminately affecting civilians*, the ICRC expressed an ethical revulsion over the "landmine carnage" and "appalling humanitarian consequences" of an-

---

[343] K Lawand and I Robinson, "Development of treaties limiting or prohibiting the use of certain weapons: the role of the International Committee of the Red Cross", in R Geiss, A Zimmermann and S Haumer (eds.), Humanizing the laws of war: the Red Cross and the development of international humanitarian law, Cambridge University Press, 2017, pp. 141–184; M Veuthey, "Public Conscience in International Humanitarian Law", in D Fleck (ed.), Crisis Management and Humanitarian Protection, Berliner Wissenschafts-Verlag, Berlin, 2004, pp. 611–642.

[344] ICRC, World War I: the ICRC's appeal against the use of poisonous gases, 1918: https://www.icrc.org/eng/resources/documents/statement/57jnqh.htm.

[345] L Doswald-Beck, "New Protocol on Blinding Laser Weapons", International Review of the Red Cross, No. 312, 1996: https://www.icrc.org/eng/resources/documents/article/other/57jn4y.htm.

ti-personnel mines in debates leading to the prohibition of these weapons in 997.[346] The recent Treaty on the Prohibition of Nuclear Weapons, adopted in July 2017 by a group of 22 States, recognizes that the use of nuclear weapons would be "abhorrent to the principles of humanity and the dictates of public conscience".14[347] The ethical underpinnings of restrictions in international humanitarian law on the use of certain weapons are not in dispute.

Civil society, medical, scientific and military experts, and the ICRC and other components of the International Red Cross and Red Crescent Movement, have played a key role in raising the attention of States to the unacceptable harm caused by certain weapons, such as anti-personnel mines and cluster munitions, building on evidence collected by those treating victims. Engagement in these endeavours by military veterans and religious figures, appeals to political leaders and parliamentarians, the testimony of victims and communication of concerns to the public were central to securing these prohibitions. In some debates, such as on blinding laser weapons, reflections by the military on the risks for their own soldiers were critical. All these various activities can be seen, in some way, as a demonstration of the public conscience.[348]

18.3   The Ethical Debate on Autonomous Weapon Systems

Ethical questions about autonomous weapon systems have sometimes been viewed as secondary concerns. Many States have tended to

---

[346] P Herby and K Lawand, "Unacceptable Behaviour: How Norms are Established", in J Williams, S Goose and M Wareham (eds.), Banning Landmines: Disarmament, Citizen Diplomacy and Human Security, Lanham, MD: Rowman & Littlefield Publishers, 2008, p. 202.

[347] UN General Assembly, Treaty on the Prohibition of Nuclear Weapons, preamble, A/CONF.229/2017/8, 7 July 2017.

[348] K Lawand and I Robinson, op. cit. (footnote 343), 2017.

be more comfortable discussing whether new weapons can be developed and used in compliance with international law, particularly international humanitarian law, and with the assumption that the primary factors that limit the development and use of autonomous weapon systems are legal and technical.

However, for many experts and observers, and for some States, *ethics* – the "moral principles that govern a person's behaviour or the conducting of an activity"[349] – *are at the heart of what autonomous weapon systems mean for the human conduct of warfare, and the use of force more broadly*. It is precisely anxiety about the loss of human control over this conduct that goes beyond questions of the compatibility of autonomous weapon systems with our *laws* to encompass fundamental questions of acceptability to our *values*.

Ethical concerns over delegating life-and-death decisions, and reflections on the importance of the Martens Clause, have been raised in different quarters, including by: more than 30 States during CCW meetings,[350] a UN Special Rapporteur at the Human Rights Council,[351] Human Rights Watch[352] (and the Campaign to Stop Killer Robots), the ICRC,[353] the United Nations Institute for Disarmament Research (UNI-

---

[349] Oxford Dictionary of English: https://en.oxforddictionaries.com/definition/ethics.

[350] Including: Algeria, Argentina, Austria, Belarus, Brazil, Cambodia, Costa Rica, Cuba, Ecuador, Egypt, France, Germany, Ghana, Holy See, India, Kazakhstan, Mexico, Morocco, Nicaragua, Norway, Pakistan, Panama, Peru, Republic of Korea, Sierra Leone, South Africa, Sri Lanka, Sweden, Switzerland, Turkey, Venezuela, Zambia and Zimbabwe.

[351] Human Rights Council, Report of the Special Rapporteur on extrajudicial, summary or arbitrary executions, Christof Heyns, A/HRC/23/47, 9 April 2013.

[352] Human Rights Watch, Losing Humanity: The Case against Killer Robots, 19 November 2012.

[353] ICRC, Statement to CCW Meeting of Experts on "Lethal Autonomous Weapons Systems", 13–17 April 2015: https://www.icrc.org/en/document/lethal-autonomous-weapons-systems-LAWS.

DIR),[354] academics and think-tanks, and, increasingly, among the scientific and technical communities.[355]

Discussions on autonomous weapon systems have generally *acknowledged the necessity for some degree of human control over weapons and the use for force*, whether for legal, ethical or military operational reasons (States have not always made clear for which reasons, or combination thereof).[356]

It is clear, however, that the points at which human control is located in the development and employment, and exercised in the use, of a weapon with autonomy in the critical functions of selecting and attacking targets may be central to determining whether this control is "meaningful", "effective" or "appropriate" from an ethical perspective (and a legal one).

---

[354] UNIDIR, The Weaponization of Increasingly Autonomous Technologies: Considering Ethics and Social Values, 2015.

[355] Future of Life Institute, Autonomous Weapons: an Open Letter from AI & Robotics Researchers, 28 July 2015; Future of Life Institute, An Open Letter to the United Nations Convention on Certain Conventional Weapons, 21 August 2017.

[356] United Nations, Report of the 2017 Group of Governmental Experts on "Lethal Autonomous Weapons Systems" (LAWS), CCW/GGE.1/2017/CRP.1, 20 November 2017, p.7: "The importance of considering LAWS ["Lethal Autonomous Weapon Systems"] in relation to human involvement and the human-machine interface was underlined. The notions that human control over lethal targeting functions must be pre-served, and that machines could not replace humans in making decisions and judgments, were promoted. Various related concepts, including, inter alia, meaningful and effective human control, appropriate human judgment, human involvement and human supervision, were discussed." United Nations, Recommendations to the 2016 Review Conference Submitted by the Chairperson of the Informal Meeting of Experts, November 2016, p. 1: "[V]iews on appropriate human involvement with regard to lethal force and the issue of delegation of its use are of critical importance to the further consideration of LAWS amongst the High Contracting Parties and should be the subject of further consideration".

A prominent aspect of the ethical debate has been a *focus on "lethal autonomy" or "killer robots" – implying weapon systems that are designed to kill or injure humans*, rather than autonomous weapon systems that destroy or damage objects, which are already employed to a limited extent.[357]

This is despite the fact that some anti-materiel weapons can also result in the death of humans either directly (humans inside objects, such as buildings, vehicles, ships and aircraft) or indirectly (humans in proximity to objects), and that even the use of non-kinetic weapons – such as cyber weapons – can result in kinetic effects and in human casualties. Of course, *autonomy in the critical functions of selecting and attacking targets is a feature that could, in theory, be applied to any weapon system.*

Ethical discussions have also *transcended the context-dependent legal bounds of international humanitarian law and international human rights law.* Ethical concerns, relevant in all circumstances, have been at the centre of warnings by UN Special Rapporteur Christof Heyns that "allowing LARs [Lethal Autonomous Robots] to kill people may denigrate the value of life itself",[358] and by Human Rights Watch that "fully autonomous weapons" would "cross a moral threshold" because of "the lack of human qualities necessary to make a moral decision, the threat to human dignity and the absence of moral agency".[359]

18.3.1 Main Ethical Arguments

Nevertheless, ethical arguments have been made both *for* and *against* autonomous weapon systems, reflecting, to a certain extent, the different

---

[357] See footnote 337 on existing autonomous weapon systems. Although the use of anti-materiel systems has not been without its problems and accidents – see, for example: J Hawley, Automation and the Patriot Air and Missile Defense System, Center for a New American Security (CNAS), 25 January 2017.

[358] Human Rights Council, op. cit. (footnote 351), 2013, p. 20.

[359] Human Rights Watch, Making the Case: The Dangers of Killer Robots and the Need for a Pre-emptive Ban, 9 December 2016.

emphases of consequentialist (results-focused) and deontological (process-focused) approaches. The *primary argument for these weapons has been an assertion that they might enable better respect for both international law and human ethical values* by enabling greater precision and reliability than weapon systems controlled directly by humans, and therefore would result in less adverse humanitarian consequences for civilians.[360] This type of argument has been made in the past for other weapon systems, including, most recently, for armed drones, and it is important to recognize that such characteristics are not inherent to a weapon system but depend on both the design-dependent effects and the way the weapon system is used.[361]

Another ethical argument that has been made *for* autonomous weapon systems is that *they help fulfil the duty of militaries to protect their soldiers* by removing them from harm's way. However, since this can equally apply to remote-controlled and remotely-delivered weapons, it is not a convincing argument for autonomy in targeting *per se*, apart from, perhaps, in scenarios where human soldiers cannot respond quickly enough to an incoming threat, such as in missile and close-in air defence.

Ethical arguments against autonomous weapon systems can generally be divided into two forms: objections based on the limits of technolo-

---

[360] See, for example on ethical compliance: R Arkin "Lethal Autonomous Systems and the Plight of the Non-combatant", in AISIB Quarterly, July 2013. And on legal compliance: United States, Autonomy in Weapon Systems, Convention on Certain Conventional Weapons (CCW) Group of Governmental Experts on "Lethal Autonomous Weapon Systems", CCW/GGE.1/2017/WP.6, 10 November 2017, pp. 3–4.

[361] For example, remote-controlled armed drones with precision-guided munitions may offer the potential for greater precision and therefore less risk of indiscriminate effects. However, if the information about the target is inaccurate, targeting practices are too generalized, or protected persons or objects are deliberately, or accidentally, attacked, then the potential for precision offers no protection in itself.

gy to function within legal constraints and ethical norms;[362] and ethical objections that are independent of technological capability.[363]

Given that technology trajectories are hard to predict, it is the second category of ethical arguments that may be the most interesting for current policy debates. Do autonomous weapon systems raise any universal ethical concerns? Among the main issues in this respect are:

- *Removing human agency from decisions to kill, injure and destroy*[364] – decisions to use force – leading to a *responsibility gap* where humans cannot uphold their moral responsibility.[365]

- *Undermining the human dignity* of those combatants who are targeted,[366] and of civilians who are put at risk of death and injury as a consequence of attacks on legitimate military targets.

---

[362] See, for example: N Sharkey, "The evitability of autonomous robot warfare", International Review of the Red Cross, No. 886, 2012.

[363] See, for example: P Asaro, "On banning autonomous weapon systems: human rights, automation, and the dehumanization of lethal decision-making", International Review of the Red Cross, No. 886, 2012; R Sparrow, "Robots and respect: Assessing the case against Autonomous Weapon Systems", Ethics and International Affairs, 30(1), 2016, pp. 93–116; A Leveringhaus, Ethics and Autonomous Weapon Systems, Palgrave Macmillan, UK, 2016.

[364] A Leveringhaus, Ethics and Autonomous Weapon Systems, op. cit. (footnote 355), 2016.

[365] See, for example: R Sparrow, "Killer robots", Journal of Applied Philosophy, 24(1), 2007, pp. 62–77; H Roff, "Killing in War: Responsibility, Liability and Lethal Autonomous Robots", in F Allhoff, N Evans and A Henschke (eds.), Routledge Handbook of Ethics and War: Just War Theory in the 21st Century, Routledge, UK, 2014.

[366] See, for example: R Sparrow, op. cit. (footnote 365), 2016; C Heyns, "Autonomous weapons in armed conflict and the right to a dignified life: An African perspective", South African Journal on Human Rights, Vol. 33, Issue 1, 2017, pp. 46–71.

- *Further increasing human distancing* – physically and psychologically – from the battlefield, enhancing existing asymmetries and making the use of violence easier or less controlled.[367]

18.3.2 Human Agency in Decisions to Use Force

In ethical debates, there seems to be wide acknowledgement of the importance of retaining human agency[368] – and associated intent – in decisions to use force, particularly in decisions to kill, injure and destroy. In other words, many take the view that "machines must not make life-and-death decisions" and "machines cannot be delegated responsibility for these decisions".[369]

Machines and computer programs, as inanimate objects, do not think, see and perceive like humans. Therefore, some argue, it is difficult to see how human values can be respected if the "decision" to attack a specific target is functionally delegated to a machine. However, there are differing perspectives on the underlying question: at which point have decisions to use force effectively been delegated to a machine? Or, from another perspective: what limits on autonomy are required to retain sufficient human agency and intent in these decisions?

---

[367] A Leveringhaus, "Distance, weapons technology and humanity in armed conflict", ICRC Humanitarian Law & Policy Blog, 6 October 2017: http://blogs.icrc.org/law-and-policy/2017/10/06/distance-weapons-technology-and-humanity-in-armed-conflict.

[368] N Castree, R Kitchin and A Rogers, A Dictionary of Human Geography, Oxford University Press, Oxford, 2013: "The capacity possessed by people to act of their own volition."

[369] See footnote 350 above listing States that have raised core ethical concerns. For example: "Germany will certainly adhere to the principle that it is not acceptable, that the decision to use force, in particular the decision over life and death, is taken solely by an autonomous system without any possibility for a human intervention." Statement to CCW Meeting of Experts on "Lethal Autonomous Weapon Systems", 11–15 April 2016.

There is a parallel in this debate with landmines, which have been described as "rudimentary autonomous weapon systems".[370]   When humans lay landmines they effectively remove themselves from the decision about subsequent attacks on specific people or vehicles. They may know where the landmines are placed but they do not know who, or what, will trigger them, or when they will be triggered. This could be seen as a primitive form of delegating the decision to kill and injure to a machine.

Some argue it is difficult to establish a clear point at which this shift in functional decision-making from human to machine happens, and human agency and intention have been eroded or lost. Rather, it may be more useful, some propose, to agree on the general principle that a minimum level of human control is required in order to retain human agency in these decisions, and then *consider the way in which humans must inject themselves into the decision-making process and at what points, to ensure this control is sufficient* – for example, through human supervision and the ability to intervene and deactivate; technical requirements for predictability and reliability; and operational constraints on the task the

---

[370] United States Department of Defense, Department of Defense Law of War Manual, Section 6.5.9.1, Description and Examples of the Use of Autonomy in Weapon Systems, 2015, p. 328: "Some weapons may have autonomous functions. For example, mines may be regarded as rudimentary autonomous weapons because they are designed to explode by the presence, proximity, or contact of a person or vehicle, rather than by the decision of the operator."

There are different views on whether the complexity of the function dele-gated to a machine affects this ethical assessment. Some distinguish be-tween an "automated function" (activation, or not, of a landmine) and an "autonomous function" with "choice" (e.g. selecting between different tar-gets), but there are no clear lines between automated and autonomous from a technical perspective, and both can enable functional delegation of decisions. See, for example: ICRC, Autonomous weapon systems: Implications of increasing autonomy in the critical functions of weapons, op. cit., 2016, p. 8.

weapon is used for, the type of target, the operating environment, the timeframe of operation and the scope of movement over an area^3[371]

18.3.3 Human Dignity: Process and Results

Closely linked to the issue of human agency, and concerns about the delegation of decisions to use force, is *human dignity*. The *central argument here is that it matters not just if a person is killed and injured but how they are killed and injured.* Where a line has been crossed, and machines are effectively making life-and-death "decisions", the argument is that this undermines the human dignity of those targeted, even if they are lawful targets (for example, under international humanitarian law). As Christof Heyns, then UN Special Rapporteur on extrajudicial, summary or arbitrary executions, put it: "to allow machines to determine when and where to use force against humans is to reduce those humans to objects; they are treated as mere targets. They become zeros and ones in the digital scopes of weapons which are programmed in advance to release force without the ability to consider whether there is no other way out, without a sufficient level of deliberate human choice about the matter."[372]

Unlike previous discussions about constraints on weapons (*see Section 2.3*), which have focused on their effects (whether evidence of unacceptable harm or foreseeable effects), the additional ethical concerns with autonomous weapon systems are about *process* as well as *results*. What does this method of using force reveal about the underlying attitude to human life, to human dignity? And, in that sense, these *concerns are particularly relevant to the relationship between combatants in*

---

[371] ICRC, Statement to the Convention on Certain Conventional Weapons (CCW) Group of Governmental Experts on "Lethal Autonomous Weapon Systems", op. cit. (footnote 337), 15 November 2017.

[372] C Heyns, Autonomous Weapon Systems: Human rights and ethical issues, presentation to the CCW Meeting of Experts on "Lethal Autonomous Weapon Systems", 14 April 2016.

armed conflict, although they are also relevant to civilians, who must not be targeted, but are, nevertheless, exposed to collateral risks of death and injury from attacks on legitimate military targets.

For some, autonomous weapon systems conjure up visions of machines being used to kill humans like vermin, and a reduced respect for human life due to a lack of human agency and intention in the specific acts of using force. In this argument, delegating the execution of a *task* to a machine may be acceptable, but delegating the *decision* to kill or injure is not, which means applying human intent to each decision.

There are *strong parallels with the broader societal discussion about algorithmic, and especially artificial intelligence (AI)-driven, decision-making,* including military decision-making[373] (*see also Section 5.1*). Through handing over too much of the functional decision-making process to sensors and algorithms, is there a point at which humans are so far removed in time and space from the acts of selecting and attacking targets that human decision-making is effectively substituted by computer- controlled processes? The concern is that, *if the connection between the human decision to use force and the eventual consequences is too diffuse, then human agency in that decision is weakened and human dignity eroded.*

The counter-argument to an emphasis on process is found in the primary argument *for* autonomous weapons systems (*see Section 3.1*) that they will offer better *results*, posing less risk to civilians by enabling the users to exercise greater precision and discrimination than with human-operated systems. However, claims about reduced risks to civilians – which remain contentious in the absence of supporting evidence – are very much context-specific, whereas ethical questions about loss of

---

[373] D Lewis, G Blum and N Modirzadeh, War-Algorithm Accountability, Harvard Law School Program on International Law and Armed Conflict (HLS PILAC), Harvard University, 31 August 2016: https://pilac.law.harvard.edu/waa.

human dignity present more of a universal concern, independent of context.

18.4 Responsibility, Accountability and Transparency

Responsibility and accountability for decisions to use force cannot be transferred to a machine or a computer program.[374] These are human responsibilities – both legal and ethical – which require human agency in the decision-making process (*see Section 3*). Therefore, a closely related ethical concern raised by autonomous weapon systems is the risk of erosion – or diffusion – of responsibility and accountability for these decisions.

One way to address this concern is to assign responsibility to the operator or commander who authorizes the activation of the autonomous weapon system (or programmers and manufacturers, in case of malfunction). This addresses the issue of legal responsibility to some extent, simply by applying a process for holding an individual accountable for the consequences of their actions.[375] And this is how militaries typically address responsibility for operations using existing weapon systems, including, presumably, those with autonomy in their critical functions.

18.4.1 Implications of Autonomy for Moral Responsibility

For the ethical debate, however, *responsibility is not only a legal concept but also a moral one.* Some argue that, in order for the commander or operator to uphold their moral responsibility in a decision to activate

---

[374]ICRC, Statement to the Convention on Certain Conventional Weapons (CCW) Group of Governmental Experts on "Lethal Autonomous Weapon Systems", op. cit. (footnote 337), 15 November 2017.

[375] Although there are still questions around whether a person can be criminally accountable in situations where they lack the required knowledge or intent of how the system will operate once activated, or where there is insufficient evidence to discharge the burden of proof.

an autonomous weapon system, their *intent needs to be directly linked to the eventual outcome of the resulting attack.* This requires an understanding of how the weapon will function and the specific consequences of activating it in those circumstances, which is complicated by the uncertainty introduced by autonomy in targeting. Uncertainty brings a risk that the consequences of activating the weapon will not be those intended – or foreseen – by the operator rises both ethical and legal concerns.

An autonomous weapon system – since it selects and attacks targets independently (after launch or activation) – *creates varying degrees of uncertainty as to exactly when, where and/or why the resulting attack will take place.* The key difference between a human or remote-controlled weapon and an autonomous weapon system is that the former involves a human choosing a specific target – or group of targets – to be attacked, connecting their moral (and legal) responsibility to the specific consequences of their actions. In contrast, an *autonomous weapon system self-initiates an attack: it is given a technical description, or a "signature", of a target, and a spatial and temporal area of autonomous operation.* This description might be general ("an armoured vehicle") or even quite specific ("a certain type of armoured vehicle"), but the key issue is that the commander or operator activating the weapon is not giving instructions on a specific target to be attacked ("specific armoured vehicle") at a specific place ("at the corner of that street") and at a specific point in time ("now"). Rather, when activating the autonomous weapon system, by definition, the user will not know exactly which target will be attacked ("armoured vehicles fitting this technical signature"), in which place (within x square kilometres) or at which point in time (during the next x minutes/hours). Thus, it can be argued, this more generalized nature of the targeting decision means the user is not applying their intent to each specific attack.

The potential technical description, or signature, for an enemy combatant is both extremely broad and highly specific (e.g. combatant, fighter or civilian that is directly participating in hostilities but not one that is *hors de combat* or surrendering) and can vary enormously from one moment to the next. It is therefore highly doubtful that a weapon system could be programmed functionally to identify "enemy combatants".[376] But, assuming this might be possible for the sake of argument, if an anti-personnel autonomous weapon system encountered the signature of an enemy combatant it would attack when the signature matches its programming. *A human decision-maker controlling a weapon system in the same circumstances still has a choice.* S/he may decide to attack, or s/he may decide *not* to attack – even if the technical signature fits – including owing to wider ethical considerations in the specific circumstances, which may go beyond whether the combatant is a lawful target.[377] (From a legal perspective, it is important to note that the principles of military necessity and humanity already require that the kind and degree of force used against lawful targets must not exceed what is necessary to accomplish a legitimate military purpose in the circumstances.)[378]

---

[376]This does not mean it is necessarily simple, functionally, to identify objects (e.g. vehicles, buildings), since they change status over time (between military objective and civilian object), and objects used by civilians and the military can share similar characteristics.

[377]A Leveringhaus, Ethics and Autonomous Weapon Systems, op. cit., pp. 92–93.

[378]N Melzer, Interpretive guidance on the notion of direct participation in hostilities under international humanitarian law, ICRC, Geneva, 2016. Chapter IX: Restraints on the use of force in direct attack, p. 82: "In situations of armed conflict, even the use of force against persons not entitled to protection against direct attack remains subject to legal constraints. In addition to the restraints imposed by international humanitarian law on specific means and methods of warfare, and without prejudice to further restrictions that may arise under other applicable branches of international law, the kind and degree of force which is permissible against persons not entitled to protection against direct attack must not exceed what is actually necessary to accomplish a legitimate military purpose in the prevailing circumstances."

In sum, from an ethical perspective, the *removal of the human intent from a specific attack weakens moral responsibility by preventing considerations of humanity*. There may be a *causal explanation* for why these combatants were attacked (i.e. they corresponded to the target signature) but we may not be able to offer a *reason*, an ethical justification, for that attack (i.e. why were they attacked in the specific circumstances?). Since the process of reason-giving and justification establishes moral responsibility, and makes people feel they are treated justly, autonomous technology risks blocking this process and diminishing it.

18.4.2 Transparency in Human-Machine Interaction

Machine control and human control have different strengths and weaknesses. As currently understood, machines have limited decision-making capacities and limited situational awareness but can respond very quickly, and according to specific parameters (although, of course, this is a fast- developing field, especially with respect to artificial intelligence (AI) – *see Section 5.1*). In contrast, humans have a limited attention span and field of perception but global situational awareness of their environment, and sophisticated decision-making capacities. *This difference gives rise to a number of problems in human-machine interaction that are relevant to discussions about autonomous weapon systems*, including: *automation bias* – where humans place too much confidence in the operation of an autonomous machine; *surprises* – where a human is not fully aware of how a machine is functioning at the point s/he needs to take back control; and the *"moral buffer"* – where the human operator shifts moral responsibility and accountability to the machine as a perceived legitimate authority.[379]

---

[379] M Cummings, "Automation and Accountability in Decision Support System Interface Design", Journal of Technology Studies, Vol. XXXII, No. 1, 2006: "… decision support systems that integrate higher levels of automation can possibly allow users to perceive the computer as a legitimate authority, diminish

This raises additional questions about how moral responsibility and accountability can be ensured in the use of an autonomous weapon system, including whether there will be sufficient transparency in the way it operates, and its interaction with the environment, to be sufficiently understood by humans. To address this concern, a human operator may need to have continuous situational awareness during the operation of an autonomous weapon system, as well as a two-way communication link to receive information and give updated instructions to the system, if necessary, as well as sufficient time to respond or change the course of action, where necessary.

These types of human-machine *problems are already evident in existing civilian autonomous systems.* One example is the accident that resulted when the pilot of a passenger aircraft had to re- take control following a failure in the autopilot system but was not sufficiently aware of the situation to respond in the correct way.[380]   Other accidents have happened with car "autopilot" systems, where drivers relied too heavily on a system with limited capacity.[381]   And there are also parallels with autonomous financial trading systems, causing so-called "flash crashes" in ways not predictable by human traders overseeing them, and not preventable owing to the extremely short time-scales involved.[382]

---

moral agency, and shift accountability to the computer, thus creating a moral buffering effect".

[380] See, for example: R Charette, "Air France Flight 447 Crash Causes in Part Point to Automation Paradox", IEEE Spectrum, 2012: https://spectrum. ieee.org/riskfactor/aerospace/aviation/air-france-flight-447-crash-caused-by-a-combination-of-factors.

[381] J Stewart, "People Keep Confusing Their Teslas for Self-Driving Cars", Wired, 25 January 2018: https://www.wired.com/story/tesla-autopilot-crash-dui.

[382] US Securities & Exchange Commission, Findings regarding the market events of 6 May, 2010. Reports of the staffs of the CFTC and SEC to the Joint Advisory Committee on Emerging Regulatory Issues, 30 September 2010.

18.5 Predictability, Reliability and Risk

Unpredictability and unreliability have been raised as key issues for any legal assessment of autonomous weapon systems, [383] as well as for the risks their use may pose, [384] in particular for civilians. However, these factors are also closely connected to ethical questions of human agency and moral responsibility (*see Sections 3 and 4*).

One way to think about predictability and reliability in autonomous (weapon) systems is as *means of connecting human agency and intent with the eventual outcome and consequences* of the machine's operation. *Predictability* is the ability to "[s]ay or estimate that (a specified thing) will happen in the future or will be a consequence of something".[385] Applied to an autonomous weapon system, predictability is knowledge of how it will likely function in any given circumstances of use, and the effects that will likely result. *Reliability* is "[t]he quality of being trustworthy or performing consistently well".[386] In this context, reliability is knowledge of how consistently the system will function as intended, i.e. without failures or unintended effects.

Degrees of unpredictability and unreliability in the use of an autonomous weapon system might: be inherent to the technical design of the

---

[383] N Davison, *Autonomous weapon systems under international humanitarian law*, *op. cit.* (footnote 337), 2017; ICRC, *Views of the ICRC on autonomous weapon systems, op. cit.* (footnote 337)*,* 11 April 2016; W Wallach, "Predictability and Lethal Autonomous Weapons Systems (LAWS)", in German Federal Foreign Office, *Lethal Autonomous Weapons Systems: Technology, Definition, Ethics, Law & Security*, 2016, pp. 295–312.

[384] See, for example: P Scharre, Autonomous Weapons and Operational Risk, Center for a New American Security (CNAS), February 2016; UNIDIR, *Safety, Unintentional Risk and Accidents in the Weaponization of Increasingly Autonomous Technologies*, 2016.

[385] *Oxford Dictionary of English*: https://en.oxforddictionaries.com/definition/predictability.

[386] Ibid: https://en.oxforddictionaries.com/definition/reliability.

weapon system; arise from the nature of the environment (e.g. uncluttered' deep sea versus 'cluttered' populated area); and/or be due to the
interaction of the weapon system with the environment. Unpredictability
and unreliability in the environment may also vary over time and within
a given area (depending on the nature of the environment).

If one recognizes the argument of the necessity for human agency
and intent in decisions to use force (*see Section 3*) and the difficulties
raised by autonomy for moral responsibility and accountability (*see Section 4*), it follows that the *use of weapon systems that lead to unpredictable and unreliable consequences, and therefore heightened risks for
civilians, will accentuate these ethical concerns.* Unpredictability and
unreliability, in that sense, are both legally and ethically problematic.
However, predictability and reliability, in themselves, do not necessarily
resolve ethical questions. For example, an autonomous weapon system
might be highly predictable and reliable in attacking combatants, but it
could still raise ethical concerns with respect to human agency and human dignity.

Of course, there are *only ever degrees of predictability and reliability
in complex software-controlled systems.* Unpredictable and unreliable
operations may result from a variety of factors, including: *software errors and system flaws; human cognitive bias* in dismissing certain
possibilities; in-built *algorithmic bias*;[387] *"normal accidents"*, where
there is no clear error, but a system still does not function as expected; and deliberate *hacking, spoofing or cyber-attacks.*

It is also important to emphasize that nothing is one hundred per cent
predictable and reliable, including non-autonomous, human-controlled,

---

[387] See, for example: A Caliskan, J Bryson and A Narayanan, "Semantics derived automatically from language corpora contain human-like biases", Science,
Vol. 356, Issue 6334, 2017, pp. 183–186; C O'Neil, Weapons of Math Destruction: How big data increases inequality and threatens democracy, Crown, New
York, 2016.

weapon systems. Although it is clear that a high degree would be demanded in safety-critical autonomous systems, such as weapon systems, questions remain about the level of predictability and reliability required to satisfy ethical (and legal) considerations.

18.5.1 Artificial Intelligence (AI) and Unpredictability

For many considering the implications of autonomous weapon systems, the key change in recent years

– and *a fundamental challenge for predictability* – *is the further development of artificial intelligence (AI)*, and *especially AI algorithms that incorporate machine learning*. In general, machine-learning systems can only be understood at a particular moment in time. The "behaviour" of the learning algorithm is determined not only by initial programming (carried out by a human) but also by the process in which the algorithm itself "learns" and develops by "experience". This can be *offline learning by training* (before deployment) and/or *online learning by experience* (after deployment) while carrying out a task.

Deep learning – where an algorithm develops by learning data patterns rather than learning a specific task – further complicates the ability to understand and predict how the algorithm will function, once deployed. It can also add to the problem of biases that can be introduced into an algorithm through limitations in the data sets used to "train" it. Or a learning system may simply have learned in a way that was not intended by the developer.

Complicating matters further, *humans' current ability to interrogate machine-learning algorithms is limited.* Such systems are often described as "back-boxes"; the inputs and outputs may be known but the *process* by which a system converts an input to an output is not known. This type of system can be tested to help determine its functioning in different environments. However, there are significant limits in current abilities to verify the functioning of these systems, a task that becomes harder the more actions there are in the repertoire of the system and the more complex the inputs. If a system continues to learn after being tested, then the verification and validation (checks to determine if a system will operate as intended in a given environment) are no longer meaningful. *This type of autonomous system would be inherently unpredictable* (owing to its technical design) and, if applied to targeting, for example, the link between human intent and eventual outcome would effectively be severed.[388]

Questions about *AI and learning algorithms in weapon systems and targeting functions are no longer theoretical.* As with civilian digital technology, big data are an increasingly important resource, and the focus of data exploitation and analysis efforts is on AI algorithms. For the military, this promises a capability advantage for decision-making in data-rich conflict environments. And despite the risks of unpredictability, which may conflict with military commanders' propensity for command and control, there is significant and increasing interest among the major powers in the military applications of AI,[389] including projects

---

[388] From a legal perspective, when considering the obligation of States to review new weapons before their deployment and use under Article 36 of Additional Protocol I to the Geneva Conventions, it is difficult to see how a weapon system that autonomously changes its own functioning could ever be approved, since what had been tested and verified at one point in time would not be valid for the future. See: ICRC, Autonomous weapon systems: Implications of increasing autonomy in the critical functions of weapons, op. cit. (footnote 336), 2016, p. 13.

[389] See, for example: United States Department of Defense, Summer Study on Autonomy, Defense Science Board, June 2016; M Cummings, Artificial Intelligence and the Future of Warfare, Chatham House, International Security Department and US and the Americas Programme, January 2017; G Allen and T Chan, Artificial Intelligence and National Security, Harvard Kennedy School, Belfer Center for Science and International Affairs, 2017; E Kania, Battlefield Singularity. Artificial Intelligence, Military Revolution, and China's Future Military Power, Center for a New American Security (CNAS), 2017; "Artificial Intelligence and Chinese Power", Associated Press, 2017; "Putin: Leader in artificial intelligence will rule world", CNBC, 4 September 2017:

underway to apply machine learning to automatic target recognition and identification.[390] AI systems may not even need to have a physical component to raise ethical (and legal) questions if their outputs, as "decision aids," are applied to targeting decisions, especially in the absence of cross-checking, or balancing, with other sources of information before human authorization to attack (as over-reliance on algorithmic output would diminish the meaning of the consequent human decision). However, if such AI systems are used directly to control the initiation of an attack by an autonomous weapon system, these concerns would be particularly serious. More broadly, there is growing appreciation of the risks of use, and misuse, of AI across the digital, physical and political domains, and the implications for international security.[391]

The degree of *predictability and reliability of autonomous (weapon) systems affects the trust of humans in that system* – especially in relation to the link between human intention and the eventual "action", or operation, of the system – and this trust is also affected by the degree to which the operation of the system can be explained – or explain itself (e.g. with in-built "explainable AI").[392]

---

https://www.cnbc.com/2017/09/04/putin-leader-in-artificial-intelligence-will-rule-world.html.

[390] See, for example: J Keller, DARPA TRACE program using advanced algorithms, embedded computing for radar target recognition", Military & Aerospace Electronics, 2015: http://www.militaryaerospace.com/articles/2015/07/hpec-radar-target-recognition.html; D Lewis, N Modirzadeh and G Blum, "The Pentagon's New Algorithmic-Warfare Team", Lawfare, 2017: https://www.lawfareblog.com/pentagons-new-algorithmic-warfare-team.

[391] Future of Humanity Institute, University of Oxford; Centre for the Study of Existential Risk, University of Cambridge; Center for a New American Security; Electronic Frontier Foundation; and Open AI, The Malicious Use of Artificial Intelligence: Forecasting, Prevention, and Mitigation, 2018: https://maliciousaireport.com.

[392] See, for example: DARPA, Explainable Artificial Intelligence (XAI): https://www.darpa.mil/program/explainable-artificial- intelligence.

There are now more and more *initiatives addressing these ethical questions for AI systems in general*, including the Institute of Electrical and Electronics Engineers (IEEE)'s Global Initiative on Ethics of Autonomous and Intelligent Systems, which is working on "ethically aligned design" standards for AI and autonomous systems,[393] *and for robotic systems, in particular.*[394]   The *Asilomar AI Principles* recently developed by the Future of Life Institute are interesting in this respect. In warning against an AI arms race,[395] they highlight ethical concerns raised by AI systems in general, noting the need for safety, failure transparency, responsibility of developers, alignment with human values and human control over delegation of decisions to AI systems.[396]

---

[393] Institute of Electrical and Electronics Engineers (IEEE), The IEEE Global Initiative on Ethics of Autonomous and Intelligent Systems, http://standards. ieee.org/develop/indconn/ec/autonomous_systems.html.

[394] See, for example: Engineering and Physical Sciences Research Council (EPSRC), Principles of Robotics, https://www.epsrc.ac.uk/research/ ourportfolio/themes/engineering/activities/principlesofrobotics/; J Bryson, "The meaning of the EPSRC principles of robotics", Connection Science, Vol. 29 No. 2, 2017, pp. 130–136.

[395] Future of Life Institute, Asilomar AI Principles, 2017: https://futureoflife.org/ai-principles/: "18) AI Arms Race: An arms race in lethal autonomous weapons should be avoided."

[396] Ibid. "6) Safety: AI systems should be safe and secure throughout their operational lifetime, and verifiably so where applicable and feasible. 7) Failure Transparency: If an AI system causes harm, it should be possible to ascertain why. ... 9) Responsibility: Designers and builders of advanced AI systems are stakeholders in the moral implications of their use, misuse, and actions, with a responsibility and opportunity to shape those implications. 10) Value Alignment: Highly autonomous AI systems should be designed so that their goals and behaviors can be assured to align with human values throughout their operation. 11) Human Values: AI systems should be designed and operated so as to be compatible with ideals of human dignity, rights, freedoms, and cultural diversity. 16) Human Control: Humans should choose how and whether to delegate decisions to AI systems, to accomplish human-chosen objectives."

18.5.2 Ethics and Risk

Unpredictability and unreliability in autonomous weapon systems *also contribute to the level of risk that the use of the weapon will lead to unacceptable consequences*, in particular for civilians, which raises ethical (as well as legal) issues. Since assessing risk requires an assessment of probability and consequence, machine-learning systems, for example, present immediate problems. Where there is inherent unpredictability in the functioning of a system it may not be possible to assess the *probability* of a certain action, and so determining risk becomes problematic. The introduction of this unpredictability into system design is therefore a significant concern in managing risk. From a purely ethical perspective, some have even argued that creating an unreasonable risk should be considered harm, and ethically wrong, even if that risk does not materialize.[397]

The level of risk also relates to the potential *consequences* of an unpredicted or unintended action, which will also be determined by the specific type of autonomous weapon system and the context of its use, including uses that were not originally foreseen. Some emphasize that the destructive power of the weapon system – in terms of size of munition or potential destructive effects – is an important factor in determining the level of risk, and therefore for an ethical assessment. For example, few would argue for development of autonomous nuclear weapon systems, even if predictability and reliability could be assured as extremely high. However, others are sceptical of a focus on the destructive power, since relatively low-power weapons – such as an autonomous machine-gun system – could still have serious consequences and be used to kill and injure many people *(see also Section 6)*. In summary, while predictability and reliability may reduce the risks of unintended consequences

---

[397] C Finkelstein, "Is Risk a Harm?" University of Pennsylvania Law Review, No. 263, 2003.

in the operation of an autonomous weapon system, they do not, in themselves, eliminate risk.

18.6   Ethical Issues in Context

Another aspect to consider is whether ethical assessments of autonomous weapon systems vary according to context. In particular, *do specific characteristics of an autonomous weapon system, and the way it is used, have an influence on its ethical acceptability?* For example: the task the weapon is used for, the type of target, the operating environment, the timeframe of operation and the scope of movement over an area.

When discussing different types of autonomous weapon systems, *in different scenarios and contexts, different views tend to emerge on ethical acceptability*. These assessments tend to vary according to the core determinations of human agency in the decision-making process and human dignity (*see Section 3*), associated moral responsibility (*see Section 4*) and, especially, the degree of predictability and risk (*see Section 5*), since contextual factors can have a significant impact on the last of these.

18.6.1 Constraints in Time and Space

A longer *timeframe* and/or increased *scope of movement over an area are major factors in contributing to uncertainty* between the point of activation of an autonomous weapon system and the eventual attack that results. As discussed, *an autonomous weapon system* – since it selects and attacks targets independently (after launch or activation) – *creates varying degrees of uncertainty as to exactly when, where and/or why the resulting attack will take place.*[398]   This is accentuated by wider temporal

---

[398]This is in contrast to a long-range non-autonomous weapon system, such as a cruise missile, which may travel long distances, with a significant delay between launch and impact, but is intended to hit a specific target at a specific point in

and spatial boundaries because of greater room for variations in the operational environment over an area, and evolution of that environment over time, both of which may affect the consequences of activation.

Uncertainties introduced by autonomy are clearly a problem from a legal perspective, to the extent that they may prevent the commander or operator from making judgements and taking decisions in line with their legal obligations – of distinction, proportionality and precautions – in carrying out attacks in armed conflict. However, uncertainties also raise concerns from an ethical perspective because they can decouple human agency and intent in the decision to use force from the eventual consequences, even if the resulting attack is lawful (*see Section 3*).

There are *different dimensions to the issue of temporal constraints.* One is the elapsed time between the point of activation of an autonomous weapon system and the point at which a resulting attack takes place. For example, there is a *significant difference in the level of uncertainty in circumstances that may result during a ten-minute flight time versus a two-day loiter time* (also depending on the operating environment). There are parallels, here, with mine warfare; a major problem with anti- personnel mines, which contributed to their indiscriminate effects and eventual prohibition, was the lack of control over the period during which they could autonomously operate. Once laid by humans, and unless fitted with self-destruct or self-neutralizing features, landmines remain activated indefinitely, and the initial user has no further control over the eventual attack and the nature of the victim.

Mines that stay active indefinitely also raise *another time-related concern: the absence of an "off switch".* With autonomous weapon systems, the uncertainty over when, where and/or why an attack takes place could be extended indefinitely if there is no capacity to deactivate the system after launch or activation. Unless the system has an automatic

---

time. (It may also have the capacity to be manually or automatically deactivated after launch.)

self-destruct or self-neutralizing feature (the reliability of which can also vary, as was the case with landmines), the ability to deactivate an autonomous weapon system would require a communication link to a human operator to be retained. Since changes in the operational environment may require deactivation at any point following activation, there is a strong argument for enabling constant human supervision and the ability to intervene and deactivate, as is the case with many existing autonomous weapon systems, such as counter-rocket, artillery and mortar weapons.[399]

A further aspect of the temporal issue is *human reaction time.* Some existing autonomous weapon systems are, by design, intended to initiate an attack quicker than is humanly possible. While speed may create a military advantage – for example, in the case of time-constrained missile and counter- rocket, artillery and mortar defence – it also erodes the potential for human intervention to prevent an unlawful, unnecessary or accidental attack. Even with continuous human supervision, it may only be possible to deactivate a weapon system after a problematic attack in order to prevent further negative consequences, and whether or not this is an acceptable risk may depend on the predictability and reliability of the weapon, the operating environment, as well as the task for which it is used and the target against which it is employed.

18.6.2 Constraints in Operating Environments, Tasks and Targets

The task for which an autonomous weapon system is used and the environment in which it is used can also be significant for ethical assessments. In situations *where there are fewer risks to civilians or civilian objects, some have argued there may also be fewer ethical concerns raised by autonomy* – in terms of reduced human agency. For example, it has been suggested that autonomous deep-sea, anti-submarine warfare

---

[399]Such a requirement could limit the utility of autonomous weapon systems where constant communication is not feasible, such as underwater.

and autonomous close-in air defence at sea may be more ethically acceptable, owing to the relatively uncluttered and simple nature of the operating environments, and the reduced numbers of civilians and civilian objects, compared with populated areas on the coast or inland – and, therefore, potentially more predictable, in terms of consequences, and lower-risk.[400]

Further, there is the issue of whether an autonomous weapon system is used for defensive or offensive tasks. Some suggest there may be an ethical distinction between a "defensive" weapon system – such as a missile or counter-rocket, artillery and mortar defence weapon, or a "sentry" weapon guarding a border – and an "offensive" system, which actively searches for targets. However, others caution that the distinction between "offensive" and "defensive" is not clear operationally (and legally, the same rules apply to the use of force or conduct of hostilities), and that a weapon system introduced for a "defensive" task may later be used in an "offensive" role.

Perhaps *the most significant contextual factor that gives rise to ethical concerns, however, is the nature of the target,* and whether the weapon system only targets objects or attacks humans directly. The fundamental anxiety in the ethical discourse is about anti-personnel autonomous weapon systems, especially, it is argued, with respect to: lack of human agency and intent in decisions to use force; the loss of human dignity on the part of those combatants targeted,[401] and of civilians that are put at risk as a consequence of legitimate attacks on military targets; and the implications for moral responsibility (*see Sections 3 and 4*).

---

[400]R Sparrow and G Lucas, "When Robots Rule the Waves?" Naval War College Review, 69(4), 2016, pp. 49–78.

[401]R Sparrow, "Twenty seconds to comply: Autonomous Weapon Systems and the recognition of surrender", International
Law Studies, 91, 2015, pp. 699–728.

18.7 Public and Military Perceptions

Although public opinion does not necessarily equal public conscience, and ethics, as a formal mode of criticism, should not be reduced
to opinion polls, it is useful to explore the perspectives on autonomous
weapon systems from different constituents of society – including the
public, the military, and the scientific and technical communities.[402]

Public opinion may not provide evidence-based answers to ethical
questions, especially when those surveyed have different understandings
of the questions and the concept of an autonomous weapon system.
*However, opinion polls can spark debate a*nd illustrate a significant interest in and engagement with the topic by different constituents, *as well*
as revealing trends related to public- conscience concerns.

18.7.1 Opinion Surveys

There have been several surveys of public opinion in this field.[403]
Many have contrasted remote- controlled armed drones with autono-
mous weapon systems, in order to differentiate reactions to autonomy
specifically from robotic-weapons platforms in general. In 2011, Moon,
Danielson and Van der Loos found greater rejection of autonomous
weapon systems (81% against, 10% in favour) than of remote-controlled
drones (53% against, 35% in favour) based on three major rationales:
preservation of human responsibility and accountability; scepticism

---

[402]R Sparrow, "Ethics as a source of law: The Martens clause and autonomous
weapons", ICRC Humanitarian Law & Policy Blog, 14 November 2017:
http://blogs.icrc.org/law-and-policy/2017/11/14/ethics-source-law-martens-
clause-autonomous-weapons.

[403]Including: L Moshkina and R Arkin, "Lethality and Autonomous Systems:
The Roboticist Demographic", IEEE International Symposium on Technology
and Society, 2008; Prof. C Carpenter, US public opinion on autonomous weapons, University of Massachusetts Department of Political Science, 2013; M
Horowitz, "Public opinion and the politics of the killer robots debate", Research
and Politics, January–March 2016.

about the technology, and therefore risks for civilians; and assertions that humans should always make life-or-death decisions.[404]

In 2015, an Open Roboethics Initiative survey gathered the views of 1000 people from 49 different countries. It, too, found a significant rejection of autonomous weapon systems (67% said all types should be banned) and stronger views based on the type of task (85% should not be used for "offensive purposes"). The rejection of autonomous weapons was also greater in comparison with remote- controlled weapons (71% would prefer their military to use remote-controlled weapons in warfare; 60% would prefer to be attacked by remote-controlled rather than autonomous weapons).[405]

A 2017 *IPSOS poll of 11,500 respondents in 25 countries also found overall opposition* to autonomous weapon systems (56% against, 24% in favour), although the poll also revealed regional variations, with the greatest opposition in Russia (69% against), Peru (67% against), Spain (66% against) and Argentina (66% against), and the least in India (31%), China (36%) and the United States (45%).[406]

While each study has its limitations, these polls reflect trends that are worth exploring further. Why do people tend to prefer attacks to be carried out by remote-controlled rather than autonomous weapon systems? How much significance is placed on reservations about the technology and its consequences, and how much on ethical concerns about human agency, human dignity and the view that machines must not take decisions on the use of force?

---

[404] A Moon, P Danielson and M Van der Loos, "Survey-based Discussions on Morally Contentious Applications of Interactive Robotics", International Journal of Social Robotics, Volume 4, Issue 1, 2012, pp 77–96.

[405] Open Roboethics Initiative, The Ethics and Governance of Lethal Autonomous Weapons Systems: An International Public Opinion Poll, 9 November 2015.

[406]IPSOS, Three in ten Americans support using Autonomous Weapons, 7 February 2017.

18.7.2 Contrasting Military and Public Perceptions

Another 2017 survey contrasted perceptions of remote-controlled armed drones and autonomous weapon systems among the public in the United States, and civilian and military personnel of the Dutch Ministry of Defence.[407] The Ministry of Defence personnel had less trust, confidence and support for the "actions" taken by autonomous weapon systems compared with remote-controlled systems but considered them equally "fair". Respondents were, generally, more anxious about the consequences of using autonomous weapon systems, and concern about a lack of respect for human dignity was one of the main objections, when compared with human-operated drones resulting in the same consequences. *In comparisons between military and public perceptions, most notable was the similar level of concern about a loss of human dignity*, which may indicate some common ground among different constituents.

18.8 Conclusions

Ethics, humanity and the dictates of the public conscience are at the heart of the debate about the acceptability of autonomous weapon systems. From the ICRC's perspective, ethics provides another avenue – alongside legal assessments and technical considerations – to help determine the necessary type and degree of human control that must be retained over weapon systems, and the use of force, and to elucidate where States must establish limits on autonomy in weapon systems.

Considerations of humanity and the public conscience provide *ethical guidance for discussions*, and there is a requirement to connect them to legal assessments via the *Martens Clause – a safety net for humanity*. These ethical considerations go beyond whether autonomous weapon

---

[407] I Verdiesen, Agency perception and moral values related to Autonomous Weapons: An empirical study using the Value- Sensitive Design approach, Masters of Science, Faculty of Technology, Policy and Management, TU Delft, 2017.

systems are compatible with our *laws* to include fundamental questions of whether they are acceptable to our *values*. And such debates necessarily require the engagement of various constituents of society.

Several ethical issues appear central to establishing constraints on autonomy in weapon systems. Perhaps the most powerful ethical concerns are those that transcend context – whether during armed conflict or in peacetime – and transcend technology – whether simple or sophisticated.[408] These are concerns about *loss of human agency in decisions to use force* – decisions to kill, injure and destroy – *loss of human dignity in the process of using force*, and *erosion of moral responsibility for these decisions*.

The importance of *retaining human agency – and intent – in these decisions* is one of the central ethical arguments for limits on autonomy in weapon systems. Many take the view that decisions to kill, injure and destroy must not be delegated to machines, and that humans must be present in this decision-making process sufficiently to preserve a direct link between the intention of the human and the eventual operation of the weapon system. It is not enough simply to say that "humans have developed, deployed and activated the weapon system". *There must be a direct connection between the human rationale for activation of an autonomous weapon system in the specific circumstances and the consequences of the resulting attack.* But questions remain about how close this connection must be, and what form it must take.

---

[408] Although there are different views among experts on the issue of technology. Some make a distinction between "automated" and "autonomous" weapons and focus their concerns on systems controlled by complex AI algorithms rather than simpler software. Others, including the ICRC, note the lack of a clear technical distinction between the two, and argue that "all such weapons raise the same core legal and ethical questions". See: ICRC, Autonomous weapon systems: Implications of increasing autonomy in the critical functions of weapons, op. cit. (footnote 337), 2016, p. 8.

Human dignity is another core ethical consideration that is linked to concerns about loss of human agency. The central argument is that it matters not just *if* a person is killed or injured but *how* they are killed or injured, and the *process by which these decisions are made is as important as the results.* If human agency is lacking to the extent that machines have effectively, and functionally, been delegated these decisions, then, according to this argument, it undermines the human dignity of those combatants targeted, and of civilians that are put at risk as a consequence of legitimate attacks on military targets. If human agency is retained, on the other hand, it is an acknowledgement of humanity in that decision to use force and the resulting consequences.

The need for human agency is also linked to *moral responsibility and accountability* for decisions to use force. These are human responsibilities (both ethical and legal), which *cannot be transferred to inanimate machines, or computer algorithms*, since it is humans that have both rights and responsibilities in relation to these decisions. From an ethical perspective, it is not sufficient only to assign legal responsibility to a commander or operator who activates an autonomous weapon system. Humans must uphold their *moral responsibility*, requiring not only a causal explanation but also a justification for the resulting use of force. Autonomous weapon systems complicate this justification because of the more generalized nature of the targeting decisions, which risks eroding – or diffusing – moral responsibility.

Predictability and *reliability* in using an autonomous weapon system are ways of connecting human agency and intent to the eventual consequences of the resulting attack. *A lack of predictability*, whether inherent to the weapon system design or due to interaction with the environment, *raises serious ethical (and legal) concerns owing to a lack of foreseeability of the consequences* and associated risks, in particular for civilians.

As weapons that self-initiate attacks, *autonomous weapon systems all raise questions about predictability*, owing to varying degrees of uncertainty as to exactly when, where and/or why a resulting attack will take place. However, the *application of AI and, in particular, machine learning, to targeting functions accentuates this problem, raising fundamental questions of inherent unpredictability* by design and heightening concerns about the loss of human agency, moral responsibility and human dignity.

Context also affects ethical assessments of autonomous weapon systems, owing to the impact on the predictability of the outcomes of their use, the nature of the consequences and the overall level of risk that results. Constraints on the *timeframe of operation* and *scope of movement over an area* are key factors, as are the *task* for which the weapon is used and the *operating environment* in which it is activated.

However, from an ethical perspective, perhaps the most important contextual factor is the type of target. *Core concerns about human agency, human dignity and moral responsibility are most acute in relation to the notion of anti-personnel autonomous weapon systems that target humans directly*. These concerns may be one reason – together with legal considerations and technical limitations – why the use of autonomous weapon systems to date has been constrained to anti-materiel systems,[409] targeting projectiles, vehicles, aircraft or other objects, even if these systems pose dangers to humans inside or in proximity to objects.[410]

---

[409]There have been reports that some anti-personnel "sentry" weapon systems have autonomous modes. However, as far as is known to the ICRC, "sentry" weapon systems that have been deployed still require human remote authorization to launch an attack (even though they may identify targets autonomously). See also footnote 336.

[410]Including through accidents. See, for example, "fratricide" incidents discussed in: J Hawley, Automation and the Patriot Air and Missile Defense System, op. cit., 2017.

18.8.1 An Ethical Basis for Human Control?

From the ICRC's perspective, ethical considerations very much parallel the requirement for a minimum level of human control over weapon systems and the use of force, to ensure compliance with international legal obligations that govern the use of force in armed conflict and in peacetime.[411]

From an ethical viewpoint, "meaningful", "effective" or "appropriate" human control would be the type and degree of control that preserves human agency and upholds moral responsibility in decisions to use force. This does not necessarily exclude autonomy in weapon systems, but it requires a sufficiently direct and close connection to be maintained between the human intent of the user and the eventual consequences of the operation of the weapon system in a specific attack. This, in turn, will necessitate limits on autonomy.

Ethical and legal considerations may demand some similar constraints on autonomy in weapon systems so that meaningful human control is maintained – in particular, with respect to: human supervision and the ability to intervene and deactivate; technical requirements for predictability and reliability (including in the algorithms used); and operational constraints on the task for which the weapon is used, the type of target, the operating environment, the timeframe of operation and the scope of movement over an area.[412]

---

[411]N Davison, Autonomous weapon systems under international humanitarian law, op. cit. (footnote 337), 2017; M Brehm, Defending the Boundary: Constraints and Requirements on the Use of Autonomous Weapon Systems Under International Humanitarian and Human Rights Law, Geneva Academy Briefing no. 9, 1 May 2017.

[412] ICRC, Statement to the Convention on Certain Conventional Weapons (CCW) Group of Governmental Experts on "Lethal Autonomous Weapon Systems", op. cit. (footnote 337), 15 November 2017.

However, the combined and interconnected ethical concerns about loss of human agency in decisions to use force, diffusion of moral responsibility and loss of human dignity could have the most far-reaching consequences, perhaps precluding the development and use of anti-personnel autonomous weapon systems, and even limiting the applications of anti-materiel systems, depending on the risks that destroying materiel targets present for human life.

19

CYBER CRIME:
THE PHILIPPINE RESPONSE

Yolanda S. Lira, Leirrand Christian A Ochotorena
Philippines

19.1 From the Philippines to the Budapest Convention

Computer security threats are ever-present and constantly evolving, seeking to match and beat existing and emerging technology. The people behind these threats constantly find new ways to, at the least, annoy and inconvenience us; at the worst, to steal our information and our identity, our money, and our property in the process.

Almost every-one uses a computer and connects to the Internet. This alone makes both companies and persons susceptible to cyber threats. However, most of us do not appreciate the importance and urgency of knowing more about cyber threats and the laws that have been passed to address them. Our limited knowledge is born out of indifference, igno-rance, or both: computer users in general have low security conscious-ness, or no regard for the safety of their official and personal digital ac-counts.

In the Philippines, it took the doings of a Filipino, Onel de Guzman, suspected to have created the "Love Bug" virus, to finally get lawmak-ers to draft the first Cyber Crime Law entitled *Republic Act 8792*, local-ly referred to as the *E-Commerce Act of 2000*. The Love Bug began its spread on May 4 of 2000, swiftly crossing international borders and disabling computers in its wake, and causing damage in places as far from Manila as the United States and the United Kingdom. The Philippine authorities filed theft and other charges against Mr. de Guzman, but ended up dropping them. At the time, the Philippines did not have laws governing computer espionage.

In Section 33(a) of R. A. 8792, Hacking or Cracking refers to unauthorized access into or interference in a computer system/ similar server or information and communication system; or any access in order to corrupt, alter, steal, or destroy using a computer or other similar information and communication devices, without the knowledge and consent of the owner of the computer or information and communications system, including the introduction of computer viruses and the like, resulting in the corruption, destruction, alteration, theft or loss of electronic data messages or electronic documents. Violators will be punished by a Minimum fine of One Hundred Thousand Pesos (P100,000.00) and a maximum commensurate to the damage incurred and a mandatory Imprisonment of Six (6) months to Three (3) years.

On November 23, 2001, the *first Convention on Cybercrime*, (also known as the *Budapest Convention on Cybercrime*) saw the signing of the first international treaty on cybercrime that became effective on July 1, 2004. It has served as the guide post for domestic legislation in the participating countries, including the Philippines. In fine, the convention covered the following[413]:

---

[413]   https://cto.int/media/events/pst-ev/2013/Cybersecurity/Alexander%20Seger-Budapest%20Convention%20on%20Cybercrime.pdf, 7. (Accessed on 16 August 2018)

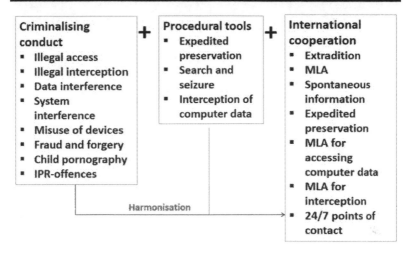

Guided by the legal framework of the Budapest Convention, the Philippines thereafter enacted the *Cybercrime Prevention Act of 2012*, recognizing the "… need to protect and safeguard the integrity of computer, computer and communications system, networks and data bases, and the confidentiality, integrity and availability of information and data stored therein, from all forms of misuse, abuse and illegal access by making punishable under the law such conduct or conducts" (Section 2, Republic Act 10175)

19.2 Cybercrime Offenses

Criminal abuse of technology is commonly referred to as cybercrime and includes three categories of offenses classified as *offenses aimed at computer systems and data,* such as hacking; *traditional offenses* such as drug trafficking or fraud committed or facilitated with the use of computer technology, and *activities concerning content* where technology is used in the making and dissemination of illicit materials.

Considered as *Cybercrime Offenses* are:

1. *Offenses against Confidentiality, Integrity and Availability of Computer Data & Systems*
   - Illegal Access/Interception
   - Data/System Interference
   - Misuse of Devices
   - Cyber-squatting

2. *Computer-related Offenses*
   - Computer-related Identity Theft
   - Computer-related Fraud
   - Computer-related Forgery

3. *Content-related Offenses*
   - Cybersex
   - Online Child Abuse/Child Pornography
   - Cyber Libel

There are three crucial components to be considered in Cybersecurity (or Computer Data Security). These are enclosed in the *CIA (Confidentiality, Integrity and Availability)* triad model. In this model, Confidentiality refers to who is authorized to access the data. Integrity points to the trustworthiness and accuracy of the data. Availability concerns whether the data is made available and/or accessible to those who are authorized to access it.

The flip side of the CIA triad is the *DAD (Disclosure, Alteration, and Destruction)* triad model, where each of these concepts are the consequences of a breach in the CIA triad. A breach in Confidentiality means that the data was leaked to unauthorized users (*Disclosure*). A breach in data integrity involves a situation where the data has been edited in some way (*Alteration*). A breach in Availability means that the data is either destroyed or made inaccessible to authorized users (*Destruction*)[414]

---

[414] Conrad, Misenar, Feldman & Greenblatt, 2010.

These provisions aim to provide computer data, computer programs and computer systems with similar protections such as those applied to corporeal objects against infliction of damages. The protected legal interest here is the integrity and the proper functioning and use of computer data, computer programs and computer systems.

Offenses against Confidentiality, Integrity and Availability (CIA) of Computer Data and Systems are defined as follows:

1. Illegal Access - where the offender enters into the whole or any part of a computer system, and such access of entry is without right or not authorized. In its simplest form, access to the computer implies an unauthorized interaction between the culprit and the targeted devices or computer components, usually by accessing the computer, using its keyboard or mouse, printing a document, browsing folders, opening files, running software and processing data stored within.

2. Illegal Interception is when there is transmission of computer data to and from, or within a computer system, including electromagnetic signals from a computer system carrying such data. Such transmission is not intended for the public and the interception is done by technical means without right or authority. It aims to protect the right of privacy of communication as traditional wire-tapping and recording of telephone conversation between two persons.

3. Data Interference is done when the offender, for purposes of committing any of the offenses under R.A. 10175, without right or authority, alters, damages, deletes or causes the deterioration of computer data, electronic document or electronic data messages, including the introduction or transmission of viruses. Such alteration, damage, deletion or deterioration must be intentional or reckless. As to system interference, the offender again without right or authority, intentionally alters or recklessly hinders or interfered with the functioning of a computer or computer network by: inputting, altering, suppressing, transmitting

computer data or program, electronic document or data message including the introduction or transmission of viruses.

4. *Misuse of Device* is committed by the offender for the purpose of
committing any of the offenses under R.A. 10175, thus, engages in the
use, production, sale procurement, importation, distribution of otherwise
making available without right, of a device, including a computer program or a computer Password, access or code, or similar data by which
the whole or any part of a computer system is capable of being accessed.

5. *Cyber Squatting* is the acquisition of a domain name over the internet, in bad faith, to profit, mislead, destroy reputation and deprive
others, from registering the same, if such domain name is similar, identical, or confusingly similar to an existing trademark or registered with
the appropriate government agency at the time of the domain name reg-
istration or identical or in any way similar with the name of a person
other than the registrant, in case of a personal name; and acquired without right or with intellectual property interests in it.

19.3 Computer-Related Offenses

Under the category, Computer-related Offenses, fall the following:

1. *Computer-related Identity Theft* is when the offender, intentionally acquires, uses, misuses, transfers, possesses, alters or deletes identifying information belonging to another and done without right or consent
from the person to whom the personal information belongs, which may
or may not result in damage;

2. *Computer-related Fraud* is when the offender, without authority
to do so, and with fraudulent intent, inputs, alters, deletes computer data
or programs; or interferes with the functioning of a computer system,
and such act may or may not result in damage to another;

3. *Computer-related Forgery* pertains to any input, alteration, or deletion of any computer data without right, resulting in inauthentic data
with the intent that it can be considered or acted upon for legal purposes

as if it were authentic, regardless whether or not the data is directly readable and intelligible. It is the act of knowingly using computer data, which is the product of computer-related forgery as defined herein, for the purpose of perpetuating a fraudulent or dishonest design.

19.4 Content-Related Offenses

The Content-related Offenses are of three types, namely: Cybersex, Online Child Abuse/Child Pornography and Cyber Libel.

1. Cybersex is the wilful engagement, maintenance, control, or operation, directly or indirectly, of any lascivious exhibition of sexual organ(s) or sexual activity, done with the aid of a computer system, and done for favour or consideration. Cybersex is "interactive prostitution by webcam."

2. Child pornography is the commission of any of the punishable acts under R.A. No. 9775 or the Anti-Child Pornography Act of 2009, done through a computer system. The law makes the penalty higher by one degree when committed in cyberspace.

3. Cyber Libel is committed by means of writing, printing, lithography, engraving, radio, phonograph, painting, theatrical exhibition, cinematic graphic exhibition or any similar means dome be, through and with the use of information and communication technology. Cyber libel in the Philippines is not a new crime since Article 353 in relation to Article 355 of the Revised Penal Code clearly punishes libel. In effect, Section 4 (c) 4, merely affirms that on-line defamation constitutes "similar means" for committing libel. Here only the author of the libellous statement or article is penalized.

R.A. 10175 (under Section 5's Other offenses) makes any person who wilfully abets or aids in the commission of any of the offenses enumerated in this Act liable. And any person who wilfully attempts to commit any of the offenses enumerated therein shall also be held liable.

Finally, Section 6 of R.A, 10175 provides that all crimes defined and penalized by the Revised Penal Code as amended and Special Laws, if committed by, through and with the use of information and communication technologies shall be covered by other provisions of this Act, provided that the penalty to be imposed shall be one (1) degree higher than what is provided for by said code and the Special Laws as the case may be.

19.5 Government Efforts in Cybersecurity

Apart from the Cybercrime Prevention Act of 2012, the Philippine government also strengthened its resolve towards building resiliency against Cyber-related incidents and Cybercrime, especially those which affect government data and systems. In its earlier campaigns and programs in ICT (Information and Communications Technologies), the DOST-ICTO (Department of Science and Technology – Information and Communications Technology Office) was the one spearheading efforts to formally recognize the increasing implications and impacts that technology have on the lives of Filipinos across different sectors.

Through the enactment of the R.A. 10844, otherwise known as the *Department of Information and Communications Technology (DICT) Act of 2015*, the government emphasized understanding the trends and impacts of computing technologies in the lives of its citizens. The government also made significant strides in making these technologies more accessible to different sectors (e.g. through its Free Public Wi-Fi projects), and also build a more robust framework handling Cyber-related incidents and/or Cybercrimes (i.e. National Cybersecurity Plan of 2022) placing special task forces such as the National Computer Emergency Response Team (CERT) which will collaborate with the Cybercrime Investigation and Coordination Center (CICC) which comprises the National Bureau of Investigation (NBI), Department of Justice (DOJ), Philippine National Police (PNP), as well as a representative from both the private sector and the academe.

For law enforcement agencies, such as the PNP, the establishment of its Anti-Cybercrime Group in March 2013 is a sign of commitment for the organization and a message to malicious elements, that the PNP is serious about the issues and challenges imposed by cybercrime in the country. It also activated its Digital Forensics Laboratories nationwide in Camp Crame (PNP's Headquarters in Quezon City), Legazpi City, Cebu City, Davao City, General Santos City, and Zamboanga City. Training and capability enhancement in the efforts towards battling cybercrimes were also conducted both locally and internationally, and a cyber training facility was commissioned through the assistance of the US Anti-Terrorism Assistance Program.[415]

With the increasing use of computing technologies, relevant issues on data privacy were also addressed in another piece of legislation, specifically *R.A.10173*, more commonly referred to as *the Data Privacy Act of 2012*. It allowed for the creation of the National Privacy Commission (NPC). This act highlights the different rights of the data subjects as stated in Chapter IV Sections 16-19 (e.g. right to access, right to be informed, right to object, right to data portability, etc.). Given the framework of the Data Privacy Act of 2012, the NPC also spearheaded programs and/or activities towards the development of the data handling, data processing and data storage methodologies through its NPC Circular 17-01 which forms the groundwork for the development of the country's first batch of Data Protection Officers (DPO) in different institutions be they public or private. With the designation of DPOs in different offices, more emphasis is given to the importance of data security to ensure that the data of the different data subjects across sectors, are well-accounted for, any form of data breach will or must be reported to the

---

[415] International Information System Security Consortium, Inc. & National Defense College of the Philippines Alumni Association Inc, 2013.

NPC which will add to its statistics of reported cybersecurity-related incidents. Being able to collect these statistics of commonly occurring cybersecurity-related incidents, the NPC, in collaboration with the DICT, will be able to step up the campaigns towards "Cyber Resiliency."

The government's thrust towards "Cyber Resiliency" is a combination of the inter-agency support from its previous framework for Cybersecurity as well as its current trainings and/or programs in technical skills development of IT specialists who will then be able to specialize further in the field of Cybersecurity and even in Digital Forensics.

19.6 Cybersecurity in the Academic World

There has been a growing interest in the academe in tackling more about these cyber-related incidents and/or cybercrimes. In fact, in the country two private schools are offering a Computer Science degree with a specialization in Cybersecurity and Digital Forensics and these are the National University and Asia Pacific College which are both located in Metro Manila. Apart from these two schools, another school is offering a Masters' degree in Cybersecurity, and this is the Holy Angel University in Angeles City, Pampanga. Other schools and/or universities are also following suit by initially offering Cybersecurity-related subjects in their curriculum.

In the current efforts of tackling Cybersecurity, Digital Forensics and Ethical Hacking in the academe, more and more focus is given to leveraging free and open source tools and/or utilities such as the ones published by OWASP (Open Web Application Security Project) and also the different Cybersecurity-centric Linux Distributions (e.g. Kali Linux and ParrotSec Operating Systems). With these tools being readily-available online, teachers are equipped with advanced utilities which can be taught to students to better understand the concepts in Web Application Security, Mobile Application Security, Systems Security, Code Security, etc. Bridging the gap between theory and actual practice, different IT companies are also making efforts through their different software development and cybersecurity seminars which aim to enhance the current skill sets and capabilities of the students so they will be more prepared in facing the challenges of the current ICT landscape.

20.7 Attack Vectors in the Philippines

Despite the information campaigns in the country regarding cyber threats and the risks associated thereof, different computer habits of Filipinos which lead to a possible breach in personal and/or sensitive data still persist. These computer habits which threaten data security of the individual involved are now seen as a regular occurrence that do little or no damage despite evidence to the contrary.

The different computer habits which risks data security of Filipinos include the following:

1. Downloading movies, games, music and software through P2P (peer-to-peer) technologies such as torrents;
2. Answering unsolicited emails and online forms from unknown sources;
3. Clicking on links, images, and attachments on unsolicited emails;
4. Plugging in a personal and even an unknown flash drive/external drive on a work computer;
5. Use of cracking software and key generators (keygen) software to unlock the full capabilities of a certain application;
6. Transacting and/or communicating with unknown entities;
7. Streaming content from unauthorized content-distribution sites;
8. Posting of sensitive data in public websites (e.g. social media sites such as Facebook, Twitter, and Instagram);
9. Re-using passwords across different sites;

10. Connecting to unsecured public Wi-Fi (Wireless Fidelity) access points.

These habits are among the problems that need to be addressed further through end-user training and awareness campaigns as these situations would allow for a large attack vector to be used by malicious entities, a.k.a. hackers. These hackers employ different techniques to gain access to computers and computer systems to be able to extract the data contained within. Given the different scenarios above, the possible attack vectors are through *Phishing, Pharming, Social Engineering, Password Attacks, Malware Attacks, Adware Bombards, Trojans, Ransomware, Botnets and Physical Security Attacks.*

In *Phishing*, individuals who often answer forms and emails from unknown sources could unwittingly give their personal data away to the hacker, allowing the hackers access to their bank accounts, social media accounts, and other valuable online accounts, effectively allowing a form of identity theft. Oftentimes, the hacker will use the identities of well-known institutions and brands as his cover. The forms submitted to the user's email are account update forms, password reset forms, and transaction verification forms to fool the user into thinking that this email communication is legitimate.

Pharming in these scenarios poses similar risks to the user, but the delivery of the attack is quite different. Pharming involves redirecting the user to a bogus website since the DNS (Domain Name System) is somehow poisoned to facilitate such a redirection. The unwitting user would misinterpret the fake website as a true and verified website. From there, a similar process as that of phishing, the data is then posted or passed to the hacker's defined server.

Social Engineering: In both Phishing and Pharming, the hackers could further their cause by creating transactions using the victim's online identities. This also causes damage to the victim's close contacts such as family members, relatives and friends.

Password Attacks would also be a cause for alarm for the end-users since their passwords can be hacked through dictionary attacks, brute-force attack, or even through social engineering. For dictionary attacks, the hackers would usually just download a word-list from their peers or from some forum sites and try that against the user passwords. Another method to employ this is to generate a list out of the combinations of the personal information taken from the user (which is usually posted in some form on the user's different social media accounts). In the brute-force method, every possible character combination given a set of parameters (e.g. the password length being 12 characters maximum and limited to alphanumeric characters) are tried against the user's password. As for the social engineering side of password hacking, the password may be placed on a user's desk where the hacker can just copy it and access the user's account, or perhaps decoded through the information which is taken directly or indirectly from the user through one-on-one conversation and other forms of communication.

Malware Attacks becomes the most complicated type of attack to cover since it encompasses a lot of forms wherein its function and/or purpose becomes its main differentiation. Filipinos are quite familiar with the term virus or computer virus, as this has become the catch-all term for everything wrong that happens with a computer, even though it was caused by another strand or type of malware altogether. Everything from the infamous windows' blue screen of death, hogging of systems resources (causing system lag) and all other computer-related problems are attributed to viruses, at least when you ask the common end-user about it. On the more technical side, malware can be differentiated whether it is adware, spyware, ransomware, a virus, a worm, a rootkit, trojan or botnet. There are other types of malware of course apart from these listed here, but these are the more commonly observed types of malware that have been downloaded or have infected computers and computer systems here in the country.

Adware Bombards the users with a lot of unsolicited advertisements, usually urging the user to install software such as a mobile game. In the case of spyware, a program is inadvertently installed on a user's computer or mobile device and leaks a user's data such as his/her browsing habits, to an external server. The delineation between a virus and a worm becomes tricky for most users in the country since the observable freezing of PCs, hiding of user's files and folders, and sometimes data corruption can be attributed to both. But, to differentiate the two, the virus needs to have a user intervention before it can propagate, whereas the worm can replicate itself on its own without the user assisting in the process.

Trojans are usually software packaged inside a useful utility program. The user usually thinks that the software will aid in movie editing, music editing, warding off viruses and other malware, etc. The program instead executes a code that opens the doors to an external attack on the user's computer or data. Similarly, rootkits are downloaded with other software (usually in cracked software) and that the rootkit digs itself deep within the internal workings of the Operating System, thus allowing it to perform many unauthorized actions (e.g. downloading a new program off a site, running a certain process and scheduling its runtime, etc.) without it being detected, since the Operating System accepts the rootkit as one of its own modules, services, or parts thus masking its presence.

When it comes to *ransomware*, the user is locked out of his/her data by the hacker using a sophisticated encryption algorithm, and the only way that the user can regain access to the data is to pay the hacker a certain amount through digital currency (e.g. Bitcoin) to receive the decryption key. The problem with this though is that there is no assurance that the hacker actually has the means to decrypt the encrypted files, and that even if the hacker has such capability, there is no assurance that the hacker will follow through after the payment has been received.

Botnets are primarily used as an agent in the Distributed Denial of Service (DDoS) Attack. In this scenario, the hackers would use the processing power and/or resources of vulnerable devices (e.g. Internet of Things (IoT) devices) to initiate an attack onto a computer and/or computer system. Basically, botnets in this case are used to overwhelm the server with a lot of requests which then render it inaccessible to the authorized users. In the CIA triad, this targets Availability.

Oftentimes, the hacking methods become quite confusing since hacking attempts usually employ hybrid methodology (combining multiple methodologies among social engineering and technical/software-based attacks). Common social engineering attacks include such methods as shoulder surfing (looking over one's shoulder to see what's on the screen), dumpster diving (digging through the trash of a user) and even the phishing attempts (including phishing through voice or vishing). The inherent hospitality of Filipinos is being exploited to gain unauthorized access to the system or its data.

Another form of social engineering involves individuals pretending to be employees of a certain institution to gain access to its valuable records.

Physical Security Attacks - going beyond the scope of the earlier scenarios - also play a part in the areas where hacking attempts can be made. Physical security attacks involve the computer or computer system being accessed by the hackers physically. This is often due to user negligence, such as leaving the computer workstation unlocked, inserting an unknown flash drive, and leaving the access door open in rooms housing vital information system assets such as the servers. Lost devices (personal or company/institution-issued) are considered as a physical security attack, the severity of which would heavily rely on the type of information that is contained in the lost devices.

19.8 What to do to Prevent Such Attempts at Hacking?

19.8.1 At the Level of Computer Scientists and Information Technology Specialists

The growing need for more Cybersecurity specialists requires that the country's Computer Scientists and Information Technology Specialists involved with the academe should adopt an interdisciplinary approach and framework in dealing with issues related to Cybersecurity, considering that these issues and concerns also involve legal frameworks (e.g. national and international legislation and agreements), and other such frameworks in the social sciences.

While it is a good step that the technicalities of the subjects of Cybersecurity, Ethical Hacking, and Digital Forensics are already incorporated into the curriculum of either *a major* or *a specialization* in the field of Computer Science and or Information Technology, this effort should also be enhanced by developing strategic partnerships with entities that deal with cyber-related incidents and/or cybercrimes such as software development companies, banks, hospitals, government agencies (including law enforcement agencies), etc.

Information campaigns should also come from practitioners of Computer Science and Information Technology, and they should spearhead efforts towards introducing the use among Filipinos of either *free and open source software*, or *officially-licensed software*, for their different productivity tasks (e.g. word processing, calculations, etc.) and other miscellaneous computer activities (e.g. multimedia content consumption). The use of pirated or "cracked" software and the consumption of multimedia content from disreputable sites and applications should be discouraged as well: they can become the entry points for attacks.

Secure coding practices and penetration testing of applications being developed by Computer Scientists and Information Technology Specialists should also be incorporated into the Software development process, *to instil the sense of proper handling, processing and storage of data* of their different clients and customers.

19.8.2 At the Level of Law Enforcement Agencies

The law enforcement agencies such as the PNP face significant challenges in Cybersecurity specifically attributed to the growing concern towards cybercrimes. The country's cybersecurity landscape plays host to the increasing number of cybersecurity-related complaints in the years 2013 to 2015. Online scams topped the list of these cybercrime cases, but by 2016, because the May presidential election was forthcoming, heated political debates took place even in cyberspace, causing online libel to emerge as the topmost complaint from victimized netizens. During this period, online scams then came in second, followed by identity theft, online threats and violations under the Anti-Photo and Video Voyeurism Act (PNP-ACU Statistics).

Police statistics show that online threats and online libel complaints blossomed with most Filipinos engaging in social media networks such as Facebook and Twitter. Mostly, the nature of complaints showed trust and affinity to a certain degree as the basic foundation of their relationship. Thus, these victims usually know who their suspects are. But police investigators say that securing digital evidences can be very difficult as it is easy to delete incriminating posts and messages. Although victims can provide their screenshots of their conversations, the investigators must still gather evidences that are admissible in court, and the cooperation or help from telecommunication companies and Internet Service Providers (ISPs) are crucial. These companies would only release transcripts upon order from the Courts. Of the 1,804 complaints received from the PNP Anti-Cybercrime Group, only 4.66% have reached the Prosecutor's Office. Almost half of these cases (40.35%) were dropped and closed and more than half of these cases (51.44%) are still ongoing.

Complaints involving money like online scams and photo and video voyeurism are easier to solve because documented evidences are available and readily obtainable. Threats and harassments that are politically-coloured and recipients of these hate messages from unknown netizens or strangers take months to investigate for obvious reasons. Brian Posey, in his article entitled Cyber-Extortion: Why it works and how to fight says: "Right now one of the on-line trends that seem to be gaining traction is cyber-extortion." And "cyber-extortion can come in many different forms, but at its simplest, it is when someone on line threatens some sort of harm unless you meet their demands. The demand is usually for money (commonly in the form of bitcoins) but an extortionist could conceivably demand just about anything."

Despite these challenges and obstacles in the Cybersecurity landscape of the country, PNP Assistant Chief of the Anti-Cyber Group Police Superintendent Jay Guillermo said that the cyber cops show ingenuity and apply street skills in ensuring other ways for successful police investigations wherein entrapment and inter-agency cooperation have been oftentimes used and proven to be effective police strategies.

Given this challenge, law enforcers should be continuously trained in handling and investigating these types of crimes. A more pragmatic approach must be adopted where these trainings are not limited to the current seminars and workshops being offered by government agencies such as the DICT. What could be done is to create short courses on Cybersecurity and Digital Forensics geared specifically for law enforcers where the learning level of difficulty increases as the topics advances further. Considering that hacking methodologies evolve and advance at a fast pace, law enforcement agencies need to capacitate and enhance capability trainings in order to develop and upgrade thier skills in combining theories and actual practice of Cybersecurity and Digital Forensics. With information readily-available online (e.g. ethical hacking tools, digital forensics software, and online courses) specifically catering to these topics and considering that there are already practitioners of Cybersecurity and Digital Forensics in various industries such as in the academe, government and private sectors, these resources would really be of great help to the efforts towards building a more robust and in-depth course and/or training for law enforcement agencies.

With the short course on Cybersecurity and Digital Forensics be in place, the levels of difficulty could be divided as being basic, intermediate and advanced so as not to burden the law enforcers to attend the same level of training more than once despite their level of competency being at a much higher level. For the basic competency-level, the cybersecurity threat landscape, common secure practices when interacting online, and basic frameworks and concepts in both fields of study can be introduced. On the intermediate level, the participants coming from the law enforcers must already possess a good theoretical grounding on the basic concepts before proceeding to this course since this will now introduce the usage of common utilities used in Digital Forensic Investigation, its methodology as well as common tools and codebase used in hacking so they will have a better understanding of the inner-workings of those who actually perpetrated the crimes as well as those who are tasked to investigate them. At the advanced level, these law enforcers would then be introduced to topics such as reverse engineering, malware, and threat analysis as well as be able to teach them how to code their own modules for use in investigation purposes since there are tools in Digital Forensics which accepts custom code coming from the user.

Another course could also be introduced which will then be called as an executive course where those who have attended the trainings could interact with their top executives and collaborate on a strategy on how to best perform a certain investigation procedure. When this will be implemented it may be very helpful in bridging the gap between the technical and the policy/decision-making officers of the organization and drive the efforts towards looking at the battle against cybercrimes in a more holistic manner (by incorporating technical know-how with the high-level strategies being thought of by the decision-makers).

19.8.3 At the Level of the End User or Netizen

For end users or the netizens, it is best that they follow safe browsing practices when dealing with any activity that they must do on their computing devices and in the Internet. They should avoid doing the computer habits (as stated in the previous section) that risk their data security as well as exercise caution when dealing with other parties in the Internet. A lot of these safe browsing practices are already being published by different government, non-government and private institutions via different channels such as in public bulletin postings and social media campaigns. As such, they should keep being updated about such practices (e.g. changing passwords on a more regular basis, investing in a good antimalware solution, updating the operating system components, updating the router firmware as well as the other Internet-connected devices at home, etc.).

Netizens should also exercise caution when dealing with unfamiliar entities online such as those who offer goods and services but are not licensed businesses. When dealing with hostile entities online be it a former friend, or colleague for the cases of cyber-extortion, and other such related cases, it is best to coordinate immediately with the proper authorities and report the incident before it escalates further. As there are plenty of cyber-extortion and on-line blackmail scams that are real, the best way to avoid becoming a victim is never do anything on line today that could embarrass you tomorrow.

These practices stated above would ensure that the netizen would be able to make full use of the Internet and its related technologies to the full extent and do away with the problems on data security – and cyber-extortion.

Bibliography

Conrad, E., Misenar, S., Feldman, J., & Greenblatt, L. (2010). Cornerstone Information Security Concepts. In E. Conrad,

S. Misenar, J. Feldman, & L. Greenblatt, *CISSP Study Guide* (pp. 7-9). Burlington: Syngress.

Cybercrime Threat Landscape in the Philippines. *SecureAsia@Manila.* Makati City: (ISC)2; NDCPAAI.

International Information System Security Consortium, Inc. & National Defense College of the Philippines Alumni Association, Inc. (2013).

Office of Cyber Crimes, Department of Justice, Philippines, R.A. 10175 otherwise known as Cyber Crime Preventjon Act of 2012 and R.A. 8792, Electronic Commerce Act of 2000

The PNP ACG website: www.acg.pnp.gov.ph.

Posey, Bryan (2017): Cyber-extortion: why it works and how to fight back, http://techgenix.com/why-cyber-extortion-works/

Seger, A. (2013): CTO Cyber Security Forum 2013, Yaoundé, Cameroon, 25 April 2013, Workshop on the Budapest Convention on Cybercrime, https://cto.int/media/events/pst-ev/2013/Cybersecurity/Alexander%20Seger-Budapest%20Convention%20on%20Cybercrime.pdf

Webroot.com, Types of Computer Security Threats and How to Avoid Them, https://www.webroot.com/us/en/resources/tips-articles/computer-security-threats

20

SPYING IN A TRANSPARENT WORLD: ETHICS AND INTELLIGENCE IN THE 21ST CENTURY

Siobhan Martin, Switzerland

Executive Summary

Is intelligence gathering ethical? [416] Three years after the Snowden revelations on mass surveillance and ten years after the emergence of extraordinary rendition scandals, the debate on the role of ethics in intelligence gathering has never been as prominent, and is dominated by opposing perspectives. On the one hand is the view that the very nature of intelligence work is unethical, but such work needs to be done to protect national security. On the other is the view that it is precisely this unethical nature that undermines the legitimacy and security of democratic states, and is therefore unacceptable. The rise of this debate is due to two trends: the increasingly transparent environment in which secret intelligence activities occur, and policymakers' public assertions on the crucial role of intelligence in protecting national and international security.

---

[416] This chapter 21 is published with permission of the Geneva Center for Security Policy GCSP, Geneva/Switzerland. First published under the same author and title as GCSP Geneva Papers, Research Series 19/16, Geneva 2016, 8-37.

The growing emphasis on intelligence has led to unprecedented concern with its practice in Western liberal democracies, particularly as a result of collection efforts in the combat against terrorism. The response from the public and civil society actors to scandals around extraordinary rendition and mass surveillance has been a resurgence of a fundamental debate on the extent to which democratic laws and values are being compromised to protect national security. This paper provides an analysis of current thinking on the relationship between ethics and intelligence in liberal democracies, the challenges posed by the increasingly complex 21st century security environment, the ethical dilemmas that emerge as a result and prospects for ethical intelligence gathering in the future.

20.1 Introduction

"Without our ability to access telecommunications call data and intercept communications [we] cannot guarantee the level of safety assurance that people expect .... The fact is that in the last eight or nine years we have stopped four mass casualty terrorist attacks ... and nipped quite a number of others in the bud at the very early planning stage."[417]

The controversies of the last decade around extraordinary rendition, enhanced interrogation techniques and mass surveillance have created unprecedented ethical concerns about the role of intelligence in democratic states. The resulting public debate has never been as prominent, and is dominated by opposing perspectives. On the one hand is the view that the very nature of intelligence work is unethical, but this work needs to be done in order to protect national security. On the other is the view

---

[417] David Irvine, Head, Australian Security Intelligence Organisation, 2009-2014. Cited in D. Hurst, "ASIO Spy Chief Defends Surveillance Network and Argues for Broader Powers", The Guardian, 21 July 2014, https://www.theguardian.com/world/2014/jul/21/asio-spy-chief-defends-surveillence-network.

that it is precisely this unethical nature that undermines the legitimacy and security of democratic states, and is therefore unacceptable. This situation becomes more complex because of the increasingly transparent environment in which secret intelligence activities now occur, in addition to policymakers' public assertions on the crucial role of intelligence in protecting national and international security.

The reliance on intelligence is reflective of a pattern in which crises are followed by a resort to reactionary policies as governments 'return to the shadows' to protect national security. This approach can be traced back to the circumstances in which professional intelligence communities first emerged, and their evolution ever since. Intelligence communities began to professionalise quite late in many democracies, in the early Cold War era, which was a very specific environment overshadowed by the fear of nuclear annihilation. The Cold War effectively became a 'spy war' between US and Soviet intelligence agencies and those of their allies, leading to the use of extreme measures and covert action in defence of opposing political ideals. The result was an era of considerable freedom and power for intelligence agencies. As the Cold War progressed, concerns over intelligence agencies' conduct began to emerge, in particular controversies surrounding covert activities abroad and spying on citizens at home.[418] An era of enquiries then began that questioned whether and how intelligence services represent the values of the states they protect. Oversight mechanisms were also developed, albeit to a limited extent.

The emphasis on intelligence dissipated in the post-Cold War period as budgets were reduced and the focus was placed on the 'peace dividend'. It was shattered by the shock of the 9/11 attacks and the so-called

---

[418] For example, Operation CHAOS in the US; see T.S. Hardy, "Intelligence Reform in the Mid-1970s", Studies in Intelligence, Vol. 20(2), 1996, https://www.cia.gov/library/center-for-the-study-of-intelligence/kent-csi/vol20no2/html/v20i2a01p_0001.htm.

global war on terror. Continuous and deadly terrorist attacks across Western liberal democracies led to extraordinary rendition and the use of enhanced interrogation techniques becoming an acceptable response – "We've got to spend time in the shadows in the intelligence world ... if we're going to be successful"[419] - followed by revelations of mass surveillance, to such a degree that the British Government Communications Headquarters (GCHQ) is reported to collect 50 billion metadata records a day.[420]4 This is countered by reflections on past mistakes and the changing transparent environment in which a return to the shadows is no longer possible because it undermines civil liberties, national interests and democracy itself.[421] In this era of governments utilising intelligence as a tool to demonstrate that they are still in control, the discussion on the role of ethics and what constitutes acceptable intelligence gathering behaviour is critical.

Yet even in democracies, the practice of intelligence is characterised by "openness with some exceptions".[422] As government actors, intelligence agencies in liberal democracies are required to adhere to laws,

---

[419] Richard Cheney, as quoted in D. Froomkin, "Cheney's Dark Side Is Showing", Washington Post, 7 November 2005, http://www.washingtonpost.com/wp-dyn/content/blog/2005/11/07/ BL2005110700793.html.

[420] N. Morris, "Edward Snowden: GCHQ Collected Information from Every Visible User on the Internet", The Independent, 25 September 2015, http://www.independent.co.uk/news/uk/home-news/edward-snowden-gchq-collected-information-from-every-visible-user-on-the- internet-10517356.html.

[421] L. Watts, "Intelligence Reform in Europe's Emerging Democracies", Studies in Intelligence, Vol.48(1), 2007, https://www.cia.gov/library/center-for-the-study-of-intelligence/csi-publications/csi-studies/studies/vol48no1/ article02.html#rfn3.

[422] L. Nathan, "Intelligence Transparency, Secrecy, and Oversight in a Democracy", in H. Born and A. Wills (eds), Overseeing Intelligence Services: A Toolkit, 2012, 52, http://mercury.ethz.ch/serviceengine/Files/ISN/157466/ ichaptersection_singledocument/22416533-d4c1-418b-8729-ad797ae62292/en/ Tool3_Nathan_EN.pdf.

norms and values, but they may also engage in "exceptional" activities to protect national security. Furthermore, ethics training is not a new concern for intelligence agencies[423], despite clear shortcomings. Consequently, extreme perspectives that portray intelligence gathering as either not, or unable to be, ethical are limited in their ability to reflect the complexity of the international security environment. Intelligence work today must be ethical and effective, in a world in which both qualities are increasingly seen to be paramount. How this can be achieved in practice and the inherent challenges of ethical intelligence gathering will be addressed in this paper.

Initially an overview will be provided of classical and current thinking on intelligence gathering and ethics in order to understand the fundamental issues that emerge. The paper will then address the specific challenges confronted by intelligence agencies in the 21st century international security environment in order to explore the key ethical dilemmas that currently exist for agencies and governments. The paper will conclude by addressing future prospects for the practice of ethical intelligence gathering.

20.2 The Context of Intelligence: An Ethical Exception?

Before examining the application of ethics to intelligence gathering, it is essential to have a clear understanding of what intelligence actually is. Defining intelligence is somewhat difficult, because its meaning varies across states and agencies, and has evolved with the changing security environment. Traditional definitions include a focus on information or

---

[423] J. Goldman, "Teaching about Intelligence and Ethics", The Intelligencer, Vol.20(2), Fall/ Winter 2013, https://www.afio.com/publications/ GOLDMAN%20Pages%20from%20INTEL_FALLWINTER2013_Vol20_ No2.pdf.

(fore)knowledge within a secret and 'foreign' political context[424], which is seen to manifest as a product, process or activity. While quite broad, the context today is as much about the domestic as the foreign sphere. Furthermore, while the emphasis on national security remains the priority, the focus is becoming increasingly international in the interlinked, interdependent world of the 21st century. The role of intelligence nonetheless remains focused on reducing uncertainty, providing early warning and informing policy decisions. As a result, intelligence can be defined as secret information, or activities conducted to produce or procure it, in order to maintain or improve national and international security. This definition introduces the need to understand the questions of who conducts what intelligence gathering activities, which are key in understanding the ethical dilemmas that arise.

Intelligence work is conducted by government agencies on behalf of the state. The traditional focus of civilian agencies is on the foreign (e.g. CIA, MI6), domestic (e.g. FBI, MI5) and technical (e.g. NSA, GCHQ) spheres. A country's executive branch of government is the primary consumer of intelligence, determines the intelligence agenda, and is, by extension, also involved in the decision to engage in ethical or unethical behaviour when it approves intelligence gathering activities. An intricate relationship, the executive has to balance the level of freedom accorded to agencies to effectively prevent threats with the risk of granting too great a zone of discretion that may lead to compromised laws and values. The situation becomes even more complicated if 'plausible deniability' is applied, as the executive may purposely remove the need for direct consent while nonetheless understanding the potential ethical risks involved in a particular activity. This increases the level of autonomy given to intelligence agencies in the 'special' context of intelligence, but also creates ethical and legal concerns.

---

[424] G. Treverton et al., Towards a Theory of Intelligence, Rand Workshop Report, 2005, 7-8, http://www.rand.org/pubs/conf_ proceedings/CF219.html.

This paper will focus on intelligence agencies, but it should also be noted that the interconnected nature of current threats requires the involvement of more and more non- security related agencies. Customs departments, finance departments and other branches of government do not just supply information, but also conduct 'operations' such as tracing funds and building legal cases against terrorist suspects. Non-traditional ministries and departments also require a rapid intelligence capacity when dealing with disasters and other crisis situations involving citizens, but do not have the level of access of traditional intelligence actors. In fact, the current context has expanded so broadly that there is a "new intelligence ecology"[425] in which we are all intelligence actors – from intelligence officers to the general public reporting suspicious behaviour to local police. The expansion of actors engaging in intelligence work makes the discussion on ethics – and what our societies agree is acceptable behaviour – even more significant.

The context in which intelligence activities take place is based on secrecy, which is "an intrinsic and necessary feature ... of [an agency's] mandate and functions"[426].10 Secrecy clearly impacts on agencies' ability to engage in unethical behaviour, but the level of secrecy required for an intelligence service to function effectively is now being questioned. For example, intelligence analysis today relies much more on open sources (reportedly up to 80 per cent)[427], but this information becomes 'secret' once it enters the intelligence process. Yet the need for secrecy

---

[425] Conversation with Prof. R. Aldrich, Warwick University, 25 May 2013.

[426] L. Nathan, "Intelligence Transparency, Secrecy, and Oversight in a Democracy", in H. Born and A. Wills (eds), Overseeing Intelligence Services: A Toolkit, 2012, 51, http://mercury.ethz.ch/serviceengine/Files/ISN/157466/ichaptersection_singledocument/22416533-d4c1-418b-8729-ad797ae62292/en/Tool3_Nathan_EN.pdf.

[427] R.A. Best and A. Cumming, Open Source Intelligence (OSINT): Issues for Congress, CRS Report, 5 December 2007, 4, https://www.fas.org/sgp/crs/intel/RL34270.pdf.

does not just apply to the information itself, but to the methods used to obtain it or the sources it comes from, the secrecy of which must crucially be maintained. Therefore, although intelligence is not only based on classified materials, secrecy is still a prerequisite to ensuring the level of knowledge necessary to prevent and forewarn against hostile threats. This need has to be taken into account for any discussion of the relationship between ethics and intelligence.

The forms of intelligence gathering activities have evolved over recent decades and reflect not only the type of threat being faced, but also political and public perception. The Cold War was an era of spies, of human intelligence ('humint'), and of moles and double agents. As technology advanced in the 1950s and 1960s, emphasis shifted to signals intelligence ('sigint'), i.e. the process of intercepting communications, because technology was seen to be more reliable than the human factor. This was also related to the negative perception that arose as a consequence of the numerous covert action scandals during the Cold War. For a time the focus on technology was less controversial. However, the shock of the 9/11 attacks demonstrated the lack of understanding of the new threat posed by terrorist groups and the need to refocus on 'humint' in response to overwhelming public pressure to prevent further attacks. In parallel, the increased technical capabilities available to intelligence agencies led to signals collection expanding to an unprecedented level, constituting the major part of intelligence gathering efforts.[428] Both are a source of concern for the public today.

Finally, failure on the part of intelligence agencies will lead to grave consequences for national and international security. This context amplifies the sense of urgency and the absolute necessity for effectiveness.

---

[428] Private information confirmed by an overview of the US intelligence "black budget"; see W. Andrews and T. Lindeman, "$52.6 Billion: The Black Budget", Washington Post, 29 August 2013, http://www.washingtonpost.com/wp-srv/special/national/black-budget/.

Consequently, our understanding of what is ethically acceptable does not apply as easily to the domain of intelligence. In considering the debate and the ability of agencies to respond to the needs of the current era, it is important to understand how the 'specialness' of intelligence is taken into account – if at all – within ethical discourse, the changes to intelligence gathering practices that have emerged in the increasingly globalised environment, and the ethical challenges they pose for intelligence agencies today.

20.3 Classical and Current Thinking on Ethics

"Tough interrogation of Al Qaeda ... thwarted more than 20 plots ... against U.S. infrastructure targets, including communications nodes, nuclear power plants, dams, bridges, and tunnels. A 'future airborne attack on America's West Coast' was likely foiled only because the CIA didn't have ... to treat Khalid Sheikh Mohammed like a white collar criminal."[429]

The use of enhanced interrogation techniques is one of many issues that have resulted in a fundamental questioning of intelligence and its role in democratic societies over the past decade. Yet the case Tenet refers to is also an example of one of multiple intelligence successes leading to the protection of many innocent lives. Deciding what constitutes ethical behaviour can be extremely complex in such scenarios and lies at the heart of this debate.

The concept of ethics is generally based on an understanding of what is acceptable and moral, as determined by the rules and values of a given society; it is "a set of behavioural guidelines based on certain beliefs ...

---

[429] George Tenet, Director, Central Intelligence Agency, 1996-2004. In M. Thompson and B. Ghosh, "Did Waterboarding Prevent Terrorist Attacks?", Time, 21 April 2009, http://content.time.com/time/nation/article/0,8599,1892947,00.html.

regarding the role of intelligence in society"[430]. These guidelines include national laws, which limit behaviour, in addition to norms relating to human rights and societal values. In considering intelligence gathering specifically (the main source of recent controversy), the discussion is quite nuanced: "Intelligence is information and information gathering, not doing things to people; no one gets hurt by it, at least not directly."[431] This is an oversimplification however, because if the information leads to a suspect being arrested and flown to an overseas location to be interrogated in a way that is contrary to human rights law, direct harm will result. In fact, ethics is closely linked with law. While the two concepts are clearly distinct, they are often intertwined in the domain of intelligence in determining what constitutes harm, but also because illegal acts are "immoral" in that they breach the rules of society.

For example, espionage in a foreign state might not directly harm an individual, but its very existence begins from an illegal – i.e. unethical – starting point. On this latter point, the most complex questions around intelligence gathering are often based on the interrelationship between ethics and law – what is morally questionable yet legal, or morally justifiable but illegal. For example, the use of enhanced interrogation techniques to prevent a terrorist attack is argued to be morally justifiable, even if illegal, because of the lives it saves. The same argument can be made regarding the collection of foreign intelligence through illegal espionage and mass surveillance. On the other hand, intelligence activities can be legal, but ethically questionable. In the so-called global war on terror, both US vice president Richard Cheney and defense secretary Donald Rumsfeld argued that members of Al Qaeda and the Taliban were not entitled to prisoner-of-war status, so international law was not

---

[430] S. Spiro as quoted in J. Goldman (ed.), The Ethics of Spying: A Reader for the Intelligence Professional, Lanham, Scarecrow Press, 2005, 37.

[431] M. Herman, "Ethics and Intelligence after September 2001", in ibid., Vol.2, 103.

applicable, allowing for 'non-white collar' treatment.[432] In another case that was technically legal but clearly unethical, the legal definition of torture was limited to such a degree that it was very difficult to prove, thus facilitating the use of enhanced interrogation techniques.[433] Intelligence gathering will not always be ethical, but neither will it always be legal. Better guidelines for ethical intelligence need to integrate ethics, the concept of harm and law.

An opportunity to do so is provided by considering that the application of ethics to intelligence is not static. The emphasis on societal values allows for ethics to evolve in conjunction with what is seen as acceptable, or legal, and therefore an understanding of ethical intelligence can change over time. The focus on guidelines is useful when considering what concrete measures can be taken to achieve the ethical practice of intelligence. Although intelligence work often takes place within a climate of extreme risk and urgency, as indicated by the case above, this is not the only reality. A distinction is needed between decisions taken and actions carried out in extreme circumstances, and day-to-day activities.

There are two classic perspectives on the application of ethics to espionage in statecraft that are also advocated by intelligence practitioners. Idealists such as Immanuel Kant believed that the use of spies was inherently wrong, that employing the "infamy of others can never be entirely eradicated", and that it will persist after war and undo any peace

---

[432] Human Rights Watch, "Summary", in Getting Away with Torture: The Bush Administration and Mistreatment of Detainees, Report, 12 July 2011, https://www.hrw.org/report/2011/07/12/getting-away-torture/bush-administration-and-mistreatment-detainees.

[433] American Psychological Association Review of Ethical Guidelines, Interrogations and Torture, "Executive Summary", Report to the Special Committee of the Board of Directors of the American Psychological Association, 2 July 2015, https://publicintelligence.net/apa-torture- report/.

that exists.[434] In order words, the use of immoral means will lead to an immoral state and therefore weaken security, and so should be forbidden. This perspective is upheld by intelligence practitioners, who see that "no area of human activity, can claim 'an a priori entitlement to require the moralist to be silent', and intelligence should be no exception"[435]. While admirable, the nature of intelligence gathering involves illegal and immoral acts, such as foreign espionage. Therefore, applying the idealist perspective (at least in the Kantian sense) essentially means conducting statecraft without an intelligence gathering capacity. This is not possible when dealing with national security, and even less so in the complex threat environment that currently exists.

While idealists focus on the means, realist philosophers interpret the use of espionage and ethics through the results obtained. Classical Machiavellian thinking acknowledged that "although the act condemns the doer, the end may justify him"[436] and so immoral methods are sometimes necessary to protect the state. Other views from intelligence practitioners range from the view that "if there is to be discomfort and terror inflicted on a few, is it not preferred to [its] being inflicted on perhaps a million people?"[437] to "the whole business of espionage is unethical .... It's not an issue. It never was and never will be, not if you want a real spy service."[438] The implications are clear. In order to maintain the civi-

---

[434]I. Kant, Perpetual Peace, 1.6, https://www.mtholyoke.edu/acad/intrel/kant/kant1.htm.

[435] M. Quinlan, "Just Intelligence: Prolegomena to an Ethical Theory", Intelligence and National Security, Vol.22(1), 2007, 2.

[436]N. Machiavelli, Discourses, 1.9, http://www.online-literature.com/machiavelli/titus-livius/9/.

[437] Unnamed British Army intelligence officer quoted in B. Hoffman, "Brutal Interrogation Techniques May Be Necessary to Gather Valuable Intelligence", in L. Gerdes (ed.), Espionage and Intelligence Gathering, San Diego, Greenhaven Press, 2004, 31.

[438] D.R. Clarridge, former CIA operative, quoted in S. Shane, "An Exotic Tool for Espionage: Moral Compass", New York Times, 28 January 2006,

lised world and to protect democratic liberties, there is a need for those who are willing to use whatever means are necessary to protect the state.

Nonetheless, the view that ethics has no place whatsoever in intelligence work is unconvincing, because it implies that the only way to protect a state is to undermine the values that constitute it. However, the less extreme perspective in which the security of the majority – the state – takes priority over that of the individual is significant in demonstrating that realists do not simply dismiss ethics; rather, they interpret its basis differently, because not engaging in intelligence work would leave the state vulnerable to threats and attacks, which is itself ethically unacceptable.

The ideas behind these classical philosophies are just as prevalent today. Societal norms do not just focus on the majority, but on the civil rights of the individual and human security. This is juxtaposed with the recent return to realist thinking, demonstrated by extraordinary actions taken in relation to rendition and mass surveillance. Nonetheless, caution must be exercised because both the idealist and realist approaches – at least in the classical sense – do not take into account the complexity of current threats. Furthermore, they do not provide concrete guidance to intelligence agencies on exceptional action.

Recent discourse allows for a more nuanced analysis in this regard, drawing on the logic of consequences. One prominent approach is the idea of an "ethical balance sheet"[439] in which the potential harm should be weighed against the potential benefits obtained through intelligence activities. This is similar to the idea of allowing for exceptions in extreme circumstances by prioritising the majority over the individual. However, this approach is seen as too restrictive, since the concept of

---

http://www.nytimes.com/2006/01/28/politics/28ethics.html?pagewanted=print&_r=0.

[439] As quoted in J. Goldman (ed.), The Ethics of Spying: A Reader for the Intelligence Professional, Lanham, Scarecrow Press, 2005, 40.

'potential harm' can be vague and not easy to understand in practice. It is difficult to assess the level of harm or potential benefits in advance of an act, while the balance can radically change after it has occurred. If a suspected terrorist is tortured due to fear of an imminent attack and is actually innocent, the 'potential' benefits would be unjustifiable in comparison to the harm done in accordance with the ethical balance sheet.

Another 'harm-focused' approach that has gained much traction in recent years is an adaption of the 'just war' theory and the argument of proportionality. It is based on the concept of 'do no harm', in which an assessment should be made of how intelligence activities can impact on an individual's 'vital interests' concretely defined as physical integrity, mental integrity, autonomy, liberty, human dignity and privacy.[440] By their nature, intelligence gathering activities will usually involve some degree of violation, but the idea is that such an assessment will allow intelligence practitioners to differentiate between "the forbidden [torture] and the essential [interrogation]"[441] by applying the following six principles:

A just cause should be evident and the threat being faced should be sufficient to justify the potential harm caused by intelligence collection; the authority to do what is required must be legitimate and represent the political community; the intention should be clear and the intelligence gathered should not be used for secondary objectives; proportionality should be applied, with potential harm weighed against perceived gains; a last resort approach should be taken in which less harmful activities

---

[440] R. Bellaby, "What's the Harm? The Ethics of Intelligence Collection", Intelligence and National Security, Vol.27(1), 2012, 96-104.

[441] T. Ricks and J. Jeffcoat, "Regaining the Moral High Ground: Time to Think about the Just Intelligence Doctrine", Foreign Policy, 18 December 2014, http://foreignpolicy.com/2014/12/18/regaining-the-moral-high-ground-time-to-think-about-just-intelligence-doctrine/.

should be conducted first; and there should be discrimination between legitimate and illegitimate targets.[442]

As a result, efforts will always be made to limit harm, and action will take place within a justified framework. Yet critics of the just intelligence approach point out that it is limited to legal activities, and refer to the obvious incompatibility of applying just war perspective to activities that are illegal and criminal.[443] Nevertheless, it can be equally argued that just war theory is suitable, given the intricate interrelationship between ethics and law in the domain of intelligence and the types of activities used to secure the state. However, there is a need to recognise that the context of intelligence requires some adaptation and flexibility.

The brief review above outlined the main theoretical approaches to the complex dialectic between intelligence work and ethics. However, a number of new trends have emerged in the practice of intelligence in the 21st century that pose challenges not only for ethics, but for intelligence work itself. An understanding of the impact of globalisation on intelligence, therefore, is key to comprehending the core dilemmas that impact on the ethical practice of intelligence gathering today.

20.4 21st Century Intelligence: New Challenges for Ethics

Although intelligence has always been a central part of maintaining state security, the era of globalisation has transformed the environment in which intelligence services operate. There has been an increase in the

---

[442] R. Bellaby, "Ethics in Intelligence", in G. Moore (ed.), Encyclopedia of U.S. Intelligence, two volumes, Auerbach Publications, 2014.

[443] J. Lunstroth, "Just War Theory and Intelligence Ethics: A Bad Fit", paper presented at the Third International Conference on Ethics in the Intelligence Community, International Intelligence Ethics Association, Baltimore, 22-23 February 2008, 9, https://docs.google.com/file/ d/0BygmT15QEBEGb EJRUXVZekNqdE0/edit?pref=2&pli=1.

number and complexity of the threats that intelligence agencies are struggling to respond to, while intelligence work increasingly occurs in the public sphere, with policymakers highlighting more and more the crucial role of intelligence in justifying policy decisions. The discussion that follows is not exhaustive, but outlines some of the main trends that have emerged and the challenges they pose for ethical intelligence gathering.

20.4.1 The Changing Nature of Threats

The threats that top national security agendas in democracies today are interconnected, borderless, state-based and vast in number. State-based threats are perhaps seen as more traditional and therefore more manageable, but the speed and unpredictability of the Arab Spring, for example, was unforeseen by intelligence agencies, while the situation in Syria is continually volatile. At the same time, the majority of security challenges are borderless, conducted by non-state actors or isolated cells that are more difficult to track, as well as by lone-wolf perpetrators loosely associated with terrorist organisations such as Al Qaeda and the Islamic State, which are extremely difficult to identify. In addition to hard security threats, intelligence agencies have seen a widening of their responsibilities: issues ranging from potential pandemics to the effects of climate change are all becoming part of the intelligence agenda. Agencies are struggling to be effective, and their ability to do so, while increasing the focus on ethics, is one of the core difficulties they currently confront. It is for this reason that the dialogue on what constitutes ethical intelligence must progress.

20.4.2 Technology

Technology has transformed the strategic environment in which intelligence agencies operate. It has enabled agencies to have a far wider reach and has given them access to more information than ever before. Yet it has exacerbated the threats that agencies are facing by significantly increasing the interaction among state entities and non-state entities threatening state security. It has also led to incredible pressure on agencies, as executive decision-makers now expect immediate, real-time intelligence, and intelligence producers have to compete with the wide variety of online, unverified information available to their consumers. While some see opportunities in the high-tech capacity of intelligence collaboration[444], which has become a necessity to protect the state, the reaction of civil rights groups raises fundamental questions about the appropriateness of technical means of intelligence gathering and their regulation. The Edward Snowden revelations brought this to the fore in illustrating the wide disconnect in public opinion on surveillance. While advances in technology should be seen as providing opportunities to intelligence agencies, how they should adapt while maintaining civil liberties remains unknown.

20.4.3 Outsourcing

In response to the pressures of current threats and the demand for real-time reporting, a significant response by agencies has been to outsource intelligence responsibilities. Edward Snowden's access as a private contractor and his leaking of up to 200,000 secret files raised key questions about the degree to which private sector companies should be used to perform state functions. Agencies have also outsourced operations and interrogation activities to private military companies who are not subject to the same regulations as state agencies, making it more difficult to monitor abuses and prosecute crimes.[445] These examples are

---

[444] D. Omand, "NSA Leaks: How to Make Surveillance Both Ethical and Effective", The Guardian,
11 June 2013, http://www.theguardian.com/commentisfree/2013/jun/11/make-surveillance-ethical-and-effective.

[445] D. Roberts, "US Jury Convicts Blackwater Guards in 2007 Killing of Iraqi Civilians", The Guardian, 23 October 2014, http://www.theguardian.com/us-news/2014/oct/22/us-jury- convicts-blackwater-security-guards-iraq.

representative of a wider trend that the overwhelming pressure to respond and the opportunities afforded by technology have led to a dramatic increase in the outsourcing of intelligence work to private sector entities. States will continue to depend on private sector support and expertise to respond to the challenges and technological environment that they face. Improved oversight and regulation are a necessity.

20.4.4 Cooperation

A global response is needed to global challenges, and the 21st century has seen a veritable explosion of intelligence sharing, which is now less the "supporting arm of defence and diplomacy, instead becoming ... the cutting edge of foreign policy"[446]. In fact, according to the CIA deputy director of operations, between 2001 and 2005 "virtually every capture or killing" of suspected terrorist was the result of international cooperation.[447] While such cooperation is logical due to the benefits of burden sharing and increasing access to equipment, expertise and technology, it lies at the crux of the tension that exists between ethics and intelligence. While many international partners have similar rules and values, others "make strange international bedfellows, with profound implications for foreign policy, civil society and human rights"[448]. Furthermore, agencies have also been accused of deliberately subcontracting intelligence activities to allied agencies, thereby technically adhering to national ethical and legal obligations, but in the knowledge that partner agencies may not or do not do so. Even if sought, agencies often

---

[446] R. Aldrich, "Dangerous Liaisons: Post-September 11 Intelligence Agencies", Harvard International Review, Fall 2002, 50.

[447] As quoted in L. Scott et al., Intelligence and International Security: New Perspectives and Agendas, London, Routledge, 2011, 37.

[448] M. Rudner, as quoted in A.D.M. Svendsen, "The Globalization of Intelligence since 9/11: The Optimization of Intelligence Liaison Arrangements", International Journal of Intelligence and Counterintelligence, Vol.21(4), 2008, 672.

have little (if any) control over how partners acquire information, and whether it is done according to the same standards and ethics as their own. Finally, agencies also provide information to partners that may or may not be used in ways that are contrary to national law and democratic values. Overall, since the majority of intelligence relationships fall under non-treaty arrangements in international law, they are flexible and not legally binding[449], making it much easier to work under the radar and avoid regulation. Moreover, public enquiries into extraordinary rendition and surveillance have demonstrated that agencies have knowingly and deliberately circumvented national laws and ethical values with the knowledge of their executive. While cooperation is necessary to respond to current threats, therefore, it has also created an ethical vacuum that allows intelligence agencies to avoid oversight and accountability.

20.4.5 Norms and Values

The 21st century has seen increased numbers and types of threats in a technologically complex world, and a resulting increase in new forms of intelligence production. The lack of clarity in deciding on what is ethically acceptable and under what circumstances is both a reality and a responsibility. The earlier discussion on ethics indicated that norms and values can be expected to change over time. Covert activities were justified by decision- makers during the Cold War, but there was strong public criticism and the reputation of intelligence agencies suffered. Currently the normative dimension of democracy is arguably stronger because of increased transparency and the multitude of stakeholders involved in governance. As a result, the return to a similarly controversial situation in which intelligence services continue to obtain information through ethically questionable or illegal methods poses serious chal-

---

[449] M. Scheinin and M. Vermeulen, "International Law: Human Rights Law and State Responsibility", in H. Born et al. (eds), International Intelligence Cooperation and Accountability, London, Routledge, 2011, 256.

lenges for democracies. Yet the reaction of the public to the more recent scandals has been quite nuanced. While there has been clear outrage among civil society groups and certain segments of the public, the perceived terrorist threat seems to have also led to a surprisingly muted reaction. Polls indicate that members of the public in several countries support mass surveillance as an acceptable method of intelligence collection.[450]

Additional surveys even indicate acceptance of enhanced interrogation techniques.[451] There is a sense that societal norms are in flux, and it is very difficult to require intelligence agencies to adhere to an ethical basis that is unclear. How this situation unfolds in the future will determine the limits of what is ethically acceptable and the context in which intelligence agencies will operate.

20.5 Three Dilemmas: Ethical Intelligence in Practice

The overview of intelligence and globalisation has highlighted a number of emerging trends. These reflect a critical debate around three

---

[450] C. Chambers, "The Psychology of Mass Government Surveillance: How Do the Public Respond and Is It Changing Our Behaviour?", The Guardian, 18 March 2015, https://www.theguardian.com/science/head-quarters/2015/mar/18/the-psychology-of-mass-government-surveillance-how-do-the-public-respond-and-is-it-changing-our-behaviour; A. Bennett, "Actually, British Voters Don't Mind Mass Surveillance", The Telegraph, 2 March 2016, http://www.telegraph.co.uk/news/uknews/terrorism-in-the-uk/12179248/Actually-British-voters-dont-mind-mass-surveillance.html; Pew Research Center, "Majority Views NSA Tracking as Acceptable Anti-terror Tactic", 10 June 2013, http://www.people-press.org/2013/06/10/majority-views-nsa-phone-tracking-as-acceptable-anti-terror-tactic/.

[451] A. Blake, "That Big CIA Torture Report? Americans Just Shrugged", Washington Post, 15 December 2014, https://www.washingtonpost.com/news/the-fix/wp/2014/12/15/that-big-cia-torture-report-americans-just-shrugged/.

specific intelligence dilemmas that may have existed as long as intelligence has been a tool of statecraft, but which are particularly complex today.

20.5.1 Ethics in Practice: Public vs Primary Goods?

At the core of the debate on ethics and intelligence is the dilemma between public goods (national security) and primary goods (individual security). This dilemma is ever present, because primary and public needs are intertwined and neither can be completely fulfilled at the same time. For example, privacy is an individual, primary good, but when information on an individual is part of an intelligence dossier, that individual's privacy becomes part of national security, which is a public good. Moral questions surrounding mass surveillance or interrogation methods become far more complex when one considers their use not as unethical as such, but as a prioritisation of national security – the security of the majority – over the security of an individual. A crucial question is whether all intelligence activities potentially involve the violation of primary goods, and whether it is possible for any intelligence activities to occur without violations. Since multiple forms of gathering exist, one must consider how different forms of intelligence impact on different vital interests and the proportionality of their use.

Proponents of open source intelligence would emphasise that its use can be justified, since the collection of information in the public domain does not involve violating privacy and intelligence actors are not responsible for placing it there, thus collecting it is not a breach of ethics. While it can be added to a secret dossier with the potential to cause either physical or mental harm, the act of using open source information alone does not do so. Because signals intelligence is based on intercepting communications, it does not cause direct physical or mental harm, but, excluding open sources, it can impact on an individual citizen's liberty, dignity and privacy to a potentially very invasive degree. It is governed by national law, in which security actors must present sufficient evidence in order to obtain a surveillance warrant. However, in recent years it is the sheer quantity of surveillance that takes place without the public's knowledge that is ethically questionable. In fact, individual cases have been declared illegal in the UK and by the European Court of Human Rights.[452] Yet one could also argue that metadata does not focus on the content of communication, but on sender- to-recipient details, therefore in the collection phase it is of limited harm. Furthermore, critical questions also emerge on how realistic privacy even is in today's online world[453] (constituting a discussion that is beyond the scope of this paper), because it can be argued that such techniques are simply a reflection of available means, and not to do so would leave intelligence agencies at a considerable disadvantage – and public security by extension.

Human intelligence, on the other hand, has the potential to cause considerable harm during its collection. National agencies may recruit foreign agents, and if their operatives are based in a foreign country under unofficial cover, this involves deception and manipulation, since espionage is illegal. From an ethical point of view, this has implications both for the intelligence operative and the individual supplying information by creating a situation that could lead to considerable mental harm, puts informants at risk of physical harm, and has obvious implications for liberty. The controversial use of enhanced interrogation tech-

---

[452] O. Bowcott, "UK-US Surveillance Regime Was Unlawful 'for Seven Years'", The Guardian, 6 February 2015. https://www.theguardian.com/uk-news/2015/feb/06/gchq-mass-internet-surveillance-unlawful-court-nsa; European Court of Human Rights, Szabo and Vissy v. Hungary, Final Judgment, 12 January 2016, http://hudoc.echr.coe.int/eng?i=001-186763; European Court of Human Rights, Roman Zakharov v. Russia, Press Release on the Final Judgment, 4 December 2015, https://www.echr.coe.int/Documents/Press_Q_A_Roman_Zakharov_ENG.PDF

[453] R. Aldrich, "Privacy Is Dead, the Future Is Fabulous", TedTalk, 7 May 2015, https://www.youtube.com/watch?v=Ml1nmdKdKV8.

niques indicates the prioritisation of public goods over primary goods, because terrorist attacks have facilitated a context of mutated norms in which torture came to be seen as necessary for combating terrorism.[454] So while legally unacceptable, it was seen as a compromise worth making, a "vital counterterrorism tool"[455] for the protection of the state and its citizens. Yet the effectiveness of torture has been increasingly called into question,[456] while there is also evidence that it was not used as an "exceptional" last resort.[457] The use of torture was facilitated not only by limiting how it was defined, as mentioned earlier, but the apparent encouragement of psychologists in the creation of "permissive ethical guidelines" to "continue to participate in harsh and abusive interrogation techniques being used ... after the September 11 attacks on the United States".[458] Such excessive and sustained efforts to permit unethical and illegal behaviour are blatantly unacceptable in the eyes of the public – and even the intelligence agencies themselves.[459]

---

[454] S. Borelli in H. Born et al. (eds), International Intelligence Cooperation and Accountability, London, Routledge, 2011, 98.

[455] Ibid, 100.

[456] D. Gardham, "Torture Is Not Wrong, It Just Doesn't Work", The Telegraph, 28 October 2011, http://www.telegraph.co.uk/comment/8833108/Torture-is-not-wrong-it-just-doesnt-work-says-former-interrogator.html.

[457] Der Spiegel, "Ex-CIA Inspector General on Interrogation Report: 'The Agency Went over Bounds and Outside the Rules'", 31 August 2009, http://www.spiegel.de/international/world/ex-cia-inspector-general-on-interrogation-report-the-agency-went-over-bounds-and-outside-the-rules-a-646010.html.

[458] American Psychological Association Review of Ethical Guidelines, Interrogations and Torture, "Executive Summary", Report to the Special Committee of the Board of Directors of the American Psychological Association, 2 July 2015, https://publicintelligence.net/apa-torture-report/.

[459] N. Hopkins and R. Norton-Taylor, "Blair Government's Rendition Policy Led to Rift between UK Spy Agencies", The Guardian, 13 May 2016, https://www.theguardian.com/uk-news/2016/may/31/revealed-britain-rendition-policy-rift-between-spy-agencies-mi6-mi5?INTCMP=sfl.

Although trade-offs between primary and public interests will be necessary in order for agencies to work with urgency and effectiveness, such circumstances must remain extraordinary. Even though support from society for extreme measures may exist, it is dependent on such measures being justified and necessary. The public enquiries and the increasing involvement of civil society demonstrate that more actors are now involved in the discussion on how intelligence agencies should balance primary and public interests. This will require considerable change to the static organisational culture of agencies, many of which have existed since the mid-20th century.

20.5.2 Ethics in Practice: Wartime Vs. Peace?

Different rules apply in war and peace. The classical debates on ethics and intelligence are based on this distinction. The challenge for the modern world is that such a distinction is no longer evident. With the ever-growing danger from asymmetrical threats, we are in a new era of instability, of conflictual peace, in which threats are heightened and pressure on intelligence agencies is increasing. The challenge is in knowing when to apply wartime exceptions in societies living according to peacetime norms.

At the heart of this dilemma is the normative debate on intelligence. Intelligence is not a case of black or white, but operates at the heart of what can be considered an ethically grey area. Our understanding of it has also evolved over time. We have moved from an era in which "no one respects the character of a spy" to perceiving intelligence as a "distasteful but vital necessity". In today's world, the nuclear risk that "justified" Cold War covert activities is distant, but the ever-present threat of terrorism has led to the "willingness to tolerate extraordinary measures to counter a threat to our survival".[460]At the same time, how wars are

---

[460] J. Olson, Fairplay: The Moral Dilemmas of Spying, Washington, DC, Potomac Books, 2006, 34-42.

fought matters considerably more today. The concept of "moral injury" has emerged:

> While perceptions of justice ... have always mattered in human conflict, they matter more in the "information age" than they ever have. These perceptions help determine the psychological aftermath of war as well as inspire and maintain the will to fight that ultimately "wins" wars.[461]

The recognition today of the need to 'win hearts and minds' applies as much to intelligence as military action. In a world in which perception has a major influence and is used so effectively by enemies of the state, governments and their agencies may need tools such as mass surveillance, but they have to be used in a way that is supported by the public. The US Patriot Act, a "vital" weapon against terrorism,[462] was created in an opaque way that did much to damage the reputation and legitimacy of US intelligence efforts among the public. In the future, one way to rebuild trust in intelligence agencies is to consider the just intelligence approach, which would be very suited to this increasingly normative context. It could provide intelligence agencies and executive decision-makers with useful guidelines on what is acceptable or not in the era of conflictual peace, thus allowing for the justification of necessary extreme measures.

20.5.3 Ethics in Practice: The Ethics-Effectiveness Trade-Off?

The need for intelligence agencies to operate at the highest levels of efficiency is crucial, considering the potentially fatal consequences for national security if they do not do so. The emphasis on ethics is often understood as placing a constraint on intelligence gathering activities,

---

[461] T. Ricks, "The Warrior and Moral Injury", Foreign Policy, 6 July 2015, http://foreignpolicy. com/2015/07/06/the-warrior-and-moral-injury-2/.

[462] N. Sales, "The Patriot Act Is a Vital Weapon in Fighting Terrorism", *New York Times*, 23 May 2014, http://www.nytimes.com/roomfordebate/2011/09/07/do-we-still-need-the-patriot-act/the-patriot-act-is-a-vital-weapon-in-fighting-terrorism.

resulting in reduced effectiveness in some form of ticking time-bomb scenario, as mentioned earlier. Indeed, the unfortunate reality is that intelligence officers are – and will continue to be – faced with impossible situations in which they have to weigh the rights of the individual against those of the public to ensure the effective protection of national security. It is to be hoped that extreme cases remain rare, but there is a need for a better understanding of what guides the decisions that are taken in this context.

The majority of intelligence work takes place in less heightened circumstances, but the application of ethical considerations is seen to impede the autonomy (and thus the effectiveness) of intelligence agencies. Such a focus is incorrect. Firstly, intelligence agencies will never be fully autonomous. They are part of the government bureaucracy, and "the very nature of democracy is that it not only does, but should, fight with one hand tied behind its back".[463] As a result, agencies currently exist and will continue to exist in a context of rules and procedures. Therefore, the juxtaposition of ethics and effectiveness is redundant. Rather, the discussion needs to focus more deeply on how to develop a more efficient balance between the two.

Secondly, the resulting implication is that unethical intelligence will be more effective. This argument is flawed. Putting open source intelligence collection aside as the least intrusive form of intelligence gathering, signals intelligence is a necessity in the modern world, and the argument is that by focusing on it, agencies are simply utilising the tools available. However, criticism has been levelled against the enormous amount of data that has to be analysed, the expensive technology required to collect it, and the continued inability of big data to explain how individuals think. Because it constitutes the most risks to vital interests, one would assume that the effectiveness of human intelligence

---

[463] M. Ignatieff, The Lesser Evil: Political Ethics in an Age of Terror, Princeton, Princeton University Press, 2004, 24.

must outweigh the ethical compromises made to assure national security. Yet reports on the quality of the information obtained through enhanced interrogation techniques have indicated the production of false and unreliable intelligence not only without any guarantee of effectiveness, as indicated earlier, but, in fact, with the potential to reduce it.[464] Furthermore, the current blurring between intelligence and police work – in prosecuting terrorist suspects, for example – means that these forms of intelligence collection are problematic, because illegally obtained information is not admissible in court. This does not mean that surveillance is without value, but an overreliance on such methods is not necessarily the most effective approach – and is certainly not the most ethical.

Consequently, it is important to understand why intelligence agency officers have used unethical methods to such an extent. It is perhaps explained by the post-9/11 environment, in which:

It felt like a 'ticking time bomb' every single day. In this atmosphere, time was of the essence. We had a deep responsibility to do everything within the law to stop another attack. We clearly understood that, even with legal and policy approvals, our decisions would be questioned years later. But we also understood that we would be morally culpable for the deaths of fellow citizens if we failed to gain information that could stop the next attacks.[465]

According to the CIA in response to the US Senate Select Committee report on rendition, legal and ethical concerns were absolutely present, but with an exclusive focus on national security. Moreover, executive involvement in approving these activities is significant. Their in-

---

[464] A. Mitchell et al., "Senate Report Finds CIA Interrogation Tactics Were Ineffective", NBC News, 9 December 2014, http://www.nbcnews.com/storyline/cia-torture-report/senate-report-finds-cia-interrogation-tactics-were-ineffective-n264621.

[465] Introduction by former CIA senior officers to the CIA Rebuttal of the Senate Select Committee on Intelligence Majority Report on the CIA's Rendition, Detention and Interrogation Program, 9 December 2014, http://ciasavedlives.com/.

volvement is often reactionary – a response to public pressure – leading to the approval of methods that might not be the most ethical or effective, and can undermine a state's reputation. Intelligence agencies are being confronted by more deadly and less traceable threats than ever before. The public and human rights groups have accepted the exceptional status of intelligence as a result.[466] If there is greater communication on the ethical framework guiding intelligence work, and if there is an unambiguous structure that balances harm and proportionality, then intelligence work can become more ethically acceptable without impacting on effectiveness. After all, intelligence will never be perfect, but the "overall test ... is whether those approving [intelligence operations] feel they could defend their activities before the public if the actions became public".[467] The 'just intelligence' approach has much to contribute in this regard.

20.6 Prospects for a 'Just Future'

Intelligence agencies are currently confronting complex threats that go beyond borders and span all domains. In order to respond to this environment, agencies need to cooperate with allies, share the burden and work with specialised private sector companies, and harness the assets available to them through technology, all while operating within the transparent, normative requirements of democratic society. The result is an awkward coexistence of ethical needs and effective intelligence, while balancing primary and public goods, in an era of conflictual peace.

---

[466] Amnesty International, Two Years after Snowden: Protecting Human Rights in an Age of Mass Surveillance, Report, https://www.amnestyusa.org/sites/default/files/ai-pi_two_years_on_from_snowden_final_final_clean.pdf; M. Knigge, "Rifkind: Intelligence Depends on Trust", Deutche Welle, 1 February 2014, http://news.ge/en/news/story/78123-rifkind-intelligence-depends-on-trust.
[467] S. Turner in J. Goldman (ed.), The Ethics of Spying: A Reader for the Intelligence Professional, Lanham, Scarecrow Press, 2005, 32.

Although the need for exceptional behaviour is accepted, the sustained extent to which norms were violated in recent scandals, not just by agencies, but with executive collusion, seems more a case of a dismissal of values rather than a trade-off, and is clearly unacceptable. It is time to dismiss the belief in both the 'inherently unethical' nature of intelligence and the 'absolute' need to be ethical without compromise. The reality is that intelligence work is already ethical, but with serious shortcomings. A just approach demonstrating proportionality, necessity, and the weighing of harm and benefits will be more effective. The debate needs to focus on how to institute such an approach as normal intelligence practice, and for this to happen more effective regulation is needed.

Consequently, one approach in moving forward should be the evolution of oversight structures that emerged as a result of numerous scandals during the Cold War and are seen as mainly reactive – "fire fighters" – within a national focus.[468] Oversight structures are naturally limited because different rules and procedures exist and the ability of oversight committees to access information is limited because of the potential consequences for security. This is even more problematic in the case of intelligence cooperation – one of the main current trends – because it is not possible to compel a foreign agency to participate in oversight procedures.

The extraordinary rendition scandals in the post-9/11 era exposed this, together with the lack of government control over how intelligence cooperation was taking place. During the enquiries that followed the rendition scandals, the executive and agencies actively impeded the accountability process, using "all legal measures" to prevent information on their activities from being revealed,[469] and in particular using the fear

---

[468] I. Leigh, in H. Born et al. (eds), International Intelligence Cooperation and Accountability, London, Routledge, 2011, 8.

[469] C. Forcese in ibid., 84.

of being cut off from valuable intelligence-sharing relationships. In 2013 the mass surveillance revelations demonstrated the dual nature of cooperation when German outrage over the tapping of Chancellor Angela Merkel's phone was followed by disclosures of the extent to which German intelligence worked closely with the US National Security Agency to produce metadata on European companies and governments.[470]

Both cases demonstrated collusion on the part of governments and set them against the public. Furthermore, the June 2016 Chilcot Report on Britain's involvement in the 2003 war in Iraq placed particular emphasis on the flawed nature of the intelligence used to justify joining the war (obtained through cooperation with the US and Germany), and on the finding that the mishandling of this intelligence "may now have permanently damaged the public's trust in [Britain's] spy agencies".[471] Intelligence cooperation is essential, but the more agencies and governments use it to circumvent national regulation and oversight, the greater the impact on their credibility and legitimacy, and on the effectiveness of the intelligence they obtain as a result.

One response to this has been the idea of creating "fair trade intelligence", in which responsibility is placed on the individual analyst to ensure that intelligence is obtained in an ethical and reliable way.[472] However, the present author acknowledges that while this may work in some cases, the reality is that agencies often do not have a choice in who provides the intelligence and we thus return to the question of prioritis-

---

[470] Deutsche Welle, "BND-CIA Collaboration Deeper than Thought", 2 May 2015, http://www.dw.com/en/report-bnd-nsa-collaboration-deeper-than-thought/a-18425290.

[471] B. Farmer, "Chilcot Report: Flawed Intelligence Led to Britain Going to War in Iraq", The Telegraph, 6 July 2016.

[472] M. Manjikian, "But My Hands Are Clean: The Ethics of Intelligence Sharing and the Problem of Complicity", International Journal of Intelligence and Counterintelligence, Vol.28(4), 2015, 703-705.

ing the primary needs of an individual (who will already have been harmed by the time the intelligence is made available to the analyst) or the public need for security in obtaining the intelligence needed to prevent an attack.

Nonetheless, frustration with state-based oversight has led to innovative and creative alternatives. Civil society actors are following intelligence agency work more closely, and there has been an increase in detailed reporting on intelligence activities by groups such as Privacy International,[473] along with a closer examination of current oversight weaknesses. This has not only taken place at the national level,[474] and the level of regional and international efforts to improve oversight capabilities has also increased.[475] There is now more interaction among actors in combining national and international efforts. The National Parliaments-EU Parliament conference on oversight, as part of the 2014-2019 agenda, is an example of this.[476]

With regard to intelligence produced from surveillance, the fundamental issue of what privacy means in the digital age and how individu-

---

[473] Privacy International and Amnesty International, Two Years after Snowden: Protecting Human Rights in an Age of Mass Surveillance, June 2015, https://www.privacyinternational.org/sites/default/files/Two%20Years%20After %20Snowden_Final%20Report_EN_0.pdf.

[474] European Parliament, National Security and Secret Evidence in Legislation and Before Courts: Exploring the Challenges, Study for the LIBE Committee, 2014, http://www.europarl.europa.eu/RegData/etudes/STUD/2014/509991/IPOL _STU%282014%29509991_EN.pdf.

[475] International Intelligence Review Agencies Conference Media Release, 7 July 2014, http://www.igis.govt.nz/media-releases/archived-media-releases/ international-intelligence-review- agencies-conference/.

[476] Conference on the Democratic Oversight of the Intelligence Services in the European Union, European Parliament–National Parliaments 2014, Overview, http://www.europarl.europa.eu/sides/getDoc.do?pubRef=-//EP//NONSGML+ COMPARL+LIBE-OJ-20150528-2+04+DOC+PDF+V0//EN; European Network of National Intelligence Reviewers, http://www.ennir.be/.

al rights are balanced against security is now being addressed. David Omand, the former director of GCHQ, has proposed a "just intelligence" approach to the use of surveillance, which would then be endorsed by national parliamentary oversight committees.[477] The United Nations (UN) has also supported such an approach, as have international civil society experts, outlining the need for the necessity and proportionality of surveillance.[478] Such proposals combine the need for an ethical framework with the need to inform and reassure the public, and indicate the adoption of the "just intelligence" approach. At the international level, regulation measures exist, for example, the UN General Assembly Resolution 69/166 on "The Right to Privacy in the Digital Age".[479]

Digital rights groups have also emerged and are interacting with other forms of oversight, for example, in organising training sessions with members of the European Parliament.[480] While these proposals can improve the oversight and regulation of ethical intelligence work, he outsourcing of intelligence activities cannot be regulated in the same way. Private military companies and other non-state partners are not subject to the same legal frameworks and obligations as state agencies. One

---

[477] D. Omand, "NSA Leaks: How to Make Surveillance both Ethical and Effective", The Guardian, 11 June 2013, https://www.theguardian.com/commentisfree/2013/jun/11/make-surveillance-ethical-and-effective.

[478] N. Pillay, UN High Commissioner for Human Rights, in C. Wong, "A Clear-eyed Look at Mass Surveillance", Human Rights Watch, 25 July 2014, https://www.hrw.org/news/2014/07/25/clear-eyed-look-mass-surveillanc; Necessary and Proportionate, 13 Principles on the Application of Human Rights to Communications Surveillance, May 2014, https://necessaryandproportionate.org/principles.

[479] UN General Assembly Resolution 69/166, "The Right to Privacy in the Digital Age", A/RES/69/166 of 18 December 2014, http://www.un.org/en/ga/search/view_doc.asp?symbol=A/RES/69/166.

[480] H. Jarvinen, "EDRi Launches Private Trainings in the European Parliament", 28 January 2015, https://edri.org/edri-launches-privacy-trainings-in-the-european-parliament/.

method would be to hold the approving government agency to account if abuses occur. However, proving an abuse is quite difficult, and even when cases of abuse are legally proven, information on approval processes is often vague[481] and so it is very difficult to hold individuals responsible. With specialised agencies, such as Booz Allen Hamilton, the risks include the vulnerabilities created by giving non-government actors access to extremely sensitive information and how to ensure that sufficient security protocols are applied. In the case of the Snowden leaks, Booz Allen was cleared of wrongdoing.[482] In the future, because governments will continue to rely on and probably increase their dependence on private actors, to do so credibly will require transparent protocols for regulation. A set of 'just intelligence' guidelines that could involve and apply to both private sector and state agencies involved in intelligence work, would facilitate the oversight process.

However, these efforts cannot be successful without the better involvement of intelligence agencies themselves. Overall, there needs to be a better understanding on the part of political leadership and the public of what intelligence agencies can and cannot do. One of the recent challenges has been the level of extreme pressure and executive collusion, creating an environment of politicisation. Organisational structures and processes are a means of controlling intelligence agencies, but also a means of instituting norms and standards. Intelligence agencies benefit and receive protection from politicisation through the standardisation of procedures and transparency regarding decision-making. It is therefore in their interests to submit to such procedures. For this to occur effectively and for regulation efforts to improve, there needs to be more equal involvement among agencies, the executive and actors involved in over-

---

[481] P. Hayezin in H. Born et al. (eds), International Intelligence Cooperation and Accountability, London, Routledge, 2011, 155.

[482] Reuters, "Air Force Clears Booz Allen of Wrongdoing in Snowden Case", 11 July 2013, https://www.rt.com/usa/air-force-booz-snowden-967/.

sight, so that the necessary changes can be introduced in a way that does not put sources and methods at risk.

It should be noted that intelligence agencies and governments have been making greater efforts to respond to the situation. In 2014, the US Directorate for National Intelligence released the "Principles of Professional Ethics" as a permanent set of guidelines for the intelligence community.[483] In the same year the Dutch Ministry of Security and Justice commissioned a report entitled "Handling Ethical Problems in Counterterrorism", which contained an inventory of methods to support ethical decision-making.[484] In 2015, the UK Intelligence and Security Committee of Parliament released a report on privacy and security, with extensive recommendations for change.[485] In 2016, the head of the BND (Germany's foreign intelligence service) was "unexpectedly" sent into retirement following criticism levied against the agency for its cooperation with the NSA on European targets, with multiple changes expected as a result of ethical concerns.[486] On the other hand, France has recently come under scrutiny for a possible "French-style Patriot Act",[487] as has

---

[483] J. Clapper, "Remarks , AFCEA/INSA National Security and Intelligence Summit", 18 September 2014, https://www.dni.gov/index.php/newsroom/speeches-and-interviews/202-speeches-interviews-2014/1115-remarks-as-delivered-by-the-honorable-james-r-clapper-director-of-national-intelligence-afcea-insa-national-security-and-intelligence-summit.

[484] A. Reding et al., Handling Ethical Problems in Counterterrorism, Rand Report, 2014, http://www.rand.org/content/dam/rand/pubs/research_reports/RR200/RR251/RAND_RR251.pdf.

[485] Intelligence and Security Committee of Parliament, Privacy and Security: A Modern and Transparent Legal Framework, London, 2015.

[486] M. Zuvela, "Germany Announces New Head of BND Foreign Intelligence Service", Deutsche Welle, 27 April 2016, http://www.dw.com/en/germany-announces-new-head-of-bnd-foreign-intelligence-service/a-19217342.

[487] France 24, "Fears of French-Style Patriot Act in Wake of Paris Attacks", 19 November 2015, http:// www.france24.com/en/20151119-fears-french-style-usa-patriot-act-following-paris-attacks-terrorism-constitution.

Australia for passing legislation to facilitate mass surveillance.[488] Yet media attention immediately focused on the opaque approach taken by these governments and the implications of the proposed legislation for civil liberties. Therefore, while agencies alone, or on the orders of their governments, may try to return "to the shadows", the opportunity to do so is becoming more limited.

20.7 Conclusions

This paper set out to analyse current thinking on the role of ethics in intelligence, the challenges posed to its practice and future prospects in this regard. Doing so required asking the question as to whether intelligence agencies can protect national security without stepping back into the shadows of secrecy and controversial behaviour that has led to decades of scandals. The response is that they must. The level of secrecy and autonomy accorded to intelligence agencies in past decades no longer exists. The main challenge for such agencies is to bridge the 20th century organisational structures and procedures with the

21st century security environment. Just as members of the public need to adapt to a new era of less privacy, so do intelligence agencies. The need for secrecy will continue to be essential, but better efforts need to be made to balance agency independence and effectiveness with individual security, democratic values and law, and how these concerns converge in intelligence gathering activities.

Three interlinked ethical dilemmas emerged as particularly complex within this context. The first centred on the prioritisation of primary (individual) security or public security. The second involved how to

---

[488] S. Ackerman and O. Laughland, "Edward Snowden on Police Pursuing Journalist Data: The Scandal Is What the Law Allows", The Guardian, 16 April 2016, https://www.theguardian.com/australia-news/2016/apr/17/edward-snowden-on-police-pursuing-journalist-data-the-scandal-is-what-the-law-allows.

adapt ethical thinking that was created on the basis of a distinction between war and peace to the demands of the modern era of conflictual peace. The third focused on the assumed juxtaposition of ethics and effectiveness in intelligence work. Of the multiple theoretical perspectives considered, the 'just intelligence' approach emerged as the most suitable in response to all three dilemmas. It allows for a balancing of the need for exceptional action with ethical guidelines reflective of current societal norms. It sets out the conditions for proportionality and the consideration of potential benefits and harm resulting from activities that impact on primary and public security. As a result, it demonstrates that ethics and effectiveness are not mutually exclusive, although balancing the two is not easy. Further efforts are required for the systematic development and inclusion of the just intelligence approach as part of day-to-day intelligence practice.

The increasingly transparent environment in which intelligence gathering takes place has only led to challenges but has also created opportunities. It has enabled the opening up of the intelligence 'black box' and the potential to change ideas, cultures, conduct and the frameworks within which intelligence agencies operate. Furthermore, the debate on the ethical practice of intelligence gathering has been strengthened by the involvement of multiple actors on the national, regional, and international levels. Although difficult ethical decisions will continue, a more inclusive approach involving all relevance stakeholders would facilitate the creation of 'just' guidelines to allow intelligence agencies and policymakers to rebuild trust and operate more effectively in today's public environment. Finally, many proposals and policies are new and unproven but they nonetheless demonstrate the opening of more channels than ever before to achieve a better balance between individual rights and national security, between ethics and effectiveness in democratic societies.

Selected Bibliography

Aldrich, R.J., "Global Intelligence Co-operation versus Accountability: New Facets to an Old Problem", Intelligence and National Security, Vol. 24(1), 2009.

Andrew, C. et al., Secret Intelligence: A Reader, London, Routledge, 2009.

Bailey, C.E. and S.M. Galich, "Code of Ethics: The Intelligence Community", International Journal of Intelligence Ethics, Vol.3(2), 2012.

Banks, C., Criminal Justice Ethics: Theory and Practice, Thousand Oaks, SAGE, 2013. Bellaby, R.W., The Ethics of Intelligence: A New Framework, London, Routledge, 2014.

Bok, Sissela, Secrets: On the Ethics of Concealment and Revelation, New York, Pantheon Books, 1983.

Colby, W.E., "Intelligence Secrecy and Security in a Free Society", International Security, Vol.1(2), 1976.

Davies, P.H.J., "Ideas of Intelligence: Divergent National Concepts and Institutions", Harvard International Review, Fall 2002.

Erskine, T., "'As Rays of Light to the Human Soul'? Moral Agents and Intelligence Gathering", Intelligence and National Security, Vol. 19(2), 2004.

Gerdes, L.I., Espionage and Intelligence Gathering, San Diego, Greenhaven Press, 2004. Gill, P. et al., Intelligence Theory: Key Questions and Debates, London, Routledge, 2009.

Gill, P. and M. Phythian, Intelligence in an Insecure World, Cambridge, MA, Polity Press, 2006.

Godfrey, E.D., "Ethics and Intelligence", Foreign Affairs, Vol. 56(3), 1978.

Herman, M., Intelligence Power in Peace and War, Cambridge, Cambridge University Press, 1996.

Jackson, P. and J. Siegel (eds), Intelligence and Statecraft: The Uses and Limits of Intelligence in International Society, Westport, Praeger, 2005.

Johnson, L.K., The Oxford Handbook of National Security Intelligence, Oxford, Oxford University Press, 2010.

Jones, C., "Intelligence Reform: The Logic of Information Sharing", Intelligence and National Security, Vol. 22(3), 2007.

Phythian, M., "The Ethics-intelligence Tension: Sources and Bypassing Strategies", International Journal of Intelligence Ethics, Vol. 3(2), 2012.

Plouffe, W.C., "Just War Theory as a Basis for Just Intelligence Theory: Necessary Evil or Sub- rosa Coloured Self-deception?", International Journal of Intelligence Ethics, Vol.2(1), 2011.

Rovner, J., Fixing the Facts: National Security and the Politics of Intelligence, Ithaca, Cornell University Press, 2011.

Sepper, E., "Democracy, Human Rights and Intelligence Sharing", Texas International Law Journal, Vol. 46(1), 2010.

Zegart, A., Eyes on Spies, Stanford, Hoover Institution Press, 2011

21

SECRET SERVICES:
CAN THEY BE ETHICAL?

Christoph Stückelberger, Switzerland

21.1 Secret Services in Present and Past

The majority of countries in the world have a Secret Service[489]. At present, 115 countries are listed in the Wikipedia overview with a total of 300 different secret service organisations/units, as many countries have different secret services for different sectors and ministries, not counting former services which have been closed or reorganised.[490]

Secret Services are governmental organisations for the secret collection of *information* through espionage (political, military, economic, religious, social), surveillance/monitoring of individuals, cryptanalyses, evaluation of public information, counter-espionage, etc. Secret services

---

[489] There are several terms used: Intelligence service, secret service, service de renseignements, Geheimdienst. We herewith use secret service as it best characterises the main character: a hidden service of espionage. The terms Intelligence Service and Service de Renseignements (information service) hide the true character.

[490] https://fr.wikipedia.org/wiki/Liste_des_services_de_renseignement. (Accessed 9 Sept 2018)

sometimes also organise *actions* such as dispersing wrong information (fake news), arms sales, kidnapping and killing.

As for *justification of Secret Services,* mainly national security is mentioned. This broad term can justify almost everything (as we see with the current government in the US), from protecting national secrets to cyber security, from economic espionage to trade war, from big data collection to the full range of anti-terrorism strategies.

Secret Services are almost as old as humanity. It mainly originated from military secret services of spying on the enemy and developing strategies of lies, subterfuge, deception, and "fake news" in order to get a strategic advantage. "The Art of War"[491] of the Chinese military strategist Sun Tzu (Spring and Autumn Period 771-476 BC) is one of the most famous military treaties which influenced not only East Asian warfare, but also Western military strategies. It justifies many means of tactics and subterfuge and describes in the last book XIII the use of spies and intelligence services. It is broadly used also for business strategies.[492]

In the 20th century, Secret Services have not only been broadly used during the World Wars I and II, but also in colonial times and especially during the Cold War. As we cannot go into details, let us just mention three examples:

Colonial and post-colonial History: Secret services have been established in colonies to protect the interests of the colonisers. After the political independence, the so-called de-colonisation, secret services continued to serve the former rulers, especially by protecting dictatorial rulers. An example is the secret service in DR Congo under Mobutu until now. A leading staff of this secret service analysed in his doctoral thesis this service, and its history. His conclusion: "While the current

---

[491] https://en.wikipedia.org/wiki/The_Art_of_War. (Accessed 9 Sept 2018)

[492] E.g. Gerald Michaelson, *Sun Tzu: the art of war for managers. 50 strategic rules*, Avon: Massachusetts, 2009.

body of knowledge on the role of intelligence services in post-colonial Africa emphasises the protection of dictatorial regimes and poor governance of the security sector as the main contributing factors to the inefficiency and ineffectiveness of African intelligence services, this book ... demonstrates that Congolese intelligence services rather efficiently protected Western interests during the Cold War period, when the West was competing with the Soviet Union over the control of the African continent. During this period, for over three decades, they incidentally protected the political leadership, which is the key role for intelligence services in virtually all states."[493]

Cold War: The Cold War between the Capitalist and the Communist world 1945-1989 led to large activities of secret services as in the bipolar world, everybody and everything was screened under the aspect of "with me or against me". The Secret Services of the US killed many dozens of political leaders in power, after WW2 in Southern Europe, and later in South America and Africa, in order to establish or keep power of pro-western regimes. This is described with detailed facts from archives in the book "The Rogue State", which in the book is not a term applied to an Islamic terrorist state but the US.[494] The book became a bestseller after it was quoted in 2006 by the terrorist Osama bin Laden who originally worked for the CIA.

Confessing Church during WW2: Karl Barth was the most famous protestant theologian in the 20th century. He was professor of theology in Bonn/Germany until 1933 when he was expelled by Hitler due to his critique of Hitler and sent back to his home country Switzerland where he became professor of theology in Basel. He was with Bonhoeffer, one

---

[493] John Kasuku, *Intelligence Reformation in the Post-Dictatorial Democratic Republic of Congo. A Critical analysis of DRC's Intelligence Service*, Globethics Publications: Geneva 2016, Theses Series no 21, back cover. Free download: https://www.globethics.net/theses-series.

[494] William Blum, *Rogue state: a guide to the World's only superpower*, HSRC: Cape Town, 2015 (first edition 2000).

of the founders of the confessing church (Bekennende Kirche) in Germany which split from the Lutheran church, which was aligned with Hitler. Since he was against National Socialism of Hitler, he was constantly observed by the Secret Service in Switzerland since 1933. Some of his publications were confiscated as they were thought to threaten national security, and his public speeches were censured. Also, after the end of WW2, he, as well as other theologians such as Paul Tillich in US, and Marquard in Berlin have been monitored by the secret services in Switzerland, and the USA.[495] Also in the present day, believers and religious institutions of all faiths are victims of secret services in violation of religious freedom.

21.2 Secret Services in a Transparent World

High Tech plays a key role in modern Secret Services: audio recording, computer intelligence blasters, video disguised cameras, face recognition, satellites, radar, submarine spy, etc.[496]

In the modern Cyber-World, the role of Secret Services may be seen as even more important than before, but they are also more controversial, ethically questionable, and needed. *Information collection* as a core justification of secret services happens in the whole cyber-world in an exponentially higher and faster way. Why should a secret service be free to collect data with rules other than those defined for the rest of the world? *Cyber-security* is of course of high importance for the security of persons and nations. But are Secret Services an appropriate instrument? *Transparency* is a key value in modern communication, financial transactions, data collection, and use. But this transparency seems to contra-

---

[495] E.g. Eberhard Busch (Eds), *Die Akte Karl Barth: Zensur und Überwachung im Namen der Schweizer Neutralität 1938-1945*, TVZ: Zürich 2008.

[496] Bayni H. Salamanca, Sammy B. Estoque, Donabell O Acils, *Police Intelligence and Secret Service*, Wiseman's Book trading: Manila 2017, 111ff. It is a detailed training handbook for police secret services in the Philippines.

dict secret services which are–by definition–non-transparent. Are such double standards not undermining international rules and regulations? *Economic espionage* is in the cyber world and still growing. But is it the role of Secret Services to fight against it or is it not the role of the normal judiciary with its economic departments?

21.3 Means and Motivations of Informants

Information collection is a key role of Secret Services. Therefore, *informants* are key actors. Their means and their motivations to give information are important for the judgment how ethical or unethical a Secret Service action is.

The *means of informants*: If corruption and bribes are unethical as it is internationally agreed, then it is also unethical for Secret Services. If torture is unethical, it is also for Secret Services. Although, if saving lives from a terrorist attack, information to a Secret Service can be ethical.

The *motives of informants* are also important for an ethical value judgment. Serving the common good/national security is more ethical than personal revenge or pure monetary greed. Here is a list of motivations[497]:

1. Reward, mercenary, money
2. Revenge, jealousy
3. Patriotism
4. Fear/avoidance of punishment
5. Friendship/please peers
6. Career development
7. Vanity
8. Civic mindedness/serve community

---

[497] Bayni H. Salamanca, Sammy B. Estoque, Donabell O Acils, *Police Intelligence and Secret Service*, Wiseman's Book Trading: Manila 2017, 86ff.

9. Repentance

10. Own fame

11. Family/community fame/revenge

12. Gaming, entertainment

13. Sex.

The following table can be used to identify which information means combined with which information motivation is ethical or unethical:

Motivations / Means	M1	M2	M3	M4	M5	M6
Common espionage, Neighbourhood						
High level espionage, conspirator						
Forced espionage, e.g. torture						
Counter Espionage, Spying the spies						
Double espionage, Two sides						
Corruption, Bribes						
Censorship Oppressing information						
Fake news False information						
Secret Societies, e.g. Free Mason						
Religious Cults, Exorcism						
Kidnapping, Killing						
Cyber Hacking, Using Darknet						
Cyber Intimidation						

Cyber Bullying						
IT-based info: audio, video, satellites, submarine						
Big data collection and analysis						
Direct communication for info gathering						
Sex for information						
Sabotage						

21.4 Ten Reasons to Withdraw the Ethical Justification of Secret Services

Secret Services are as old as humanity; but they are outdated in a Cyber world. Their role of protecting national security has to be carried out by existing or new national and multilateral entities. In light of the strong existence of Secret Services, one may say it is an illusion to abolish Secret Services e.g. with an international convention even though ethically, it would be worth discussion. Governments would not agree as most of them have such services and superpowers with vested interests in secret services of their smaller allies. On the other hand, we have to say:

Secret Services violate key ethical principles. Therefore, from an ethical point of view, we have at least to withdraw the ethical justification for Secret Services. Even if they may continue to exist, they cannot count on the ethical blessing and their budgets and number must be reduced. They operate in most cases, against and not in favour of ethical values and not in line with the principles and values of the other "non-secret" political activities of the country of the Secret Service. They often serve - at least in non-democratic countries – a rather small elite who defend their political, economic or religious self-interests instead of the common good of the country and the world.

Let me – only as short food for thought – mention *ten reasons for withdrawing the ethical justification of Secret Services:*

1. *Transparency* is a key value in modern communication, financial transactions, data collection and use. Secret services are by definition non-transparent. Such double standards undermine international rules and regulations.

2. *Honesty: Lies and fake news.* Honesty is a key virtue for all activities. Lies and fake news are core instruments of Secret Services. Therefore, they are directly undermining the everyday private and public ethics.

3. *Collusion with Criminals*: Secret services, in order to be successful, often cooperate willingly or unwillingly with (Cyber) Criminals. The criminals are used by Secret Services until they become their enemies, as the famous case of Osama Bin Laden shows who was originally supported and used by the CIA. Successful cyber criminals are forced by Secret Services to serve them in the respective country or to be killed, as it was reported for Russia.[498]

4. *Darknet:* The darknet was originally developed by the FBI for their hidden communication outside the normally accessible internet. It is now broadly used by cyber-criminals of all kind, from dark e-commerce dealing with drugs and arms to the whole range of cybercrimes. Secret Services directly and indirectly serve cyber-criminals and vice versa.

5. *Security Threat:* Secret Services aim at increasing national security. National security is certainly ethically justifiable, as long one agrees that national sovereignty and armed defence are ethically justified to protect life and communities in a given legal entity. The problem occurs that Secret Services often undermine national security,

---

[498] The famous case of the cyber-criminal with the (fake?) name Kempinsky who according to him was forced to serve Russian secret service but escaped to US where he died.

a) in bilateral relations by all kind of "accidents" of spying, counter-spying, disinformation, information stealing, influencing political processes such as elections in the other country etc.[499], b) by giving doubtful information to political or military decision makers which leads to play with the fire as the war against Iraq, secret killings of leaders etc.

6. *Trust instead of mistrust: Security through human relations.* Community development shows: the best human security are not fences, walls, cameras and security staff for the night, but neighbourhoods, trustworthy relations and community instead of loneliness. Such community is built on trust, but secret services mainly work with mistrust, control, and monitoring as key of spying. Spying often destroys trust and communities.

7. *Protection of (dictatorial) political leadership:* Secret Services are often used to keep dictators in power or to remove leaders which are not aligned. They use means to reach goals which politically and diplomatically cannot be justified. This is ethically unacceptable. Changing of governments has to be done with transparent, democratic, political, economic, social and cultural means.

8. *Need for Ethical Norms*: As Secret Services are per definition secret, their control is often shaky even if there is a legal basis for these services and even if there are monitoring commissions of parliaments. Paul Ericson from the CIA states, "The ethics attendant to the intelligence business are, at best, complicated. Each day many of us face formidable ethical choices. It is no accident that we are concerned about the ethical standards of potential employees. ... This Agency [CIA] can no longer permit the 'slips', 'errors' and

---

[499] The news are full of examples: Edward Snowden stealing secret information, Russia being accused of influencing elections in various countries, China being accused of economic espionage, secret services hacking even the mobile phones of friendly government representatives such as Angela Merkel etc.

'misjudgements' which naturally evolve from an environment where our officers are often left to their own judgment when shifting through the maze of sometimes conflicting signals regarding proper behaviour. ... Ethical issues are not always fully and formally addressed within corporate training programs."[500]

9. *Strengthening other governmental units:* Police, Military, and Judiciary can implement most of the tasks of a secret service. E.g. Interpol already has four core functions: communication services, data services, operational support, and training/development services.

10. *Funding:* Secret Services are expensive and according to experts often not very efficient. It may be more efficient to put these expenses in the police and judiciary institutions on national, regional, and international levels. The economic criminality units in the courts are understaffed in many countries and need more means, Interpol must get more competencies against cyber-crime, school children and students need more protection against cyber-bullying, small and medium enterprises need more protection against cyber-attacks etc. Instead of secret services pushing for wars such as the war against Iraq, based on dubious secret information, such money is much better used for the immediate security needs of the population which needs financing from public budgets.

---

[500] Paul G. Ericson, *The Need for Ethical Norms. A personal perspective*, published 8 May 2007, updated 4 Aug 2011, by Center for the Study of Intelligence of CIA. https://www.cia.gov/library/center-for-the-study-of-intelligence/kent-csi/volume-36-number-1/html/v36i1a02p_0001.htm (Accessed 9 Sept 2018)

PART VII

CYBER MEDIA, CYBER EDUCATION
AND ETHICS

22

CYBER ETHICS REQUIRES
CRITICAL THINKING OF CITIZENS

Ingo Radermacher, Germany

The flood of information and dealing with a constantly growing amount of knowledge is – contrary to the perception of many people – not a new problem. It has been occupying people for a very long time: at the latest since the 16th century. With the arrival of the printing press and the industrial production of books, the problem of classifying and managing new knowledge arose. Gottfried Wilhelm Leibniz lamented the excessive demands of book printing because there were "too many books". His concern was that "the terrible mass of books" would throw mankind back into barbarism. Today we may smile at this, knowing that the opposite was, in fact, the case: book printing led to a boom in the development of knowledge. Leibniz possibly felt that a philosopher could no longer have an overview of all areas of knowledge, which was of course incredibly frustrating and frightening for him as an intellectual "universal scholar" (Gleick 2011, 437f). A feeling that many people may also understand today.

Because it has never been as easy to obtain information as it is today. And so another development seems to run contrary to this: that it has never been so difficult to find one's way around the seemingly indiscriminate nature of infinitely available information. Instead, many people find that with the almost unlimited availability of information and the density of that information, the ability to differentiate information, and in particular to evaluate it, is dwindling. Users are responsible – and increasingly unable to cope with this responsibility – for judging to what extent claims, statements and information coming at them from all angles and for all reasons can and should be considered valid arguments at all. Thus, it is Incumbent upon educated people today to develop the ability to discriminate and classify, which leads to an appropriate judgment.

22.1 Digital Reality Captures Us 'Completely'

When new technologies reach a society as a whole – at all levels and in all areas – in such transformation processes – especially in the early days – very extreme views often receive special publicity. These then posit either auspicious or apocalyptic scenarios: for utopians digitization is an incomparable opportunity to solve almost all humanity's problems – from disease to death – that eclipses anything that has existed before. Or, at the other extreme, the exaggerated risk that the digital could destroy all previous – and perceived as vulnerable – lifestyles and living conditions, as well as all existing social certainties and social customs.

Of course, upon closer inspection, both perspectives prove to have one thing in common: they are exaggerated. Instead, a prudent and enlightened response to new technological possibilities would be: to examine, evaluate and analyse their modes of action and then to integrate them wisely into the existing environment; in the spirit of an evolutionary technological development process.

Back to the digital. Looking at the widely proclaimed digital transformation, we note that: what is new about digital is that we are fully geared to digital not only technologically but also socially. Thus, the still widely prevalent idea that the digital and physical worlds can or will coexist proves to be one thing above all: wrong. Digital networking and the ubiquity of the digital increasingly shape the physical world, keyword: The Internet of Things. This is how the analogue and digital worlds network and interlink. At the same time the digital captures us completely. This can also be seen, for example, in the way we acquire or define ownership today: when buying a book, it is often no longer the cultural capital objectified in a book that is acquired, but merely access to the basically infinite virtual storage of all kinds of cultural products. In this way, digitization leads to a reduction in the value of property compared to access and usage rights. This is particularly true for property-oriented societies: a completely new (revolutionary) approach.

Digitization and its intertwined concepts such as the "Internet of Things" or the economic perspective of "Industry 4.0" are therefore meandering through almost all private, social, cultural and, in particular, economic areas of responsibility as a result of the extent of the transformation.

In technological terms, there are also unprecedented options for action; for example, in data acquisition (sensor technology), data evaluation (big data) and data interpretation (artificial intelligence). Taking advantage of these opportunities, organizations and, above all, globally active corporations have turned the collection of (user) data into a functioning and profitable business model. This is made possible by the fact that users are predominantly willing to disclose their data, provided that the service of a digital offer provides visible added value. However, this is less about the classic information such as name or date of birth; rather, it is about very private data packages such as movement profiles and health data, which (for example in fitness apps) are willingly placed in the hands of commercially active companies. But this is just one side of the coin.

At the same time, however, in the course of digitization, people also have the opportunity to enjoy an informational freedom that hardly any previous generation has been able to experience before: News and reports from people all over the world (e.g. in blogs) can be consumed, as well as large parts of books and also the world knowledge that has been made digitally distributable in writing, images or otherwise, available to everyone and at any time.

22.2 Who Defines the Boundaries

But in addition to this apparent self-empowerment of the people concerning information and its liberal use, there is also commercialization of comparable degree. The longer the World Wide Web exists, it is not (any longer) only public sector and non-profit organizations – such as universities – that technically provide information, but rather profit-orientated, classically profit-driven companies. For them, freedom of information is only a partial aspect and above all just another tool for business. In addition to the collection of user data, these companies practically run roughshod users' informational freedom in favour of their economic interests, in particular by providing personalized content. One could say that the search results of many Internet services basically only lock users 'in the garden of their own desires and thoughts'. Many already know this so-called "filter bubble" from the analogue world. This was formed from the (few) people with whom one usually exchanged and negotiated knowledge and from whom one learned "new things". But it was exactly this "bubble" that it was thought we had all escaped from, thanks to the Internet and the informational freedom it offers. However, the commercialization of information research appears to have misled us. We have merely changed who is involved in the filter.

If we go further, we find that established social institutions and works predominantly operate on a collectively agreed or negotiated – and in particular transparent – set of shared values. In contrast, the Internet has always seen itself as a fundamentally value-free space – "by design" existed without control and management. In the meantime, however, the above developments have led us to conclude that in this area (too) the (economic) might is right and because of that, in contrast to a democratically negotiated set of values, a set of shared values that is based on economic interests is being established.

This insight is decisive, for example, with regard to the value of "privacy". For many people in these digital times, this seems to be a relic from the old days of a bourgeois society. Either it has no value to them, so there's no reason to defend it; or it seems hopeless to defend it in a restless and insatiable data and information society. However, privacy and the necessity of it is clearly underestimated. Because it is an fundamental element of human freedom. This manifests itself in the possibility of an interplay between privacy and publicity, concealment and disclosure. In this way we open ourselves to the disclosure of something always willingly and under the assumption in the respective context – for example during a doctor's visit – that the disclosed data will remain in the chosen context and not passed on without our consent. We have a mental model that represents what we assume to be the flow of information and we expect it to be based on more than just habits and conventions. Instead, we assume that there are – as Hellen Nissenbaum puts it – "key organizing principles of social life, including moral and political ones" (Nissenbaum 2009, p. 231).

For example, the phenomenon that personal digital data is preserved "forever" could raise the question to what extent this is compatible with the paradigm that the most fundamental prerequisite for individual freedom is also the ability of man to constantly reinvent himself. Finally, the informational self-determination of man as an expression of human dignity was the determining basis for the judgment of the Federal Constitutional Court on the 1983 census (Horn 2017, 4).

The fact that there is a real war for privacy and user data going on is also evident in some users' guerrilla tactics, which are directed against moral standards prescribed by providers, digital giants and platforms. With regard to social networks, for example, this means that the following motto is applied: "Never enter your real data" (Capurro 2011). In view of the requirement in the general terms and conditions of these networks to always use one's own "real name", the ethically explosive question arises: "Am I lying if I do this?" Furthermore: "Would such a lie be justified if, conversely, I was unaware of what happens to my data (and exactly which of my data is collected, stored and evaluated)?"

If we now regard individual freedom in our western societies as "good" and "desirable", then in digital times, for example, this should be reflected in our ability to decide for ourselves – to have the freedom – to hide or reveal ourselves. Such a freedom to conceal (for example, our identity), however, opposes the imperative of total revelation and exhibitionist principles which are, for example, characteristic of social media. Instead of individual privacy, there is a fierce competition in the digital world: to create the impression of having the most attractive, interesting or extreme life and to have the most prolific social media presence of all your friends. Awaiting as a reward: a high profile, (perceived) admiration, status and above all "likes" and "followers" in digital reality. Occasionally, such extensive public displays give the impression of a relapse of modern, enlightened, thinking people into roles and clichés typical of what is known as the "Stone Age" stage of socialization and life.

22.3 Ethics in the Digital Age

In terms of the relationships that determine human life, in a society shaped by digital technologies, one gets the impression that life circumstances and lifestyles are changing so fast that morality and the law can barely keep up. In this respect, it would make sense to address ethical issues much more strongly. The need to address ethical issues of this kind can also be explained by the new forms of exploitation and oppression that (can) accompany digital transformation. New job profiles are being created in knowledge-intensive areas in particular, while many other people are being used or even exploited in jobs, which may simply no longer exist in a few years' time as a result of digitization efforts. On the labour market side, highly skilled knowledge workers will, as "Tech Bohemians", be the beneficiaries of a new industrial conflict. In contrast, however, a "cybertariat" is developing, whose supposed freedoms basically only bring about a drastic deterioration in employment conditions. Platform economics is an economic model in which an algorithm in the background sets the pace of work, an app replaces the business and the workforce of the digital proletariat can be hired, monitored and managed with maximum flexibility. The associated rethinking process in global societies may not bring an unconditional basic income into play as an "option", but will make it absolutely necessary, since at the end of the digital transformation process there will no longer be enough for everyone.

But as digitization records and changes people's ways of life, some good and some not so good new conventions are emerging. To problematize these new morals is, as claimed by the French philosopher Michael Foucault, a task of ethics. Thus, an ethical debate can offer support through ethical theories and analyses – by giving an explanation of the options for action and the impact on the person affected. This involves uncovering prejudices, problematising (seemingly) unambiguous terms and analysing options for action with their effects, and thus addressing others – in terms of new perspectives – from their own language and culture. However, the affected person is not held responsible for his decision and its consequences.

But the *ethical fields of conflict of the digital world* are often not where they might be expected. The first and most frequently discussed issue in this context is the *increasing automation and associated decision-making abilities of machines* – or more precisely, the algorithms integrated in them. Applications and devices formed from algorithms are meanwhile endowed with human characteristics – such as the ability to "feel" or make decisions – so that they could be regarded as our counterparts, communication partners and also as bearers of responsibility for action. Automation, algorithmic decision-making processes and cooperative human-machine interaction also have an *impact on social and economic development* – not only within countries, but across the world. However, the ethical field of conflict here does not lie in the algorithm itself, but in the question of the image of man and the understanding of values that lies behind the algorithms – and thus in the minds of the developers of digital offerings and developments.

In addition, important ethical areas of conflict lie in an *evaluation of the information available digitally, its reception and how it can be influenced* by conscious or controlled misinformation and false information. And they can be found in very practical requirements of ethical issues such as image rights and the publicity or publication of photos: when considering how to balance one's own and other people's privacy – how to proceed between disclosure and related publication of injustice, guilt and things that need to be changed.

But sometimes the issues raised with regard to ethical issues in the context of the digital world seem to be rather droll: they deal with marginal topics that are often already known to the public, instead of venturing into the actual conflict areas. Thus, mock battles are conducted, which are underpinned by the assertion that completely new ethical questions arise in such circumstances. However, this is often not the case. For example, one theoretical dilemma which is repeatedly reported is that of a self-driving car which has to avoid an obstacle and runs over a pensioner or a child. But this question is by no means as new as many modern thinkers claim. The "Plank of Carneades" is one example of this kind of philosophical thought experiment, which has existed for a very long time: "Imagine the situation of two castaways whose only salvation is a plank that can only support one person. One of the two shipwrecked men kills the other to save the plank for himself and to be rescued afterwards. Should the survivor now be convicted of murder or can the killing be justified (on what grounds and within what legal framework)?"

The trolley dilemma is another example: "A tram threatens to drive into five people. The tram can be diverted to another track by moving a switch. Unfortunately, there is another innocent person there. Is the death of this man, by shifting the switch, acceptable, in order to save the lives of the five others?". We recognize: these questions are by no means new and a human being will always make the decision – both in analogue and digital times. Ultimately, an ethical understanding is "programmed" into the decision algorithm of a self-driving car.

Digital ethics should therefore not be reduced to individual questions, but, should instead be seen as a critical reflection on the "good life" in a world shaped by digitization. The pioneering work was done by Norbert Wiener and Joseph Weizenbaum in the 1940s, when they established a professional ethic for computer scientists with computer ethics. Wiener and Weizenbaum were already aware that the consequences would manifest themselves in the overall social impact of computer technology. Cyber Ethics therefore now asks about the "good" and "right" in digital change and the associated discursive orientation in order to shape the digital transformation with all its opportunities and possibilities as well as its dangers and risks in a freedom-enhancing manner (Horn 2017, p1).

22.4 Acting Responsibly in the Digital World

Anyone who asks about the "good" must inevitably also ask where this "good" is defined and negotiated. Traditionally, "throughout western civilization, places such as the ancient Greek agora, the New England town hall, the local church, the coffeehouse, the village square, and even the street corner have been arenas for debate on public affairs and society" (Poster 1995). But in the meantime, *the Internet* has taken this place. It has become a *new public sphere* to which all people – not least due to the triumphant advance of smartphones – have access in almost all parts of the world. It remains to be seen, however, whether this public sphere is indeed democratic, as it is often implicitly assumed and accepted to be in Western societies. Because appearances can – especially with a view to a well-founded and sophisticated discussion and debate – be clearly deceptive. Although the Internet reduces barriers to expression and allows people to speak on an equal footing, rational arguments – especially when looking at the commentary and opinion columns in social networks – seem to be rather rare. Martin Luther King Jr. is said to have once put it this way: "History will have to record that the greatest tragedy of this period of social transition was not the strident clamour of the bad people, but the appalling silence of the good people".

It is therefore a rather arrogant statement when modern people today in our free, rich Western capitalist society claim either to have "no choice" or to be able to make "no difference" by their choice. And if you think about it, one would even have to state that it is also an equally arrogant assertion about oneself: "I'm sorry, but I'm unfortunately too stupid and incompetent – despite my good education and my, by global standards, outrageously high income and living standards and the amount of free time, mobility and life options I have – to make a good, smart decision for the benefit of the well-being of the world and its peoples. Unfortunately, there's nothing I can do". Yes, what do these poor, pitiful creatures say about the state of our societies?

Given this wealth of information available, the digital age has therefore become much more apt to become a "battlefield of argument". And everyone who takes part in this digital world is called upon to enter into the discourse – at least within his domain of knowledge – and to engage in an argumentative manner. However, first of all it would be necessary to clarify what is meant by argumentative participation and to clarify the question: What is an argument? An argument can be considered as presentation of evidence in support of an assertion. This definition is independent of the purpose of the argument – whether a judgment or decision is to be made or a discussion is to be held. An argument provides a solid foundation and an assertion can – and this is important – be examined in a certain context and compared or combined with other assertions. Assertions can be true or false, right or wrong, and may or may not be worthwhile with regard to an action. Argumentation usually comes to a standstill when sufficient evidence has been provided for or against an assertion, so that serious discussion or debate is no longer necessary to reach a consensus (Inch 2001).

But instead of careful argumentation, however, rumours are quickly spread – often informally – in digital contexts, informed by a mixture of fantasy, irony and suspicion and presented to the world as facts. These quickly attract the attention of many users, attention which is just as quickly lost again. Instead of examining evidence for such an assertion, further assertions based on new events, images and statements are constantly being developed in the digital world, thus prolonging the lines of conflict even further. The possibility of seeking and finding a consensus is abandoned in favour of constantly new associated connections. The objective of attracting the interest and attention of users seems to dominate well-argued debate.

Populists, radical groups as well as individual politicians of democratic systems use this. Thanks to this attention-seeking mind set, they can – despite all the information available – increasingly argue without any facts and still gain supporters. The much-quoted catchword "post-truth era" has long since made the rounds and should not surprise us at all in view of the possibilities of the digital age. But if, out of convenience, you no longer attach importance to facts, then you are heading towards a dangerous future.

Thus, the new public debate is often formed and shaped by catchy headlines instead of profound content – who still reads article, such as this one, right to the end? And this trend is ubiquitous. As Ernst Pöppel points out, the phenomenon has even infected scientific journals. And so, he sees today's expectation that researchers were creating as bold a headline as possible on their manuscripts so as not to jeopardise the chance of publication. More and more – whether in science or in the publicity-generating media Industry – it is all only about attention management (Lossau 2016).

Everyday life – especially in view of the abundance of information in the digital world – is full of concepts, which are then often and readily adopted without question. Not doing so would be to approach conceptual meanings with questions. For example: "What is unethical?", "What does it mean to act responsibly?" or "What is good leadership?". However, this would require independent, critical thinking and logical argumentation. But this would be time-consuming. Instead, it is easier to make use of empty phrases and pompous words and the resulting wealth of terminology – especially in the digital world.

Almost without thinking, many people (therefore?) seem willing to agree with opinions that others have already preformed. Such behaviour could be seen as a regression into a self-inflicted immaturity. The following applies: those who think vaguely can only act vaguely. However, independent, critical thinking is a prerequisite for wise action. Especially in turbulent digitally shaped times it should be important to take responsibility and to think about upcoming questions – and above all the important things in life.

Especially with regard to argumentative-led discussions and knowledge-negotiating, clarifying discourses, another obstacle many times is that the identity of the participants can remain hidden. This is illustrated by a cartoon from the 1990s, which apparently depicted two enthusiastically technophile dogs sitting at a desk. In front of the two were keyboard and PC – no webcam – and one of them was probably chatting. Anyway, he says, obviously enthusiastically, to the second dog, who is squatting on the floor next to the desk and looking up at him questioningly: "On the Internet, nobody knows, that you are a dog ...". This cartoon, which dates back to the early days of digitization, still holds much more truth today than it did then: the more diverse the digital communication channels – the greater the possible gap between the actual counterpart and what is presented or presenting. Be it "copy & paste", a speechwriter or ghost-writing. The fact that the actual competence of the presenter lags far behind what is presented, whether spoken or written, is a disappointing experience that has to be expected more and more. "On the internet, nobody knows, that you are a dog ..." (Radermacher 2017, 136).

22.5 Critical Thinking – the Solution

The way out of the social but above all the ethical consequences and requirements of the digital transformation was already made above: *it is especially important in the digital age to think for oneself.* What is more: it's important to think not only for oneself but also critically (Radermacher 2018, 42). At first, critical thinking is an invisible process, because it is inherent to human beings. The ability and practice of critical thinking becomes visible when it finds its expression in a communication – both verbally and in writing. A clever and appropriate argumentation is the result of a critical thought process and the thus possible critical discourse can be regarded as an achievement of the "human condition". The argumentation is of course already available in the old, analogue world. It is not a new achievement of the digital. But especially in view of the interconnectedness, the availability of information and the presence of ubiquitous mass communication, the need for rational-critical thinking is greater than ever before. Because the ability to think independently is an important achievement, both in one's private life and in exchange with others, which must be defended.

Critical thinking can be defined as the ability to think clearly and rationally and to understand the logical connection between ideas and arguments and to form and understand connections. It is the ability to think about something in an active, independent and reflective manner, and expresses itself in the ability to reason intelligently. In this way prejudices as well as manipulations become visible and a person's problem-solving competence as well as their ability to make decisions is strengthened. But the description of what characterizes critical thinking is complex. Ennis describes it thus: "Critical thinking is reasonable and reflective thinking focused on deciding what to believe and what to do" (Ennis 2011, 1); While others point out that critical thinking, "involves calling into question the assumptions underlying our customary, habitual ways of thinking and acting and then being ready to think and act differently on the basis of this critical questioning" (Brookfield 1987, 1) and that critical thinking is "responsive to and guided by intellectual standards. The standards include clarity, accuracy, precision, relevance, depth, logic, and breadth" (McLean 2005, 6).

Critical thinkers first question ideas presented to them and try to determine whether they are valid. They look for and identify inconsistencies as well as errors in their own argumentation as well as in the statements made by others. They therefore also reflect on and rethink the reasons behind, content of, and goals of their own beliefs, thoughts, and values.

However, critical thinking has – unfortunately, one might say – negative connotations for many people. To them it sounds like scepticism, distrust and perhaps dismissive theoretical rationality. To some extent they are right. Because critical thinking does not mean choosing or trusting answers, simply because they feel right. Instead, all available possibilities and information should be subjected to critical examination. The goal of critical thinking is to separate what is meaningful and serious from what is just different. For critical thinking, it is first of all imperative to understand what you are looking for.

Critical thinking can be seen as asking challenging questions and finding diverse and meaningful answers. Here, "critical" is not meant to be disapproving, but understood as the art of judging, of differentiating between assumptions and facts and questioning arguments and interpreting facts (Wohlrapp 2008, 213). In doing so, such critical thinking builds on existing facts and thus raises questions that explore the correctness and truth of the various views and examine their conditions. Furthermore: even one's own thinking undergoes criticism and asks which standards are used to examine a matter or from which point of view it is considered (Jahn 2013, 2).

Maturity and the escape of humanity from a self-inflicted immaturity requires thinking – man must think for himself. Immanuel Kant described this as: "Enlightenment is man's release from his self-incurred tutelage. Tutelage is man's inability to make use of his understanding without direction from another. Self-incurred is this tutelage when its cause lies not in lack of reason but in lack of resolution and courage to use it without direction from another. Sapere aude! 'Have courage to use your own reason!'- that is the motto of enlightenment". (Kant 1784).

It remains an open question to what extent the (technical) possibilities of the digital age can support or even promote enhance thinking. "As technology has played a bigger role in our lives, our skills in critical thinking and analysis have declined" (Wolpert 2009). This becomes visible when blind belief in technology and untested confidence in technology leads to the suppression of one's own ability to think: "If my weather app says it's not raining, then I don't need an umbrella – even if the road is wet and storm clouds are passing overhead". This is in no way about demanding or even preaching a hostile attitude towards technology. But despite all the potential of technology, it is still in the hands of and remains the responsibility of people, to use and exploit it appropriately – that is to say: wisely.

But it would seem that the assumption of the (self-) "thinking man" today cannot be taken for granted. After all, how else could one explain the need for recognition and excessive ambition in professional but especially private everyday life, as well as, at the same time, a perceptible indifference to social-political participation and unbridled private consumption? Is not mankind, as either the crown of creation or the hero of evolution, something particularly unique? Whose skill of reflective-critical thinking, is a uniquely important distinguishing feature?

Another obstacle to establishing and, in particular, implementing critical thinking is the lack of time. In these digital times we appear to be too happy to do away with this, while the answers we require are only too readily available – keyword: convenience. In a time when there seems to be more answers than questions, and basic questions are (no longer) dealt with due to convenience and a lack of time. The digital marketplace of ideas, theories, hypotheses, facts and false reports in particular requires the characteristics of mature evaluation and wise judgement.

And this is where critical thinking comes in: It serves the development of cognitive abilities and training as well as the cultivation of prudent judgement. Because critical thinking enables the formulation of flexible, open, reasonable and appropriate argumentation and thus offers the basis for a discursive and comprehensive exchange of knowledge. However, this thinking is not only suitable to the outside world and for argument-led debates with those with a different viewpoint; rather, critical thinking also goes hand in hand with the ability to develop self-correcting thinking.

Critical thinking can therefore, in many cases, simply be regarded as reflective thinking. But for this it is necessary to actively, persistently and above all thoroughly weigh up every belief or every supposed form of knowledge. In this way, both the reasons that support the supposed knowledge and the conclusions it tends to draw are examined (Dewey 1938, 9). At the same time, "as technology has played a bigger role in our lives, our skills in critical thinking and analysis have declined" (Wolpert 2009). In digital times, instead of critical thinking, we cultivate our visual abilities and allow ourselves to be guided by them. Images and videos now dominate social media in particular and have even become the core business purpose of successful and partly dominant Internet services – such as Instagram or Snapchat. The only question is to what extent our visual abilities have increased or can keep pace with this shift. Because our attention is increasingly required to follow so-called "real-time requirements", which, however, "do not allow time for reflection, analysis or imagination". (Wolpert 2009).

Worrying, in this context, is an experiment by Kimberley Wade. She and her team at the University of Wellington in New Zealand showed subjects an old black-and-white photograph showing them in a hot-air balloon. What the test persons did not know: one of their relatives had secretly sent the scientists a photo of each test person. The researchers used it for a photomontage – and the hot-air balloon flight was apparently supported by an historical document. This was then presented to the participants – the result: The photo reminded every third subject of previous experience that had never actually happened. The researchers then asked the subjects to think again about the event at home. In the end, one in two believed that the flight had actually taken place – and some of the subjects even remembered details (Wade 2002).

A study by Elizabeth Loftus comes to a similarly striking conclusion: a Disneyland brochure was presented to test subjects. Besides the usual, expected advertising photos, it also contained pictures of the cartoon rabbit Bugs Bunny. Later, a third of the test persons stated that they had met this character while visiting the amusement park. 62% of this group said that they shook hands with a wearer of this rabbit outfit and almost one in two thought they were embraced by the cartoon hero. The surprising thing about this memory: you can't meet Bugs Bunny in Disneyland, because the rights to this character are owned by Warner Bros Inc. and not by the World Disney Company (Loftus 2002).

The importance of the ability to think critically in our digital age is also highlighted in the current "Future of Jobs Report" by the "World

Economic Forum". This report lists skill of critical thinking in second place, among the skills required from employees for 2020; directly behind the ability to solve complex problems and even before such frequently desired abilities as creativity, leadership or emotional intelligence (WE Forum 2016). In this respect, critical thinking training is an educational requirement in the digital age. This is also supported by Facione, who reminds us where critical thinking should be taught and, at the very least, known: as a central element of university education (Facione 1995, 2).

22.6 Essential: Education which Promotes Critical Thinking

In most countries, the majority of pupils and students continue to leave educational institutions without having learned anything worth mentioning about data protection, algorithms and networking – not to mention the connection between the digital and critical thinking. However, particularly in the field of information technology knowledge is essential – in addition to the ability to judge and make decisions and to classify information – in order to educate people to become self-determined individuals in the digital world. Thus, an informatics understanding of contexts and a capacity for self-learning is intrinsically interwoven with the skill of critical thinking.

The demand I have already raised elsewhere that all active participants in a digital and knowledge-oriented society should continue their training to become "part-time computer scientists" can also be justified by the need for critical thinking in these times (Radermacher 2017, 99). Computer scientists – similar to philosophers – usually already learn informal logic, pragmatism and linguistics skills during their training. In this way, as long as the teachers keep this in mind, they acquire a basic knowledge of critical thinking.

In the context of the debates on digitization in the education sector, it must immediately be pointed out, that the acquisition and introduction of technology in educational institutions alone will not solve the existing and more worrying educational problems currently hindering successful participation in the digital world. For it is less about technology than about the interaction between education and its requirements such as freedom, linguistic ability and personality – all elements need each other. Freedom of education is both a necessity and a consequence, and the same applies to language ability and personal development. This cannot be outsourced to technological systems, but requires individual responsibility and cooperation.

It is therefore completely irrelevant whether a person obtains knowledge and understanding from digital or analogue (printed) sources. Rather, competent classification skills and judgement is required. This can take place in particular through (communicating) one's own knowledge and the resulting open local and/or global discourse for sound knowledge negotiation. Not only knowing but also using these possibilities is a requirement for those in the know, in this digital age.

Anyone who has learned to think critically is also able to think differently and, in this way, to defend himself, in particular against opinion leaders or even opinion dictators. Such an option for self-determination, which can ultimately express itself in a revolution, was also put forward by the American writer and philosopher Henry David Thoreau; he wrote: "all men recognize the right of revolution; that is, the right to refuse allegiance to, and to resist, the government, when its tyranny or its inefficiency are great and unendurable" (Thoreau 1849). But having rights and proclaiming oneself also means having the necessary knowledge and education.

With regard to (school) education, it would thus be necessary for students to have enough freedom to practice critical thinking. To this end, however, existing structures would have to be changed in such a way that this skill of critical thinking can also be repeatedly applied in the learning process and thus improved. But those who want to – and should – think critically also need a sufficient knowledge base for such thinking. In this respect, the question of the content of learning and the canon of knowledge also arises. With regard to the schools' products and also highly regimented studies, however, one has rather the impression of a pseudo- education, which does not adequately question the opinions of other people or things and remain uncritical.

In digital times, however, one hears in many places that given the round-the-clock availability of all information on the Internet, it is no longer relevant and necessary to impart knowledge. Instead, the focus is on the ability to acquire knowledge. However, this often pragmatic and modern definition of a skill set is far too limited. This might make it easy to remove some special knowledge from the curricula – but it is precisely this knowledge, if properly conveyed, that can also stimulate further learning and the strengthening of skills. Furthermore, unless the highest level of pragmatics is applied and only theoretical knowledge acquisition is taught, it would remain open who can define the "limits". To offer learning corridors in which students can follow their curiosity in a serious and individually significant way means leaving room for other things in addition to obligatory areas of learning. However, it is and remains certain that pupils should also deal with some central (life) issues, such as for example: Who am I? Why is democracy important? As well as questions like: How do I behave in the company of people from other cultures? Or: How do you unite individual and group interests in a community? – In this way, the right learning content can expand not only knowledge but also thought horizons.

Instead of titbits of knowledge, schools and universities should provide "maps of knowledge". Through the knowledge of theories, works of art and languages, people are enabled to look "differently" at the world. It is necessary to rethink which concepts, initial thoughts and cultural assets have a "value" in a digitally-networked, globalized world. It is the fundamental question: What are the central questions and content that every person should deal with in order to lead a good life in a digitally globalized world?

22.7 Conclusion

Digital transformation is not limited to the technological sphere; it also affects the analogue reality and the environment around us. In this way, ethical questions and areas of conflict emerge, which must be dealt with appropriately. Ideally, the first goal is always a critical reflection on a "good life" – even in a digital world. However, the "good" contained in it needs to be continuously reviewed, defined and negotiated. The necessary and desirable ingredient of such argumentative negotiation is: critical thinking. Even in an information-flooded hodgepodge of opinions, this enables a reflected independence of thought and a focus on understanding, locating, distinguishing and ultimately assessing changes as well as the "new formulations" of the "good" that may be necessary in a process of transformation.

On the whole, one could say that there is an interaction between critical thinking and Cyber Ethics: critical thinking requires values derived from ethical principles so as not to be arbitrary. At the same time, ethical principles demand a critical (over-) thinking of real or anticipated changes in order to examine them appropriately for the "good". In this respect, even in digital times, people remain called upon to participate in society and the world in a responsible manner and to behave in an ethical manner: to be inquisitive, to be able to argue and above all – or in particular – to think for oneself and to think critically.

Bibliography

Brookfield, Stephen D., *Developing critical thinkers: Challenging adults to explore alternative ways of thinking and acting.* San Francisco, CA: Jossey-Bass, 1987.

Capurro, Rafael, *Never enter your real data*, 2011, http://www.capurro. de/ realdata.html, (Accessed 30 June 2018).

Dewey, John, *Experience and Education*, New York: Kappa Delta Pi, 1938.

Ennis, Robert H., *The Nature of Critical Thinking: An Outline of Critical Thinking Dispositions and Abilities,* 2011, http://faculty.education.illinois.edu/rhennis/documents/Th eNatureofCriticalThinking_51711_000.pdf. (Accessed 30 June 2018)

Facione, Peter A.; Giancarlo, Carol A.; Facione, Noreen C.; Gainen, Joanne, *The disposition toward critical thinking*, In: Journal of General Education, No. 44, 1998, 1-25.

Gleick, James, *Die Information: Geschichte, Theorie, Flut*, München: Redline Verlag, 2011.

Horn, Nikolai, *Denkimpuls Digitale Ethik,* https://initiatived21.de/app/ uploads/2017/08/01_denkimpulse_ag-ethik_grundlagen-der-digitalen-ethik.pdf. (Accessed 30 June 2018)

Inch, E. and B. Warnick, *Critical Thinking: The use of reason in argument.* Boston: Allyn & Bacon, 2001.

Loftus, Elizabeth F.; Braun, Kathryn A.; Ellis, Rhiannon: *Make my Memory*, In: Psychology & Marketing, Vol. 19, No. 1, 2002, 1-23.

Lossau, Norbert, *Wir verlassen uns darauf, dass für uns gedacht wird*, https://www.welt.de/wissenschaft/article159033795/Wir-verlassen-uns-darauf-dass-fuer-uns-gedacht-wird.html, 2016 (Accessed 30 June 2018)

Poster, Mark (1995): The net as a public sphere?, 10. January 1995, Wired, URL: https://www.wired.com/1995/11/poster-if/, Revision: 30. June 2018/McLean, Cheryl (2005): Evaluating Critical Thinking Skills: Two Conceptualizations, In: Journal of Distance Education, Vol. 20, No. 2, S. 1-20

Nissenbaum, Helen (2009): Privacy in context – Technology, Policy and the Integrity of Social Life, Stanford: Stanford University Press

Radermacher, Ingo (2017): Digitalisierung selbst denken, Göttingen: BusinessVillage

Radermacher, Ingo (2018): Denk klar, Göttingen: BusinessVillage

Thoreau, Henry David (1849): Resistance of Civil Government, In: Elizabeth P. Peabody (1849): Aesthetic Papers, New York: G.P. Putnam

Wade, Kimberley A.; Garry, Maryanne; Read, J. Don; Lindsay, Stephen (2002): A picture is worth a thousand lies, In: Psychonomic Bulletin & Review; Vol. 9; No. 2; S. 597-603

WE Forum (2016): The Future of Jobs – Employment, Skills and Workforce Strategie, URL: http://www3.weforum.org/docs/WEF_Future_of_Jobs.pdf , Revision: 30. June 2018

Wolpert Stuart (2009): Is technology producing a decline in critical thinking and analysis?, URL: http://insciences.org/article.php?article_id=1759, Revision: 30. June 2018.

23

CYBER BULLYING

Saakshar Duggal, India

23.1 Introduction

The *Center Against Cyber Bullying* (CACB) is an organization which aims to educate all relevant stakeholders in the education ecosystem about the huge challenges that cyber bullying as a phenomenon presents, be it students, youth, parents, teachers, schools, colleges and universities on online safety. The Centre further seeks to impart education about cyber bullying to cyberspace users and netizens.

23.2 What is Cyber Bullying?

Cyber Bullying in simple terms can be defined as bullying that takes place over digital devices like cell phones, computers or tablets. Cyber bullying can occur through any social platform. It can also occur through SMS, text, apps, forums or gaming where people can view, participate or share content.

Cyber bullying includes, amongst others, sending or posting images of the other person and causing embarrassment and humiliation to that person. Cyber Bullying may not sound very important, but in reality, stopping cyber bullying is the need of the hour.

23.3 Who is a Cyber-Bully?

A cyber-bully can be defined as a person who uses the cyber space as a medium, to cause bullying online. A cyber bully can be from any country, of any age or gender, which simply means that anyone can be a cyber-bully on the internet. A cyber bully can use a number of mediums to perform the act of bullying; he simply requires a social media platform where the bully can exploit or humiliate the other person. Cyber bullying can also be done through *different forms*. Some of them are mentioned below:

- Posting any kind of humiliating content of the victim;
- Stalking by means of cell phone, laptop etc;
- Threats of child pornography;
- Hacking into the victim's account;
- Extending threats to commit acts of violence.

The Ryan Halligan case of Vermont happened in 2003 was the first case that dealt with the issue of cyber bullying in which the defendant was not held liable for cyber bullying the girl because criminal law could not applied in that matter[501].

23.4 Signs of Cyber Bullying

These signs are not always visible, that is why these have to be taken into account. It is important for the parents to have close observation on the child since there are lot of signs from which one can interpret that the child is facing the problem of cyber bullying. Some of these signs of cyber bullying may vary but may include as follows:

- Avoiding school or gathering;
- Changing moods or behaviour, sleep or appetite;
- Withdrawal from family members, friend circle and other activities;

---

[501] https://cyber.laws.com/ryan-halligan. (Accessed 9 Sept 2018)

- Wanting to stop using the computer or cell phone;
- Avoiding discussions about computers, social activities, social media.
- Being emotionally upset during or after use of the internet or the phone.

Cyber bullying is actually a phenomenon where the person who is the victim, is experiencing a number of negative feelings, like confusion, dissatisfaction, vulnerability, humiliation etc. Sometimes, the student who is being bullied feels as if the entire world knows what is going on with him. At times, the stress of dealing with cyber bullying can cause kids to feel like the situation is going out of their hands. Since cyber bullying is done in the cyberspace, one knows that once something is posted on a social media platform then it will always be out there. Therefore, when the cyber bullying occurs in the form of nasty posts, text messages, humiliating messages etc., it can lead to intense feeling of humiliation in the person who is the victim. Cyber bullying can also cause a self-complex if the person is constantly being bullied online as he has to face lot of nasty comments, due to which his/her self-confidence is just shattered. This can easily be shown in his/her daily activities. For example, if a person is fat and there would be a lot of nasty and humiliating posts posted on the physical appearance of the person, the self-confidence of that person will automatically be very low and this would later result into depression.

Generally speaking, people consider depression as a normal thing but technically speaking, depression is actually a psychological disorder. Victims of cyber bullying often feel depressed since the cyber bullying erodes one's self-esteem and self-confidence. In addition, there is a lot of stress of coping with cyber bullying on a regular basis. It diminishes the feelings of happiness and contentment.

23.5 Suicidal Tendencies

One of the major consequences of cyber bullying are suicidal tendencies. The victims are constantly humiliated on social media platforms. These messages often lead to feeling of hopelessness. In many cases, they even begin to feel like the only way to escape the pain of this humiliation is through suicide. At that point of time, suicide appears to be the only option left, for them. In fact, some of them say suicide is actually the way to end all of this but that is not true. Suicide will in any case end one's life and all of the bright future that one could have had. It is a sincere request from me that both the parents and children should have a daily communication in case if any parent or child is bullied. Do not dismiss their feelings, trust me that would create a blunder. Parents need to clearly understand that parents are the ones, who have to guide their children and no one can guide children better than their parents in any scenario whatsoever.

23.6 The Role of Children and Duty of Parents

Our *Center Against Cyber Bullying* has conducted lot of interviews with children who are in schools and with their parents. After interviewing and interacting with them, one trend is clear. There are several factors which people usually don't talk about that are the actual reasons for the rampant increase of cyber bullying. There is always a gap between the children and their parents, especially in the cases of cyber bullying. There are lots of things that are going on in a victim's mind that have to be discussed.

There are some points which both the parents and their children should keep in mind whenever an incident of cyber bullying occurs. In such a situation, children are usually in a state of confusion, whenever they face or become the victims of cyber bullying. Often, half of them don't even know that it is a crime and they are being victimized; they think their parents will not be able to understand what is happening. In some cases, they are scared for example, when the child himself is guilty of sharing explicit pictures or content and with the result, faces threats in the form of cyber bullying. Sometimes, children feel that their parents would punish them and as a result, children often think like that and act accordingly since they are immature and which further leads to complication of problems.

In case of parents, they always want the best for their child and want to protect their child from this harsh world. But the fact is that sometimes they have to understand the child's problem with an open mind. If you discover that your child is being a victim of cyber bullying, offer comfort or support to him/her talking about any bullying experiences you had in your childhood, which might help the child feel less alone. You should praise your child for doing the right thing by talking to you about it. Let your child know that it is not his/her fault and the bullying says more about the bully than the victim. Parents should let someone at school or anywhere e.g. Principal or School Nurse or Counsellor or Teacher know about the situation. Many schools in schools-districts often have protocols regarding cyber bullying. In some schools, there are also specific cells to deal with these matters.

I think that encouragement, support and comfort is the key. If you are able to give your child that in that situation, wherein he has all sorts of trouble and confusion, then this can really help to create a bond of trust between the child and his parents.

23.7 Limiting Access of Technology

There are other certain measures that the parents as well as children need to keep in mind, before dealing with the matter. First, block the bullying. Many devices as well as social platforms such as Facebook, Snapchat etc. have this setting which allows the user to block another user electronically.

Although, I know it is very difficult these days for a teenager to leave that phone for a few days on which he/she spends 6-8 hours every day but trust me, this will actually work and will make you feel better. One can search for a number of ways on the internet to keep oneself secure online. There are a lot of sites which help and do give steps to prevent being a victim of cyber bullying.

23.8 When your Child is the Bully?

At this juncture, I actually wanted to discuss the scenario when you discover that your child is himself the cyber bully. We often talk about cyber bullying from the perspective of the victim, in the sense that he is being victimized, humiliated etc. The fact that we don't talk about is that when one's own child is the bully. More and more children are wanting to be the cyber bully, as they want to give vent to their sadistic tendencies, while hiding behind the cloak of anonymity.

This unfortunately is a reality. Victims of cyber bullying get cyber bullied as there are cyber bullies present in the cyberspace ecosystem. There are a lot of recommendations for parents of cyber bullies. Parents need to understand the problem of their child, as to why he/she has become a cyber-bully. Finding out that one's own child is the cyber bully or is always behaving badly can be upsetting and heart breaking for any parent but it is important to address the problem head on and not wait for it to go away.

Talking to the child firmly and making him understand about the negative impact, his/her actions are creating, is a good strategy moving forward. It is equally important to make the child understand the legal ramifications of his/her acts. The child needs to be told that his/her behaviour is unethical and that the child would not relish if the same behaviour is targeted to the child or to his family members. Sometimes the child also is unaware of the fact that he is the one who is committing the cyber bullying. Hence, it becomes more important that the child must be sensitized about the disastrous, unethical consequences of his/her cyber bullying behaviour.

Joking and teasing might seem harmless to one person but can be really a sign of bullying behaviour to another. Bullying in any form is unacceptable. There can be permanent consequences arising out of cyber bullying behaviour in schools, home and other communities, if this continues.

There can also be other ways to talk to children and prevent them from going in the wrong direction. For example, to get to the heart of the matter, talking to teachers, counsellors and other school officials can help identify situations that lead kids to bully others. If the child has trouble managing his/her behaviour, then there is a need to consult and talk to a therapist, who can easily help the child to cop up with negative emotions of anger or frustration etc. Parents need to also set a good example in front of the child. Inculcating model good online habits to help your kid to understand the benefits and danger of life in the digital world, is the right step in the right direction.

All stakeholders need to realize that cyber bullying in its intrinsic sense, is an unethical activity that is done in cyberspace. Such a behaviour is against ethical standards in the real world as well as cyber space. Such an activity runs contrary to the foundation principles of cyber ethics. Numerous countries have sought to grant penal sanction against cyber bullying by coming up with special legal provisions governing cyber bullying. However, in numerous jurisdictions, we find that cyber bullying is not specifically covered under the provisions of existing law. All stakeholders have a common duty to keep cyberspace a secure space for all netizens. Massive capacity building programmes targeted at cyber bullying is the need of the hour. We as internet users, have an ethical duty towards all other users of the Internet as well as the future generations. We must all unite to join hands to fight the menace of the unethical menace of cyber bullying, from all directions.

24

CHILD PROTECTION ONLINE:
UNICEF INDIA RECOMMENDATIONS

UNICEF India

Child online protection against cybercrime, cyberbullying, online sexual abuse etc. is a global huge challenge. UNICEF India is very active in prevention, education and legislation as the following excerpts show.[502]

24.1 Prevention Through Education for Digital Literacy and Safety

24.1.1 The Role of Parents and Children

A unique set of issues is emerging as a result of the expansion of ICT and use of the Internet. Dynamic technology and the irrelevance of national boundaries to the transfer of information in cyberspace make it nearly impossible to control access. The affordability and

---

[502] The following contribution is from UNICEF India, *Child Online Protection in India,* New Delhi 2016, 68-75 and 94-97. The full Report with analysis of online risks and threats for children, child online protection response system and legislation and policies to protect children online for free download at http://unicef.in/Publications and http://unicef.in/PressReleases/418/UNICEF-India-launches-the-first-comprehensive-report-on-Child-Onl. See also the *Handbook on Cyber Crimes against Children and Investigation Methodologies for Law Enforcement Agencies.* Co-published with www.cyberpeace.org.

accessibility of mobile phones further provides a level playing field to "haves", "have nots" and "have lots", giving them greater agency than ever before. As a result, it is imperative to inform children and parents about potential threats and safeguards to influence their use of digital devices and technology.

A protective family environment also demands an open dialogue, negotiation and coordination based on a shared understanding of the risks of online social networking, protective capacity of communities and families and their own life skills, knowledge and participation.

One of the key gaps identified as part of this assessment is the lack of understanding of the risks and threats posed to children by ICT and social media among professionals, policymakers and society as a whole. Children often indulge in a wide array of risky behaviours online that remain undetected by the parents, as early exposure to ICT and social media has made them more adept than their parents at using technology in their daily lives.

Research among urban Indians reveals that children and parents are equally concerned about online risks. Sharing of personal information and its ramifications was predominant, followed closely by contact with strangers online. While parents and children are universally aware of the prevalence of online risks, children demonstrate a wider spectrum of awareness of those risks. This awareness gradient is perhaps explained by digitally native children habitually seeking information online as well as in conversation with their peers, both offline and online.

About 60 per cent of parents across eight metro areas shared that their children had consulted them about things that bothered them online. Despite claims of asking parents about online risks, almost two thirds of children keep some aspects of their online behaviour a secret from their parents. When asked, most children say they do not want their parents to know what they do with their friends. Clearing browsing history, deleting messages, using privacy settings, using mobiles instead of desktops or laptops and minimizing the browser in the presence of an adult are among the many stratagems used to safeguard their privacy.[503] Most children and parents do not understand the full extent of the risks. In the United States, for example, parents largely seem to be content using offline means and discipline to protect their children online, eschewing available online tools and apps. Indian parents, with relatively lower levels of sophistication, show similar behaviours. Norton Security, a firm dealing with online security and protection, found that awareness of risks among adult Indians was significantly lower than global levels of concern based on the "it won't happen to me" syndrome. The same misplaced confidence probably extends to the risks faced by children online.

Children appear to share their concerns with parents primarily when encountering cyberbullying, either as a witness or victim. Parental engagement in informing and educating them about online protection is limited. Very few claim to report, fewer still challenge the bullies and a substantial proportion does nothing.

Experiences from other countries show that children and young people have a large role to play in safeguarding themselves and their peers from child online abuse. Examples of a few promising practices include the constitution of peer groups in schools called cyber congress, scouts or cyber security ambassadors. However, such practices have not been properly documented in India and there is little understanding of how digital literacy and safety programmes can be implemented effectively.

It is commonly argued that technological innovations would provide the best response given the technological nature of the chal-

---

[503] Intel Security, Teens, Tweens and Technology Study, Delhi, 2015.

lenges. The ICT sector has a key role to play in the prevention of, and response to, child online abuse and exploitation. However, it is clear that no single sector or agency can ensure the safety of children from online or ICT-mediated violence. Relevant government institutions, the private sector, international organizations, academia and civil society need to work together to build structures, mechanisms and capacities to prevent and respond to child online abuse, violence and exploitation in India. A safe online ecosystem for children requires a high degree of preparedness, collaboration and coordination among the stakeholders as well as adequate technological solutions.

24.1.2 The Role of the Government

DEITY, part of the Ministry of Communications and Information Technology, has launched a five-year project on information security education and awareness. One of the activities under this programme is to widely promote information security awareness among children, home users and non-IT professionals. C-DAC Hyderabad, which has been assigned the responsibility of executing this project, is expected to prepare information security awareness material and coordinate with participating institutes to organize various events. Useful information for children, students and parents is made available through messages, periodic competitions on safety issues and a website (www. infosecawareness.in). CERT-In also disseminates information and creates awareness on security issues through its website (http://www.cert-in.org.in) while police cybercrime cells undertake outreach activities in schools to raise awareness about the safe use of the Internet.

24.1.3 The Role of the ICT Sector

Many ICT companies and service providers conduct periodic surveys with the objective of improving and expanding the quality and reach of their services. The understanding of emerging trends in the behavioural and usage patterns of the users enables ICT companies to take strategic decisions about their products and to provide a better and safer experience to existing and potential consumers. It is worth noting that while available surveys provide interesting insights, they have tended to be confined to relatively high-end, urban ICT and Internet users. There are few enquiries covering different sociocultural and economic groups and these are usually limited to certain geographical areas. However, ICT companies and service providers can play an important and critical role in preventing and responding to child online abuse and exploitation. Some companies in India have already started to play a key role in addressing the issue.

The DSCI, a body set up by NASSCOM, has been conducting social awareness campaigns to inform and educate individuals and end users, including children, in Tier II and Tier III cities[504] about cybersecurity and cybercrimes through week-long social awareness campaigns. These campaigns use open group discussions, quizzes and conferences to target students, home users and working professionals. Cyber labs under DSCI also conduct some outreach programmes in schools. A school outreach programme was conducted for students and parents in collaboration with Telenor.

IAMAI has organized outreach programmes on safe web surfing and digital wellness through a consultant reaching approximately 100,000 students in schools and colleges over the last five years. Individual schools have cyber safety champions advising children on online safety and netiquette.[505] Intel Security's Cybermum is a digital

---

[504] Tier II cities have a population of 1 million and Tier III cities have a population of less than 1 million.

[505] Rakshit Tandon has reached 1.5 million students through a safe surfing programme since 2008, and currently supports Cyber Congress in about 100 schools. He has been supported by IAMAI, Facebook, Intel and Telenor in this

evangelist who champions the cause of online safety for children through an active blog on Wordpress, the Intel Security portal, Twitter and Facebook. With about 600 Facebook friends and over 13,400 followers on Twitter, Cybermum has a follower base comprising parents, academicians, parent bloggers and other parent influencers. She analyses popular studies and their relevance for children and has blogged about issues such as cyberbullying. Since September 2014, Intel Education's Digital Wellness Curriculum has been providing digital education among schools in India in an effort to ensure grass-roots education on cyber safety and digital wellness. In 2014 alone, the programme reached over 108,000 students in India.

Telenor's WebWise initiative seeks to introduce first-time users and young children to the potential of the Internet for information and learning but also informs them of the online risks and threats of bullying, abuse and malware. A Telenor report highlighted that Indian children face the worst risks due to a combination of high rate of access to mobile phones and low resilience due to a lack of formal or informal counsel to create awareness of or control over their Internet activity. In response, Telenor started a school outreach programme aimed at creating awareness of Internet safety among children and helping parents to monitor and educate their children about Internet safety. The programme, named WebWise, was started in February 2014 with Telenor volunteers reaching out to schools and parents to run Internet safety workshops for children. The first phase of the programme reached 15,000 children and the initiative continued into 2015.

As part of the India Digital Literacy and Internet Safety Campaign, Google's Web Rangers programme empowers teens to promote safe use of the Internet among their peers.

---

effort. His Facebook page on safe surfing provides a platform for responding to queries.

Web Rangers are students who have been equipped to serve as ambassadors for safe and responsible use of the web in their schools. They are trained to create cyber safety campaigns among their peers to encourage thinking about online behaviour and how to keep each other safe online. The initiative enrolled young people aged 14–17 years, representing 50 schools in Hyderabad, Bangalore and New Delhi.

Microsoft's Stand Up To Online Bullying quiz and Digital Citizenship in Action toolkit, in conjunction with the results of the 2012 Global Youth Online Behaviour Survey, provide adults with tools and resources to help start the conversation with children about how to stay safer online. The quiz is designed to walk adults through a series of scenarios in which, upon answering, they receive immediate guidance on how to talk about, identify and respond to the range of online behaviours from meanness to bullying and beyond. The toolkit is an interactive educational guide which teaches users about responsible use of technology.[506] Microsoft also partners with organizations like iKeep Safe, iLook Both Ways and the Anti-Defamation League to provide professional development to teachers and school staff with courses on online bullying, public awareness campaigns and cyber safety education.

24.1.4 The Role of Civil Society

Few civil society organizations have chosen to address child online protection issues, which can be attributed to a deficit of technological know-how required to meet the complex and ever-evolving nature of cyber offences against children. Agencies that have engaged with child online protection issues have either been

---

[506] The interactive online quiz and the toolkit can be downloaded as a teaching tool by organizations and schools.

working against child sexual abuse and exploitation, for meaningful education, or seek to highlight critical emerging social issues.

Chennai-based Tulir-Centre for the Prevention and Healing of
Child Sexual Abuse has extended its offline work for public awareness on child sexual abuse, prevention and support services for child
victims and policy advocacy related to the online space. It provides
guidance and support to child victims of online exploitation and
abuse, whether the cases are registered with the police or not. In addition, Tulir lobbies for the integration of cyber safety in the school
curriculum in Tamil Nadu and advocates against online abuse and
exploitation of children at the national and international levels.

New Delhi-based Breakthrough has used the digital space for its
media campaigns and dialogue with young audiences against gender-
based violence and discrimination. The group has also taken up issues of online harassment and violence against women and girls and
methods for addressing them. Breakthrough has used the online
space to create a dialogue with young boys and girls to examine
their own beliefs and social norms related to gender relations and
violence against women and girls.

The Cyber Peace Foundation incorporated child online protection in its programs via two initiatives: the 'E-Raksha Seminars' in
schools to raise awareness of children of the risks and threats when
using internet and social media; and, the 'I-Safe Project' specifically
targeting youth to sensitize them on cyber-abuse, cyber-harassment
and cyber-extremism implemented in collaboration with the Policy
Perspective Foundation Bachpan Bachao Andolan ran an online
campaign on child sexual abuse called Full Stop in 2015. This included aspects of online abuse and exploitation of children including
cyberbullying, cyberstalking and sexting. The information addressed children, care providers and survivors of sexual abuse online
and offline through a school outreach programme. The group's specif-

ic focus is on online child sexual abuse, trafficking, child pornography and extortion through engagement with key stakeholders on the international dimensions of child trafficking.

Freedom from Abuse of Children from Technology (FACT), the brainchild of the Asian School of Cyber Laws, provides information for parents and children on some of the threats that exist online and safe behaviours to mitigate them.

Although civil society organizations are doing a commendable job of creating public awareness about digital safety and building resilience among children to deal with potential harm online, the narrow focus or limited reach of their initiatives does not adequately address the growing need for informed and responsible use of technologies. Taking these interventions to scale remains a major challenge. A coordinated response – including common content focus, sharing of lessons and the evolving concerns of children through a common platform, coordination of action and resources, institutionalization through inclusion in the school curriculum, and peer education – could guide the way forward.

24.1.5 Partnerships Between the ICT Industry and Civil Society

A number of initiatives for digital safety, digital wellness, netiquette education and awareness programmes have been initiated by ICT companies and service providers in collaboration with civil society organizations. For instance, Facebook has been working with NGOs on programmes and guides for adolescents and parents on how to stay safe online and offline. Moreover, the Safety Centre on the Facebook site seeks to help people learn about how to stay safe while using the platform.

Both Google and Facebook have supported the Learning Links Foundation (LLF), which works actively with education stakeholders, leaders and policymakers to improve education systems, enhance curricula, reform assessments and leverage technology solutions to enhance teaching and learning processes. LLF has been able to reach 300,000 students over 11 years of age with cyber safety and wellness awareness in 19 states of India. The partnership with Facebook has resulted in Internet safety campaigns reaching 52,000 students in 10 states.

Digital Citizenship: Preparing Children for a Digital World

There is an urgent need to address and mitigate the risks associated with widespread use of ICT (i.e., online threats, abuse and misuse of information, and physical and mental health hazards) while simultaneously taking advantage of the opportunities afforded by these technologies. Children and young people in a digital world need to be equipped with appropriate knowledge, skills and attitude to leverage and enjoy the potential benefits of ICT while being resilient to the risks.

The concept of digital citizenship helps teachers, technology leaders and parents to understand what children, students and users of technology should know to use technology appropriately and responsibly. More than a teaching tool, it is a way of preparing them for current challenges. The proactive approach of digital citizenship education could foster a favourable environment to encourage responsible and safe use of ICT among children and youth with support from schools, teachers, parents/guardians, policymakers, industry leaders and other key stakeholders.[507] The following are some of the critical components of digital citizenship education:

- Internet safety
- Privacy and security
- Relationships and communication

---

[507]   www.unescobkk.org/education/ict/resources/publications/elibrary-themes/ teaching-and-learning/fostering-digital-citizenship-through-safe-and-responsible-use-of-ict.

- Cyberbullying and digital drama
- Digital footprint and reputation
- Self-image and identity
- Information literacy
- Creative credit and copyright.

The much older partnership with Google has led to the cybersecurity Web Rangers programme in 15 states. In November 2015, the Family Online Safety Institute recognized LLF for its outstanding work on online safety.

Twitter is developing the "Twitter for Good" initiative with five vertical areas dealing with freedom of expression, women in technology, emergency crisis response, improving access and inclusion, and digital citizenship focusing on privacy, safety and prevention of child sexual exploitation. Its outreach programme for women in technology seeks strong collaboration with organizations working for women's empowerment and rights to deal with issues of harassment and vitriolic abuse.

The Mumbai-based initiative, Aarambh India, works on the issue of child sexual abuse. Its website is the first national resource portal on online child sexual abuse and exploitation, which it seeks to locate within the broader framework of child protection in India and elsewhere. It also has a separate section on online safety for children with videos and other resources. Aarambh provides support services for child victims of online abuse and exploitation. Recognizing the threat posed by websites that carry CSAM, it is collaborating with the United Kingdom-based IWF. A reporting button on its website links to the IWF hotline for reporting CSAM. IWF assesses material and, if illegal, takes steps to remove it.

24.2 Recommendations for Priority Interventions

24.2.1 Leadership and Partnerships for Child Online Safety in India

- Identify key organizations and potential partnerships to lead, coordinate and monitor inter-agency efforts to ensure appropriate prevention and response to child online exploitation and abuse

- Develop a National Framework for Child Online Safety and a multi-agency action plan to be implemented through multi-sectoral partnerships and collaboration; including clear definitions of roles and responsibilities

- Build awareness and capacity of key partners including ICT companies, government bodies, law enforcement agencies, media, civil society actors, etc.

24.2.2 Evidence, Research and Data on Child Online Safety in India

- Carry out a study of the risky and harmful online behaviours of children in and out of school

- Carry out a study of the production, distribution and use of CSAM based on data available from law enforcement agencies, ICT companies, Childline India and media reports

24.2.3 Education for Digital Literacy, Citizenship and Safety

- Bring key education actors together to agree on a common action plan on digital literacy and safety

- Develop a plan to institutionalize and mainstream digital safety and literacy to reach a very large proportion of children, caregivers and relevant professionals

- Develop an age-appropriate 'Digital Safety, Literacy and Citizenship' Curriculum to be integrated and mainstreamed in the school curriculum across subjects, particularly as part of the ICT curriculum

- Ensure active and meaningful engagement of children and adolescents in protecting themselves and their peers from online abuse and exploitation
- Enable and empower parents and caregivers to play an active role in preventing and protecting children from child online abuse and exploitation

24.2.4 Legislation and Policies to Protect Children from Online Abuse and Exploitation

- Review and revise cyber laws related to child online abuse and exploitation
- Invest in the implementation of cyber laws and legislation via improved child- centred guidelines, structures, capacities and resources
- Develop approaches that do not criminalize children and adolescents for harmful online behaviours

24.2.5 Reporting and Removing Online Child Sexual Abuse Material (CSAM)

- Invest long term in an India-based Hotline able to remove high volumes of CSAM
- Establish and reinforce collaboration between the ICT industry and law enforcement actors to ensure effective reporting and removal of online CSAM
- Raise awareness of mechanisms for the reporting and removal of CSAM among children, parents and professionals
- Monitor, analyse and review data on the reporting and removal of CSAM

24.2.6 Legal Investigation and Prosecution of Online Child Sexual Abuse and Exploitation

- Invest in the capacities and resources of the police workforce and cyber forensic professionals
- Clarify and strengthen processes and procedures for cybercrime investigations involving children
- Improve coordination and collaboration between cybercrime cells, police and ICT industry
- Apply a child-centred approach to reporting of CSAM and to the legal investigation and prosecution of child online abuse and exploitation

24.2.7 Services for Child Victims of the Worst Forms of Child Online Abuse and Exploitation

- Integrate and mainstream child online protection in existing processes and ongoing efforts to strengthen child protection systems; including defining a specific intervention package for end-to-end support for child victims of online exploitation and abuse
- Map the responsibilities and skills required by key actors (law enforcement, child protection service providers, etc.) to effectively prevent and respond to child online exploitation and abuse
- Develop a programme to strengthen capacities for child online protection across the child protection system
- Develop capacities for online counselling of child victims and child offenders involved in online abuse and exploitation (e.g., Childline India).

25

CYBER-ETHICS RESEARCH CENTRES AND NETWORKS

Collected by Christoph Stückelberger.
Status 30 September 2018

The list is only a teaser and does not claim to be comprehensive.

➤ United Nations Global Pulse, about Big Data for development,
https://www.unglobalpulse.org/about-new

➤ International Telecommunication Union ITU, AI for Good,
https://www.itu.int/en/ITU-T/AI/Pages/default.aspx

➤ UNESCO Ethics of Science and Technology,
https://en.unesco.org/themes/ethics-science-and-technology

➤ UNESCO Global Ethics Observatory,
http://www.unesco.org/new/en/social-and-human-sciences/themes/global-ethics-observatory/

➤ UNESCO, ICT in Education, https://en.unesco.org/themes/ict-education

➤ The European Group on Ethics in Science and New Technologies (EGE),
https://ec.europa.eu/research/ege/index.cfm

➤ Globethics.net, largest online library on ethics, free access.
www.globethics.net and with a special collection with over 7000 professional codes of ethics, https://www.globethics.net/web/codes-of-ethics?layoutPlid=4297674&screenName=no

> Centre for the Study of Ethics in the Professions of the Illinois Institute of Technology, with an Ethics Code Collection, http://ethics.iit.edu/ecodes/

> World Economic Forum, Centre for the Fourth Industrial Revolution. https://www.weforum.org/centre-for-the-fourth-industrial-revolution.

> International Centre for Information Ethics. https://www.i-c-i-e.org/home

> 4TU.Centre for Ethics and Technology of three technical universities in the Netherlands (Delft, Eindhoven, Twente), https://ethicsandtechnology.eu

> Centre for Technology, Ethics, Law and Society TELOS, Kings College London, https://www.kcl.ac.uk/law/research/centres/telos/index.aspx

> Yale Interdisciplinary Center for Bioethics, https://bioethics.yale.edu/

> MIT LAB, The Ethics and Governance of Artificial Intelligence Initiative. https://aiethicsinitiative.org/

> University of Oxford, Ethics for Artificial Intelligence. Towards a code of ethics for AI, https://www.cs.ox.ac.uk/efai/

> Computer Ethics Institute, Washington, http://computerethicsinstitute.org/

> WashLaw. Legal Research on the Web, on cyberspace ethics, http://www.washlaw.edu/subject/cyberethics.html

> IEEE (Advancing Technology for Humanity) Tech Ethics https://techethics.ieee.org/

> Google AI Ethics Principles: https://www.blog.google/technology/ai/ai-principles/

> AI Research Center of Alibaba with Nanyang Technological University in Singapore,

> UK Centre for Data Ethics and Innovation, in formation.

> Agency for Science, Technology and Research, Singapore, https://www.a-star.edu.sg/Research/Research-Quality-Excellence/Research-Ethics

> African Centre of Excellence for Information Ethics, University of Pretoria, South Africa, https://www.up.ac.za/african-centre-of-excellence-for-information-ethics

> Centre for Applied Ethics, Stellenbosch University, South Africa, https://www.sun.ac.za/english/faculty/arts/cae

➢ Dubai AI

➢ Leeds Beckett University, GB, Research Ethics,
http://www.leedsbeckett.ac.uk/studenthub/research-ethics/

➢ SAP AI Ethics Advisory Panel (the first European Company to establish this), https://news.sap.com/2018/09/sap-first-european-tech-company-ai-ethics-advisory-panel/

CONTRIBUTORS

Editors

Christoph Stückelberger, Geneva/Zurich, Switzerland, is Founder and President of Globethics.net Foundation and Professor of Ethics (emeritus in Basel, Visiting Professor in Enugu/Nigeria, Moscow/Russia, Beijing/China). He is author and editor of numerous books and over 1000 articles on applied ethics in economy, environment, technology, politics, peace, sustainability, media and others. He serves in different ethics commissions in governmental and private sector institutions. stueckelberger@globethics.net.   www.christophstueckelberger.ch

Pavan Duggal, New Delhi, India, Dr. iur, is an Advocate of Supreme Court of India. He is an internationally renowned expert authority on Cyber Law and Cybersecurity Law. He has been acknowledged as one of the top four Cyber lawyers in the world. He is also the Chairman of International Commission on Cybersecurity Law and member of the Board of Foundation of Globethics.net.
pavan@pavanduggal.com   www.pavanduggal.com

Authors (sorted by the number of the article)

1 Christoph Stückelberger see above under Editors

2 Pavan Duggal see above under Editors

3 Globethics.net Foundation, Geneva/Switzerland, is a global network on ethics with its head office in Geneva and ten regional offices on all continents and 200,000 registered participants. It has the new focus on

Ethics in Higher Education with a global consortium of universities and training courses. www.globethics.net

4 Erny Gillen was born in 1960 and works as an ethicist and theologian. He was a professor of theological ethics in Luxembourg for more than twenty years and taught at the Catholic University of Applied Sciences in Freiburg for ten years. He was President of Caritas in Luxembourg and President of Caritas Europa for two terms until 2015 and First Vice-President of Caritas Internationalis in Rome. From 2011 to 2015 he was Vicar General of the Archdiocese of Luxembourg.

5[a] Julia Bossmann, Director Strategy Fathom Computing. Graduate, Singularity University GSP; MSc (Hons) in Neuroscience, Psychology, University of Southern California and University of Dusseldorf. Former: Co-Founder, Anticip8 Analytics; McKinsey Fellow; Research Scientist, Bosch Research & Technology. Currently, Vice-President, Special Projects, Foresight Institute; Founder, Synthetic. Global Shaper, World Economic Forum. Lectures on brain interfaces, artificial intelligence, technological progress, and how technology transforms society.

5[b] Rob Smith is former Senior Reporter at the publications and now Account Manager at Formative Content, a digital communications provider company for global companies and institutions.

5[c] Mauro F. Guillén Anthony L. Davis Director of The Lauder Institute, Dr. Felix Zandman Professor of International Management, The Wharton School, University of Pennsylvania.

5[d] Srikar Reddy Managing Director and Chief Executive Officer, and a member of the Board of Directors of Sonata Software Limited and Sonata Information Technology Limited. Reddy has an engineering degree from the Regional Engineering College (now the National Institute of Technology), Tiruchirapalli, and a post graduate degree in management from IIM, Kolkata.

6 Troy Wilkinson, Las Vegas/USA, is a highly recognized Law Enforcement Expert: a lead bomb investigator, prosecuting child pornography. Under George W Bush and Barack Obama a top U.S. cyber investigator seconded to the United Nations and European Union to lead investigations into political corruption, organized crime, war crimes, financial crimes and terrorism. With a team he built the first IT forensics lab in the European Union Mission in Kosovo. He is CEO of Axiom Cyber Solutions to secure America's businesses against cybercriminals with self-healing cyber security platforms. troy.wilkinson@axiomcyber.com

7 International Labor Organisation (ILO), the UN special agency for labor standards, policies and decent work programmes, celebrates in 2019 its 100th anniversary with a focus on "Social Justice and Decent Work". ILO is the only UN organization with a tripartite governing structure with equal representatives of governments, employers and workers of 187 member states. www.ilo.org

8 Yuval Noah Harari, Jerusalem/ Israel, got his PhD from the University of Oxford and is Professor of History at the Hebrew University in Jerusalem. His book Homo Deus is a global bestseller, translated in many languages and got various awards in 2017. http://www.ynharari.com/

9 Christoph Stückelberger see above under Editors.

10 Bruno Gransche, Dr. Phil, is postdoc researcher at the research programme "Zukunft menschlich gestalten" (for a humane future) of the University of Siegen/Germany and before at the Fraunhofer Institute for Systems and Innovation Research ISI, Karlsruhe, Germany, with a focus on futurist research. bruno.gransche@uni-siegen.de

11 Michael Mosimann from Zug/ Switzerland (Zug is a centre city for Blockchain and cryptocurrencies). He is a lawyer with a particular focus on legal aspects of Blockchain businesses. He is a Counsel with Prager Dreifuss Ltd., a well-known business law firm in Switzerland.

He has been and is advising many clients in the crypto sector with regard to legal aspects of their business model and potential token sales and to their corporate legal and regulatory questions.

12a Aharon Aviram, Negev/ Israel, is Philosopher of Education, Professor and Chair of the Center for Futurism in Education at the Ben-Gurion University of the Negev in Israel. He is the Israeli representative to the Intergovernmental Council for UNESCO's Information for All Programme IFAP. His focus is on the impact of postmodernity and ICTs on society and education. roniav@bgu.ac.il

12b Tapan Patel has a Master of Technology in Civil Engineering from the Indian Institute of Technology Madras. For his focus on the social, psychological and ethical impacts of technology he joined Ben Gurion University in Israel and has been working with Prof. Aharon Aviram.

13[a] Vayena Effyaa, Health Ethics and Policy Lab, Department of Health Sciences and Technology (D-HEST), ETH Zurich (Swiss Federal Institute of Technology), Switzerland

13[b] Haeusermann Tobias, Department of Sociology, University of Cambridge, UK. Contact for the authors: blasimme@hest.ethz.ch

13[c] Adjekum Afua, PhD student in Digital Health Ethics & Policy at ETH Zurich

13[d] Blasimme Alessandro, PhD in Bioethics, Senior Researcher at Department of Health Sciences and Technology, ETH Zurich.

14 Dan Shefet, Paris/France, holds a philosophy and a law degree and specialises in technology law and in particular how it impacts Human Rights. He is a frequent speaker at international conferences and advises governments and international organizations on IT regulations, accountability and jurisdiction. shefet@shefet.com

15 Narayan Toolan, Geneva/Switzerland, is a legal futurist and earth-advocate based in Geneva. He has experience in human rights, finance, intellectual property and technology law; at International Bridges to Justice, Royal Courts of Justice and the Clifford Chance Legal Aid Centre. He founded a chapter of Legal Hackers in Geneva, and is a graduate of the LSE (Lecturer's Prize in Jurisprudence) and UCLA School of Law. narayantoolan@gmail.com

16 Pavan Duggal see above under Editors.

17 Johan Rochel, Zurich, Switzerland, Dr. iur, MA Political Philosophy, is a post-doctoral researcher at the University of Zürich and co-founder of ethix: Lab for innovation ethics. His works focus on the ethics of innovation, philosophy of law and immigration ethics. rochel@ethix.ch.

18 International Committee of the Red Cross (ICRC) is an independent, neutral global organization ensuring humanitarian protection and assistance for victims of armed conflicts and other situations of violence. It takes action in response to emergencies and also promotes respect for international humanitarian law, its implementation in national law and its further development related to new challenges such as new technologies. www.icrc.org.

19[a] Yolanda S. Lira, Manila/ Philippines, was Regional Director (Capital Region of Manila) of the National Police Commission, is Dean of the Philippines School of Criminology in Manila and Founding President of ALCCDA, the Association of Licenced Criminologists, Criminology Deans and Administrators. She is also Director of Globethics.net Philippines. alccda.ph@gmail.com.

19[b] Leirrand Christian A. Ochotorena, Manila/ Philippines, is Head off Office at the Data Protection/IT Security Office at the Western Mindanao State University and Police Instructor. He teaches Cybersecurity, Digital Forensics and Ethical Hacking.

20 **Siobhan Martin**, Geneva/Switzerland, PhD, is a Senior Programme Officer in the GCSP's Leadership, Crisis and Conflict Management Programme. She is the director of the GCSP's eight-month Leadership in International Security Course, and is also involved in developing and leading courses on "New Frontiers in Intelligence" and "International Geneva: Responding to 21st Century Peace and Security Challenges". She has a PhD in International Relations/Political Science from the Graduate Institute of International and Development Studies, Geneva. Research focus on intelligence, international cooperation, leadership issues and transnational threats.

21 **Christoph Stückelberger** see above under Editors.

22 **Ingo Radermache**r, Germany, is Computer Scientist and Founder/CEO of Radermacher Consulting for strategic IT development. He is lecturer at the International Institute for Management at the University of Flensburg and the University for applied sciences in Bonn-Rhein-Sieg. ingo@radermacher-consulting.de

23 **Saakshar Duggal** is Youth Coordinator at the Centre against Cyber Bullying (CACB) in New Delhi, India. He is third year student of Bachelor of Law (LL.B). duggalsaakshar@gmail.com.

24 **UNICEF** India, New Delhi/ India, is the India Office of UNICEF, die United Nations' children agency for child protection and inclusion. Child protection in the digital world is one of the programmes. www.unicef.in

***

Globethics.net Publications

The list below is only a selection of our publications. To view the full collection, please visit our website.

All volumes can be downloaded for free in PDF form from the Globethics.net library and at www.globethics.net/publications. Bulk print copies can be ordered from publictions@globethics.net at special rates from the Global South.

The Editor of the different Series of Globethics.net Publications Prof. Dr. Obiora Ike, Executive Director of Globethics.net in Geneva and Professor of Ethics at the Godfrey Okoye University Enugu/Nigeria.

Contact for manuscripts and suggestions: publications@globethics.net

Global Series

Christoph Stückelberger / Jesse N.K. Mugambi (eds.), *Responsible Leadership. Global and Contextual Perspectives*, 2007, 376pp. ISBN: 978–2–8254–1516–0

Heidi Hadsell / Christoph Stückelberger (eds.), *Overcoming Fundamentalism. Ethical Responses from Five Continents*, 2009, 212pp.
ISBN: 978–2–940428–00–7

Christoph Stückelberger / Reinhold Bernhardt (eds.): *Calvin Global. How Faith Influences Societies*, 2009, 258pp. ISBN: 978–2–940428–05–2.

Ariane Hentsch Cisneros / Shanta Premawardhana (eds.), *Sharing Values. A Hermeneutics for Global Ethics*, 2010, 418pp.
ISBN: 978–2–940428–25–0.

Deon Rossouw / Christoph Stückelberger (eds.), *Global Survey of Business Ethics in Training, Teaching and Research*, 2012, 404pp.
ISBN: 978–2–940428–39–7

Carol Cosgrove Sacks/ Paul H. Dembinski (eds.), *Trust and Ethics in Finance. Innovative Ideas from the Robin Cosgrove Prize*, 2012, 380pp.
ISBN: 978–2–940428–41–0

Jean-Claude Bastos de Morais / Christoph Stückelberger (eds.), *Innovation Ethics. African and Global Perspectives*, 2014, 233pp.
ISBN: 978–2–88931–003–6

Nicolae Irina / Christoph Stückelberger (eds.), *Mining, Ethics and Sustainability*, 2014, 198pp. ISBN: 978–2–88931–020–3

Philip Lee and Dafne Sabanes Plou (eds), *More or Less Equal: How Digital Platforms Can Help Advance Communication Rights*, 2014, 158pp. ISBN 978–2–88931–009–8

Sanjoy Mukherjee and Christoph Stückelberger (eds.) *Sustainability Ethics. Ecology, Economy, Ethics. International Conference SusCon III, Shillong/India*, 2015, 353pp. ISBN: 978–2–88931–068–5

Amélie Vallotton Preisig / Hermann Rösch / Christoph Stückelberger (eds.) *Ethical Dilemmas in the Information Society. Codes of Ethics for Librarians and Archivists*, 2014, 224pp. ISBN: 978–288931–024–1.

Prospects and Challenges for the Ecumenical Movement in the 21st Century. Insights from the Global Ecumenical Theological Institute, David Field / Jutta Koslowski, 256pp. 2016, ISBN: 978–2–88931–097–5

Christoph Stückelberger, Walter Fust, Obiora Ike (eds.), *Global Ethics for Leadership. Values and Virtues for Life,* 2016, 444pp. ISBN: 978–2–88931–123–1

Dietrich Werner / Elisabeth Jeglitzka (eds.), *Eco-Theology, Climate Justice and Food Security: Theological Education and Christian Leadership Development*, 316pp. 2016, ISBN 978–2–88931–145–3

Obiora Ike, Andrea Grieder and Ignace Haaz (Eds.), *Poetry and Ethics: Inventing Possibilities in Which We Are Moved to Action and How We Live Together*, 271pp. 2018, ISBN 978–2–88931–242–9

Christoph Stückelberger / Pavan Duggal (Eds.), *Cyber Ethics 4.0: Serving Humanity with Values*, 503pp. 2018, ISBN 978–2–88931–264-1

Theses Series

Kitoka Moke Mutondo, *Église, protection des droits de l'homme et refondation de l'État en République Démocratique du Congo*, 2012, 412pp. ISBN: 978–2–940428–31–1

Ange Sankieme Lusanga, *Éthique de la migration. La valeur de la justice comme base pour une migration dans l'Union Européenne et la Suisse*, 2012, 358pp. ISBN: 978–2–940428–49–6

Kahwa Njojo, *Éthique de la non-violence*, 2013, 596pp. ISBN: 978–2–940428–61–8

Carlos Alberto Sintado, *Social Ecology, Ecojustice and the New Testament: Liberating Readings,* 2015, 379pp. ISBN: 978-2–940428–99–1

Symphorien Ntibagirirwa, *Philosophical Premises for African Economic Development: Sen's Capability Approach*, 2014, 384pp.
ISBN: 978–2–88931–001–2

Jude Likori Omukaga, *Right to Food Ethics: Theological Approaches of Asbjørn Eide*, 2015, 609pp. ISBN: 978–2–88931–047–0

Jörg F. W. Bürgi, *Improving Sustainable Performance of SME's, The Dynamic Interplay of Morality and Management Systems*, 2014, 528pp.
ISBN: 978–2–88931–015–9

Jun Yan, *Local Culture and Early Parenting in China: A Case Study on Chinese Christian Mothers' Childrearing Experiences*, 2015, 190pp.
ISBN 978–2–88931–065–4

Frédéric-Paul Piguet, *Justice climatique et interdiction de nuire*, 2014, 559 pp.
ISBN 978–2–88931–005–0

Mulolwa Kashindi, *Appellations johanniques de Jésus dans l'Apocalypse: une lecture Bafuliiru des titres christologiques*, 2015, 577pp. ISBN 978–2–88931–040–1

Naupess K. Kibiswa, *Ethnonationalism and Conflict Resolution: The Armed Group Bany2 in DR Congo.* 2015, 528pp. ISBN: 978–2–88931–032–6

Kilongo Fatuma Ngongo, *Les héroïnes sans couronne. Leadership des femmes dans les Églises de Pentecôte en Afrique Centrale*, 2015, 489pp. ISBN 978–2–88931–038–8

Bosela E. Eale, *Justice and Poverty as Challenges for Churches: with a Case Study of the Democratic Republic of Congo*, 2015, 335pp,
ISBN: 978–2–88931–078–4

Andrea Grieder, *Collines des mille souvenirs. Vivre* après *et* avec *le génocide perpétré contre les Tutsi du Rwanda*, 2016, 403pp. ISBN 978–2–88931–101–9

Monica Emmanuel, *Federalism in Nigeria: Between Divisions in Conflict and Stability in Diversity*, 2016, 522pp. ISBN: 978–2–88931–106–4

John Kasuku, *Intelligence Reform in the Post-Dictatorial Democratic Republic of Congo*, 2016, 355pp. ISBN 978–2–88931–121–7

Fifamè Fidèle Houssou Gandonour, *Les fondements éthiques du féminisme. Réflexions à partir du contexte africain*, 2016, 430pp. ISBN 978–2–88931–138–5

Nicoleta Acatrinei, *Work Motivation and Pro-Social Behaviour in the Delivery of Public Services Theoretical and Empirical Insights*, 2016, 387pp. ISBN 978–2–88931–150–7

Texts Series

Principles on Sharing Values across Cultures and Religions, 2012, 20pp. Available in English, French, Spanish, German and Chinese. Other languages in preparation. ISBN: 978–2–940428–09–0

Ethics in Politics. Why it Matters More than Ever and How it Can Make a Difference. A Declaration, 8pp, 2012. Available in English and French. ISBN: 978–2–940428–35–9

Religions for Climate Justice: International Interfaith Statements 2008–2014, 2014, 45pp. Available in English. ISBN 978–2–88931–006–7

Ethics in the Information Society: the Nine 'P's. A Discussion Paper for the WSIS+10 Process 2013–2015, 2013, 32pp. ISBN: 978–2–940428–063–2

Principles on Equality and Inequality for a Sustainable Economy. Endorsed by the Global Ethics Forum 2014 with Results from Ben Africa Conference 2014, 2015, 41pp. ISBN: 978–2–88931–025–8

Focus Series

Christoph Stückelberger, *Das Menschenrecht auf Nahrung und Wasser. Eine ethische Priorität,* 2009, 80pp. ISBN: 978–2–940428–06–9

Christoph Stückelberger, *Corruption-Free Churches are Possible. Experiences, Values, Solutions,* 2010, 278pp. ISBN: 978–2–940428–07–6

—, *Des Églises sans corruption sont possibles: Expériences, valeurs, solutions,* 2013, 228pp. ISBN: 978–2–940428–73–1

Benoît Girardin, *Ethics in Politics: Why it matters more than ever and how it can make a difference,* 2012, 172pp. ISBN: 978–2–940428–21–2

—, *L'éthique: un défi pour la politique. Pourquoi l'éthique importe plus que jamais en politique et comment elle peut faire la différence,* 2014, 220pp. ISBN 978–2–940428–91–5

Willem A Landman, *End-of-Life Decisions, Ethics and the Law,* 2012, 136pp. ISBN: 978–2–940428–53–3

Corneille Ntamwenge, *Éthique des affaires au Congo. Tisser une culture d'intégrité par le Code de Conduite des Affaires en RD Congo,* 2013, 132pp. ISBN: 978–2–940428–57–1

Elisabeth Nduku / John Tenamwenye (eds.), *Corruption in Africa: A Threat to Justice and Sustainable Peace,* 2014, 510pp. ISBN: 978–2–88931–017–3

Dicky Sofjan (with Mega Hidayati), *Religion and Television in Indonesia: Ethics Surrounding Dakwahtainment*, 2013, 112pp. ISBN: 978–2–940428–81–6

Yahya Wijaya / Nina Mariani Noor (eds.), *Etika Ekonomi dan Bisnis: Perspektif Agama-Agama di Indonesia*, 2014, 293pp. ISBN: 978–2–940428–67–0

Bernard Adeney-Risakotta (ed.), *Dealing with Diversity. Religion, Globalization, Violence, Gender and Disaster in Indonesia*. 2014, 372pp. ISBN: 978–2–940428–69–4

Nina Mariani Noor/ Ferry Muhammadsyah Siregar (eds.), *Etika Sosial dalam Interaksi Lintas Agama* 2014, 208pp. ISBN 978–2–940428–83–0

B. Muchukiwa Rukakiza, A. Bishweka Cimenesa et C. Kapapa Masonga (éds.), *L'État africain et les mécanismes culturels traditionnels de transformation des conflits*. 2015, 95pp. ISBN: 978–2–88931– 042–5

Dickey Sofian (ed.), Religion, *Public Policy and Social Transformation in Southeast Asia*, 2016, 288pp. ISBN: 978–2–88931–115–6

Symphorien Ntibagirirwa, *Local Cultural Values and Projects of Economic Development: An Interpretation in the Light of the Capability Approach*, 2016, 88pp. ISBN: 978–2–88931–111–8

Karl Wilhelm Rennstich, *Gerechtigkeit für Alle. Religiöser Sozialismus in Mission und Entwicklung*, 2016, 500pp. ISBN 978–2–88931–140–8.

John M. Itty, *Search for Non-Violent and People-Centric Development*, 2017, 317pp. ISBN 978–2–88931–185–9

Florian Josef Hoffmann, *Reichtum der Welt—für Alle Durch Wohlstand zur Freiheit*, 2017, 122pp. ISBN 978–2–88931–187–3

Cristina Calvo / Humberto Shikiya / Deivit Montealegre (eds.), *Ética y economía la relación dañada*, 2017, 377pp. ISBN 978–2–88931–200–9

Maryann Ijeoma Egbujor, *The Relevance of Journalism Education in Kenya for Professional Identity and Ethical Standards*, 2018, 141pp. ISBN 978–2–88931233–7

African Law Series

D. Brian Dennison/ Pamela Tibihikirra-Kalyegira (eds.), *Legal Ethics and Professionalism. A Handbook for Uganda*, 2014, 400pp. ISBN 978–2–88931–011–1

Pascale Mukonde Musulay, *Droit des affaires en Afrique subsaharienne et économie planétaire*, 2015, 164pp. ISBN: 978–2–88931–044–9

Pascal Mukonde Musulay, *Démocratie électorale en Afrique subsaharienne: Entre droit, pouvoir et argent*, 2016, 209pp. ISBN 978–2–88931–156–9

Pascal Mukonde Musulay, *Contrats de partenariat public privé : Options innovantes de financement des infrastructures publiques en Afrique subsaharienne*, 2018, ISBN 978-2-88931-244-3, 175pp.

China Christian Series

Yahya Wijaya; Christoph Stückelberger; Cui Wantian, *Christian Faith and Values: An Introduction for Entrepreneurs in China*, 2014, 76pp. ISBN: 978–2–940428–87–8

Christoph Stückelberger, *We are all Guests on Earth. A Global Christian Vision for Climate Justice*, 2015, 52pp. ISBN: 978–2–88931–034–0 (en Chinois, version anglaise dans la Bibliothèque Globethics.net)

Christoph Stückelberger, Cui Wantian, Teodorina Lessidrenska, Wang Dan, Liu Yang, Zhang Yu, *Entrepreneurs with Christian Values: Training Handbook for 12 Modules*, 2016, 270pp. ISBN 978–2–88931–142–2

Christoph Stückelberger / Li Jing, *Philanthropy and Foundation Management: A Guide to Philanthropy in Europe and China*, 2017, 171pp. ISBN: 978-2-88931-195-8

Christoph Stückelberger / Vanessa Yuli Wang, *Faith at Work. Directory of Christian Entrepreneurs and Workers*, 2017, 126pp. ISBN: 978-2-88931-207-8

马提阿斯奈格鲍尔（Matthias Neugebauer），茨温利的伦理学 *Ulrich Zwingli's Ethics*, 2017, 329pp. ISBN 978-2-88931-214-6

理查德·希金森（Dr. Richard Higginson）著，刘殿利（Dr. Dianli Liu）译，信仰、希望与全球经济：一种为善的力量 *Faith, Hope & the Global Economy: A Power for Good*, 2017, 319pp. ISBN 978-2-88931-228-3

Faith-based Entrepreneurs: Stronger Together. Report of the International Conference Geneva 2018, 2018, 88pp. ISBN 978-2-88931-258-0

China Ethics Series

Liu Baocheng / Dorothy Gao (eds.), 中国的企业社会责任 *Corporate Social Responsibility in China*, 459pp. 2015, en Chinois, ISBN 978–2–88931–050–0

Bao Ziran, 影响中国环境政策执行效果的因素分析 *China's Environmental Policy, Factor Analysis of its Implementation*, 2015, 431pp. En chinois, ISBN 978–2–88931–051–7

Yuan Wang and Yating Luo, *China Business Perception Index: Survey on Chinese Companies' Perception of Doing Business in Kenya*, 99pp. 2015, en anglais, ISBN 978–2–88931–062–3.

王淑芹 (Wang Shuqin) (编辑) (Ed.), *Research on Chinese Business Ethics [Volume 1]*, 2016, 413pp. ISBN: 978–2–88931–104–0

王淑芹 (Wang Shuqin) (编辑) (Ed.), *Research on Chinese Business Ethics [Volume 2]*, 2016, 400pp. ISBN: 978–2–88931–108–8

Liu Baocheng, *Chinese Civil Society*, 2016, 177pp. ISBN 978–2–88931–168–2

Liu Baocheng / Zhang Mengsha, *Philanthropy in China: Report of Concepts, History, Drivers, Institutions*, 2017, 246pp. ISBN: 978–2–88931–178–1

Liu Baocheng / Zhang Mengsha, *CSR Report on Chinese Business Overseas Operations*, 2018, 286pp. ISBN 978-2-88931-250-4

Education Ethics Series

Divya Singh / Christoph Stückelberger (Eds.), *Ethics in Higher Education Values-driven Leaders for the Future,* 2017, 367pp. ISBN: 978–2–88931–165–1

Obiora Ike / Chidiebere Onyia (Eds.) *Ethics in Higher Education, Foundation for Sustainable Development*, 2018, 645pp. IBSN: 978-2-88931-217-7

Obiora Ike / Chidiebere Onyia (Eds.) *Ethics in Higher Education, Religions and Traditions in Nigeria* 2018, 198pp. IBSN: 978-2-88931-219-1

Readers Series

Christoph Stückelberger, *Global Ethics Applied: vol. 4 Bioethics, Religion, Leadership,* 2016, 426. ISBN 978–2–88931–130–9

Кристоф Штукельбергер, *Сборник статей, Прикладная глобальная этика Экономика. Инновации. Развитие. Мир*, 2017, 224pp. ISBN: 978–5–93618–250–1

John Mohan Razu, *Ethics of Inclusion and Equality, Vol. 1: Politics & Society*, 2018, 452pp., ISBN:978–2–88931–189-7

CEC Series

Win Burton, *The European Vision and the Churches: The Legacy of Marc Lenders*, Globethics.net, 2015, 251pp. ISBN: 978–2–88931–054–8

Laurens Hogebrink, *Europe's Heart and Soul. Jacques Delors' Appeal to the Churches*, 2015, 91pp. ISBN: 978–2–88931–091–3

Elizabeta Kitanovic and Fr Aimilianos Bogiannou (Eds.), *Advancing Freedom of Religion or Belief for All*, 2016, 191pp. ISBN: 978–2–88931–136–1

Peter Pavlovic (ed.) *Beyond Prosperity? European Economic Governance as a Dialogue between Theology, Economics and Politics*, 2017, 147pp. ISBN 978–2–88931–181–1

CEC Flash Series

Guy Liagre (ed.), *The New CEC: The Churches' Engagement with a Changing Europe*, 2015, 41pp. ISBN 978–2–88931–072–2

Guy Liagre, *Pensées européennes. De « l'homo nationalis » à une nouvelle citoyenneté*, 2015, 45pp. ISBN: 978–2–88931–073–9

Copublications & Other

Patrice Meyer-Bisch, Stefania Gandolfi, Greta Balliu (eds.), *Souveraineté et coopérations: Guide pour fonder toute gouvernance démocratique sur l'interdépendance des droits de l'homme*, 2016, 99pp. ISBN 978–2–88931–119–4 (Available in Italian)

Reports

Global Ethics Forum 2016 Report, Higher Education—Ethics in Action: The Value of Values across Sectors, 2016, 184pp. ISBN: 978–2–88931–159–0

African Church Assets Programme ACAP: Report on Workshop March 2016, 2016, 75pp. ISBN 978–2–88931–161–3

Globethics Consortium on Ethics in Higher Education Inaugural Meeting 2017 Report, 2018, 170pp. ISBN 978–2–88931–238–2

This is only selection of our latest publications, to view our full collection please visit:

www.globethics.net/publications

Printed in Poland
by Amazon Fulfillment
Poland Sp. z o.o., Wrocław